THE CORRESPONDENCE OF SAMUEL CLARKE AND ANTHONY COLLINS, 1707-08

broadview editions
series editor: L.W. Conolly

THE CORRESPONDENCE OF SAMUEL CLARKE AND ANTHONY COLLINS, 1707-08

edited by William L. Uzgalis

broadview editions

Library and Archives Canada Cataloguing in Publication

Clarke, Samuel, 1675-1729
The correspondence of Samuel Clarke and Anthony Collins, 1707-08 / edited by William Uzgalis.

Includes bibliographical references and index.
ISBN 978-1-55111-984-7

1. Clarke, Samuel, 1675-1729—Correspondence. 2. Collins, Anthony, 1676-1729—Correspondence. 3. Philosophers—Great Britain—Correspondence. 4. Freethinkers—Great Britain—Correpondence. 5. Consciousness. 6. Mind and body. I. Collins, Anthony, 1676-1729 II. Uzgalis, William III. Title.

B1365.Z7A4 2011 192 C2011-900982-X

Broadview Editions
The Broadview Editions series represents the ever-changing canon of literature by bringing together texts long regarded as classics with valuable lesser-known works.

Advisory editor for this volume: Michel Pharand

Broadview Press is an independent, international publishing house, incorporated in 1985.

We welcome comments and suggestions regarding any aspect of our publications—please feel free to contact us at the addresses below or at broadview@broadviewpress.com.

North America
PO Box 1243, Peterborough, Ontario, Canada K9J 7H5
2215 Kenmore Ave., Buffalo, New York, USA 14207
Tel: (705) 743-8990; Fax: (705) 743-8353
email: customerservice@broadviewpress.com

UK, Europe, Central Asia, Middle East, Africa, India, and Southeast Asia
Eurospan Group, 3 Henrietta St., London WC2E 8LU, United Kingdom
Tel: 44 (0) 1767 604972; Fax: 44 (0) 1767 601640
email: eurospan@turpin-distribution.com

Australia and New Zealand
NewSouth Books
c/o TL Distribution, 15-23 Helles Ave., Moorebank, NSW, Australia 2170
Tel: (02) 8778 9999; Fax: (02) 8778 9944
email: orders@tldistribution.com.au

www.broadviewpress.com

This book is printed on paper containing 100% post-consumer fibre.

PRINTED IN CANADA

Contents

Acknowledgements

First I would like to thank John Perry for organizing the informal seminar at Stanford in 1989 that introduced me to the Clarke-Collins correspondence, for his help in getting this volume published all these years later and for commenting on a draft of the introduction. I would also like to thank the other members of that seminar, especially Ezio Vailati. Thanks to Trip McCrossin for typing the first version of this edition twenty years ago. I would also like to thank my colleagues Jon Dorbolo and Jon Kaplan for commenting on a draft of the introduction and Kaplan for help in getting the book published. I owe thanks to Kyle Klain for help in proofreading. I especially owe thanks to both the Oregon State University Center for the Humanities and the Hundere Endowment in Culture and Religion for providing time off from my teaching duties to work on this project. I would especially like to thank the staff at Broadview Press, who from the beginning to the end of the process of producing this book have been friendly, helpful, and unfailingly committed to making this the best book they could. I am so impressed!

I would also like to thank the publishers of the translations of the various Latin passages in the text for their permission to use these translations:

Reprinted by permission of the publishers and the trustees of the Loeb Classical Library from Cicero, Volume 18, Loeb Classical Library Volume 141, *The Tusculan Disputations* translated by J.E. King, Cambridge, Mass., Harvard University Press, Copyright 1927 by the President and Fellows of Harvard College. The Loeb Classical Library is a trademark of the President and Fellows of Harvard College. Pp. 26-27; 30-31. The first of these is a translation of one of the epigraphs for Collins' "A Reply to Mr. Clarke's Defense of his Letter to Mr. Dodwell," p. 65 of this edition. The second is one of the epigraphs for Collins' "Reflections on Mr. Clarke's Second Defense of an Argument," p. 115 of this edition.

Reprinted by permission of the Society for the Propagation of Christian Knowledge (SPCK) from Tertullian, *Of the Resurrection of the Flesh*, translated by Ernest Evans, SPCK Publishing & Sheldon Press, 1956. This appears as a translation of one of the epigraphs for "Reflections on Mr. Clarke's Second Defense of an Argument," p. 115 of this edition.

The passages from Ralph Cudworth's *The True Intellectual System of the Universe* are from the facsimile edition of Friedrich Frommann Verlag (Gunther Holzboog), Stuttgart-Bad Cannstatt, 1964.

I would like to thank the Hackett Publishing Company, Inc. for permission to include a portion of note L of Bayle's Historical and Critical Dictionary as one of the supplementary readings in this volume (Appendix A3):

Pierre Bayle, *Historical and Critical Dictionary: Selections*, translated by Richard Popkin. Copyright 1991 by Hackett Publishing Company Inc. Reprinted by permission of Hackett Publishing Company Inc.

Introduction

The public correspondence of 1707-08 between Samuel Clarke and Anthony Collins is an extended debate about the relation of mind and matter, the origins of life and consciousness, personal identity, and free will, and determinism as well. The roots of the controversy can be traced back into the seventeenth century and earlier. The correspondence is the most philosophically significant clash between the Newtonians (Clarke in this case) and the eighteenth-century free thinkers (Collins). It set the terms of the debate over materialist theories of mind and personal identity in England for much of the rest of the eighteenth century, and on the continent. There are clear echoes of it in the nineteenth-century controversy about evolution and twentieth- and twenty-first century debates about personal identity and the emergence of consciousness.

Consciousness is a hot topic in contemporary philosophy, but the term was quite new in English philosophy at the time of the correspondence. Ralph Cudworth in *The True Intellectual System of the Universe* (1678) and John Locke in *An Essay Concerning Human Understanding* (1689) had raised it to philosophical prominence. It is central to the debate between Clarke and Collins. Is it possible for a material system like a brain to be conscious? Collins claims that it is possible, while Clarke denies that possibility. Clarke gives a spectacular and full-blooded defense of mind/body dualism just as that doctrine was going into three centuries of decline. Clarke claims, along with others in the seventeenth and eighteenth centuries, that there is nothing in common between dead and unconscious matter and living and conscious beings that would allow the former to cause the latter. We will call this, following Ezio Vailati, the Homogeneity Principle.[1] Further, the nature of matter is different from mind. Matter and its essential properties can be

---

1 Vailati, 1997, p. 57. David Hume, in attacking this principle (see Appendix B1), claims this is a Scholastic principle and so very likely its origins are earlier than the seventeenth century. Still, as used by Cudworth, Bayle, and Clarke, it seems to have been the mainstay in the defense against materialism in the late seventeenth and early eighteenth centuries.

composed into wholes or the wholes divided into parts. Call this the Composition Principle. In Clarke's view mind and consciousness are so unified that they cannot be compounded into wholes or divided into parts — thus they do not conform to the Composition Principle. So, mind and consciousness must be distinct from matter. Anthony Collins, by contrast, is a perceptive advocate of a materialist account of mind, who defends the possibility that thinking and consciousness are emergent properties of the brain — some 130 years before Mill's treatment of the subject in his *System of Logic* (Appendix B2). The second main topic of debate is personal identity. Can we explain personal identity over time in terms of consciousness rather than the soul? Locke claimed that we can and Collins develops a materialist version of Locke's theory of personal identity. Clarke mounts powerful arguments against both accounts. There is also a tertiary debate over free will and determinism. Collins holds a determinist position similar to that of Hobbes, while Clarke is a sophisticated contra-causal free will theorist. The correspondence itself has a number of virtues. The two authors stick to the issues, give arguments and explanations, and given the intensity of their disagreement, they are remarkably civil to one another.

Samuel Clarke and Anthony Collins

Samuel Clarke (1675-1729) was perhaps "the most important British philosopher in the generation between Locke and Berkeley."[1] Born at Norwich on 11 October 1675, he received his BA from Cambridge in 1695. His tutor introduced him to Newtonian physics and urged him to provide a new annotated Latin translation of Jacques Rohault's *Treatise on Physics* (1671). This was first published in 1697 with Clarke's comments on it from the perspective of Newtonian physics. As the book went through edition after edition it became, in effect, the first textbook of Newtonian physics used in the universities. In addition to his interest in science, Clarke was a theologian whose basic interests were metaphysical. He gave the Boyle lectures in both 1704 and 1705, which were published together as *A Demonstration of the Being and Attributes of God.* In 1706 Clarke published a Latin translation of Newton's *Opticks* (*Optices*, published by Smith and

1 Vailati, 2008.

Walford in 1706), thus becoming a leading figure in Newton's inner circle. He was Newton's neighbor for years. In 1706 Clarke responded to a book by a renowned biblical scholar Henry Dodwell, in which Dodwell claimed mainly on the basis of scripture that the soul was naturally mortal. Clarke refuted Dodwell's scriptural citations and, in response to a passage that suggested that the soul is material, he offered a single philosophical argument in the form of a thought experiment to show that it was not possible for consciousness to belong to a material system. This provoked a public letter from Anthony Collins claiming that he could show that Clarke's argument for the immateriality of the soul was inconclusive. Thus the Clarke-Collins correspondence began.

Clarke was later to engage in perhaps the most famous exchange of philosophical letters in the history of philosophy — the Leibniz-Clarke correspondence of 1715-16. He also continued his public dialogue with Collins by reviewing Collins' *A Discourse of Free Thinking* (1713) and *A Philosophical Enquiry Concerning Human Liberty* (1717). Though Collins was unaware of this at the time of his correspondence with Clarke, Clarke was (like Newton) an anti-Trinitarian or Arian. This heterodoxy kept Clarke from rising in the Church and becoming Archbishop of Canterbury. Clarke died in 1729 — the same year as Collins.

Anthony Collins (1676-1729), along with John Toland, was the most significant member of a close-knit circle of radical free thinkers that arose in England in the first three decades of the eighteenth century. This group included such men as Samuel Bold, Matthew Tindal, Thomas Woolston and William Wollaston. Born in Heston, Middlesex on 21 June 1676 into a family of lawyers, he went to Eton and then King's College, Cambridge, in 1693. Though he had not graduated from Cambridge, Collins went to the Middle Temple in 1694 to study law. He didn't like the profession and was never called to the bar. In 1698 he married the daughter of a rich London merchant, Sir Francis Child. She died in childbirth in 1703. At the time of his marriage he received some property in Essex from his father. Together with his wife's dowry, this made him a very rich man indeed. Collins met John Locke on a visit to Oates in Essex in 1703, visited Locke five times over the next eighteen months and carried on a correspondence with him about various philosophical topics.

In one of his letters to Collins, Locke remarked: "Believe it, my good friend, to love truth for truth's sake is the principal part of human perfection in this world, and the seed bed of all other virtues; and if I mistake not, you have as much of it as I have ever met with in anybody." (Locke to Collins, in de Beer, vol. 8, letter 3361, p. 97). In 1707, three years after Locke's death, and in the year the Clarke-Collins correspondence began, Collins published anonymously his first book, *An Essay Concerning the Use of Reason in Propositions, the Evidence Whereof Depends on Human Testimony*. Clarke was able to deduce who wrote the book and teased Collins about inconsistencies between his views in the correspondence and the book.

Collins' later works take up the issue of free will and determinism broached in the Clarke-Collins correspondence and he continued being an anti-clerical advocate for free thinking and rational religion along with raising a variety of objections to Anglican orthodoxy and Christianity more broadly. Perhaps his most famous work — *A Discourse of Free Thinking* (1713) — provoked considerable outrage among orthodox Anglicans.[1] He continued to spar with Newtonians such as William Whiston about such topics as Biblical prophecies and miracles. What, then, brought these two figures into opposing sides on such a variety of issues?

Natural Philosophy, Religion and Dualism in the Seventeenth Century

The seventeenth century in Europe saw the rise of a new natural philosophy marked by empirical enquires, remarkable discoveries in mathematics, an emphasis on mechanical explanations, and analogies between the world perceived by the senses and the corpuscularian or atomic constituents of the things in that world. This was the scientific revolution, even if scholars have now traced continuities and influences back into the medieval world. The seventeenth century was a time of enormous intellectual ferment and crisis. It saw, for example, the acceptance of atomism in England and elsewhere in Europe, though the debate over whether matter was infinitely divisible or not was

1 For more extensive treatments of Collins' life and works, see O'Higgins, 1970, and Uzgalis, 2008.

lively and disturbing to many of the new natural philosophers.[1] There are clear reverberations of this debate in the Clarke-Collins correspondence.

The attitude of religious people towards these developments ranged from seeing the new natural philosophy as an ally of religion to seeing it as a destructive threat. The Protestant Reformation narrowed Catholic attitudes. Galileo was put under house arrest for championing Copernican ideas. Descartes, prominently, combined a mechanical account of bodies, up to and including human bodies, with a robust substance dualism and saw the passivity of matter as the key to preserving God's role in the universe. Descartes was also a Copernican and never got the approval of his work from the doctors of the Sorbonne that he so much craved. The Cambridge Platonist, Henry More (1614-87), while at first welcoming Descartes' dualism, grew dissatisfied with it in several important respects. More held that Descartes' conception gave God too small a role in the universe and while he accepted the immateriality of the soul he rejected the Cartesian notion that the soul was unextended. So, he argued that the soul was immaterial, had no parts and yet was extended (see Appendix A1). More's views about the soul and the nature of space may well have influenced one of his students — Isaac Newton. This view of the soul, though without some of its baroque ramifications, is the one defended by Samuel Clarke in the Clarke-Collins correspondence.

There was some reason for concern about the new natural philosophy. Insofar as mechanical explanations (explanations involving matter in motion and the impact of one body on another) were becoming more popular and effective, they also contributed to the rise of materialistic and deterministic explanations of the universe. The most prominent of these voices was that of Thomas Hobbes (1588-1679) in England. The views of Benedict de Spinoza (1632-77) in the Dutch Republic, though rather different from those of Hobbes, were also perceived as materialistic and thus a threat to religion. By the beginning of the eighteenth century, the discussion of animal souls and animal consciousness both on the continent and in England

---

1 For an account of the acceptance of atomism in England see Kargon, 1966. For a discussion of the problems associated with the infinite divisibility of matter during this period see Holden, 2004.

led a number of writers to suggest that the human soul might be material.[1]

The Cambridge Platonist Ralph Cudworth (1617-89) attacked these materialistic and deterministic tendencies in his book *The True Intellectual System of the Universe* (1678). John Yolton comments that for Cudworth's contemporaries *The True Intellectual System of the Universe* "must have been a major source book of ancient versions of materialism, as well as for an array of arguments to combat it."[2] Cudworth distinguished four different kinds of ancient atomists spanning inert, passive, and senseless matter to that endowed with active principles, including thought, volition, and consciousness. Cudworth characterized modern materialists such as Hobbes in terms of these ancient schools. He introduced the term "consciousness" in arguing against Hobbes and claimed that consciousness was immaterial. Some of Clarke's central arguments for dualism are well articulated in Cudworth's book (see Appendix A2). On the continent, Pierre Bayle invoked the Homogeneity Principle to refute materialism in notes C and L of the article "Dicaearchus" in his *Historical and Critical Dictionary* (1696) and, like Cudworth, anticipated Clarke's central argument in the Clarke-Collins correspondence against materialism (see Appendix A3).

Robert Boyle (1627-91), Isaac Newton (1643-1727), and Samuel Clarke (among others), all members of the British Royal Society, sought to forge an alliance between science and the Anglican religion. In his will Robert Boyle left a legacy to establish the Boyle lectures and the Newtonians used them to attack Hobbes, Spinoza, and the Deists and Free Thinkers, and to try to use Newtonian natural philosophy to bolster Anglican orthodoxy.[3] As early as the first Boyle lectures in 1692, Richard Bentley had taken up several versions of the thinking matter doctrine and refuted them (Bentley, 1976). Samuel Clarke, as noted earlier, gave the Boyle lectures for 1704 and 1705 and these, published as *A Demonstration of the Being and Attributes of God* and *A Discourse Concerning the Unchangeable Obligations of Natural Religion and The Truth and Certainty of the Christian Revelation*, set the position and provided some of the main

1 O'Higgins, 1970, pp. 69-70.

2 Yolton, 1983, p. 4.

3 See Jacob, 1976, for an account of this effort.

arguments that Clarke was to defend and present in the Clarke-Collins correspondence.

John Locke and the Clarke-Collins Correspondence

John Locke (1632-1704) expressed views in his monumental *An Essay Concerning Human Understanding* (1690) that played a significant role in both provoking the correspondence between Clarke and Collins and in shaping the arguments given in the correspondence. Locke's argument for the existence of an immaterial God (Appendix A4c) plays a role in the correspondence, as does his view that substance is unknowable — a view accepted by Clarke and rejected by Collins. Locke was much less convinced than many other seventeenth-century philosophers that one needed to show that the soul was simple and immaterial in order to defend certain fundamental Christian doctrines such as the immortality of the soul and the resurrection of the dead (Appendix A4b). Locke also offered a revolutionary treatment of personal identity in which he replaced the soul as the bearer of personal identity with consciousness (Appendix A4a, sec. 9).

In his discussion of personal identity (Book II, Chapter 27, "Of Identity and Diversity"), added to the second edition of the *Essay* in 1692, Locke embedded his theory of personal identity within a general account of identity and individuation. In this general account of identity and individuation Locke contrasts the individuation of bodies with that of living things. Bodies are individuated by the material particles that compose them at a time, however organized. If a collection of particles gains or loses a single atom it becomes a different body. Living things, by contrast, are individuated by their functional organization and the preservation of the same life and not by their constituents (Appendix A4a, sec. 4). This distinction is needed, Locke thinks, to explain how living things remain the same through growth and change, i.e. the flux of the particles that constitute them. This leads to a claim that living things can persist through changes in the substances that compose them at a time. This distinction between individuation by constituents and individuation by function may well be at the heart of Collins' strategy for showing that there are properties possessed by a whole that are not possessed by its parts.

The claim that living things can persist through changes in the substance that composes them at a time also serves as an analogy for persons continuing to exist through changes in the thing that thinks in us (Locke, Essay II. xxvii, 11). For persons, the continuance of the same consciousness is the analogue of the continuance of the same life in plants and animals. What is the substance in persons that corresponds to the particles that make up an oak tree or a horse at a time? Locke acknowledged (sec. 25) that the most probable opinion was that the underlying substance was a single immaterial soul. Yet he crafted a theory that was neutral as to what kind of substance thinks in us. He did this, in part, by making consciousness and not the soul the bearer of personal identity. Thus, Locke's account of personal identity would be basically the same even if it turned out that the substance that thinks in us is material and compounded or immaterial and simple, or any other combinations of these possibilities. Still, Locke may have had his doubts about materialist theories of personal identity. At another point in the chapter "Of Identity and Diversity," he remarks that how far treating memories as representations "may be an argument against those who would place Thinking in a system of fleeting animal Spirits, I leave to be considered" (Appendix A4a, sec. 13). Collins was one of those who placed Thinking in a system of fleeting animal spirits. He produced a materialist version of Locke's theory of personal identity and saw memories as both acts and representations and representations as the key to the success of his account of memory.

In another passage (Appendix A4b), Locke claims that he saw no need to argue for the immateriality of the soul in order to ensure the immortality of the soul. And earlier in the same passage Locke claims that we will probably never know whether it is as easy for God to superadd the power of thinking to a material system as it is for him to connect an immaterial soul to a material body.[1]

1 What is "superaddition"? It is the idea that some being, in this case God, could add some power to something that it does not naturally or essentially possess. Michael Ayers argues for an epistemological interpretation of superaddition in regard to Locke's thinking matter hypothesis rather than a metaphysical interpretation. Thus Ayers writes: "... for Locke whatever is not 'visibly' impossible or self-contradictory ought piously to be regarded as within God's power to create — even though, for all we know, it might be in itself impossible" (Ayers, 1991, 2, 150f). Collins certainly seems to have taken Locke to be thinking in this way. Clarke is claiming that he can show that Locke's suggestion is metaphysically impossible and thus not epistemically possible either.

Descartes' difficulties in explaining the relation between mind and body presumably informed this suggestion.

It was this "thinking matter" passage that became the centerpiece of the Clarke-Collins correspondence. In rejecting Locke's thinking matter suggestion, Clarke is defending mind/body substance dualism, while in defending the suggestion Collins is promoting the possibility of a materialist account of mind. Collins had talked to Locke about some of the responses to this controversial passage before Locke's death in 1704. This issue of whether matter could think continued to be debated for most of the rest of the eighteenth century.[1]

Clarke, Dodwell, and Collins

At the beginning of the eighteenth century, a number of writers had considered the possibility that the soul was mortal and some had maintained that this was compatible with Anglican orthodoxy. Henry Dodwell was a well-known and enormously respected biblical scholar. When he wrote a book, *An Epistolary Discourse proving from the Scriptures and the first Fathers that the Soul is a principle naturally mortal, but immortalized by the pleasure of God* (London, 1706), in which he claimed that scripture supported the thesis that the soul was naturally mortal, Dodwell's reputation led Clarke to respond. In the late seventeenth and early eighteenth century the thesis of the natural mortality of the soul might have been associated with the Socinian heresy,[2] but it might also have been associated with materialism and ancient atomism in particular. If the soul were naturally mortal, perhaps the most obvious explanation of that fact would be that it was material and compounded. Samuel Clarke wrote a public *Letter to Dodwell* (1706) objecting to his claim that the soul is naturally mortal and charging that Dodwell's view was destructive of religion.[3] Clarke's letter is largely taken up with the refutation of Dodwell's citations from the Bible and the Church fathers.

---

1 See Yolton, 1983, and Martin and Barresi, 2004, for extended discussions of the eighteenth-century repercussions of Locke's thinking matter suggestion.

2 The Socinians believed in the annihilation of the wicked, which implies that the soul is naturally mortal and that God must act to make the souls of those going to heaven immortal.

3 See Fergusen, 1974, p. 138.

There is in the letter, as Anthony Collins noted, one philosophical argument against the possibility of consciousness belonging to a material system, and it is to this argument that Collins addresses himself. Since Collins quotes the argument in full in his *Letter to Dodwell*, there seemed no need to reprint Clarke's very lengthy *Letter to Dodwell*.[1]

The main conclusion of Clarke's sole philosophical argument in his *Letter to Dodwell* is that since "matter is a divisible substance, consisting always of separable, nay of actually separate and distinct parts; it is plain that unless it were essentially conscious, in which case every particle must consist of innumerable separate and distinct consciousnesses, no system of it in any possible composition or division can be an individual conscious being" (p. 47). Clarke is here invoking the Composition Principle to show that the difference between consciousness and matter precludes consciousness from being a property of a material system.

In Clarke's thought experiment we are asked to imagine three or three hundred particles of matter at a mile or any given distance from one another. Clarke rhetorically asks if these separate parts could be an individual conscious being? Clarke clearly thinks the answer to his rhetorical question is "No! Absolutely not!" He is perhaps depending on our intuition that being separated the particles cannot be one thing, though it is possible to think of counter-examples of single things with spatially separated parts; for example, a watch that has been taken to pieces, or perhaps the original state of Bangladesh, its two parts geographically separated by Pakistan. Later, however, Clarke is going to make a much stronger claim, namely that individual beings don't have parts. An entity with spatially separated parts would certainly not count as an individual being in Clarke's terms.

Clarke next invites us to imagine these three or three hundred particles brought together into a system so as to touch one another. He asks whether by any motion or composition the particles will become any the less truly distinct beings than they were at a greater distance? Again, clearly he expects "No!" for an answer. The final question is whether, in this case, any possible system could be an individual being. And the expected answer is once again "No!"

---

1 The letter is reprinted in the Garland edition of *Clarke's Collected Works*, Vol. 3, pp. 719-47.

Clarke is clearly discounting and rejecting the unity that organization might confer on particles as well as the new functions that organization makes possible. Clearly there are vast and important differences in the amount of unity possessed by a heap of sand, a table, and a living being. Clearly also there are powers and capacities that tables and living things have that are not had by heaps of particles. But, because in Clarke's account individual beings don't have parts, he can dismiss the unity provided by any organization simply because an organization is an organization of parts and individual beings don't have parts.[1] One of the fundamental differences between Clarke and Collins is that Collins claims that the organization of matter is crucial to the individuation and differential functioning of things while Clarke denies the ontological importance of organization.

Collins' Letter to Dodwell

Collins read Clarke's *Letter to Dodwell* and apparently talked to Dodwell before writing his own letter to him.[2] The ostensible purpose of Collins' letter is to defend freedom of religious speech from the kind of bullying Collins thought Clarke was engaged in. Collins proposed to show that Clarke's one philosophical argument was inconclusive. In his short, five-page *Letter to Dodwell*, Collins makes some brief preliminary remarks, then quotes Clarke's argument from his letter to Dodwell and then raises a series of five objections to it. The structure of Collins' letter is that each succeeding objection supposes that the one before it has been answered. The first is that since matter consists of actually separate and distinct parts it surely meets the condition proposed for being an individual being, and thus is capable of thinking. The second is that God could surely render matter, when united into one system, an individual being; that is, God could make it so there could be no division or separation of parts of it by natural causes, thus making that system capable of thinking. In the course of stating this objection, Collins states what seems to have been the central insight that led Locke to

1 See Mijuskovic, 1974, and Rozemond, 2008, for accounts of the role that this kind of unity played in arguments for dualism and the immortality of the soul and in Clarke's arguments in the correspondence.

2 See Berman, 1975, p. 62.

make his thinking matter suggestion — that there is nothing about a solid extended substance that would keep God from superadding the power of thought to it.

The third objection is that even if matter cannot possibly be an individual being, still Collins sees no reason why an individual power could not reside or inhere in a material system. So, Collins sees no reason why inhering in individual being is a necessary condition for an individual power. At the end of the objection, Collins goes on to remark that he sees no particular reason why thinking should even count as an individual power. Collins claims there are many counter-examples all about us to Clarke's claim that individual powers must inhere in individual beings. Collins offers the power of a rose to produce its sweet smell in us as one such example. He points out that the particles of the rose separately do not have this power, but properly organized they do. And he offers this as an analogy for the brain and consciousness (p. 49). This is not only an example of an individual power, but also what we would call an emergent property. Collins never employs this language; indeed the term "emergent property" is first used only in the late nineteenth century. However, it is clear that Collins needs examples where the whole has properties not possessed by the parts individually, since the particles of the brain are dead and unthinking, while the brain is part of a living organism that thinks and is conscious. Being a property possessed by a whole that is not possessed by its parts is exactly what the language of emergent properties is intended to capture. This turns out to be the central matter of debate in the correspondence.

The fourth objection is that even supposing that Clarke had proved that consciousness could reside in an individual being, and that the individual being must be immaterial, the soul would still not be proved to be immortal, and so all the pains to show that it was immaterial would "signify nothing" (p. 49). Collins' point is that even if the substance of the soul were to continue, it is not clear that thinking would. If the soul were essentially a thinking thing, it would always be actually thinking. But following Locke, Collins takes thinking to be an action of the soul that can begin after the soul exists and perish while the soul still remains. Trying to prove the immortality of a thinking thing in this way is as futile as claiming the body is immortal because matter can only perish by annihilation. So, Clarke's argument is of no use for the ends and purposes of religion, and thus no use or influence on our lives or actions.

Supposing all the previous objections are met, Collins claims that all animals with sensations will be in the same condition as humans; that is, being made capable of eternal happiness. To avoid this consequence, Collins claims Clarke faces a dilemma: either all these creatures are machines and thus have no souls, or their souls will be annihilated at the death of their bodies; that is, that they are naturally mortal. Since animals are remarkably similar to humans in that they have sensations and seek pleasures and avoid pains and learn from experience how to do these things better, if the operation of animals is not sufficient to distinguish them from machines such as clocks, the operations of men will not serve to show them superior to machines. Collins goes on to claim that, should Clarke adopt the second horn of the dilemma, it would show that the assumption that immateriality ensures immortality is false.

Collins finishes by remarking that they are debating the merits of the argument, not the conclusion. He believes in the immateriality and natural immortality of the soul, not on the basis of uncertain reason, but on the basis of the New Testament. Thus, he claims neither he nor Clarke should be suspicious of the other's orthodoxy. One may wonder what the subtext to this remark is. It seems that insofar as revealed religion and natural religion do not deliver the same message, this is so much the worse for natural religion, or perhaps only a more limited conclusion — so much the worse for the efforts of the Newtonians to use natural philosophy to bolster Anglican orthodoxy.[1]

The Remainder of the Correspondence: The Central Issues

The rest of the correspondence largely develops from the five objections that Collins makes in his letter to Dodwell. The exceptions are the discussion of free will and determinism and personal identity. These topics develop from Collins' claims that Clarke's views are useless to religion. In reply, Clarke claims that Collins' determinism and his account of personal identity are not just useless to religion; they are dangerous. Here are the central issues:

---

1 The differing views of James O'Higgins and David Berman on whether Collins was an atheist or not turn largely on whether Collins' rejected natural religion or not. See O'Higgins, 1970, and Berman, 1975.

Emergent Properties

The issue of the possibility of wholes having properties not possessed by their parts, i.e. the possibility of emergent properties, remains a fundamental point of contention between Clarke and Collins for the remainder of the correspondence.

Clarke's Position

Clarke's chief strategy for denying that there are wholes that have properties not possessed by their parts is to give an enumeration of all the kinds of properties that exist and to claim that there are no real emergent properties.

To prove this, Clarke distinguishes qualities into three kinds that are similar in some ways to the Boyle/Locke distinctions between primary, secondary, and tertiary qualities, though there are also significant differences.

Clarke's Categories

1. REAL PROPERTIES INHERING IN A SUBSTANCE

A. Properties of Matter such as **magnitude** and **motion**, where the properties in the parts sum to the property in the whole. These are similar to **primary qualities**.

B. Properties of individual beings that are so unified that they do not have parts that can be compounded or divided, e.g. c**onsciousness**.

2. SECONDARY QUALITIES

These properties are real but inhere in some other substance than the one they originate from, e.g. **the smell of a rose**.

3. ABSTRACT (FICTIONAL) PROPERTIES

Magnetism, electricity, gravitation are not real properties but the effects of the action of one substance on some other substance.

The first class of qualities is composed of those properties that do "strictly and properly ... inhere in the substance to which they are ascribed" (p. 56). There are, Clarke claims, two different subclasses of qualities that do this. The first subclass of these properties (A in the list of categories above) are qualities of material systems such as figure and motion where the property in the whole material system is precisely the sum or aggregate of properties of the same kind inherent in the parts — roughly primary qualities. Thus, these properties all conform to what we may call the Composition Condition — that the properties of the parts will sum to the same properties of the whole (and that the properties of the whole can be divided into the parts). Magnitude and motion, Clarke's prime examples, are both subject to composition and division.

Along with this Composition Principle goes Vailati's Homogeneity Principle. Clarke says: "Composition or division of magnitude, varied in infinite matters to eternity, can produce nothing in the whole system, no quality or power whatsoever, but magnitude" (p.56). So, qualities of one kind can only cause or produce a quality of the same kind. This principle had been enunciated previously by both Cudworth (1678) and Bayle (1696) and applied to make precisely the same point: that one cannot get thought from motion or consciousness from figure because thought and consciousness are not of the same kinds as figures and motion. The Composition Condition clearly makes emergent properties impossible in that class of properties to which it applies. The Homogeneity Principle, while a quite distinct principle, has the same consequence. It is the violation of the Homogeneity Principle that generates all the contradictions that Clarke claims to follow from the assertion that wholes can have properties not possessed by their parts. Both principles require some form of an heirloom theory of causality — that is a theory that asserts that the cause must have in it whatever property is inherited by its effect.

The members of the second subclass of real properties that strictly and properly inhere in the substance to which they are ascribed (B in the list of categories above) are individual powers that belong to individual beings. This is a second class because such properties are so unified that they are not subject to composition or division and can only inhere in individuals that are similarly unified. The soul is so unified as to have no parts and so is consciousness. Descartes offered precisely this difference between bodies that have parts and minds that do not as one of his arguments for the real distinction between bodies and minds in Meditation VI (Descartes, 1988, pp. 119-20). Consciousness is a real property and it does strictly and properly inhere in the soul, but neither consciousness nor the soul satisfies the Composition Condition, and so they must make another subclass of qualities of the first kind. Instead of the Composition Condition, they conform to another condition that we might dub the Individual Being Condition. Inhering in an individual being is a sufficient condition for a quality being an individual power, though only a necessary condition for an individual being to be conscious.

The second of Clarke's three classes of properties can be characterized as what Boyle and Locke called secondary qualities and Clarke, along with Descartes, "sensible qualities." Clarke tells us that there are other qualities besides the first class that "are vulgarly looked upon as individual powers, resulting from and residing in the whole system without residing in each or any of its single and original parts, such as the sweetness of certain, bodies, the colors etc" (p. 57). But this is, he claims, a vulgar and gross error. For these properties do not reside in or result from the same system in any proper sense. Rather they are not individual powers residing in the material system to which they are supposed to belong, but rather effects occasionally produced in some other substance and are really qualities or modes of that other substance. So, Clarke's answer to Collins' counter-example of the sweetness of the rose is that "the sweetness of the rose is well known not to be a quality really inhering in the rose, but a sensation, which is merely in him that smells it, and is a mode of the thinking substance that is in the man"[1] (p. 57).

---

1 For the full exchange about the smell of the rose see p. 57, where Clarke treats the example of the smell of the rose as a secondary quality and speaks as if Collins is ignorant of the distinction between primary and secondary qualities; p. 75, where Collins protests that he understands perfectly well what secondary qualities are, but what he was referring to was not the smell but the power of the particles in the rose so organized that they produce that smell — a property none of them possesses individually. Clarke replies at pp. 102-03. He explains that he regards the texture of the rose (insofar as it differs from the magnitude, figure, and motion of the parts, as a "mere abstract Notion, and nothing really in the thing itself." He rejects the analogy between the rose and the brain because the power in the rose produces an effect in some other subject, while the power in the brain is supposed to produce an effect in the same subject. But there are always differences in analogies. Clarke assumes that this difference is crucial and the analogy fails in consequence. There is no reason to think that this is correct.

Clarke goes on to claim that insofar as these properties can be ascribed to the system of matter that produces them they are not individual powers. In the bodies that produce them, they are only specifically, not individually single powers, that is: "they are only a number of similar motions or figures of the parts of the bodies" (p. 57). Clarke goes on to deny that they are even always specifically the same, given the compound color green (which is an individual mode in the thinking substance that perceives it) which is composed of motions or figures that are specifically different — namely blue and yellow. This might very well seem like a violation of the Homogeneity Principle, but Clarke will claim that green is not a new quality — to think so would be the fundamental mistake that leads one astray in these matters. "Green" is simply a new name for a mixture of blue and yellow and not really a new quality at all.

The so-called qualities in the third class are not real qualities at all residing in any subject, "but merely abstract names to express the effects of some determinate motions of certain streams of matter." In this class are included electricity, magnetism, and gravity. At this point, because of the difficulties involved in gravity acting at a distance, the Newtonians are treating gravity as the operation of God on bodies, and not as a property of bodies. Only later was Newton to abandon this hypothesis in favor of the ether. Clarke treats these properties as fictions, and as the correspondence progresses the number of such fictions swells.

Having given this enumeration of all the kinds of qualities there are, the question becomes in which of these does consciousness fall. Clarke claims that it surely is not going to be in either of the last two of his classes of qualities, so it must be in one of the subclasses of the first. But if consciousness is claimed to belong to a material system, then it must belong to all of the parts proportionally, and thus one gets Clarke's original argument. So, consciousness must belong to the second subclass of the first kind of qualities — it must be an individual power of an immaterial substance — the soul.

Given Clarke's enumeration of properties, it is plain that there are no such things as emergent properties. To suppose there are wholes that have properties not possessed proportionally by their parts would involve one in a whole series of contradictions. It would suppose "either a universal to exist without particulars; or an effect to be produced without a cause, or to have more in it than was in the cause, or that a quality is made by God so as to arise out of nothing, as to be superadded to a subject without inhering in that subject, to which at the same time it is supposed to belong" (p. 58). Clarke concludes that it is thus manifestly impossible for the brain to either naturally produce consciousness or for that power to be superadded to it. Clarke also claims that he has not begged the question in claiming that an individual power like consciousness can only reside in an individual being. He has proved it.

Collins' Position

Collins sees organization of parts into wholes as fundamental to the creation of different kinds of things and their individuation.[1] Locke's account of the individuation of living things in his chapter "Of Identity and Diversity" in *An Essay Concerning Human Understanding* is most likely the inspiration for Collins' views on the importance of the organization of matter, although one can find Ralph Cudworth in *The True Intellectual System of the Universe* (1678) and Pierre Bayle (1647-1706) in the article "Dicaearchus" in his *Historical and Critical Dictionary* (1697) rejecting similar positions and for much the same reasons that Clarke does (see Appendix A2 and A3 respectively). The strategy that Collins adopts is, indeed, one of the few available to materialists to solve the problem of the origin of life and consciousness.

In section 1 of Collins' response to Clarke's *Defense of an Argument*, Collins claims that Clarke's enumeration of the three kinds of qualities is an argument from ignorance. Clarke, Collins asserts, needed to prove that there are no other powers in matter but has not done so. Collins claims that it is possible that different portions of matter have different properties and argues that if different parts of matter have different powers, then these powers might well combine to produce new powers, ones that

1 The Clarke-Collins correspondence took place before the development of modern chemistry and molecular biology, with the multitude levels or organization from atoms to molecules, to biological molecules to single cells and so on, that would have provided Collins with much stronger evidence for the position he was arguing. What is perhaps notable about the correspondence in this regard is how ignorant both of the protagonists were about the nature of matter.

differ from any possessed by the parts. He uses this point to justify his analogy between the rose and the brain — these are both cases where parts with different powers combine to produce new powers and where the particles making up those parts do not have the power that results. He also considers the possibility that all atoms are the same in structure. In this case, all of the differences between things in the world would be the result of matter being organized in different ways rather than being composed of different kinds of atoms (p. 71).

Collins makes another point on behalf of his claim that there are systems of matter that are not sums or aggregates of the powers of the same kind in their parts. First he defines power as "an actual ability to make or receive any change. To act or be acted on" (p. 72). He claims that it is not only magnitude and motion that are necessary to the making or receiving some kind of change, but the texture or organization of any particular being. The organization of ears, eyes "or any other part of man, is essentially different from the texture of other beings, and the texture of the parts of the being itself" (p. 72). He goes on to develop the example of the power of the eye to see to show that this class of powers is a different class of powers from magnitude and motion. For in the case of magnitude and motion, divide the matter as much as you will some determinate of magnitude and motion remain. But cut an eye in half and the power to see perishes because the organization that made it possible has perished. This is one of Collins' best efforts to show that there is a class of real qualities and powers that Clarke's taxonomy had failed to identify. As Robin Attfield notes in his article "Clarke, Collins and Compounds":

> We should not wish to say that propositions about a horse's running or a horse's life boil down simply to propositions about the functioning of (its) members, so long as they are related in a certain way. It is true not that the members, when suitably placed, run or live but that the horse runs and lives. Again it is implausible that a clock's showing the time consists in its parts showing the time, however well we describe their relations, unless we specify that they are *parts of a clock*, which we cannot say if we are to avoid circularity.[1]

---

1 Attfield, p. 52.

Clarke had already denied that such properties genuinely inhere in the substance to which they belong. He makes this point in his discussion of the roundness of a globe that perishes when divided (p. 60). Still, what makes Collins' eye example so compelling is that the organization of the eye seems to be essential to its being an eye and of its having the power to see. So, denying that this is a real quality inhering in a subject suggests that if this is not a real property, then eyes are not real. It is true that there are sightless eyes. But it is also plain these are defective eyes — eyes that fail to perform their function. The latter are parasitic on the former. The status of compound entities that are distinguished into kinds by their functional organization is one of the fundamental differences between Clarke and later Butler on the one hand, and Locke and Collins on the other.

In his *Reflections of Mr. Clarke's Second Defense*, after rehearsing Clarke's objections to his examples of wholes that have properties different from their parts, Collins makes a distinction between numerical and generical powers that he says will show that his examples — such as the texture of the eye — are pertinent. In making this distinction Collins has in mind not only Clarke's objections, but those of Bayle in "Dicaearchus." Collins is evidently trying to find a scheme that will both make a place for Clarke's kinds of qualities (among generical powers) and his own class of emergent properties (among the numerical) and answer Bayle's quite different objection about modes. Clarke finds the distinction unconvincing, but it leads him to write the *Third Defense* to show Collins that it will not do.

Collins quotes Cicero's account of Dicaearchus' position as an epigraph to his *Reflections on Mr. Clarke's Second Defense of an argument* presumably because he plans to deal with Bayle as well as Clarke. He takes up Bayle's position after he has made the distinction between numerical and generical powers. Bayle's original argument was that if you once supposed that the soul is not separate from the body, as Dicaearchus did, that it is only a power equally distributed through all living things and that it makes but one simple being with the bodies that are called living, then Bayle claims, you have to maintain that this power always accompanies the body. For what is not distinct from the body is essential to the body, and it followed from this that the power of feeling does not cease in dead bodies and that when they decay the parts of living bodies carry away with themselves their life and soul, which is quite counter-intuitive. Not only that but, about the view Bayle is attacking, he claims there can be no distinction between living and non-living matter. Bayle, having thus refuted Dicaearchus to his own satisfaction, then takes up an objection to the argument he has given against Dicaearchus, which he himself had thought up.

"Someone will tell me that feeling could be a modification of the body. From which it would follow that matter, without losing anything essential to it, could cease to feel as soon as it was no longer enclosed in the organs of a living machine."[1] Bayle claims this theory is absurd, "for all the modifications of which we have any knowledge are of such a nature that they cease only to give way to another of the same kind. There is no figure but what is destroyed by another figure, nor is any color driven out but by another color."[2] Presumably Bayle thinks this "feeling is a modification of body" version of the position will not save it from the absurd consequences he attributes to Dicaearchus' position. Presumably, also, if the soul is separate from the body and immortal, modes of the same kind will continue to succeed one another in it.

Finally, Bayle turns in note L to a point raised by an unnamed objector who, the evidence suggests, was, in fact, John Toland.[3] This new position is that Dicaearchus (or a Cartesian) need only say that it is organization rather than matter that contributes life to answer Bayle's argument. Then, when the organization ceased, so would life. (At least from Cicero's account, this in fact, seems to have been Dicaearchus' real position anyway.) Bayle's reply is to forcefully invoke the Homogeneity Principle (see Appendix A3).

Collins believes that he can answer both Bayle's objection about modifications of the same kind always being replaced by modifications of the same kind and disarm the Homogeneity Principle by making his distinction between numerical and generical powers. Thus Collins writes:

---

1 Bayle, 1991, p. 66.

2 Ibid.

3 Sullivan's *John Toland and the Deist Controversy* identifies Toland as the unnamed author (p. 177 and note 12). Jacopo Agnesina, who consulted Gianluca Mori on my behalf, first cleared up this point for me. Thanks to them both!

> Now if thought be supposed a species of motion, then it never ceases indeed but to make room for some other motion (the particles of all bodies being in perpetual action, as well as under some figure of color). But it follows not that the succeeding motion must always be a thought for the reasons and examples already alleged, no more than that the motion of a going clock existed in the several parts of it before, or continues after, they are separated. (p. 127)

Perhaps Collins' efforts to answer both objections have led him into confusion. In answering Clarke he claims that emergent properties like consciousness are numerical, while properties that obey the Composition condition are generical. Yet in answering Bayle he also says (as in the quotation above) that some numerical properties are, in effect, emergent (motions that are thoughts) and others are not. What he could have said that might have rendered his view consistent, is that some numerical properties are emergent and others are not, and that generically all motions obey the Composition Principle. It is worth comparing this supposition with Mill's treatment of the topic in his *System of Logic* (Appendix B2).

However, given what he did say, Collins' distinction allows him to deal with the Homogeneity Principle by restricting its application to generical powers. Thus, while consciousness as a mode of motion is generically the same as modes of motion that are not conscious, it is numerically different. Clarke had ended his *Second Defense of an Argument* with a fifteen-proposition summary of his position. In responding to Clarke's ninth proposition it becomes quite clear that this is how Collins thinks the distinction is going to help him. Clarke had claimed:

> 9 *No real quality can result from the composition of different qualities, so as to be a new quality in the same subject of a different kind or species from all and any one of the compound qualities.* (p. 146)

Collins' response is in terms of the distinction between numerical and generical qualities:

> According to Mr. Clarke's explication of this proposition, I allow this likewise to be true. *For from motion nothing but motion can arise, and from figure nothing but figure.* But this reaches not the case of numerical powers, and particularly reaches

not the case of consciousness. A real numerical power, as I suppose consciousness to be, and such as roundness is, may result from the composition of different qualities, as roundness does from different species of figures, and is consequently a new quality in the same subject of a different kind or species from all the component qualities considered together.

But motion, being a generical power, does I agree, consist of the motions of the parts. And did consciousness answer to figure and motion, that would likewise consist of the consciousness of the parts. (p. 146)

This passage leads us to the next major position that Collins takes in his *Reflections on Mr. Clarke's Second Defense* — and that is that he allows that thinking may be a mode of motion. I suspect one reason that Collins does this is to pick a quality that Clarke regards as real and that he therefore cannot reduce to his third kind. It is also plausible from a materialist perspective that consciousness would be a form of motion in the brain.

Clarke is unimpressed by both of these moves. In his *Third Defense* Clarke rejects Collins' account of the numerical/generical distinction, claiming that all real powers are numerical and that all generical powers are fictions. Clarke's response to the claim that consciousness is a mode of motion in the brain is to invoke the Homogeneity Principle. He elaborates his account of the Homogeneity Principle in terms of categories — it is not possible for something that belongs to one category to produce something belonging to another category with which it has not a single idea in common, so consciousness cannot be a mode of motion. The differing answers that Cudworth, Bayle, and Clarke on the one hand and Locke, Toland, and Collins on the other, give to whether the organization of matter can produce new qualities not possessed by the parts is one of their most fundamental and important differences.

This fundamental difference ramifies into differing metaphysical systems. Clarke makes a distinction in the correspondence that was later given a name by Clarke's protégé Bishop Joseph Butler (1692-1752) in his essay on personal identity appended to his *Analogy of Religion* (1736).[1] The distinction is between

1 Butler in Perry, pp. 99-105. Clarke's authorship of the distinction was first noted in Ducharme, 1986.

identity in the strict and philosophical sense and identity in the loose and popular sense. Things that are identical in the strict and philosophical sense are so because they remain the same substance over time, while things that are identical in the loose and popular sense do not. On this account, living things are not identical in the strict and philosophical sense because the substance (the collection of atoms) that makes them up at a given time changes over time. They are only identical in the loose and popular sense — not really identical but called identical for pragmatic and practical purposes. The most prominent of the things that are identical in the strict and philosophical sense are souls. Locke had rejected the soul as the bearer of personal identity in favor of consciousness. Both Clarke and Butler believe this to be a serious mistake on Locke's part. This brings us to the second major topic in the remainder of the Clarke-Collins correspondence: personal identity.

Personal Identity

From the beginning of the correspondence, Collins had been goading Clarke by claiming that Clarke's view was useless to religion. In the *Third Defense of An Argument*, besides giving an extensive refutation of Collins' distinction between numerical and generical powers, Clarke takes the offensive and offers spectacular arguments to show that Collins' account of personal identity is incoherent and therefore dangerous to such religious ideas as the resurrection. Since Clarke has a same substance view of identity, his view is that the immaterial soul is the bearer of personal identity, and the role of consciousness and memory is to inform us that we are the same person who did such and such a deed in the past, and if we look forward to being rewarded or punished for that deed, it will be the same soul that is punished or rewarded. Thus, consciousness contains not only the representation of deeds done, but also the direct awareness that it was I who did them. Bishop Butler shared this view of personal identity. Anthony Collins, on the other hand, develops a materialist version of Locke's account of personal identity. He holds that it is consciousness that constitutes personal identity and that personal identity is preserved through changes in the substance that composes the body and the brain by memories being revived and imprinted over again on the brain as the particles that make up the brain change over time. It is the transference of this memory information that preserves personal identity over time. For an echo of this view and Clarke's response to it, see Appendix B3), from Charles Darwin's *The Descent of Man*.

Clarke's response to this account of personal identity is to raise powerful arguments to show that it is inadequate. In his third and fourth *Defenses*, Clarke claims that consciousness cannot be transferred from one substance to another, so as soon as the particles in the brain change, one will have a new substance and hence a new person. That person may be qualitatively quite similar to the previous one, but they will not be identical. Both Clarke and Butler explicitly attribute this sort of successive person view to Collins, and Butler claims that this is an extension of Locke's too hasty account of personal identity.[1]

Perhaps the most interesting and important of Clarke's arguments (briefly referred to but not repeated in detail by Butler) is his Reduplication Argument. Clarke seems to have come by this argument by misreading or reading his own concerns into one of the more enigmatic sections in Locke's account of personal identity — section 13. Clarke claims that on the Locke/Collins account of personal identity it would be possible for God to create two or two hundred persons with the same memories, either in this life or the next. He claims that on Collins' account these two or two hundred would not be like the original person: they would each one be the original person. Thus, the Locke/Collins account of personal identity violates the notion that identity should be a one-one relation. On the other hand, Clarke claims that his own substance account of personal identity is not open to this objection because, presumably, not even God is capable of making copies of souls. As Barresi and Martin have convincingly shown in *The Naturalization of the Soul* (2004), Clarke's reduplication argument was reduplicated many times in the course of the eighteenth-century debate about materialism and personal identity. The argument was then forgotten and reinvented in the mid-twentieth century by Anthony Flew (1951), Arthur Prior (1957), and Bernard Williams (1957).

---

1 Some modern scholars seem to have accepted that this charge is true. See, for example, Martin and Barresi, pp. 58-59. For an account of the successive person view and reasons to think the charge not well founded, see Uzgalis, 2008.

Free Will and Determinism

A third issue, free will and determinism, arises in the same context as the issues about personal identity. Clarke claims that Collins' view that the soul might be material leads to a determinism that is dangerous to religion. By the time of Hobbes' debate with Bishop Bramhall in the 1640s the Anglican Church had abandoned the theological determinism of Luther and Calvin for free will. Hobbes defended his deterministic views on both theological and scientific grounds. Collins' views are similar to those of Hobbes. He sees free action as compatible with determinism and he raises powerful objections to free will. He claims, for example, that it is impossible for different effects to follow from the same causes, as would be the case if we had free will and could do otherwise. While the discussion of free will and determinism is relatively brief in the correspondence, Collins was later to write a book on the subject (O'Higgins, 1976) that was reviewed by Clarke, and there is still another book, *A Dissertation on Liberty and Necessity; With some remarks upon the late Reverend Dr. Clarke's reasoning on this point. And an epistle dedicatory to truth* ... (J. Shuckburgh, London, 1729), published the year of Collins' death and signed A.C. that responds to Clarke's review. Scholars are divided about whether A.C. was Anthony Collins or not. Clarke's sophisticated views on free will are best found in "Letters to Dr. Clarke concerning Liberty and Necessity from a Gentleman of the University of Cambridge, with the Doctor's Answers to them" and Clarke's review of Collins' *A Philosophical Inquiry Concerning Human Liberty*."[1]

Some Other Issues

A fourth issue, which is only briefly touched on in the correspondence, has to do with the origin of life. The issue is debated in relation to the question of how chicks develop in eggs. Collins maintains that the origins of life are material, while Clarke denies this. It thus, to a large degree, mirrors the debate about consciousness.

A fifth issue has to do with Clarke's account of the soul as extended. Collins raises a whole series of puzzles based on the

1 See Vailati, 1997, pp. 134-37.

parity of problems involving the extension of matter and the extension of the soul. Clarke's basic response to these difficulties is to claim that they are irrelevant to the main issue and that if one finds an extended immaterial soul unacceptable one can adopt the hypothesis that the soul is immaterial and unextended and vice versa. However, Ezio Vailati has suggested that Collins scored some real points against Clarke in this regard.[1] After all, if the soul is divisible in the way matter is, Clarke's whole argument founders; or one is forced to the view that the soul is immaterial and then one is faced with the mind/body problem that plagued Descartes' dualism.

Evaluating the Clarke-Collins Correspondence

One might very well hold that Clarke prevailed in the debate. He certainly gives some spectacular arguments against Collins' position, and from a rhetorical point of view maintains a superior attitude towards it throughout. He also got the last word. In his biography of Collins, James O'Higgins dismisses his arguments as poor, claiming, in effect, that it is only because Collins had history on his side that we find his views of any interest.[2] Martin and Barresi, while more positive, also have faint praise of this kind for Collins. They write: "His faltering, but often successful attempts to reformulate traditional metaphysical issues empirically, embodies the birth pangs of a new approach."[3] I hope this introduction has persuaded the reader that Collins' views are more interesting than these assessments might suggest, though they do have some truth to them. Collins certainly does give some bad arguments. For example, I have suggested that his distinction between numerical and generical properties is confused and perhaps inconsistent, though it is certainly possible that this problem could be fixed. Yet Collins sometimes does better than his defenders allow and Clarke sometimes worse than even his critics have noted.

Given the polarization over the issues involved, materialists in the eighteenth century tended to adopt Collins' views, while the defenders of the immaterial soul sided with Clarke. The

1 See Vailati, 1993, pp. 213-28.
2 O'Higgins, pp. 99-105.
3 Martin and Barresi, p. 51.

correspondence had gone through six editions (either both sets of letters being published separately or together) by 1731. The publication of correspondence in Clarke's *Works* in 1738 was, in effect, the seventh edition. Through the rest of the eighteenth century philosophers, theologians, and scientists read the correspondence and rehashed its arguments.[1] David Hume was clearly aware of the *Correspondence* and offers a rejection of the Homogeneity Principle in the chapter in the *Treatise of Human Nature* entitled "Of the Immateriality of the Soul" (see Appendix B1).

In the nineteenth century the Clarke-Collins correspondence was forgotten, though emergent properties got a new and consistent treatment from Mill in his *System of Logic* (Appendix B2) and, as noted earlier, one can find an echo of some of the issues Clarke and Collins struggled with in the debates over evolution (Appendix B3). The doctrine of evolution seems to provide reasons for thinking that the seventeenth- and eighteenth-century philosophers who maintained that the Homogeneity Principle showed that life and mind cannot come from matter were wrong. Rather, evolution suggests that the Principle of Homogeneity is satisfied in the evolution of living things from non-living ones, and then satisfied again in the evolution from simple organisms up to humans and the emergence of consciousness.

In the twentieth century, philosophers like Paul Grice, Quinton Skinner, Sydney Shoemaker, and John Perry have revived neo-Lockean theories of personal identity (see Perry, 2008), while Roderick Chisholm (Care and Grimm, 1969) revived the distinction between identity in the strict and philosophical and the loose and popular senses in opposition to neo-Lockeanism. It was only discovered late in the twentieth century that the kind of reduplication arguments offered by Flew, Prior, Williams, Shoemaker, Wiggins, and others, had first been offered by Samuel Clarke in 1708. Thus contemporary debates about consciousness, personal identity, and emergent properties explain the renewed interest that both scholars and philosophers are taking in the Clarke-Collins correspondence of 1707-08.

---

1 For the history of the Clarke-Collins correspondence in the eighteenth century, see O'Higgins, 1970, chapter XI; Yolton, 1983; and Martin and Barresi, 2004. Fox, 1988, gives both a good account of the controversy itself and of its antecedents and consequences in eighteenth-century English literature.

Samuel Clarke and Anthony Collins: A Brief Chronology

1675	11 Oct. Samuel Clarke born in Norwich.
1676	21 June. Anthony Collins born in Heston, Middlesex.
1693	Collins attends King's College at Cambridge University for a year.
1694	Collins enters the Middle Temple to study law but is never called to the bar.
1695	Clarke receives his BA from Cambridge.
1697	Publication of Clarke's translation of Rohault's *Treatise on Physics*. Clarke is introduced to Newton and becomes a member of his inner circle.
1699	Publication of Clarke's *Three Practical Essays on Baptism, Confirmation, and Repentance.*
1698	Collins marries Martha Child, daughter of Sir Francis Child.
1701-02	Publication of Clarke's *A Paraphrase on the Four Evangelists.*
1702	Clarke marries Katherine Lockwood.
1703	Collins meets John Locke at Oates. Visits Locke five times and corresponds with him until Locke's death eighteen months later. 19 Apr. Death of Collins' wife.
1704	Death of Locke.
1704-05	Clarke delivers the Boyle lectures two years in a row, making him a famous philosopher in England. The first year's lectures are subsequently published as *A Demonstration of the Being and Attributes of God.* This work set much of the position Clarke would defend in the Clarke-Collins correspondence.
1706	Publication of Clarke's *A Discourse Concerning the Unchangeable Obligations of Natural Religion, and the Truth and Certainty of the Christian Revelation*, a continuation of *A Demonstration.*

	Publication of Clarke's translation of Newton's *Optics* into Latin.
	Publication of Clarke's *Letter to Mr. Dodwell*, bringing about the Clarke-Collins correspondence of 1707-08.
1707	Publication of Collins' *An Essay Concerning the Use of Reason in Propositions, the Evidence whereof Depends on Human Testimony.*
1707-08	The published correspondence between Anthony Collins, Henry Dodwell, and Samuel Clarke.
1709	Clarke's public dispute for doctor of divinity at Cambridge.
	Clarke made rector of St. James, Westminster.
	Publication of Collins' *Priestcraft In Perfection.*
1710	Publication of Collins' *A Vindication of the Divine Attributes, in some Remarks on His Grace the Archbishop of Dublin's Sermon entitled "Divine Predestination Consistent with the Freedom of Man's Will."*
1711	Collins and Tindal meet frequently with Clarke and Whiston at the house of Lady Calverly and Sir John Hubern for friendly debates about the truth of the Bible and the Christian religion.
1712	Publication of Clarke's *The Scripture-Doctrine of the Trinity: Wherein Every Text in the New Testament Relating to that Doctrine is Distinctly Considered,* whose heterodox doctrines prevented Clarke from further advancement in the Church of England.
1713	Publication of Collins' *A Discourse of Free Thinking,* his most famous book, advocating the use of reason in the study of religion and the study of comparative religions.
1714	Clarke becomes a close adviser to the Princess of Wales the future Queen Caroline.
1715	Collins moves to Mowden Hall, Essex, where he builds a huge research library and holds a variety of important posts in local government, including Treasurer of Essex.
1715-16	Clarke's correspondence with Gottfried Leibniz, perhaps the most famous philosophical correspondence in history.

1717	Publication of Collins' *A Philosophical Inquiry Concerning Human Liberty.* Clarke publishes a review of Collins' *Inquiry.*
1723	Collins' only son dies.
1724	Collins marries his second wife, Elisabeth. Publication of Collins' *A Discourse on the Grounds and Reasons of the Christian Religion* as well as *An Historical and Critical Essay on the Thirty Nine Articles of the Church of England.*
1726	Publication of Collins' *The Scheme of Literal Prophecy Considered.*
1728	Publication of Clarke's *On the Proportion of Force to Velocity in Bodies in Motion.*
1729	Publication of Collins' *A Discourse Concerning Ridicule and Irony in Writing.*
1729	Publication by an author identified only as "A.C." of *A Dissertation on Liberty and Necessity; With some remarks upon the late Reverend Dr. Clarke's reasoning on this point. And an epistle dedicatory to truth.* 17 May. Samuel Clarke dies after a short illness. 13 Dec. Anthony Collins dies.

A Note on the Text

This edition of the Clarke-Collins correspondence of 1707-08 is based on the 1738 edition in Vol. 3 of Clarke's *Works* as reprinted by Garland in 1978. The present edition omits Clarke's original letter to Henry Dodwell, as well as Clarke's comments on a book on the life of Milton (Clarke, 1978). Typography and spelling both in the correspondence and in some of the supplementary readings in the appendices have been modernized. Some printing errors have also been corrected and very occasionally awkward words or phrases have been replaced with more readable ones, short phrases added where sentences were difficult to understand because of elision, or long Latinate sentences shortened in the few cases where the punctuation of the sentence made this possible. Editor's additions, deletions, and replacements are marked with [–ed.] or noted in footnotes. Latin and French passages and words or phrases in Greek and Latin have been translated.

The notes on the side of the page in the 1738 edition have been turned into footnotes and, where possible, page numbers added to make them useful in finding references by Clarke and Collins to earlier letters, to Clarke's Boyle lectures, and to other works. Where page numbers are given in the text of the correspondence, the page numbers to this Broadview edition of the correspondence or to the Boyle lectures follow in the text where possible. It should be noted that as these page numbers are the choice of the editor and not the original authors, it is possible that there are cases where the editor's choice is in error. Still, it was thought that the usefulness of adding page numbers to these notes vastly outweighs the possibility of error in some cases.

Explanatory footnotes have been written where these seemed appropriate. Thus there are three kinds of footnotes. First, footnotes of the authors in the original letters; second, side notes that have been turned into footnotes with page numbers added where possible; third, the editor's explanatory notes and notes about changes from the text of the 1738 edition. These are always marked with [–ed.] to distinguish them from the original footnotes of the authors.

THE CORRESPONDENCE OF SAMUEL CLARKE AND ANTHONY COLLINS, 1707-08

Anthony Collins (1676-1729), oil on canvas by Jonathan Richardson (1665-1745). © Trustees of Leeds Castle Foundation, Maidstone, Kent, UK/ The Bridgeman Art Library.

Anthony Collins

A Letter to the Learned Mr. Henry Dodwell

Containing Some Remarks on a (pretended) Demonstration of the Immateriality and Natural Immortality of the Soul, in Mr. Clarke's *Answer to his late* Epistolary Discourse, etc.

Sir,

There is nothing more unreasonable than to imagine there is any dangerous consequence in allowing men fairly to examine the grounds of received opinions, or to suspect the good intentions of those who do examine. For, until men have something besides *reason* for their direction, it is their duty to follow *that light* wherever it leads them. And how they can use their reason when there is a restraint laid on their tongues and pens is as unconceivable to me as how people should be Christians in *Japan,* or Protestants in *Spain.* Every man has the faculty of reasoning, but without the use and exercise of that faculty will make little or no progress in any science.

And what makes such suspicions; if possible, still more unaccountable is that examination is really a mark of sincerity, since the hazard of suffering lies more on the side of examination, than on that of submitting to prevailing opinions. And, to be sure, it is a disposition of mind much more favorable to truth than the contrary one, because reason being the same in all men, we should more of us light upon truth, did we rely on the use of the same common faculty, than we possibly can, by following the contradictory orthodoxies of the several countries in the world.

But, since through the artifices of designing men, they who sincerely search after truth meet with such discouragement — especially if there be any blot in their characters, or anything done in the whole course of their lives that is capable of having an invidious turn given to it — I publicly return *you* my thanks for your late *Epistolary Discourse,* wherein you have showed a noble example of freedom and liberty in attacking the received opinion of the *natural immortality of the soul.* Your character of piety towards God, charity to the necessitous, and patience under affliction, occasioned by adhering to your principles (which were once thought doctrines of the Church of *England*), is too well established in the world by the applause of those men who now endeavor to make you as little in the judgment of others as you were great in theirs before, not to derive some credit on those who pursue your steps, or at least to abate the edge of satire and invective against them. For the world has now a great instance not only of the consistency of zeal for religion with liberty of thinking, but that it is evidently your zeal for religion which has occasioned the liberty you have taken.

Under the protection therefore of your authority, I shall propose some of my thoughts to the world on the great subject of the *natural immortality of the soul,* with all the brevity that perspicuity will allow, and in some respect promote the design of your late Discourse. For though I do not pretend to prove the *natural mortality of the soul* by reason, yet if I can show the inconclusiveness of the most cogent argument for its *natural immortality,* they who lay a stress on that argument will be better prepared to receive those proofs from the *Scriptures and the first Fathers,* urged in your *Epistolary Discourse* to show that *the soul is a principle naturally mortal.*

The principal argument for the *natural immortality of the soul* is founded on the supposition of its immateriality. And therefore great endeavors have been made use of to prove the soul an immaterial being, and particularly by the reverend and learned *Mr. Samuel Clarke,* who in his *Letter* to you proposes *to demonstrate that the soul cannot possibly be material.* And what he has there said being urged with very great acuteness and dexterity, I shall impartially consider it.

By *soul,* I suppose, Mr. *Clarke* means a substance with a power of thinking, or, as he expresses himself, with an *individual consciousness.*

By saying *the soul cannot possibly be material,* I conceive is meant, that the substance which has solidity added to it, cannot have a power of thinking added to it. Or, that the same substance cannot be both solid and have the power of thinking.

To demonstrate the impossibility of this, it should be declared what is to be understood by the word *substance,* and then in what the identity of the same substance does consist. But these things being omitted, I shall observe, that after an enumeration of *arguments which,* he says, *have been urged by the wisest and most considerate men in all Ages* (so it is said, and so let it pass), we are told: *the same thing is demonstrable from the single consideration of bare sense or consciousness. For,* says he, *matter being a divisible substance, consisting always of separable — nay of actually separate and distinct parts — it is plain, unless it were essentially conscious — in which case every particle of matter must consist of innumerable separate and distinct consciousnesses — no system of it in any possible composition or division can be an individual conscious being. For, suppose three or three hundred particles of matter at a mile, or any given distance, one from another. Is it possible that all those separate parts should in that state be one individual conscious being? Suppose then, all these particles brought together into one system, so as to touch one another. Will they thereby, or by any motion or composition whatsoever, become any whit less truly distinct beings than they were at the greatest distance? How then can their being disposed in any possible system, make them one individual conscious being? If you suppose God, by his infinite power, superadded consciousness to the united particles, yet, still those particles, being really and necessarily as distinct beings as ever, cannot be themselves the subject in which that individual consciousness inheres, but the consciousness can only be superadded by the addition of something which in all the particles must still itself be but one individual being. The soul therefore, whose power of thinking is undeniably one individual consciousness, cannot be possibly a material substance.*

I have set down Mr. *Clarke*'s argument at length, and in full force of his own expressions, that a judgment may be made more easily of the pertinency or impertinency of the following observations.

1. Since it is only required that a thing be an individual being in order to its being a proper subject of a power of thinking, or at least that it may be possible for God to superadd to it a power of thinking, it is evident, by Mr. *Clarke*'s own account of matter — which he makes to consist of *actually separate and distinct parts* (though I wonder that at the same time he should make it *divisible,* when by its consisting of separate and distinct parts it is actually divided) — that those *separate and distinct parts* are capable of having a power of thinking, or an individual consciousness superadded to each of them. Because the want of individuality or distinctness is the sole reason urged why a system of matter cannot have a power of thinking, or an individual

consciousness. And consequently, according to Mr. *Clarke*'s own reasoning, matter may have a power of thinking, or an individual consciousness.

2. Since an individual being, according to Mr. *Clarke*, can only be the subject of a power of thinking, why may not several particles of matter, when united in one system, become an individual being, and be by the power of God rendered incapable of any division or separation by natural causes, and consequently be a subject capable of thinking? If several particles of matter can be so united as to touch one another, or closely to adhere, wherein does the distinctness or individuality of the several particles consist? The distinctness or individuality is as much lost to me by this supposed union, as the distinctness of the parts (if I may so speak) of an immaterial being, upon supposition that extension is not excluded out of the idea of immateriality, as it is not by Mr. Clarke, if I rightly apprehend him. For if the union of material particles be complete and entire, I can as well conceive an *immaterial being* capable of [division –ed.], as conceive those particles so united capable of division from one another. All the difference perceivable by us between such a material substance and an immaterial substance, besides solidity in one and want of solidity in the other, lies in this: that one perhaps continues as it was created, and the other becomes, by the power of God, what the other was by creation. And what difference that will make as to one's being capable of the power of thinking, and the other's not being capable of that power, does not appear to me, and never will, until thinking and solidity are proved to be incompatible in the same subject.

3. But let us suppose with Mr. *Clarke,* that a material substance in any manner disposed is not an individual being. Yet I cannot see but that an individual power may reside in a material system — which consists of actually separate and distinct parts — and, consequently, that an individual being is not indispensably necessary to be the subject of an individual power. Now if an individual power can be lodged by God in, or superadded to, that which is not an individual being, or follows from the composition or modification of a material system — consisting of actually separate and distinct particles — the very soul and strength of Mr. *Clarke*'s demonstration is gone. And matter of fact is so plain and obvious, that a man cannot turn his eye but he will meet with material systems wherein there are individual powers which

are not in every one, nor in any one, of the particles that compose them when taken apart and considered singly. Let us instance, for example, in a *rose*. *That* consists of several particles, which separately and singly want a power to produce that agreeable sensation we experience in them when united. And therefore, either each of the particles in that union contributes to the individual power, which is the external cause of our sensation, or else God Almighty superadds the *power* of producing that sensation in us upon the union of the particles. And this, for ought I can see, may be the case of matter's thinking. Those particles which compose the brain may, under that modification, either have the power of thinking necessarily flowing from them, or else may have the power of thinking superadded to them by the power of God — though singly and separately they may not have the power of thinking. The fallacy of Mr. *Clarke*'s argument, by which, as I take it, he deceives himself, lies in this: that by an individual power he understands a power that can only proceed from, or reside in, an individual being — which is a plain begging of the question, or supposing the thing in dispute, that *thinking is such an individual power*. To prove which, he has not, though all he says depends on it, offered so much as one word, and I conceive cannot, until he is perfectly acquainted with the nature of thinking. I readily acknowledge that we can distinguish the various modes of thinking from one another. But whether thinking is such a kind of operation as proceeds from an individual being, or whether it proceeds from a being which consists of actually separate and distinct parts, I must be content to be ignorant, until some better proof is produced to place it in an individual being than by calling it an individual power.

4. But after all, supposing Mr. *Clarke* had proved that consciousness could only reside in an individual being, and that that individual being must be an immaterial being, the soul would not then be proved to be naturally immortal. And consequently all the pains taken to prove the soul immaterial signify nothing. Nothing is proved naturally immortal by the supposition of the soul's immateriality, but the substance of the soul. Now, the soul is supposed to be a thinking immaterial being, and unless a thinking immaterial being can be proved naturally immortal, the soul cannot be proved naturally immortal. But how this can be done, I know not, but by showing the inseparable connection between immaterial being and thinking. And until then we have

as much reason to believe that thinking is an action which may commence after the existence of its subject, and may perish or cease to exist its subject still remaining. And thus there is no more progress made in the proof of the natural immortality of the soul by proving its immateriality, than there would be in proving the natural immortality of men's bodies, which are laid in the grave, by showing that matter can only perish by annihilation. For, as in the last case, no proof is made of the necessary continuance together of the several particles that compose our bodies, so, in the other case, we have no proof that thinking is an inseparable property of immaterial being. Of what use then is this argument to the ends and purposes of religion? For if we have no security that we must hereafter exist in a state of perception, as by only proving the natural immortality of the substance of the soul we have not, it can be of no use to influence our lives and actions.

5. But let us suppose that from the power of thinking, or individual consciousness, we can prove the immateriality of the soul, and from its immateriality prove its natural immortality, and then see what will be the consequence. All the numerous sensible creatures in the universe are put in the same condition with man, and made capable of eternal happiness as well as he. Now, to avoid this consequence, there are two things principally urged.

1. That all those creatures (which I call sensible) are only mere machines. Or,

2. That their souls shall be annihilated upon dissolution of their bodies.

To the first I answer, that experience as much convinces us that they perceive, think, etc., as that men do. They avoid pain and seek pleasure, and give as good marks of uneasiness under the one, and satisfaction under the other, as men do. They avoid pain and seek pleasure by the same motive that men do — *viz.* by reflecting on their past actions, and the actions of their fellows, with the consequences of them, which is apparent from their acting more to their own advantage the more experience they have had. But if, after all, brutes are only mere machines, the difficulty of proving the soul immaterial will be increased. For if the operations of brutes are not sufficient to distinguish them from clocks and watches, the operations of men will not prove *them* to be superior to machines.

To the second objection I answer that if the souls of brutes are annihilated upon the dissolution of their bodies, then the proof of the natural immortality of men's souls from their immateriality tends not to prove that their souls shall really be immortal. Because mere natural immortality is not a security from annihilation, as is supposed in the objection.

I shall now only add, that under the uncertainty in point of reason, both of the soul's immateriality and natural immortality, I am not the less certain of man's immortality from the Gospel of Christ. And therefore, for the sake of those who may be offended with me for my freedom, I shall observe that the same zeal which engages one man to maintain that a certain argument has a great deal of force in it to prove the immortality of the soul, may engage another man to maintain that it is weak and dangerous. They both aim at the same end. They differ only in judging of the nature of an argument. They ought both to abstain from all suspicious expressions — to abstain, I say, not in saying they will abstain, for that makes an ill impression, but by a perfect silence.

I am, *Sir, your humble servant.*

Samuel Clarke (1675-1729), oil on canvas by an unknown London artist.

Samuel Clarke

A Defense of an Argument

Made Use of in a Letter to Mr. Dodwell To Prove the Immateriality and Natural Immortality of the Soul.

In a Letter to Mr. *Dodwell,* upon occasion of his late *Discourse* concerning the nature of the *soul,* the following argument was among others particularly made use of to prove the *immateriality* and *natural immortality* of the soul.

"The same thing, *viz.* that *the soul cannot possibly be material,* is moreover demonstrable from the single consideration even of bare sense and consciousness itself. For, matter being a divisible substance, consisting always of separable — nay of actually separate and distinct parts — it is plain, unless it were essentially conscious — in which case every particle of matter must consist of innumerable separate and distinct consciousnesses — no system of it in any possible composition or division can be an individual conscious being. For, suppose three, or three hundred particles of matter, at a mile, or any given distance, one from another. Is it possible that all those separate parts should in that state be one individual conscious being? Suppose then, all these particles brought together into one system, so as to touch one another. Will they thereby, or by any motion or composition whatsoever, become any whit less truly distinct beings, than they were at the greatest distance? How then can their being disposed in any possible system make them one individual conscious being? If you suppose God, by his infinite power, superadded consciousness to the united particles. Yet still those particles, being really and necessarily as distinct beings as ever, cannot be themselves the subject in which that individual consciousness inheres, but the consciousness can only be superadded by the addition of something, which in all the particles must still itself be but one individual being. The soul therefore, whose power of thinking is undeniably one individual consciousness, cannot possibly be a material substance."[1]

To invalidate the force of this argument, the following objections have been offered to the public.[2]

"I. That an individual power *may* reside in a material system which consists of actually separate and distinct parts. *That* an individual power *can* be lodged by God in, or superadded to, that which is not an individual being, *or it may* follow from the composition or modification of a material system consisting of actually separate and distinct particles, *and if so, then* the very soul and strength of the *foregoing* demonstration is gone. *That as to this,* matter of fact is so plain and obvious, that a man cannot turn his eye but he will meet with material systems wherein there are individual powers, which are not in every one, nor in any one of the particles that compose them, when taken apart and considered singly. *That* a rose, *for example,* consists of several particles which separately and singly want a power to produce that agreeable sensation we experience in them when united. And therefore, either each of the particles in that union contributes to the individual power which is the external cause of our sensation, or else God superadds the power of producing that sensation in us, upon the union of the particles. *That* this may be the case of matter's thinking. Those particles which compose the brain may, under that modification, either have the power of thinking necessarily flowing from them, or else may have the power of thinking superadded to them by the power of God — though singly and separately they may not have the power of thinking. *And that* the fallacy *of the fore-mentioned argument* lies in this: that by an individual power *is there meant* a power that can only proceed from, or reside in, an individual being — which is a plain begging of the question."

"II. *That though* a system *of matter were allowed not to be capable of thinking, yet* it is evident that, *according to the foregoing argument,*

1 *Letter to Mr. Dodwell.* [This reference is to Clarke's original letter to Dodwell, which is not included in this edition. –ed.]

2 A Letter containing some Remarks on a pretended Demonstration, etc. [This refers to Collins' *Letter to Mr. Dodwell*, pp. 45-51 of this edition. –ed.]

the separate and distinct parts of matter are capable of having a power of thinking, or an individual consciousness, superadded to each of them. Because the want of individuality or distinctness is the sole reason urged why a system of matter cannot have a power of thinking or an individual consciousness. *And* it is only required that a thing be an individual being in order to its being a proper subject of a power of thinking, or at least *in order to its being a subject to which* it may be possible for God to superadd a power of thinking."

"III. *That though it were allowed,* that consciousness could reside only in an individual being, and *also* that that individual being must be an immaterial being, yet *even* then the soul would not be proved to be naturally immortal. *That is, the* thinking immaterial being *would not be proved to be immortal,* but only the bare immaterial subject or substance *itself. Because* thinking is an action which may commence after the existence of its subject, and may perish or cease to exist, its subject still remaining."

"IV. *That if* an individual being can only be the subject of a power of thinking, *then, according to the foregoing argument, either it will be proved that material substance is capable of thinking, or else that neither is immaterial substance capable of it. Because either* several particles of matter, when united in one system, may become an individual being — and be by the power of God rendered incapable of any division or separation by natural causes, and consequently be a subject capable of thinking — *or else* immaterial substance *also* may as well be conceived capable of division, upon supposition that extension is not excluded out of the idea of immateriality."

"V. *That if* from the power of thinking, or individual consciousness, we can prove the immateriality of the soul, and from its immateriality prove its natural immortality, *then* the consequence will be that all the numerous sensible creatures in the universe are put in the same condition with man, and made capable of eternal happiness as well as he. *Or else,* to avoid this consequence, *it must be supposed, either* that all those creatures are only mere machines, *or else* that their souls shall be annihilated upon the dissolution of their bodies. *And if so,* then the proof of the natural immortality of men's souls from their immateriality tends not to prove that their souls shall *really be* immortal."

The question being of great importance, and the objections very ingenious — as containing in brief all that can be said in favor of *matter's* being capable of thinking — it is presumed it may be acceptable to the impartial reader to see a clear answer given to each of them as they are here represented in their full strength (though, for method's sake, in somewhat different order than they were at first published).

I. To the first — *viz.* that *an individual power* may *reside in a material system, as sweetness in a rose, and that thinking may be supposed to do so as well as any other individual power* — it is answered that it is so far from being true, as is alleged, that *matter of fact is so plain and obvious that a man cannot turn his eye but he will meet with material systems wherein there are individual powers which are not in every one, nor in any one, of the particles that compose them, when taken apart and considered singly.* This, I say, is so far from being true that, on the contrary, it is both absolutely false in fact and impossible, and a direct contradiction in the nature of the thing itself that *any power whatsoever* should *inhere* or *reside in* any system or composition of matter different from the powers residing in the single parts. For the clearer and more distinct explication and proof of which doctrine, it is to be observed that all *powers* or *qualities* may be distinguished into three sorts. 1*st,* some qualities there are which do, *strictly* and *properly* speaking, *inhere* in the substance to which they are ascribed. And concerning these, it is evident at first sight, that every power or quality that is, or can be, *inherent* in any system of matter is nothing else than the sum or aggregate of so many powers or qualities *of the same* kind inherent in all its parts. The *magnitude* of any body is nothing but the sum of the magnitudes of all its parts. Its *motion* is nothing but the sum of the motions of all its parts. And if *cogitation* in like manner could possibly be a quality really *inherent* in a system of matter, it must likewise necessarily be the sum and result of the cogitations of the several parts. And so there would be as many distinct consciousnesses as there are particles of matter of which the system consists — which, I suppose, will be granted to be very absurd. Compositions or divisions of *magnitude*, varied in infinite manners to eternity, can produce nothing in the whole system, no quality or power whatsoever, but *mere magnitude:* Compositions and variations of *motion*, nothing but *mere motion.* And *sound* may as well be added to a *color*, or *color* to a *smell* — or any *quality* be made to subsist without any *subject* at all — as that any power whatsoever should be superadded to, and really made to *reside* in, any compositum or system of matter, without being made to inhere *proportionably* in the parts of that whole, taken singly as well as together. This, I say, is evidently at first sight true of all real qualities which truly and properly *inhere* in the subject to which they belong, such as are *magnitude* and *motion* in matter. 2*dly,* other qualities there are which are *vulgarly* looked upon as *individual powers,* resulting from and residing in the whole system without residing particularly in each or any of its single and original parts — such as are the *sweetness* of certain bodies, their *colors,* etc. But this is only a *vulgar* and very *gross* error. For neither do these qualities reside in, or at all result from, the whole system in any *proper sense.* Neither in *any sense at all* in which they can be ascribed to that body or system of matter to which they are vulgarly supposed to belong are they truly individual powers. In the *first* place, they are not *really* qualities of the system, and evidently do not at all in any *proper sense* belong to it, but are only *effects* occasionally produced by it in some other substance, and truly qualities or modes of that other substance in which they are produced. Thus the *sweetness of a rose* is well known not to be a quality really inhering in the rose, but a *sensation* which is merely in him that smells it, and a mode of the *thinking substance* that is in the man. In the *next* place, these qualities, in no sense wherein they can be ascribed to the system of matter, are *individual powers.* They are individuals only as they are modes of the thinking substance that perceives them. But in the bodies themselves, they are *only specifically,* not *individually,* single powers. That is, they are only a number of *similar motions* or *figures* of the parts of the body. Nay, they are not always so much as *specifically* single powers. Thus compound colors — as certain *greens,* for example — which are *individual modes* in the thinking substance that perceives them, may in the objects be nothing but a number of figures or motions *even specifically* different — namely such as usually represent both *blue* and *yellow.* And the same may be said of *heat, light, taste, sound,* and all those others which we call *sensible qualities.* 3*dly,* other powers — such as *magnetism* and *electrical attractions* — are not *real qualities* at all residing in any subject, but *merely abstract names* to express the *effects* of some determinate motions of certain streams of matter. And *gravitation* itself is not a *quality inhering in* matter, or that can possibly *result* from any texture or composition of it, but only an *effect* of the continual and regular operation of some other being upon it, by which the parts are all made to tend one towards another. Under these *three* heads must necessarily be contained all possible qualities, modes or powers whatsoever. They must either be *qualities really inhering in the subject to which they are usually ascribed,* or *modes produced by it in some other subject,* or else *mere abstract names signifying certain powers or effects that do not properly reside in any subject at all.* And now the question is among which of these *three* sorts of powers must *consciousness* or *thinking* be reckoned. I suppose it will neither be said to be a *mere abstract name,* nor yet *an effect* produced in or upon a foreign substance (as the *sweetness* or *color* of a rose is not any individual power in the rose itself, but merely a *sensation* excited in him that smells or sees it), but that it is certainly a *power* or *quality* truly and *really inhering* in the thinking substance itself. And therefore, if that thinking substance be a *system of matter,* the former reasoning holds strictly and demonstratively true, that the consciousness must inhere in all and every one of the particles of that system, taken singly as well as together. To suppose any power or quality of this kind arising from, or belonging to, any *whole* system of matter, without belonging to the *several parts* of which that whole consists, is a direct and express contradiction. It is supposing either a *universal* to exist without *particulars,* or an *effect* to be produced without a *cause* — or to have more in it than was in the *cause* — or that a *quality* is, by the power of God, made so to arise out of nothing, as to be supperadded to a *subject,* and to subsist without inhering in that subject to which it is at the same time supposed to belong. By this, I presume it sufficiently appears with what possibility of truth it is alleged that *the particles of matter which compose the brain may, under that modification, either have the power of thinking necessarily flowing from them, or else may have the power of thinking superadded to them by the power of God, though singly and separately they may not have the power of thinking.* And it will easily be judged, whether it be indeed a *fallacy,* and *a plain begging of the question,* to affirm that *an individual power,* properly and strictly speaking — such as consciousness or thinking must needs be acknowledged to be — *can only proceed from, or reside in, an individual being,* or whether the contrary be not rather demonstrated to be a plain contradiction.

II. To the second — *viz.* that according to the argument now under consideration, if not a *system of matter,* yet at least *the separate and distinct parts of matter are capable of having a power of thinking, or an individual consciousness, superadded to each of them,* seeing *it is only required that a thing be an individual being in order to its being a proper subject of a power of thinking* — it is answered, first, that supposing any particle of matter could be truly an individual — that is, an indivisible or indiscerptible being — yet it would not therefore follow that it could be capable of thinking. For though divisibility or discerptibility in any subject is a sufficient proof that that subject is not capable of such an individual power of thinking, yet it does not from thence presently follow, on the contrary, that whatever is indiscerptible is therefore capable of thinking. Though the present argument proves indeed only that whatever is discerptible cannot think — that is, that individuality is a *sine qua* non [that without which –ed.], or a necessary qualification without which no subject can be capable of thinking — yet it does by no means exclude other considerations, or at all imply that whatever has this property of individuality must therefore necessarily be capable of thinking, and cannot by any other property be rendered, or by any other argument proved to be, incapable of it. Though *the want of individuality or distinctness is* indeed *the sole reason urged* in the present argument *why a system of matter cannot have a power of thinking, or an individual consciousness,* yet it ought not therefore to be said that *it is only required that a thing be an individual being in order to its being a proper subject of a power of thinking.* Besides, supposing any particle of matter could be truly an individual being, and also that upon that account (which yet is by no means necessary) it could be capable of thinking, yet still the principal part of the question would be certain and unavoidable: that a thinking being must be, if not immaterial, yet however *naturally immortal.* For whatever is indiscerptible, though it were supposed material, could not by any power of time, or any force in nature, receive any such alteration, but that not only its substance, but even all its qualities also, must naturally remain forever unchanged. But then, secondly, it is answered further that the supposition itself of this objection is utterly impossible, *viz.* that any particle of matter can be truly an individual or indiscerptible being. For it is necessarily included in the nature of solid substance, how *small* so ever it be conceived to be, to consist still of parts not essentially connected, and not at all depending on each other for their existence. So that it is absolutely impossible and contradictory to suppose any particle of matter so truly an individual, but that by the power of God (for the *powers of nature* here are nothing to the purpose) it may be divided into two or more particles, which shall each of them separately be as perfect and complete matter, and continue to have all the very same properties as the whole particle had before it was divided. Suppose then the smallest imaginable particle of matter, endued with consciousness or thought. Yet, by the Power of God, this particle may be divided into two distinct parts, and then what will naturally and consequently become of its power of thinking? *If* that power will continue in it unchanged, then there must either be two distinct consciousness in the two separate parts; or else the power continuing in the intermediate space, as well as in the parts themselves, must there subsist without a subject; or else, not the material substance, but some other thing, is the subject of the consciousness. *If* the power of thinking will remain only in one of the separated parts, then either that one part only had at first the power residing in it — and then the same question will return, upon the supposition of *its* being likewise divided — or else it will follow that one and the same individual quality may be transferred from one subject to another, which all philosophers of all sects in the world have always confessed to be impossible. *If*, in the last place, it be said that, upon the division of the particle, the power of thinking which was in it will wholly cease, then it will follow that that power was never at all a real quality inhering or residing in the substance (in which mere separation of parts makes no alteration), but that it was *merely an external denomination,* such as is *roundness* in a globe, which perishes at its being divided. And this, I suppose, will be granted to be sufficiently absurd. There is no way to evade this argument, but by affirming either that a particle of matter may be so small as that it shall not be in the power of God to divide it; or that if it be divided it will consequently and necessarily be annihilated (neither of which, I suppose, will be affirmed); or else that the same may be argued concerning immaterial substance also, which is the *fourth* objection, and will be considered presently in its proper place.

III. To the third — *viz.* that though *consciousness* were allowed necessarily to infer *indivisibility*, and *indivisibility* to infer *immateriality*, yet even then not *the soul*, the *thinking immaterial being*, but only the *bare immaterial subject or substance* itself, *would be proved to be naturally immortal*, since *thinking is an action* (a *power* it should rather have been called) *which may commence after the existence of its subject, and may cease its subject still remaining* — it is answered that the contrary is evidently true. Namely, that not only the *bare immaterial subject*, but the *subject* and the *power* together, the *thinking immaterial being* itself, is hereby proved to be *naturally immortal*. Because, whatever substance is wholly *indiscerptible* is plainly, by virtue of that property, not only *itself* incapable of being destroyed by any natural power (for so also is the most *discerptible* substance likewise), but all its *qualities* and *modes* also are utterly incapable of being affected in any measure, or changed in any degree, by any power of nature. For all real and inherent qualities of any substance are either modifications of the substance itself, or else powers superadded and connected to the substance by the immediate power of God. And in either of these cases, it is manifest no *quality* can be altered by any natural power, which is not able to affect and make some alteration (in the disposition of the parts at least) of the *substance* itself, which in an *indiscerptible* substance it is evident cannot be done. The *soul* therefore, the *whole conscious being*, the *power of thinking* that resides in it, as well as the *bare immaterial subject or substance itself* (whatever may be said concerning the *power of God* in this question), will clearly, notwithstanding what any *finite* power can do, of necessity be *naturally immortal*. The truth of this reasoning is evident from what we cannot but observe even in the *material world* — namely, that all the changes which are caused therein by any powers of nature are nothing but changes of the order and disposition of the parts of compound bodies. The original and perfect solid particles of matter which are (not indeed absolutely in themselves, but) to any power of nature indiscerptible, are utterly incapable of having not only their substance, but even any of their qualities or properties, altered in any measure by any power of nature. As is evident from the form or species of those we vulgarly call simple or elementary bodies, remaining always unalterably the same, and indeed continually with the same powers and qualities.

IV. To the fourth — *viz.* that, according to the argument we are now considering, either a *system of matter*, being by a strict union of parts made an individual being, may become *capable of thinking*, or else *immaterial substance* also *may as well be conceived capable of division*, and consequently incapable of thought, *supposing extension not excluded out of the idea of immateriality* — it is answered, that the case is very different. Because some of the *first* and *most obvious* properties which we *certainly know* of *matter* — as its having *partes extra partes* [parts beyond parts — meaning that they exist independently of one another. –ed.], strictly and properly speaking; that is, its consisting of such parts as are *actually unconnected*, and are *truly distinct beings*, and *can* (as we see by experience) *exist separately*, and have *no dependence one upon another* — do necessarily and confessedly imply *discerptibility*. But in *immaterial beings* we do *not know* of any such properties, as any wise imply discerptibility. It cannot be collected from any property we know of *them*, but that they *may* be such beings as can no more be divided than annihilated — that is, whose whole essence may be necessarily one, and their substance essentially indivisible, upon the same ground as their existence continues. Nay, the *only* properties we *certainly and indisputably* know of them, namely *consciousness* and its modes, do prove (as has been before shown) that they *must necessarily* be such indiscerptible beings. As evidently as the *known properties* of *matter* prove it to be certainly a *discerptible substance*, whatever other *unknown properties* it may be endued with, so evidently the *known and confessed properties* of *immaterial beings* prove them to be *indiscerptible*, whatever other *unknown properties* they likewise may be endued with. How far such *indiscerptibility* can be reconciled and be consistent with some kind of *expansion* — that is, what *unknown properties* are joined together with these *known ones* of consciousness and indiscerptibility — is another question of considerable difficulty, but of no necessity to be resolved in the present argument. Only this: as the parts of *space* or *expansion* itself can demonstrably be proved to be *absolutely indiscerptible*, so it ought not to be reckoned an insuperable difficulty to imagine that all *immaterial thinking substances* (upon supposition that expansion is not excluded out of their idea) may be so likewise.

V. To the fifth — *viz.* that by the fore-mentioned argument, *all the sensible creatures in the universe are put in the same condition with man, and made capable of eternal happiness as well as he;* or else that, *to avoid this consequence, all those creatures must either be supposed to be only mere machines,* or else *that their souls shall be annihilated upon the dissolution of their bodies;* and if so, *then the proof of the natural immortality of* men's *souls from their immateriality, tends not to prove that their souls shall* really be *immortal* — it is answered that, though all sensible creatures have certainly in them something that is immaterial, yet it does not at all follow either that they must needs be annihilated upon the dissolution of their bodies, or else that they must be capable of eternal happiness as well as man. This is just such an argument, as if a man should conclude that whatsoever is not exactly like himself can therefore have no being at all. Or that all the stars of heaven, if they be not exactly like our globe of earth, cannot possibly be any globes at all. Certainly the omnipotent and infinitely wise God may, without any very great difficulty, be supposed to have more ways of disposing of his creatures than we are at present let into the secret of. He may indeed, if he please, annihilate them at the dissolution of their bodies (and so he might, if he thought fit, annihilate the souls of men, and yet it would be never the less true that they are *in their own nature immortal*), or he may, if he pleases, without either annihilating them or suffering them to fall into a state of entire inactivity dispose of them into *numberless* states, concerning the particular nature of which we are not now able to make the least conjecture. I suppose that man does not do any great honor either to God, or to the Christian religion, who will needs contend that through a boundless eternity there shall never exist anything in the immense universe, but what must needs partake of happiness or misery of *mankind*.

Anthony Collins

A Reply to Mr. Clarke's Defense of his Letter to Mr. Dodwell

With a Postscript relating to Mr. Milles' Answer to Mr. Dodwell's Epistolary Discourse

—Jesus Christ, who hath abolished Death, and hath brought Life and Immortality to Light through the Gospel, 2 Tim. i. 10.

M. Evolve igitur librum Platonis qui est de animo: amplius quod desideres, nihil erit. A. Feci mehercule & quidem sæpius: sed nescio quomodo dum lego, assentior; cum posui librum, & mecum ipse, de immortalitate animorum, cœpi cogitare, assensio omnis ilia elabitur.

M.T. Ciceronis Tusculanarum Qucestionum lib. 1.

Marcus Tullius Cicero: Turn over, therefore, the pages of Plato's book about the soul; you will need nothing further. Atticus: I have done so, be sure, and done so many times: but somehow I am sorry to say, I assent while reading; yet when I have laid the book aside and begin to reflect in my own mind about the immortality of souls, all my previous sense of agreement slips away.

M.T. Cicero Tusculan Disputations, Questions Bk. 1
Trans. J.E. King

Sir,

The importance of the *question* concerning the possibility of matter's thinking, and the ability of Mr. *Clarke* to urge to the best advantage whatever can be said on that side of it which he espouses, make me presume it will not be unacceptable to the impartial reader to see what answer can be given to his *Defense of an Argument, Made Use of in a Letter to Mr. Dodwell, to Prove the Immateriality and Natural Immortality of the Soul* by the author of the objections to that *Argument;* who still thinks it inconclusive, and proposes to show its inconclusiveness in the following papers, and thereby to contribute towards the establishment of the immortality of man on that evidence only that God has thought fit to afford us of it — and by a *new instance* assert the freedom and liberty, so peculiar to the country wherein we live, of examining the grounds and reasons of prevailing opinions. But if he happens to fail in the execution of his design — either through the weakness of his cause, or his own inability to deal with so learned an adversary — yet he is very sure not to err in anything but a matter of speculation. He is not disposed to use any foreign or unmannerly mixture in any debate, much less when engaged with a gentleman who, by confining himself solely to the argument, set so unusual an example of fair dealing in controversy.

The argument made use of by Mr. *Clarke*, to prove the immateriality and natural immortality of the soul, was *that the soul cannot possibly be material is demonstrable from the single consideration even of bare sense and consciousness itself. For matter being a divisible substance, consisting always of separable — nay, of actually separate and distinct parts — it is plain, unless it were essentially conscious — in which case every particle of matter must consist of innumerable consciousnesses — no system of it, in any possible composition or division, can be an individual conscious being. For, suppose three or three hundred particles of matter at a mile or any given distance one from another. Is it possible that all those separate parts should in that state be one individual conscious being? Suppose then, all these particles be brought together into one system, so as to touch one another. Will they thereby, or by any motion or composition whatsoever, become any whit less truly distinct beings than they were at the greatest distance? How then can their being disposed in any possible system make them one individual conscious being? If you suppose God by his infinite power superadded consciousness to the united particles, yet still those particles being really and necessarily as distinct beings as ever, cannot be themselves the subject in which that individual consciousness inheres, but the consciousness can only be superadded by the addition of something which in all the particles must still itself be but one individual being. The soul therefore, whose power of thinking is undeniably one individual consciousness, cannot possibly be a material substance.*

Against this argument I offered several objections, which I shall repeat and defend, in the same order that Mr. *Clarke* has thought fit to consider them. The first is as follows:

[*Sect.* 1] "Let us suppose, with Mr. *Clarke,* that a material substance in any manner disposed, is not an individual being. Yet I cannot see, but that an individual power may reside in a material system — which consists of actually separate and distinct parts — and, consequently, that an individual being is not indispensably necessary to be the subject of an individual power. Now if an individual power can be lodged by God in, or superadded to, that which is not an individual being, or follows from the composition or modification of a material system — consisting of actually separate and distinct particles — the very soul and strength of Mr. *Clarke*'s demonstration is gone. And matter of fact is so plain and obvious, that a man cannot turn his eye but he will meet with material systems wherein there are individual powers which are not in every one, nor in any one, of the particles that compose them when taken apart and considered singly. Let us instance, for example, in a *rose* that consists of several particles, which separately and singly want a power to produce that agreeable sensation we experience in them when united. And therefore, either each of the particles in that union contributes to the individual power, which is the external cause of our sensation, or else God Almighty superadds the power of producing that sensation in us upon the union of the particles. And this, for ought I can see, may be the case of matter's thinking. Those particles which compose the brain may, under that modification, either have the power of thinking necessarily flowing from them, or else may have the power of thinking superadded to them by the power of God — though singly and separately they may not have the power of thinking. The fallacy of Mr. *Clarke*'s argument, by which, as [I –ed.] take it, he deceives himself, lies in this: that by an individual power he understands a power which can only proceed from, or reside in, an individual being — which is a plain begging of the question, or supposing the thing in dispute, that *thinking is such an individual power.* To prove which, he has not, though all he says depends on it, offered so much as one word, and I conceive cannot, until he is perfectly acquainted with the nature of thinking. I readily acknowledge that we can distinguish the various modes of thinking from one another. But whether thinking is such a kind of operation as proceeds from an individual being, or whether it proceeds from a being which consists of actually separate and distinct parts, I must be content to be ignorant, until some better proof is produced to place it in an individual being than by calling it an individual power."

To answer this objection Mr. *Clarke* says, *that all powers and qualities may be distinguished into three sorts. (i) Some qualities there are which do, strictly and properly speaking, inhere in the substance to which they are ascribed. And concerning these, it is evident that every power or quality that is or can be inherent in any system of matter is nothing else than the sum or aggregate of so many powers or qualities of the same kind inherent in all the parts. The magnitude of any body is nothing else but the sum of the magnitudes of all its parts. Its motion is nothing else but the sum of the motions of all its parts. And if cogitation in like manner could possibly be a quality really inherent in a system of matter, it must likewise necessarily be the sum and results of the cogitations of the several parts. And so there would be as many distinct consciousnesses as there are particles of matter. (ii) [There are] other powers, which are vulgarly looked on as individual powers, resulting from and residing in the whole system without residing particularly in each or any of its single and original parts — such as the sweetness of certain bodies, their colors, etc. But [supposing] this is only a gross and vulgar error. (iii) Other powers — such as magnetism and electrical attractions — are not real qualities at all residing in any subject, but merely abstract names to express the effects of some determinate motions of certain streams of matter. And gravitation itself is not a quality inhering in matter, or that can possibly result from any texture or composition, but only an effect of the continual and regular operation of some other Being upon it, by which the parts are all made to tend one towards another. Under these three heads must necessarily be contained all possible qualities, modes or powers whatsoever. And now the question is among which of these three sorts of powers must consciousness or thinking be reckoned. I suppose it will neither be said to be a mere abstract name, nor yet an effect produced in or upon a foreign substance (as the sweetness and color of a rose is not any individual power in the rose itself, but merely a sensation excited in him that smells or sees it), but that it is a quality or power truly and really inhering in the thinking substance itself. And therefore, if that thinking substance be a system of matter, the former reasoning holds strictly and demonstratively true, that the consciousness must inhere in all and every one of the particles of that system, taken singly as well as together. To suppose any power or quality of this kind arising from, or belonging to, the several parts of which the whole consists, is a direct and express contradiction. It is supposing either a universal to exist without particulars, or an effect to be produced without a cause, or that a quality is, by the power of God, made so to arise out of nothing, as to be superadded to a subject, and to subsist without inhering in that subject to which it is at the same time supposed to belong.*

1. Before I make any return to this answer of Mr. *Clarke,* it will not be improper to fix and determine the precise significations of some words on which the question turns. The question being whether a system of matter can have a power of thinking, or an individual consciousness, superadded to it, or flow from any modification of that system, it is evident that by a *power of thinking* is understood, not a *capacity to think,* but *actual thinking,* for else *consciousness* could not be properly employed, by Mr. *Clarke,* to signify the same thing with a *power of thinking.*

2. The term individual, when applied to power, must likewise signify barely *one power,* without any determination whether that *power* proceed from an individual or an actually divided, or divisible, being. For if an *individual power* signifies a power which proceeds from, or inheres in, an individual being, and consciousness be supposed such an individual power, and the question is, whether consciousness or any individual power can reside in a system of matter, or a being that is not individual, there is no ground to dispute whether a system of matter can have consciousness, or any other individual power, on such suppositions. It is evident that on those suppositions a system of matter cannot possibly think. For a system of matter being supposed to consist of parts, and thinking or consciousness being supposed to be a power incapable of residing in a being that consists of parts, the question of matter's thinking will amount to this: *whether that which cannot think, can think.* I do not, by what I have said, exclude Mr. *Clarke* from contending for consciousness or thinking's being a power that can only reside in an individual being. He is at his liberty to make that a question whenever he thinks fit, and I shall be very glad to see what so able a gentleman can say to give me light into the nature of thinking. But all that I contend for is that thinking be not supposed an individual power, in a sense that begs the question between us, till it be proved an individual in that sense and then I will allow that there is no ground to dispute whether a system can think. These things being cleared, I answer to Mr. *Clarke*'s argument.

1. That it is nothing else but *argumentum ad ignorantiam* [an argument from ignorance –ed.]. For by enumerating his three

sorts of powers or qualities of matter, and showing that the two last of his sorts are improperly called powers or qualities, he does suppose that a system of matter has, and can have, only powers of one sort or kind — such as magnitude and motion — which are only the sum or aggregate of powers of the same kind. Which, what is it else but to argue that because we know of no other powers of a different kind in matter from magnitude and motion, therefore it has, and can have, no other powers of a different kind from magnitude and motion? Whereas he ought to have demonstrated, if he would have proved the point he undertook to prove, that there can be no other power in any system of matter but what is the sum or aggregate of powers of the same kind. And then there might have been some ground to conclude *that if consciousness be really inherent in a system of matter it must be the sum or result of the consciousnesses of the several parts*. For until it is demonstrated that there can be no other power in any system of matter but what is the sum or aggregate of powers of the same kind, it may as well be supposed that there are powers of different kinds in different particles of matter, or that God can superadd different kinds of powers to the different parts of a material system. And then the action or power exerted, resulting from them when united, will be of a different sort or species from any power inhering in the particles singly considered, and so far from being the sum or aggregate of powers of the same kind, that the new power will be the sum or aggregate of powers of a different kind. And if so, then Mr. Clarke must prove that consciousness is not an action or actual power resulting from a union of different kinds of powers, or else he will not be able to prove the impossibility of matter's thinking from its divisibility, or its being actually divided *in infinitum*. For on supposition that there are powers of different kinds in different parts of the same material system, and that consciousness cannot be proved to be, properly speaking, an individual power, or a power which can only reside in an individual being, there will be no reason to conclude *that if consciousness be really inherent in a system of matter, it must be the sum or result of the consciousnesses of the several parts*. But, on the contrary, that if consciousness does inhere in a system of matter, it must not be the sum or result of the consciousnesses of the several parts. And all Mr. *Clarke*'s difficulties founded on matter[1] consisting of actually separate and distinct parts will be removed. For it

1 Replacing "matter's" –ed.

will then be no *contradiction to suppose a power arising from matter without belonging to the parts of which the whole consists,* no more than it will be to conceive that a whole is not the same with a piece of a clock. For the power resulting from the different contributing powers in the system neither belongs to any part of the system when considered by itself, nor is it of the same sort or kind with any power in any part of the system. Nor will there be any ground to *suppose a universal to exist without particulars,* but a particular power existing to which several particular powers contribute — as every man is a particular man, though various powers are necessary to constitute him of the species. Nor, lastly, to *suppose an effect produced without a cause,* for the different powers in the single and separate parts of a system of matter, by uniting in one operation or power to operate, are the cause of the existence of that power which did not exist in the particles singly considered. And thus it may be conceived that there may be a power in all those particles which compose the brain to contribute to the act of thinking before they are united under that form, though while they are disunited they have no more of consciousness than any being which produces sweetness in us (that is made up of parts wherein different powers inhere) when under a particular form has a power to produce sweetness in us when its parts are disunited and separated.

2. Though I have supposed different parts of matter in the same system to have actual powers essentially different, yet I will allow that matter is everywhere, under the same circumstances, endowed with the same powers; and that, taking the whole material world together, every particle thereof is capable of contributing to all the actual powers of matter equally with any other particles whatever. But then if these actual powers exist but only under such and such regulations, and that a disposition of parts by motion be necessary to the exertion of every power, it will equally follow that the power of every system will not be the sum of powers of the same kind, but be the sum of powers of different kinds. Because by the different situation of parts in a system, a different power is exerted in every particle, though each of them would exert the same power under the same circumstance or position. And I much rather take this to be the case, than to suppose really different powers founded on different capacities in the different parts of matter. For by experience we see that everything by change of form becomes everything. The same parts of matter become parts of *dung, earth, grass, corn, sheep,*

horses, men, etc., and act their parts under these mutations. And, I would add, as what seems equally matter of fact to me, that the matter of which an egg consists does entirely constitute the young one, and that the action of sensation began under a particular disposition of the parts by motion, without the addition of an immaterial and immortal soul — as the powers of vegetation, gravitation, of producing the sensation of heat, cold, red, blue, yellow, are performed without the addition of an immaterial and immortal soul — had not the system-makers of *Europe* thought fit to deny it, in order to etch out their hypotheses.

3. Mr. *Clarke* has not rightly enumerated the known powers of matter. In order to make that appear, let us consider what we mean by power. By power I understand, in the question between us, *an actual ability to make or receive any change, to act or be acted on*. The question then will be whether there is in any system of matter a power to make or receive a change, to act or be acted on, that is not the sum or aggregate of powers of the same kind? Now that there are powers in systems of matter that are not the sum or aggregate or powers of the same kind is apparent from this consideration, that not only mere magnitude and motion is necessary to the making or receiving some sort of change, but the particular texture of a being. Now the texture, let it be of the eye, ear, or any other part of a man, is essentially different from the texture of other beings, and the texture of the parts of the being itself. And it is from its texture, as well as from its magnitude and motion, that the matter of which the eye consists, has a power to make or receive a change, to act or be acted on — which power depends so entirely on the particular texture that, upon the least alteration of some parts of the eye, it ceases to have a power of being operated on by external objects, or of contributing to the act of vision. And if the powers of a system of matter may entirely cease upon the least alteration of a part of that system, it is evident that the powers of the system inhere not in its parts in the same sense with magnitude and motion. For divide and vary the parts of matter as much as you will, there will be magnitude, and may be motion. But divide or vary the least part of the eye, and the power of contributing towards the act of vision is entirely at an end.

4. I had said, "that the fallacy of Mr. *Clarke*'s argument, by which, as I took it, he deceived himself, lies in this: that by an individual power he understands a power which can only proceed

from, or reside in, an individual being — which is a plain begging of the question, or supposing the thing in dispute, that thinking is such an individual power. To prove which he has not, though all he says depends on it, offered so much as one word, and I conceive cannot, until he is perfectly acquainted with the nature of thinking. I readily acknowledge that we can distinguish the various modes of thinking from one another. But whether thinking is such a kind of operation as proceeds from an individual being, or whether it proceeds from a being that consists of parts, I must be content to be ignorant, till some better proof is produced to place it in an individual being, than by calling it an individual power."

To manifest this, and show yet farther the weakness of Mr. *Clarke*'s argument, I observe that Mr. *Clarke* proposed to demonstrate that a power of thinking or consciousness cannot inhere in a system of matter, *from the single consideration of bare sense or consciousness itself.* His argument is in short as follows. *Matter is a substance consisting always of actually separate and distinct parts. Consciousness is an individual power. An individual power cannot be added to a substance, consisting of actually separate and distinct parts, but by being added to all those parts of which that substance does consist. Whereby instead of one consciousness, there will be as many distinct consciousnesses as there be distinct parts of that substance.* This, if I mistake not, comprehends the entire strength of his argument, with relation to which I shall lay down the following particulars.

(i) That our idea, signified by the term matter in this dispute, is of a solid being, which does consist of actually separate and distinct parts.

(ii) Saying, *that consciousness is an individual power* (be they ever so many that say so) is but calling consciousness by another name. It is not giving an account of what consciousness is, wherein it does consist, which is requisite to demonstrate from consciousness that consciousness cannot be added to a being that consists of actually separate and distinct parts. If a man should say that consciousness is a quality that makes the being to which it is added not to consist of distinct parts, he would (allowing the truth of his assertion) prove that it cannot inhere in a being that consists of parts, because of the obvious repugnancy there is between the coexistence of these two properties, affections, qualities (or call them as you please) in the same being. But it is not enough to demonstrate that consciousness cannot be superadded to a being that consists of parts to call consciousness by another name. If one should undertake to demonstrate to me that consciousness can only inhere in a system of matter, and for this purpose should tell me that consciousness is an organic operation, I should desire him to tell me wherein thinking or consciousness does consist? For if he would do that I should be able to know whether it is an organic operation or not. Whereas his telling me that it is an organic operation leaves me as ignorant what thinking is, in what it does consist, as I was before those sounds reached my ear: and does as much suppose the thing in dispute — *that matter can only think* — as Mr. *Clarke*'s calling consciousness an individual power, in his sense of individual power, is supposing that matter cannot think.

(iii) Therefore before it can be demonstrated from consciousness that consciousness cannot reside in a being that consists of actually separate and distinct parts, it must be demonstrated that consciousness is *an individual power* in Mr. *Clarke*'s sense of those words, or that it is a power which can only reside in an individual being. But Mr. *Clarke* has not said anything to this question, but barely by calling consciousness *an individual power.* His argument therefore, stripped of all doubtful expressions, and resting on the proofs by which he supports it, is this. *Matter is a substance consisting always of actually separate and distinct parts. Consciousness cannot reside in a being which consists of actually separate and distinct parts. Therefore matter cannot think, or be conscious.* To support which connection he has no intermediate ideas, but by saying *consciousness* is *an individual power, and an individual power cannot reside in a being that consists of parts, therefore consciousness cannot reside in a being which consists of parts.* Which carries the matter not one jot further than merely supposing consciousness to be a power which can only reside in an individual being.

(iv) Having made good my charge against Mr. *Clarke*'s argument, as it stands in his Letter to Mr. *Dodwell,* which only could lie before me when I made my objections, and from whence Mr. *Clarke* has urged nothing in his Defense to show that he did not beg the question, I shall consider what I can find in his *Defense* to show that thinking is a power which must reside in an individual being. He says, *that every power or quality that is or can be inherent in any system of matter is nothing else but the sum or aggregate of powers of the same kind, inherent in all its parts. And if cogitation could be a quality really inherent in matter, it must be the sum and result of the consciousnesses of the several parts — which is apparently absurd.* Now though this does not suppose thinking to be a power which can only reside in an individual being, as Mr. *Clarke*'s argument did, yet it supposes another proposition: *that all the powers of any system of matter are nothing else but the sums or aggregates of powers of the same kind.* From whence he infers, that consciousness cannot reside in a system of matter, or, which is all one, that it is an individual power in his sense and therefore it lies upon him to prove that there can be no power in a system of matter, but what is the sum and result of powers of the same kind.

(v) Having fully examined the main argument of the first article of Mr. *Clarke*'s Defense, I proceed to take notice of two or three particular incidents in it. As,

a. Mr. *Clarke* charges me with saying, *sweetness is in a rose*, whereas I say quite the contrary in these words "that a rose consists of particles which singly and separately want a power to produce that agreeable sensation we experience in them when united." And therefore Mr. *Clarke* had no reason to show the *vulgarness and grossness* of believing that sweetness exists in bodies to me who agreed with him, as appears by my own words. I know no one more capable of instructing others than Mr. *Clarke,* and therefore I wish he had chosen some topic wherein we differed, and then how well and closely so ever he had argued, I should have had the satisfaction either of seeing myself ingeniously opposed, or else have been convinced by him. Wherein now I appear ignorant where I am not so, and Mr. *Clarke* by no means [appears –ed.] advantageously, when he gives himself the trouble to dispute with a man in print, that he makes ignorant of the first rudiments of Natural Philosophy.

b. Mr. *Clarke* says *that the powers in a rose are nothing else but a number of similar motions or figures.* Wherein there are two things to be proved: (i) that the mere figure and motion of the parts of a rose do produce, or are the sole external cause of, the sensation caused by them; (ii) that those motions and figures are perfectly similar.

c. Mr. *Clarke* says *that gravitation is the effect of the continued and regular operation of some other Being on matter.* Whereas it does not appear but that matter gravitates by virtue of powers originally placed in it by God, and is now left to itself to act by those original powers. And it is as conceivable that matter should act by virtue of those powers, as that an immaterial being should originally put it into motion, or continue it in motion.

Sect. 2. It was objected, "since it is only required that a thing be an individual being in order to its being a proper subject of a power of thinking, or at least that it may be possible for God to superadd to it a power of thinking, it is evident by Mr. *Clarke*'s own account of matter — which he makes to consist of *actually separate and distinct parts* (though I wonder at the same time he should make it *divisible,* when by its consisting of separate and distinct parts it is actually divided) — that those *separate and distinct parts* are capable of having a power of thinking, or an individual consciousness superadded to each of them. Because the want of individuality or distinctness is the sole reason urged why a system of matter cannot have a power of thinking, or an individual consciousness. And consequently, according to Mr. *Clarke*'s own reasoning, matter may have a power of thinking, or an individual consciousness." To this Mr. *Clarke* answers, *that supposing any particle of matter could be truly an individual — that is, an indivisible or indiscerptible being — yet it would not therefore follow that it could be capable of thinking. For though divisibility or discerptibility in any subject is a sufficient proof that that subject is not capable of such an individual power as thinking, yet it does not from thence follow, on the contrary, that whatever is indiscerptible is therefore capable of thinking.*

1. But if indiscerptibility be what is only required, in Mr. Clarke's argument, for a subject of a power of thinking, then it must follow, not only that what is discerptible cannot think, but that whatever is indiscerptible is capable of thinking — until Mr. Clarke thinks fit to add such considerations to his *argument,* whereby an individual material being is excluded from a capacity of thinking, and an individual immaterial being is not. For if indiscerptibility is all that is mentioned as requisite in a subject for a power of thinking, then wherever there is indiscerptibility there is all that is required by that argument. And so though it does not, from *discerptibility in any subject being sufficient proof that that subject* is *not capable of thinking,* universally follow *that whatever* is *indiscerptible* is *therefore capable of thinking;* yet it may and does follow from Mr. *Clarke*'s argument, as it stands at present — and I desire him to show me any one principle, in the present argument, from whence it cannot be as well inferred — that an individual material being is a proper subject of a power of thinking, as an immaterial being.

But Mr. *Clarke* says *though the want of individuality or distinctness* is *the sole reason urged in the present argument why a system of matter cannot think, yet it ought not therefore to be said that it* is *only required that a thing be an individual being in order to its being a proper subject of a power of thinking.* Upon which I observe that Mr. *Clarke* owns the truth of my reasoning upon the supposition that individuality is only required by him in a subject of a power of thinking, but denies that I have any reason to infer that individuality is only required *from the want of individuality's being the sole reason urged why a system of matter cannot have a power of thinking.* Which I cannot help thinking to be all one, until there is a difference assigned between *only required* in the present argument, and *the sole reason urged* in the present argument.

2. Had I affirmed, from the consideration of Mr. *Clarke*'s argument, *that whatever is indiscerptible* is *therefore capable of thinking,* I cannot see how Mr. *Clarke,* consistently with the principles on which his argument proceeds, can urge any considerations whereby an individual material being is excluded from a capacity of thinking. And if he cannot, then it follows universally from his argument that whatever is indiscerptible is therefore capable of thinking. This I would show, but that Mr. *Clarke* does *deny the supposition on which this objection is grounded* — viz. *that any particle of matter can be truly an indiscerptible being* — and therefore I shall spare the reader by not arguing longer on a supposition denied on both sides. Though when I urged it, I took it to be Mr. *Clarke*'s opinion, because he said *matter consisted of actually separate and distinct parts,* by which words — since he understands improper parts, or parts that seem so to us (for according to him matter has no parts) — I own the ground of my objection, as founded on his words, is entirely taken away.

Sect. 3. It was objected, "Supposing Mr. *Clarke* had proved that consciousness could only reside in an individual being, and that an individual being must be an immaterial being, the soul would not then be proved naturally immortal. And consequently all the pains taken to prove the soul immaterial signify nothing. Nothing is proved naturally immortal by the supposition of the soul's immateriality, but the substance of the soul. Now the soul is supposed to be a thinking immaterial being, and unless a thinking immaterial being can be proved naturally immortal, the soul cannot be proved naturally immortal. But how this can be done, I know not, but by showing the inseparable connection between immaterial being and thinking. And until then we have as much reason to believe that thinking is an action which may commence after the existence of its subject, and may perish or cease to exist its subject still remaining. And thus there is no more progress made in the proof of the natural immortality of the soul by proving its immateriality, than there would be in proving the natural immortality of men's bodies which are laid in the graves, by showing that matter can only perish by annihilation. For, as in the last case, no proof is made of the necessary continuance together of the several particles that compose our bodies, so, in the other case, we have no proof that thinking is an inseparable property of immaterial being. Of what use then is this argument to the ends and purposes of religion? For if we have no security that we must exist hereafter in a state of perception, as by only proving the natural immortality of the soul we have not, it can be of no use to influence our lives and actions."

To this Mr. *Clarke* answers, *that all the qualities and modes of an indiscerptible being are utterly incapable of being affected in any degree by any power in nature. For all real and inherent qualities of any substance are either modifications of the substance itself, or else powers superadded and connected to the substance by the immediate power of God. And in either of these cases, it* is *manifest no quality can be altered by any natural power, which* is *not able to affect and make some alteration (in the disposition of the parts at least) of the substance itself, which in an indiscerptible substance cannot be done.*

1. Upon this answer I observe that it is inconsistent with matter of fact, or else supposes the soul a material being. For we know by experience that the soul or thinking being undergoes several changes or alterations. It has not only different passions as anger, love, etc., at different times, which are modifications of the soul that begin and have their period, but has qualities or powers such as seeing and hearing, which by the defect of our organs plainly cease for a time. Now when Mr. *Clarke* reconciles our having different passions at different times, and our enjoying of powers and then losing of them, with his notion *that all the qualities and modes of an indiscerptible being are utterly incapable of being affected in any measure, or changed in any degree, by any power of nature,* I promise him to account for the possibility of thinking's ceasing in an immaterial being by the powers of nature. But if he cannot, what remains, but from the actions of our souls which must then, according to him, be inconsistent with their existence in an indiscerptible being, to conclude the soul to be material?

2. *The powers of nature* signify material and finite immaterial beings, and their several powers and operations one on another. Now until Mr. *Clarke* has a complete idea of both sorts of beings, their powers and operations one on another, it is impossible for him, in many respects, to tell how far they can affect one another's operations. For instance, there are beings in the world that think, of whose substance I have no other idea but that it is indiscerptible by the powers of nature. But yet I understand not the manner how these indiscerptible beings think, nor how they are capable of other qualities, nor what other qualities and powers they have. Nor do I understand all the powers of material or other immaterial beings, and the manner of their operations. How then can I possibly tell how that of which I have no idea may affect an action or power of another being of which I have no idea — how it is performed, how it inheres in its subject, or wherein the nature of that power consists?

3. But Mr. *Clarke* says *no quality or mode can be altered by any natural power, which is not able to affect and make some alteration of the substance itself, which in an indiscerptible substance cannot be done.* In answer to which I ask Mr. *Clarke* whether God can destroy a mode or quality in an immaterial being without making some alteration in the substance itself? If Mr. *Clarke* replies that God can destroy a mode or quality without making some alteration in the substance itself, then there is no repugnancy in the nature of the thing that a mode or quality may be destroyed, without any alteration of the parts of that substance which was the subject of that mode or quality. If he says that God can destroy a mode or quality in an immaterial substance, without making any alteration in the substance, but that a created being by any powers that it is capable of receiving from the hand of God cannot, I desire him to give me any argument upon his principles to prove created beings cannot, that will not equally conclude against God's destroying such a power unless at the same time he annihilates the subject of that power. He cannot make it impossible for the powers of an immaterial being to cease, by the operations of created beings on it, from its indiscerptibility, without excluding God from putting an end merely to those powers. For, according to Mr. *Clarke*, God himself can no more make any alteration in the parts of an immaterial substance than a created being can. If Mr. *Clarke* replies that God cannot destroy a mode or quality of an immaterial being without making an alteration in the parts of the substance, I answer

that if God does make any alteration in the parts of the substance upon destroying the power or quality that he superadded, then an immaterial substance is plainly as discerptible by the power of God as a material substance, and all Mr. *Clarke*'s arguments against the possibility of matter's thinking turn upon him, for alteration of parts in a finite being is as much an evidence of discerptibility as solidity is. But, lastly, if Mr. *Clarke* replies that no power or quality can be destroyed without the annihilation of the subject of that power, I desire a reason may be given why God can *superadd a power* to an immaterial being, as Mr. *Clarke* acknowledges he can, and not cause it to cease, its subject remaining as it was before the power was superadded.

4. But to give him all the satisfaction I can, I shall instance in a quality of immaterial being that may owe its continuance to the actions of created beings, and may cease without making any alteration in the substance itself. Extension not being excluded out of Mr. *Clarke*'s idea of immaterial being, it is plain whenever our bodies are carried from one place to another our souls must likewise move along with them, though motion is no doubt incompatible with immaterial being in case immaterial being has no extension. Now this supposed motion of our souls is entirely owing to external and material causes, not only as to the degree of motion, but as to the determination of the motion. For both the degree of motion, and the particular determination thereof, will cease upon withdrawing the external material causes. And if any particular motion of an immaterial being be owing to external material causes, then all its motions, for all we know to the contrary, may be so too. And if so, there can be no repugnancy in supposing it possible for an immaterial being to be destitute of the quality of actual motion. And if there is no repugnancy in supposing that motion may be continued in an immaterial being by the powers of nature, and may cease by withdrawing of those powers, then Mr. *Clarke*'s affirmation *that no quality of an immaterial being can be altered by any natural power, which is not able* to *make an alteration (in the disposition of the parts at least) of the substance itself,* is very precarious.

5. Lastly, supposing Mr. *Clarke* had proved in this article, what I conceive he has not, that the whole soul, the thinking immaterial being, is indivisible by the powers of nature, or naturally immortal in that sense, yet this indivisibility, this natural immortality, is no more than he allows to some particles of matter. For he says, *that there are original and perfectly solid particles which are to any power of*

nature indiscerptible. And he corrects me for calling any particle of matter an *individual being* because it cannot be divided by natural causes, or the powers of nature. And therefore if a particle of matter, notwithstanding its indiscerptibility by natural causes, is not naturally immortal, or indivisible, in that sense in which Mr. *Clarke* requires the substance of the soul to be — *viz.* to be indiscerptible by the power of God — neither can the whole thinking being be proved naturally immortal in that sense, unless it can be showed that the whole thinking being is indiscerptible by the power of God. But to that question he has not said anything, and therefore, I may conclude, that supposing *thinking* must reside in an individual being, or a being that is indiscerptible by the power of God, yet it does not follow that the thinking immaterial being is indiscerptible by the power of God, or naturally immortal.

[*Sect.* 4.] It was objected, "since an individual being can only be the subject of a power of thinking, why may not several particles of matter, when united in one system, become an individual being, and be by the power of God rendered incapable of any division or separation by natural causes, and consequently be a subject capable of thinking? If several particles of matter can be so united as to touch one another, or closely adhere, wherein does the distinctness or individuality of the several particles consist? The distinctness or individuality is as much lost to me by this supposed union, as the distinctness of the parts of an immaterial being, upon supposition that extension is not excluded out of the idea of immateriality, as it is not by Mr. *Clarke*, if I rightly apprehend him. For if the union of material particles be complete and entire, I can as well conceive an immaterial being capable of division, as conceive those particles so united, capable of division from one another. All the difference perceivable by us between such a material substance [and an immaterial substance –ed.], besides solidity in one and want of solidity in the other, lies in this: that one perhaps continues as it was created, and the other becomes by the power of God what the other was by creation. And what difference that will make as to one's being capable of the power of thinking, and the other's not being capable of that power, does not appear to me, and never will, until thinking and solidity are proved to be incompatible in the same subject."

To this Mr. *Clarke* answers *that the case is very different,* between such a material being and an immaterial being, though it be supposed to be extended. *Because some of the first and most obvious properties, which we certainly know of matter — as its having* partes extra partes [parts beyond parts –ed.], *strictly and properly speaking, and its consisting of such parts as can exist separately, and have no dependence on one another — do necessarily and confessedly imply discerptibility. But in immaterial beings we do not know of any such properties as any wise imply discerptibility.*

The case is not different between such a material being as I have described, and a finite extended immaterial being. For though all matter does consist of parts that have no dependence on one another for their existence, yet by the supposition in the objection it is as indiscerptible by natural causes as an immaterial being. Now this supposition Mr. *Clarke* is so far from denying to be possible, that he grants it to be true in fact *that there are particles of matter which are to any powers in nature indiscerptible.* And if there are or may be systems of matter which imply indiscerptibility by natural causes, though they are allowed discerptible by the power of God, there can be no difference between those systems of matter and any other finite extended beings, as to their divisibility by the powers of nature. Nor can there be any difference as to their divisibility by the power of God, for all finite extended beings must so far consist of parts, that the part of one side is not the part of the other side. They can only consist in a continuity of the same substance, and why such a substance should not be as divisible as a perfectly continued solid substance I can see no reason. Let Mr. *Clarke* show that a continued solid substance is discerptible by the power of God, and the same argument will equally show the discerptibility of any other finite continued substance. Suppose the substance of the soul to be four inches square (for when once extension is allowed to the soul, such a supposition becomes reasonable), I ask Mr. *Clarke* if that substance at its creation did not depend entirely on the will of God as to the degree of its extension, as much as any of those perfectly solid particles of matter did, which are allowed to be indiscerptible by the powers of nature? And whether God could not have made it two inches square, had he pleased, as well as any of those particles smaller? Both which, I suppose, Mr. *Clarke* will allow. Then I ask him, if God can make immaterial beings of different dimensions, what can hinder him from making an immaterial being less than when he first created it that will not hinder him from making a *continued* solid being less than when he first created that? It does not appear to me that an inch on one side of an immaterial being is more dependent on an inch on the other side, as to each other's existence, than two sides of a perfectly solid particle of matter are. So that I think we have as clear evidence *we do as much know* of a property in immaterial substance which implies discerptibility as we do in some particles of matter, continued extension in a being as much implying discerptibility as continued solidity. But Mr. *Clarke* says *as the known parts of space can demonstrably be proved to be absolutely indiscerptible,* so *it ought not to be reckoned an insuperable difficulty to imagine extended immaterial substance may be* so *likewise.* Though the known parts of space can be demonstrated to be absolutely indiscerptible, yet it may be and is an insuperable difficulty to imagine an immaterial substance may be so likewise, because space is infinitely extended, and because it is nothing but the mere absence or place of bodies, whereas immaterial being is something extended and finite. Now if all finite extended beings are divisible by the power of God, then all Mr. *Clarke* says against matter's thinking has equal force (if it has any at all) against an immaterial being's thinking, as will appear by his own words if we put immaterial or extended being in the place of the term matter or material being. *Suppose,* says he, *an extended being as small as you please, indued with consciousness or thought. Yet if, by the power of God, this* extended being *may be divided into two parts, what will naturally and consequently become of its power of thinking? If that power continues in it unchanged, then there must be two distinct consciousnesses in the two separate parts; or else the power continuing in the intermediate distance or space, as well as in the parts themselves, must there subsist without a subject; or else, not the* [*im* –ed.] *material substance, but some other thing* is *the subject of the consciousness. If the power of thinking will remain only in one of the separated parts, then either that one part only had at first the power residing in it — and then the same question will return upon the supposition of its being likewise divided — or else it will follow that one and the same individual quality may be transferred from one subject to another, which all philosophers of all sects in the world have always confessed to be impossible. If, in the last place, it be said that upon the division of an* extended being, *the power of thinking which was in it will wholly cease, then it will follow that that was never or at all a real quality inhering and residing in the substance (in which mere separation of parts makes no alteration), but that it was a mere external denomination, as the roundness of a being, which perishes at its being divided.* And this, *he supposes,* will be granted to be sufficiently absurd.

[*Sect.* 5.] It was objected, in the fifth and last place, "but let us suppose that from the power of thinking, or individual consciousness, we can prove the immateriality of the soul, and from its immateriality prove its natural immortality, and then see what will be the consequence. All the numerous sensible creatures in the universe are put in the same condition with man, and made capable of eternal happiness as well as he. Now to avoid this consequence there are two things principally urged.

1. That all those creatures (which I call sensible) are only mere machines. Or,

2. That their souls shall be annihilated with their bodies.

To the first I answer, that experience as much convinces us, that they perceive, think, etc., as that men do. They avoid pain and seek pleasure, and give as good marks of uneasiness under the one, and satisfaction under the other, as men do. They avoid pain and seek pleasure by the same motive that men do — *viz.* by reflecting on their past actions, and the actions of their fellows, with the consequences of them, which is evident from their acting more to their own advantage, the more experience they have had. But if, after all, brutes are only mere machines, the difficulty of proving the soul immaterial will be increased. For if the operations of brutes are not sufficient to distinguish them from clocks and watches, the operations of men will not prove *them* to be superior to machines.

To the second objection I answer that if the souls of brutes are annihilated on the dissolution of their bodies, then the proof of the natural immortality of men's souls from their immateriality tends not to prove that their souls really be immortal. Because mere natural immortality is not a security from annihilation, as is supposed in the objection."

To which Mr. *Clarke* answers *that, though sensible creatures have certainly something in them that is immaterial, yet it does not at all follow either that they must needs be annihilated upon the dissolution of their bodies, or else be capable of eternal happiness as well as man. This is just such an argument, as if a man should conclude that whatsoever is not exactly like himself can therefore have no being at all.* The strength of this answer lies in my supposing either a necessity of annihilation of the souls of brutes on the dissolution of their bodies, or else that they become capable of eternal happiness as well as man. Which, should I allow to be what I intended, yet it would not be *just such an argument as if a man should conclude that whatsoever* is *not exactly like himself can therefore have no being at all.* Because it does not place opposition between a capacity of the soul's eternal happiness and not existing at all, but between a capacity of eternal happiness and not existing after the dissolution of their bodies. And therefore though it may follow from the argument that whatever immaterial being has not a capacity of eternal happiness cannot exist after the dissolution of the body to which it was joined, yet it by no means follows that no immaterial being or soul can exist at all unless it has a capacity of eternal happiness as well as man — or, in Mr. *Clarke*'s words, *is not exactly like himself* as to that capacity. But it was very far from my intention to argue that there was either a necessity of the annihilation of the souls of brutes on the dissolution of their bodies, or else that they would be capable of eternal happiness as well as man, but only to argue either the necessity of annihilation some time or other, or else that brutes would be capable of eternal happiness as well as man. For when I objected to myself *that the souls of brutes shall be annihilated with the dissolution of their bodies,* I considered that those who would suppose an annihilation of the souls of brutes would be most likely to pitch on the dissolution of the body as the proper term or period for the existence of their souls — as I could show from the several answerers of Mr. *Dodwell* who only from his supposing the soul to be naturally mortal, though capable of immortality, conclude the time of the dissolution of the body the proper time for the actual mortality of the soul. And therefore I crave leave to understand Mr. *Clarke*'s argument after this manner *that though all sensible creatures have certainly in them something that is immaterial, yet it does not at all follow either that they must needs be annihilated, or else that they must be capable of eternal happiness as well as man.* To which I reply that since Mr. *Clarke* does allow that all the sensible creatures in the universe are not mere machines, by acknowledging *that they have all something in them that is immaterial,* I desire him to tell me, consistently with the principle of his foregoing argument for the natural immortality of the thinking immaterial being in us, what else remains reasonable but that they be supposed sometime or other to be annihilated, or else be supposed capable of eternal happiness as well as man. For they, having something immaterial in them, must, according to Mr. *Clarke,* forever, without annihilation, enjoy the power of perception. And if they must have forever a power of perception, they must have either agreeable or disagreeable perceptions. And if they must have either agreeable or disagreeable perceptions, they must be supposed capable of eternal agreeable perceptions, unless Mr. *Clarke* will say, that they are only capable of an eternal mixture of agreeable and disagreeable perceptions, or only capable of eternal disagreeable perceptions — which, since they are unreasonable suppositions, and would destroy all proof of man's capacity for a happy immortality from the argument now in question, I dare say he will not affirm.

My last objection therefore, cleared from all doubtfulness arising from expression, and to which I should be glad to receive a good answer, stands thus. That if from the power of thinking we can prove the immateriality of the soul of man, and from its immateriality prove its natural immortality, and consequently its capacity of eternal happiness, the power of thinking must prove the immateriality of the souls of brutes, the immateriality of their souls must prove their natural immortality, and consequently their capacity of eternal happiness. If it be supposed that the souls of brutes may be sometime or other annihilated, then this argument is not useful to the end for which it is intended, because natural immortality will then be no proof of the real immortality of the soul of man.

Postscript[1]

Since the finishing this Reply to Mr. *Clarke,* I have met with Mr. *Milles'* Answer to Mr. *Dodwell*'s *Epistolary Discourse,* in the preface whereof he has endeavored to defend Mr. *Clarke*'s *Argument for the Immateriality and Natural Immortality of the Soul*

1 Thomas Milles, as Collins explains, wrote a reply to Dodwell's *Epistolary Discourse* entitled *The Natural Immortality of the Soul, asserted and proved from the Scriptures and first Fathers; in Opposition to Mr. Dodwell's Epistolary Discourse* (London, 1707) in which he defends Clarke's argument against Collins' objections, but quite fails to understand that Clarke holds that the immaterial soul is extended and yet has no parts. Thus Mr. Milles bolsters Collins' objections instead of answering them. –ed.

against my objections — but upon Principles which entirely overthrow it, and by putting such a sense on Mr. *Clarke*'s words as is inconsistent with what Mr. *Clarke* understands by them in his *Defense.* As for instance, Mr. *Milles* says *if that which thinks within us be extended it must consist of parts;* and *that by individual being, in Mr.* Clarke's *reasoning, we are to understand an unextended being;* and again, *that I did not rightly apprehend Mr.* Clarke *when I said extension was not excluded by him out of his idea of immateriality.* Whereas Mr. *Clarke* is so [far –ed.] from objecting any such mistake to me, and from supposing *that if that which thinks in us be extended it must consist of parts,* that in the fourth article of his *Defense* he argues with me as not mistaking his meaning by allowing *extension not to be excluded out of his idea of immateriality*, and gives up his argument in case I prove that whatever is finitely extended must consist of parts — that is, prove what Mr. *Milles* grants to be true, and insists on in Defense of Mr. *Clarke.* Therefore instead of returning any particular answer to Mr. *Milles'* observations, I refer him for satisfaction to Mr. *Clarke*'s *Defense,* where he may not only see that he has mistaken Mr. *Clarke*'s meaning, but that Mr. *Clarke*'s argument cannot be defended by him until he retracts his *Preface.* For if an immaterial being or soul be, according to Mr. *Clarke,* an extended being, and yet indiscerptible both by the powers of nature and the power of God, then Mr. *Milles'* assertions *that if that which thinks in us be extended it must consist of parts, and that it is impossible that what has parts should be the subject of thought,* do overthrow Mr. *Clarke*'s demonstration of the immateriality of the soul. For if whatever is extended must consist of parts, and if that which consist of parts cannot think, then Mr. *Clarke*'s immaterial being cannot think, and consequently the immateriality of the soul, in Mr. *Clarke*'s sense, is destroyed by Mr. *Milles'* defense. And therefore if Mr. *Milles* undertakes again Mr. *Clarke*'s defense, he must first retract this principle in his preface *that if that which thinks in us be extended it must consist of parts,* before he can demonstrate the indiscerptibility of an extended being — that is, before he can prove the immateriality and natural immortality of the soul, in Mr. *Clarke*'s sense.

Though Mr. *Milles* has thus egregiously mistaken Mr. *Clarke,* yet it is but just to let the reader see the reason he assigns why Mr. *Clarke* must understand by immaterial being unextended being. *The remarker,* says he, *has done Mr.* Clarke *a great deal of wrong in saying he does not exclude extension out of the idea of immateriality, since it is plain our argument would have no force but upon supposition that the immaterial thinking substance within us is proved not* to *be extended.* For which argument I shall not return him the civility he bestows on me, in supposing that I despise logic, but take the liberty to attribute it to a more indisputable cause — notwithstanding he has the modesty to say, *he has taken the liberty* to *imitate the great Mr.* Chillingworth *throughout his treatise.*

As Mr. *Milles* does not sufficiently agree with Mr. *Clarke* in principles in order to defend him, so Mr. *Milles* and I are not sufficiently agreed in common principles to dispute with one another. In a matter of speculation it is not the authority of *Tully* himself [Marcus Tullius Cicero (106-43 BCE), the great Roman philosopher. –ed.], could his opinions be known (I say could they be known, because he does not always tell us on what side he is in his philosophical dialogues), nor all the philosophers that ever lived, much less the Fathers of the Church, that has any weight with me. It is reason alone, from what hand so ever it comes, to which I am ready to pay my submission, and it is by that alone that Mr. *Clarke* and I propose to be determined. And therefore when Mr. *Milles* urges no other argument to prove the power of thinking inseparable from immaterial being, but by saying *the power of thinking has been always looked upon, and is now by every one acknowledged to be, a necessary property of immateriality,* I think it fruitless to contend with a man who knows not that the question between Mr. *Clarke* and me is not a question that depends on the opinion of any man, nor that Mr. *Clarke* proposes only by the *argument* I have examined to demonstrate the immateriality and natural immortality of the soul by reason. In short, his argument from fact is as foreign to the matter, as if I should use some topical arguments to prove the Fathers profound philosophers, when that question can only be determined by an induction of particular passages out of their works, to which end Mr. *Milles'* and Mr. *Dodwell*'s writings may perhaps be allowed very useful.

Samuel Clarke

A Second Defense of an Argument

Made Use of in a Letter to Mr. Dodwell, To Prove the Immateriality and Natural Immortality of the Soul. In a letter to the Author of A Reply to Mr. Clarke's Defense, etc.

Sir,

In abstract and *metaphysical* speculations, it is hardly possible that anything should ever be so clearly expressed, or so strongly proved, but those who are not very much versed in such enquiries will perpetually be apt to misapprehend what is said, and men of wit and parts will always be able to raise new difficulties, and perplex their readers with intricate and endless disputations.

Since you have not thought fit in your *Reply* to offer any new arguments, but only to urge again the same objections which you had before advanced against what I persuade myself I have already explained with as much clearness as can reasonably be expected in questions of this nature, I think I might very well, without entering into any further debate, have now left it wholly to the judicious and impartial reader to consider and determine with himself on which side the greatest strength of reason and argument lies. Nevertheless, the candor and ingenuity with which you have written have once more engaged me to endeavor to give you satisfaction in this matter, by pointing out to you some of the principal instances wherein you seem either to have mistaken the question itself, or to have misunderstood my argument upon it. But hereafter, unless any new objections shall be proposed, and not merely repetitions and ingenious representations of the former difficulties, you must excuse me if I think not myself obliged to do so anymore.

In repeating my answer to your first objection, you cite my words thus: *to suppose any power or quality of this kind arising from, or belonging to, the several parts of which the whole consists, is a direct and express contradiction.*[1] Whereas my words were: *to suppose any power or quality of this kind arising from, or belonging to, [any whole system of Matter, without belonging to] the several parts of which the whole consists, is a direct and express contradiction.*[2] I make no question but this is only a fault of the press in your *Reply.* Yet it was proper to take notice of it, because perhaps every reader will not be at the pains to compare the books, and it happens as the passage stands in your citation to give a very disadvantageous representation of my sense. In your preliminary defining the signification of the terms,[3] I cannot see any reason (unless it be to perplex the reader with a new question — *whether the soul always actually thinks or not* — which is wholly foreign to the matter at present in dispute) I cannot see any reason, I say, why you should affirm that *consciousness cannot be properly employed to signify the same thing with a power of thinking, unless by a power of thinking, be understood, not a capacity to think, but actual thinking.* For the thing to be proved being this, that a divisible substance is not capable of a power of thinking, what difference can it make whether by a *power of thinking* you understand *actual thinking* or a *capacity to think?* For I presume you will not deny but whatever is proved incapable of *actual thinking* is also proved incapable (pardon the expression) of a *capacity of thinking,* and whatsoever is proved incapable of a *capacity of thinking* is also proved incapable of *actual thinking.* Wherefore there was no need of endeavoring at this time to perplex and multiply the question by any such disputable distinction. Which kind of difficulties, foreign to the thing at present under consideration, they who are desirous to come at truth, and to come at it [in –ed.] the nearest way, ought always very carefully to avoid.

Consciousness, in the most strict and exact sense of the word, signifies neither a *capacity of thinking,* nor yet *actual thinking,* but the *reflex act by which* I *know that* I *think, and that my thought and actions are my own and not another's.* But in the present question, the reader needs not trouble himself with this nicety of distinction, but may understand it indifferently in all or any of these significations, because the argument proves universally that matter is neither capable of this *reflex act,* nor of the first *direct act,* nor of the *capacity of thinking* at all.

1 Reply. [p. 68 of this edition. –ed.]

2 Defense. [p. 58 –ed.]

3 Reply. [p. 69 –ed.]

By an *individual power* I mean (in the sense that logicians commonly use the word *individual* when they oppose it to *specific*) such a power as is *really and truly* in the nature of the thing itself *one power,* in opposition to its being such merely in our *abstract complex notion.* For instance, when I speak of my own consciousness, and call it an *individual power,* I mean thereby to express that it is really and truly one undivided consciousness, and not a multitude of distinct consciousnesses added together. But when I speak of the blueness (suppose), or redness, or sweetness of a body, as a *single power* belonging to that body, it is evident [that –ed.] I can mean that only that it is such merely in the *abstract complex notion* or *idea* I frame in my mind — that is, in the same sense as we say an *army* or a *city* is *one* — but that really and indeed is a vast multitude of bluenesses, rednesses, or sweetnesses, or rather (to speak strictly and properly) a vast multitude of such parts as excite in us the sensations of blueness, redness, or sweetness. Now the thing to be proved was that such an individual power as consciousness cannot possibly inhere in, or result from, a divisible substance. And this I did prove, not by *defining* or *supposing* an *individual power* to be *a power that cannot possibly inhere in, or result from, a divisible substance* (which would indeed have been begging the question), but by *demonstrating* that it would necessarily imply a plain and direct contradiction, for any power which is really *one* and not *many* (such as yourself acknowledged consciousness to be by confessing it does not reside in the single and separate parts of the brain) to inhere in or result from a divisible substance. Wherefore it is altogether without reason that you endeavor to perplex your reader by telling him that a *system of matter being supposed to consist of parts, and thinking being supposed to be a power incapable of residing in a being that consists of parts, the question of matter's thinking will amount to this, whether that which cannot think can think,* when you well know that I made use of no such supposition, but endeavored to *prove* (and, I hope, *have proved* with some strength and clearness) what you seem to insinuate as if I only have *supposed.*

I. You reply to my answer to your first objection, that it is nothing else but *argumentum ad ignorantiam*: that *in enumerating the sorts of powers or qualities of matter, I suppose that a system of matter has, and can have, only powers of one sort or kind — such as magnitude and motion — which are only the sum or aggregate of pow-*

ers of the same kind. Which, what is it else but to argue that because we know of no other powers of a different kind in matter from magnitude and motion, therefore it has, and can have, no other powers? Now I cannot think, Sir, but a man of your understanding, if you please to consider the matter a second time, will find it is by no means *argumentum ad ignorantiam*. For if a disjunction be complete (as that in which I enumerate the several sorts of powers of which matter is capable either is, or else you ought to have proved that another member could be added to it, to show that it was not), it contains in it all the possible particulars, as well the *unknown*, as those that are ever so well *known*. For how many particulars so ever be supposed to be *unknown*, and how impossible so ever it be supposed to come at the knowledge of those particulars, yet if the heads or kinds be rightly distributed, they must of necessity contain under them all the *unknown* particulars as certainly as those that are the *most known*. All the possible qualities, I said, or powers of matter (whether *known* or *unknown*), must of necessity be either *qualities really inhering in the subject itself to which they are ascribed,* or *modes produced by it in some other subject,* or else *mere abstract names signifying certain powers or effects that do not properly reside in any subject at all.* Now if this disjunction be true, and thinking be at all a quality or power of matter, and be confessed not to belong to either of the two latter sorts, it must of necessity (how *unknown* so ever the nature of it be otherwise supposed to be), be included in the former. And then the argument holds unanswerably good that *thinking* (or, if you please to imagine any other even more abstruse quality or power of matter, even these also), as well as magnitude and motion which I instanced in, and whatever else may be reducible to this kind by truly and really inhering in the subject itself, must of necessity inhere in all and every one of the particles of the system, taken singly as well as together. Because, as I said before, to suppose any power or quality of this kind arising from, or belonging to, any *whole* system of matter, without belonging to the *several parts* of which the whole consists, is a direct and express contradiction. It is supposing either an *universal* to exist without particulars; or an *effect* to be produced without a *cause*, or to have more in it than was in the *cause*; or that a *quality* is by the power of God made so to arise out of nothing, as to be superadded to a *subject*, and to subsist without inhering in that subject to which it is at the same time supposed to belong.

To this you reply that *to suppose a power arising from matter without belonging to the parts of which the whole consists* is *not to suppose an* universal *to exist without particulars, but a* particular *power existing to which several particular powers contribute — as every* man *is a* particular *man, though various powers are necessary to constitute him of that species.* But, Sir, if the whole or result, which you call a *particular* power, be entirely and *specifically* different from all and every one of the particular powers contributing to it — as *thinking* manifestly is from all the powers of particles not indued with *thought* — you will find, if you please to consider it carefully, that it is as certain and evident as any *arithmetical* demonstration that such a *particular* power is a *whole* bigger than *all its parts,* a *whole* that contains something in it besides all and every one of its *parts* — that is, I think, an *universal* without *particulars.* It is exactly as if you should assert that a *smell* and a *color* could be joined together to make a sound or as if hardness and figure could be the particulars contributing to constitute a *motion.* A *man,* if you mean the whole man, the thinking person (as the reader may be apt to think you do), and suppose him to be constituted of mere matter, whose single particles are none of them indued with thought, is such a contradictory whole. But if you mean (as you seem to do) the body only, with its mechanical powers, then there is nothing in it differing from the powers of the single parts, except only the bare name, the abstract notion of its being a *whole,* which is a complex idea in our mind. But in the thing itself it is nothing at all but its being the sum of the magnitudes, figures and motions of all the several parts, from which constituent parts no whole can (without an evident contradiction) differ any otherwise than as in numbers a *thousand* differs from *ten hundred,* or as in weights a *pound* differs from *sixteen ounces,* or as an *army* differs from all the *men* that compose it — that is, nothing but the bare *name.*

You add: *Neither is a supposing an effect produced without a cause, for the different powers in the single and separate parts of a system of matter, by uniting in one operation or power to operate, are the cause of the existence of that power which did not exist in the particles singly considered. And thus in those particles which compose the brain, etc.* Now here, Sir, I really cannot but wonder how a gentleman so well skilled in philosophy as you are can suffer himself to be imposed upon by so very gross and palpable a fallacy. For though the different powers in the single and separate parts of a system of matter (as, for instance, their magnitude, situation, figure and motion), may by uniting in one operation or power to operate, be the cause of the existence of another power *of the same species,* which did not exist in the particles singly considered; that is, may constitute another magnitude, another figure, another motion, than was in the single particles, just as twenty different numbers added together constitute a new number different from any of the particulars: yet those powers cannot, without an evident contradiction, be the cause of the existence of any other power of a *different species* (as *thinking* is confessedly of a *different species* from *magnitude, figure, motion,* or whatever other properties may belong to *unthinking* particles of matter) for the same reason as the addition of different numbers in arithmetic cannot without a manifest contradiction be the cause of the existence of a line or a figure, or the mixture of tastes constitute a color; Namely, because thus the *effect* would contain more in it than was in the *cause* — that is, something would without any efficient [cause] be produced out of nothing. In like manner, though the different powers in the single and separate parts of a system of matter (their magnitude *suppose,* situation, figure and motion) may, by uniting in one operation or power to operate, be the cause of the existence of a power *to affect some foreign substance,* which power did not exist in the particles singly considered, that is, certain particles united may prick the skin and cause pain, which the single ones could not do; or may strike the eye so as to excite the sensation of blue or red, which the single ones could not do, just as a wedge may force itself a passage where a body of some other shape could not; yet those powers cannot, without an evident contradiction, be the cause of the existence of any new quality *really inhering in the subject itself* (as *thinking* confessedly is a quality *really inhering in the thinking being itself,* and not barely an *abstract notion,* or *power of affecting some foreign substance*) for the same reason as the sharpening of a point of a needle cannot possibly be the cause that the needle itself should feel pain.

From hence it easily appears how defective your similitude is, when you say it is *no contradiction to suppose a power arising from matter without belonging to the parts of which the whole consists, no more than to conceive that a whole is not the same with a piece of a clock.* Wherein *the power resulting from the different contributing powers in the system, neither belongs to any part of the system when considered by itself, nor is it of the same sort or kind with any power in any part of the system.* For that which you call the *power* of a clock to show the time of day is evidently nothing *in the clock itself*, but the figure and motion of its parts, and consequently not anything of a different sort or kind from the powers inherent in the parts. Whereas *thinking*, if it was the result of the powers of the different parts of the machine of the body, or of the brain in particular, would be something really inhering *in the machine itself*, specifically different from all and every one of the powers of the several parts out of which it resulted — which is an express contradiction, a supposing the *effect* to have more in it than the cause. And therefore, though you are pleased to make use of it as a *similitude*, yet in reality this power of thinking, which truly and properly inheres in its subject, has not in any respect the least appearance of *likeness* to the *power of a clock* to show the time of the day, which is merely an *abstract complex notion* in the man that beholds it, and nothing at all really in the clock itself.

In like manner, when you say *it may be conceived that there may be a power in all those particles which compose the brain to contribute to the act of thinking before they are united under that form, though while they are disunited they have no more of consciousness than any being which produces sweetness in us (that is made up of parts wherein different powers inhere) when under a particular form has a power to produce sweetness in us when its parts are disunited and separated,* you fall again into the same fallacy. For the power of a body to excite in us the idea of sweetness is nothing else but a certain figure and motion resulting from different figures and motions of its original constituent parts, just as the power of a pin to cause pain in us is nothing but its motion and the sharp figure of its point, resulting from different motions, figures, and situations of its constituent parts. And if the effect of the powers by which the several particles that compose the brain contribute (as your phrase is) to the act of thinking was likewise only the exciting of certain *thoughts* in something which was before a *thinking substance,* your similitude would have something of likeness in it. But that particles which in themselves have no *thought* should ever contribute anything towards making the substance, which they constitute a *thinking* being, this I am sure you can no more be able to clear from being an express contradiction (though I doubt not but you can argue upon it as acutely as anyone) than if you should undertake to prove that a solid mass of marble is made up of particles which, without having any solidity themselves, contribute by other unknown powers to constitute a solid mass; or that a foot-square of any matter is made up of particles which, without having any extension themselves, contribute by other different and unknown powers to constitute an extended solid quantity.

And here I cannot but take notice that, besides the contradictions before-mentioned, you have, by choosing to annex consciousness to so flux a substance as the brain or the spirits in it, fallen into another very great absurdity. For if the brain or spirits be the subject of consciousness, and the parts of the brain or spirits be (as they certainly are, whatever question may be made concerning any original *solid stamina* of the body) in perpetual flux and change, it will follow that that consciousness by which I *not only remember* that certain things were done many years since, but also *am conscious that they were done by me, by the very same individual conscious being* who now remembers them — it will follow, I say, that that consciousness is transferred from one subject to another; that is to say, that it is a real quality which subsists without inhering in any subject at all.

But to return to the argument before us. You suppose that the particles which compose the brain, though themselves *void of consciousness* when taken singly, may yet by other different powers contribute towards the making up one *conscious whole.* This I affirm to be, and I think I have proved to be, an express contradiction — an assigning more to the *effect* than was in the *cause,* a making the *whole* bigger than all its *parts,* and specifically different from all and every one of them. The occasion, the common ground and foundation, of men's erring in this whole matter, I have elsewhere largely discovered, and shall here repeat what I think may be sufficient to satisfy an inquisitive and unprejudiced person.[1] "Whatever can arise from, or be compounded of, any things, is still only those very things of which it was compounded. And if infinite compositions or divisions be made eternally, the things will still be but eternally the same, and all their possible effects can never be anything but repetitions of the same. For instance, all possible changes of *figure* are still nothing but *figure,* [all possible variations, compositions and divisions of *magnitude* are still nothing but *magnitude,*] all possible compositions or

1 Demonstration of the Being and Attributes of God. Prop. 8. Sect. 2. [Clarke, 1998, pp. 39-43 –ed.]

effects of *motion* are still nothing but *mere motion*." All compositions of *magnitude, figure* and *motion* together are still nothing but *magnitude, figure* and *motion*. And how many other qualities so ever, *known* or *unknown*, the particles of matter be supposed to be indued with, those qualities can never in any composition or division produce any new power specifically different from themselves, unless a *cause* could give more to the *effect* than is in itself. And consequently, if the matter of the brain be the subject in which consciousness inheres, that consciousness cannot possibly be the result of any other known or unknown powers of the several constituent particles, but what must themselves have been originally of the same *species* — that is to say, so many several consciousnesses. "That which has been apt to deceive men in the matter is this, that they imagine compounds to be somewhat really [specifically] different from the things of which they are compounded. Which is a very great mistake. For all the things of which men so judge either, if they be really different, are not compounds nor effects of what men judge them to be, but are something totally distinct — as when the vulgar thinks colors and sounds to be properties inherent in bodies when indeed they are purely thoughts of the mind — or else, if they be really compounds and effects, then they are not different, but exactly the same that ever they were — as when two triangles put together make a square, that square is still nothing but two triangles, or when a square cut in halves makes two triangles, those two triangles are still only the two halves of a square, or when the mixture of blue and yellow powder makes a green, that green is still nothing but blue and yellow intermixed, as is plainly visible by the help of microscopes. And, in short, everything by composition, division or motion, is nothing else but the very same it was before, taken either in whole or by parts, or in different place and order, [so as to excite in our minds different *complex notions*, and occasion *abstract names* of things, but by no means to produce any new quality in the things themselves, such as *consciousness* is agreed to be, inhering truly and properly in the subject it is ascribed to]."

The true state of this case seems, in brief, to be this. Sometimes we consider one and the same quality of a thing, in different circumstances and respects, and with relation to other different things. Which relation may be changed by the alteration or removal of those other things, and a new effect be produced without any alteration at all of the thing itself or any of its qualities. And yet, then we give it a *new name,* and are apt to think that *new name* a *new quality.* Sometimes we consider several distinct qualities of different parcels of matter together and, because some new effect is thereby occasioned in some other being, we give the *imaginary whole* a *new name,* and think that *new denomination* a *new quality.* But with how little reason this is done will abundantly appear by the following instances. The same particle of matter which makes a point in the surface of a *globe* may, by other parts being shaved off, become the point of the angle of a *cube* without undergoing any alteration itself, and produce an effect which it could not produce before. But is this truly a *quality* or *power* in the point itself? *Blue* and *yellow* powder mingled together occasion a new effect, and are called by a *new name: green.* But is this really a new *quality* or *power?* Is it not plainly the same two qualities, which they had when separate, acting still distinctly as appears in a microscope? That *particular and determinate degree of velocity* in a wheel, whereby it turns once round precisely in twelve hours, is that which you call the *power of a clock* to show the time of the day. And because such a determinate *velocity of motion* is made use of by us for the measure of time, and has an *abstract name* given it to express that use, is it therefore really a new *quality* or *power* distinct from the *motion* itself? And to mention no more, when a *weight* in one scale of a balance does, by taking out part of the weight that was in the other scale, begin to *preponderate,* which it did not before, is this any new *quality* or *real power* in the weight that is not altered, different from what it had before?

I shall observe but one thing more upon this head, and that is that whereas I affirmed *every power or quality that is, or can be, inherent in any system of matter to be nothing else than the sum or aggregate of so many powers or qualities of the same* kind *inhering in all the parts* — meaning that the powers inhering in the several parts must be of the *same kind,* or species *of that power, which is the result of the whole* — you seem all along to understand it as if I had asserted that the powers or qualities inhering in the several parts must needs be all of *the same kind* or species *one with another,* thereby diverting your reader from the true strength of the argument and perplexing him with that which has no relation to the question. For, whether the powers of the several parts be all of the *same kind one with another,* or of ever so *different kinds one from another,* that which I affirmed is still equally certain and necessary: that the power of the whole, being but the sum or mixture of the powers of the parts, cannot possibly be of a *different kind* or species from all the several powers of the parts, as *thinking* is of necessity specifically different from all and every one of the powers, known or unknown, of particles which are confessed to be *void of thought*. Wherefore when you say, *he ought to have demonstrated, if he would have proved the point he undertook to prove, that there can be no other power in any system of matter but what is the sum or aggregate of powers of the same kind;* and that *until it is demonstrated that there can be no other power in any system of matter but what is the sum or aggregate of powers of* the same *kind, it may as well be supposed that there are powers of* different *kinds in different particles of matter;* and that it is *so far from being the sum or aggregate of powers of the* same *kind, that the new power will be the sum or aggregate of powers of a* different kind; and that *the power of every system will not be the sum of powers of the* same *kind, but the sum of powers of* different *kinds.* All this is entirely besides the purpose.

Your supposition *that the matter of which an egg consists does entirely constitute the young one, and that the action of sensation began under a particular disposition of the parts by motion, without the addition of an immaterial and immortal soul,* is in every part contrary to all the discoveries in anatomy, and to all true philosophy. For, so far is it from being true that the matter of the egg, by any particular disposition of its parts by motion, is formed into, or *entirely constitutes,* the young one, that it does not *constitute it at all,* not so much as the *body* of it, but only serves it for *nourishment and growth* — it being as impossible that the organized body of a chicken should by the power of any mechanical motions be formed out of the unorganized matter of an egg, as that the sun, moon, and stars should by mere mechanism arise out of a chaos. And that *sensation* should be added to it by arising from a *particular disposition of the parts by motion* is still more impossible, because it is supposing something to come out of that in which it never was, that than which nothing in the world can be a more express contradiction. You think it ridiculous to recur to the *addition of an immaterial and immortal soul.* Let it be so, I can as easily suppose, if you must needs have a hypothesis, that the immaterial substance was not *added* afterwards, but was in it from the beginning, from the time that the seminal principle itself of the organized body was framed. And who shall tell us when that was? The deeper discoveries every age makes in anatomy by microscopical observations, the further all these things are found to be removed backwards from the search and common notions even of the most inquisitive men. Suppose therefore we could not frame any probable hypothesis at all *when* and *how* the immaterial principle of sensation came in, yet why ought this to incline any man to doubt the truth of a certain proof which shows him that there is such a principle. Any more than the difficulty (which is altogether as great a one) of framing an hypothesis *how* and *where* the organized body came, makes him disbelieve his senses which discover it to him?

You tell me again that I have *not rightly enumerated the known powers of matter.* To prove which charge, you repeat what you had before said concerning *aggregates of powers of the same kind,* wherein I have already shown that you lay stress upon that which is wholly foreign to the question. And what you add concerning the *particular texture of a body,* as being something that is different from the *magnitude* and *motion of its parts,* and on which depend certain powers — as the power of the *eye,* for instance, to *be operated upon by external objects* and to *contribute to the act of vision;* which power, because it ceases *wholly* upon the least alteration of the texture of *any part* of the eye, it is evident does not *inhere* in *the parts* of the system in the same sense with *magnitude* and *motion* — this also is altogether foreign to the question. For the *eye's power of seeing* is not, as your argument supposes, one of those powers which I ranked under the *first* head — that is, a power which really inheres in the system, and consequently in all the parts of it. But it is one of those powers which I called the *third* sort — *viz.* which are *mere abstract names signifying certain powers or effects which do not at all reside in the subject.* For the *eye* does not *see* in the same sense as the *thinking* substance *thinks,* but *seeing* in the *eye* is what *magnetism* is in the *load-stone* — not a real inherent quality, but merely a situation of parts and pores so as to be the occasion of an effect wholly extrinsic to itself, an effect produced in some other substance by rays transmitted through the pores of the eye, just as the magnetic effluvia are through a load-stone, a corn through a sieve. So that you might exactly as well have compared the power by which the soul *thinks* to the power by which a *sieve* transmits *corn,* as to the power by which the *eye sees.*

You observe that *saying consciousness is an individual power is but calling consciousness by another name, and not giving an account of what consciousness is, or wherein it consists, which is requisite to demonstrate from consciousness that consciousness cannot be added to a being that consists of actually separate and distinct parts.* It is true; my affirming consciousness to be an individual power is not giving an account of what consciousness is. Neither was it intended to be so. Every man feels and knows by experience what consciousness is better than any man can explain it — which is the case of all simple ideas. And it is not at all necessary to define more particularly what *it is,* but abundantly sufficient that we know and agree what it *is not* — viz. that it is not a multitude of distinct and separate consciousnesses — in order to prove that it does not and cannot inhere in a being that consists of a multitude of separate and distinct parts. You yourself acknowledge that the parts which constitute the brain are not separately and distinctly conscious — that is, that the consciousness of a man is not a multitude of consciousnesses, but one. This is all that I *suppose* when I call consciousness an individual power, and from hence I think it is *proved* strongly that consciousness cannot reside in a being that consists of a multitude of separate and distinct parts. Because if it could, it must necessarily follow either that it would become a multitude of distinct consciousnesses, contrary to the supposition which you yourself allow; or else, that an individual quality of each single particle would become the individual quality of every one of the rest likewise, which is a contradiction in terms; or else, that the consciousness would be one power resulting from the contributing powers of all the several separate and distinct particles, in which case, it would be, as I have before proved in enumerating the several kinds of powers, a *mere abstract name* or *complex notion,* and not a real quality residing in any subject at all. It is therefore wholly without reason that you say *Mr.* Clarke's *calling consciousness an individual power, in his sense of an individual power, is* supposing *that matter cannot think,* and that you insinuate to your reader *that consciousness being an individual power, in Mr.* Clarke's *sense of those words, is* supposing *that it is a power which can only reside in an individual being,* to prove which *he has not said anything but barely by calling consciousness an individual power.* For an *individual* power, in my sense of the word, does not *mean in the definition a power which can only reside in an individual being,* but it signifies *one power,* in opposition to *a multitude,* and I have *proved* that such a power can only reside in an individual being (not by supposing it, but) by reducing the contrary supposition to an express contradiction.

What you say, again, concerning sums and aggregates of powers of the same kind is repeating the same mistake, which I have before shown you to have fallen into, in understanding powers *of the same kind* with *one another* instead of powers of the *same kind* [or species] with the *whole that results from them.*

You are pleased to entertain yourself and your reader upon my accusing you with supposing *sweetness to be in the rose.* But I hope that this will appear very pardonable, since it seemed necessary to me to understand you as I did because I could not otherwise apprehend what you said concerning it to be pertinent to your purpose. For you compared the power which results from the several particles of a *rose* without being in the particles themselves separately and singly to the power which results from the several particles of the *brain* without being in the particles themselves separately and singly. Now the power which you say results from the disposition of the several particles of the brain is *consciousness residing in the brain itself.* Either therefore by the power resulting from the disposition of the several particles of the *rose,* you must mean *something residing* likewise *in the rose itself,* or else your similitude is not at all parallel. Now that power which resides in the rose itself, as consciousness does in the brain, and yet belongs not to the several constituent particles of the rose, can neither be *magnitude,* nor *figure,* nor *motion* (for these belong to the several parts singly), nor *texture* (for that, so far as it differs from the former, is nothing but a *mere abstract notion,* and nothing really in the thing itself) but must be either sweetness itself, or something else equally unintelligible and inexplicable. If you will say you mean a power not residing *in* a rose at all, but resulting *from* it, then (besides that, as I said before, it is not pertinent to your purpose) what is it but supposing a power subsisting without any subject at all — a *mere name?*

In my assertion that the powers in a rose are nothing else but a number of *similar* motions or figures, you tell me *there are two things to be proved.* (i) *That the mere figure and motion of the parts of a rose do produce, or are the sole external cause of the sensation caused by them.* (ii) *That those motions and figures are perfectly similar.* By *similar* I meant that they were so far *similar* as the smell or color of the rose was similar or homogeneous. But whether they are *similar,* or no, is of no concern at all in the present question, unless you still continue in your former mistake about powers of *the same kind* with *one another,* instead of *with the whole.* And as to the other thing which you say wants proof, I think I may appeal to yourself whether you can find or conceive anything else in the rose which can be the cause of our sensation besides the mere *magnitude, figure, situation,* and perhaps *motion* of its parts.

You find fault with me for asserting that gravitation is the effect of the continued and regular operation of some other being on matter, *whereas,* you think, *it does not appear but that matter gravitates by virtue of* powers *originally placed in it by God, and is now left to itself to act by those original powers.* This opinion of yours I cannot but think, Sir, to be a great mistake in your philosophy. For when a stone that was at rest does of itself, upon its support being removed, begin to fall downward, what is it that causes the stone to begin to move? Is it possible to be an effect produced without cause? Is it impelled without any impeller? Or can a *law* or *power* — that is to say a *mere abstract name* or *complex notion,* and not any *real being* — impel a stone and cause it to begin to move? In any other case you would not doubt but this implied an absolute contradiction.

II. When, in my answer to your second objection, I said that though the want of individuality is indeed the sole reason urged in the *present argument* why a system of matter cannot think, yet it ought not therefore to be said that individuality is the *only thing required* to render a being a proper subject of a power of thinking (because I would not exclude any *other argument* by which other inquisitive persons might prove other conditions also, as well as individuality, to be necessary requisites in order to a subject's being capable of thinking. You hereupon make the following remark: *Upon this I observe that Mr.* Clarke *owns the truth of my reasoning upon the supposition that individuality is only required by him in a subject of a power of thinking* (you should have added, and upon supposition also, that a particle of matter could be truly an individual), *but denies that I have any reason to infer that* individuality *is only required from the* want of individuality's *being the sole reason urged why a system of matter cannot have a power of thinking, which I cannot help thinking to be all one, until there is a difference assigned between* 'only required *in the present argument*', *and* 'the sole reason urged *in the present argument*'. Now this is a very unfair observation, because the difference to be assigned, and which I did assign expressly, was between *the sole reason urged* in the *present argument,* and what was *only required* (not in *the present* but) in any *new argument* which others might make use of.

III. The question concerning the *alterations of the modes and qualities* of immaterial beings seems indeed to have some difficulties in it, but not such as any way affect our present argument. The thing you objected was that though the substance of the soul were proved to be both immaterial and immortal, yet it would not follow that it must be an immortal *thinking* substance, because its *thinking* might perish though its *substance* did not. To this I replied that the *power of thinking* could no more be destroyed by any natural power than the *substance* itself, because the qualities or modes of any substance not being alterable otherwise than by some alteration in the substance itself. It is manifest that an indiscerptible substance not being itself alterable by any natural power, it must follow that neither can any of its qualities be altered by any natural power. When therefore I said that all its qualities and modes are utterly incapable of being affected in any measure, or *changed* in any degree, by any power of nature, you had no reason to understand this as if I had asserted that an indiscerptible substance could not be *acted upon at all* by any power of nature. But my meaning was that it could not be so acted upon as to *destroy, change,* or *alter* any of its inherent qualities or powers, which was all that the thing in question required me to prove. And that this was my meaning, you might have understood from the comparison I used of the original and perfectly solid particles of matter. For as those particles, being (not absolutely in themselves, but) to any power of nature indiscerptible, are evidently incapable of having any of their qualities or properties altered in any measure by any power of nature. That is, their figure, their magnitude, their hardness, and all the respective effects or powers depending upon these, can by no natural means be changed. And yet you could not imagine me to mean but these particles might be *acted upon,* might be *struck* by each other, might be removed this way or that way, upwards or downwards, all which makes no real alteration in them. So an indiscerptible immaterial thinking substance, though it may be transferred from one part of the universe to another, though it may be *acted upon* by a multitude of things, though it may have different ideas represented to it, though the organs of the senses may at times transmit different species, or hinder them from being transmitted to it, yet all this makes no real alteration either in the substance or its inherent powers. Nor can its power of *thinking* (which was the thing in question) be destroyed or altered by these or any other natural powers, any more than the *mobility* or *hardness* of the original perfectly solid particles of matter can be destroyed by any of their actings one upon another.

There is still less weight in what you add: *Now until Mr.* Clarke *has a complete idea of both sorts of beings* [material and immaterial], *and of their powers and operations one on another, it is impossible for him, in many respects, to tell how far they can affect one another's operations.* This is true indeed, but what follows from it? Because, in *many respects,* I cannot tell how far they *can* affect one another's operations, does it therefore follow that I cannot in *any respect* tell wherein they *cannot* affect one another's operations? All that I pretend to is to deny the possibility of such effects as plainly imply a contradiction. And this, I presume, I may be allowed to do, though I were in *most respects* ignorant how far material and immaterial beings *can* affect one another.

As to the *power of God* to destroy any mode or quality in an immaterial indiscerptible substance, I said nothing concerning it, neither is our question at all concerned in it. But since you have thought fit to put the question whether, according to my principles, God can destroy a mode or quality in an immaterial being without making some alteration in the substance itself, I cannot but take notice that all the answers you have made for me to this question are such as I cannot approve, and that therefore I am not concerned in any of their consequences. The answer I would make for myself is that supposing God to destroy any mode or quality in an immaterial being, it is reasonable to imagine that he must do it by making some such *alteration in that substance* as may be analogous or equivalent to *altering the disposition of the parts in a material substance.* But you ought not to have jumbled these two things together (which I carefully distinguished) by supposing me to answer that God must do it by making an alteration in the *parts of the* immaterial substance (to which it is not *proper* to ascribe any *parts*) and thence concluding that an immaterial substance is *as discerptible* by the power of God as a material substance.

Lastly, you tell me that, after all, I make the immaterial thinking substance to be in no other sense *immortal* than I make the original solid particles of matter to be *indiscerptible.* That is to say, that the one is *immortal* and the other *indiscerptible*, only with respect to the powers of nature, but that in respect to the power of God, neither is the one *indiscerptible* nor the other *immortal*. Your expressions in the whole section lie under so much obscurity that I can hardly be sure whether I understand you right or not. But if this be your sense, I confess I do indeed make it so, and I suppose no considerate man ever made the soul *immortal* in any other sense. For though I believe it is not *discerptible* even by the power of God, yet he is undoubtedly able to destroy it either by *annihilating* it, or perhaps by otherwise *depriving* it of all its faculties in ways which we can know nothing of.

IV. To the difficulties arising from the *supposition* of immateriality not excluding extension, I answer:

1. That all these difficulties are wide of the main question, for if the foregoing proof that matter is incapable of thinking cannot be shown to be defective, it follows necessarily that the soul must be an *immaterial indiscerptible substance*. But the difficulties that arise from any following hypothesis concerning other properties of that immaterial indiscerptible substance, as to whether it be *extended* or *unextended*, whether it ever acts *wholly separate*, or always *in some material vehicle*, finer or grosser, and the like — the difficulties, I say, that arise from any of these particular hypotheses affect the particular hypothesis from which they arise, and not at all the foregoing general proof. I take it to be demonstrated that the soul is an *immaterial indiscerptible substance*. He that thinks the difficulties arising from the supposition of that immaterial indiscerptible substance being *extended* to be insurmountable, may try if he can find fewer difficulties in supposing it *unextended*. And he that thinks the difficulties that arise from supposing it *unextended* are not to be got over, may try to solve the difficulties that arise from supposing it extended. But the main argument remains firm either way, and no difficulty arising from following hypotheses can be so great as to lessen the force of the foregoing positive proof.

2. But conceiving immateriality not to exclude extension, and supposing the difficulties arising from that hypothesis to be such as could not be clearly answered, yet this would not weaken the foregoing proof unless that argument could oth-

erwise be shown to be in itself defective. For there are many demonstrations, even in abstract mathematics themselves, which no man who understands them can in the least doubt of the certainty of, which yet are attended with difficult consequences that cannot perfectly be cleared. The *infinite divisibility of quantities* is an instance of this kind. Also the *eternity of God,* than which nothing is more self-evident, and yet the difficulties consequent upon it are such as have reduced most of the Schoolmen to entertain that unintelligible notion of a *nunc stans* [the eternal now –ed.]. And his *immensity,* attended with much the like difficulties.

3. But neither is this the true state of the case. For the difficulties arising from the supposition of immaterial indiscerptible extension are by no means like those before-mentioned. Space (which you *unphilosophically* call the mere absence of bodies, and yet confess it to be positively infinite) is without difficulty confessed by you to be an instance of such an extension — an extension whose parts (improperly so called) depend on each other for their existence, not only because of its infinity, but because of the contradiction which a separation of them manifestly would imply. And the only thing required in the present case is to conceive that God can create a finite substance which shall not — like the solid, rigid, determined extension of matter — consist of parts which are actually so many distinct beings independent of each other,[1] but be a substance perfectly and essentially one, so that to suppose any division of it shall necessarily infer a destruction of the essence of that substance. This must indeed be confessed to be a considerable difficulty. But if the difficulties upon any other hypothesis be (as they certainly are) *at least* as great, nothing can thence be inferred to the weakening of the foregoing proof.

Your applying the argument by which I proved that matter could not think, in the same words, to prove that neither could immaterial substance be capable of thinking, is fallacious in the first sentence. For the supposition of the substance being by *the power of God divided into two parts* — which, concerning matter, is confessed to be always possible — may, concerning immaterial substance (even though extension not be excluded), be denied

1 Replacing "on each other for their existence" –ed.

to be possible, as being a supposition which destroys the very *essence* of the substance itself.

V. As to your last difficulty concerning brutes, I answer that your disjunction is still imperfect when you say they must either necessarily be annihilated some time or other, or else be capable of eternal happiness *as well as man.* For though they should never be annihilated, yet why must they needs be capable of eternal happiness *as well as man* — any more than their present subsisting implies that they must needs be capable of the *expectation* and *condition* of eternal happiness *as well as man?* But what is all this to our purpose? Cannot God, if he pleases, cause them to perish at the dissolution of their bodies? Or cannot he, if he pleases, annihilate them at any other time when he shall so think fit? Or cannot he, if he pleases, without ever annihilating them at all, dispose of them into states suitable to their particular natures, which yet may in no propriety of speech be styled a capacity of eternal happiness as that of *man* is?

Having thus at large endeavored to give you particular satisfaction in every one of the difficulties you proposed, I shall conclude with briefly repeating the strength of the argument in a few plain and easy *propositions,* and so leave it to the judgment of the inquisitive and impartial reader.

(Note: by consciousness *in the following propositions, the reader may understand indifferently either the* reflex act — by which a man knows his thoughts to be his own thoughts *(which is the strict and* most proper sense of the word) — *or* the direct act of thinking, *or* the power or capacity of thinking, *or (which is of the same import)* simple sensation, *or the* power of self-motion or beginning motion by the will — *the argument holding equally in all or any of these senses, as has been before said.)*

I. Every *system of matter* consists of a *multitude of* distinct *parts.*

This, I think, is granted by all.

II. Every *real quality* inheres in some *subject.*

This also, I think, is granted by all. For whatever is called a *quality,* and yet inheres not in any *subject,* must either subsist of itself — and then it is a *substance,* not a *quality* — or else it is nothing but a *mere name.*

III. No *individual* or *single quality* of one particle of matter can be the *individual* or *single quality* of another particle.

The *heat* of one particle is not the *heat* of another. The *gravity,* the *color,* the *figure,* of one particle is not the same individual *gravity, color,* or *figure* of another particle. The *consciousness* or *sensation* of one particle (supposing it to be a quality of matter) is not the *consciousness* or *sensation* of another. If it were,[1] it would follow that the same thing could be *two,* in the same sense and at the same time that it is but *one.*

Note, from hence may be drawn an evident confutation of that absurd notion which Mr. *Hobbes* suggests in his *Physics* (ch. 25, sect. 5) that *all matter* is essentially *endued with an obscure actual sense and perception,* but that there is required a number and apt composition of parts to make up *a clear and distinct sensation or consciousness.* For from this notion it would follow that the resulting *sensation* or *consciousness* at last, being but one distinct *sensation* or *consciousness* (as is that of a man) the *sensation* or *consciousness* of every one of the constituent particles, would be the individual *sensation* or *consciousness* of all and each of the rest.

IV. Every *real simple quality* that resides *in* any *whole material system* resides *in* all the *parts* of that system.

The *magnitude* of every *body* is the sum of the *magnitude* of its several *parts.* The *motion* of every *body* is the sum of the *motions* of its several *parts.* The weight of every body is the weights of its several parts. The *heat* of every *body* is the sum of the *heat* of its several *parts.*[2] The *color* of every *body* is the sum of the *color* of its several *parts.* And the same is universally

1 Replacing "was" –ed.

2 Note, by heat here is meant that motion which causes in us the sensation of heat, by color, that magnitude and figure which causes particular rays to be transmitted to us, etc.

true of *every simple quality* residing *in* any *system.* For residing in the *whole* and not residing in the *parts* is *residing* in a thing and not *residing* in it at the same time.

V. Every *real compound quality* that resides *in* any whole material *system* is a number of simple qualities residing *in* all the *parts* of that system — some in one part, some in another.

Thus in the instance of *mixed colors* — when the simples *blue,* suppose, *and yellow* make the *whole* appear *green* — in this case, that *portion* of the system in which any one of the particular simple qualities resides is a *whole* system with respect to that quality, and the quality residing in it resides in the several *particles* of which that *portion of the system* is constituted. And so of the rest.

VI. Every *real quality, simple* or *compound,* that *results from* any whole material *system,* but does not *reside in it* — that is, neither in all its distinct parts, nor in all the parts of some portion of it — according to the explication of the two foregoing propositions, is the mode or quality of some *other substance,* and not of *that.*

All sensible secondary qualities — *heat, color, smell, taste, sound,* and the like — are of this kind, being in reality not *qualities* of the *bodies* they are ascribed to, but *modes* of the *mind* that perceives them.

VII. Every *power, simple* or *compound,* that *results from* any whole material *system,* but does not *reside in it* — that is, in all its parts, in the manner before explained — nor yet resides in any *other substance* as its subject, is no *real quality* at all, but must either be itself a real substance (which seems unintelligible), or else it is nothing but merely an *abstract name* or *notion,* as all *universals* are.

Thus the power resulting from the texture of the *rose* to excite in us the sensation of sweetness is nothing but an *abstract name,* signifying a particular motion and figure of certain parts emitted. The power of a *clock* to show the hour of the day is nothing but one *new complex name,* to express at once the several motions of the parts, and particularly the *determinate velocity* of the last wheel to turn round once in twelve hours: upon the stopping which *motion* by the touch of a finger or any other impediment, without making any alteration at all in the number, figure, or disposition of the parts of the clock, the *power* wholly ceases. And upon removing the impediment, by which nothing is restored but *mere motion,* the *power* returns again — which is therefore no new real quality of the *whole,* but only the *mere motion* of the *parts.* The power of a *pin* to prick is nothing distinct from its mere figure permitting it to enter the skin. The power of a *weight in one scale of a balance* to ascend or descend, upon increasing or diminishing the counterpoint in the other scale, is not a *new real quality* distinct from its *absolute gravity,* though it occasions a new *effect,* there being no alteration at all made in *the weight itself.* The *power of the eye to see* is not a real quality of the *whole eye,* but merely an *abstract name* signifying a transmitting and refracting of the rays of light in a certain manner through its several parts — which effect, by the interposition or removal of an opaque body, is destroyed or renewed without any alteration at all in the eye itself. A *key,* by having many new locks made fit to it, acquires a *new power* of producing effects which it could not before, and yet no new real quality is produced, nor any alteration at all made in the *key* itself. And so, universally, of all powers of this kind. If these powers were anything else but *mere abstract names,* they would signify qualities subsisting without any subject at all — that is, such as must themselves be distinct substances — which is unintelligible.

VIII. *Consciousness* is neither a *mere abstract name* (such as are the *powers* mentioned in prop. VII), *nor a power of exciting or occasioning different modes in a foreign substance* (such as are all the *sensible qualities* of bodies, prop. VI), but *a real quality truly and properly inherent in the subject itself, the thinking substance.*

If it were[1] *a mere abstract name,* it would be nothing at all in the person that thinks, or in the thinking substance itself, but only a notion framed by the imagination of some other being. For all those powers which are only *abstract names* are not at all in the *things whose powers they are called,* but are only *notions* framed in imagination by the mind that observes, compares, and reasons about different *objects without itself.*

If it was a *power of exciting or occasioning different modes in a foreign substance,* then the *power of thinking* must be before in that

1 Replacing "was" –ed.

foreign substance, and that foreign substance alone would in reality be conscious, and not *this* which excites the different modes in *that foreign substance.* For the power that is in one substance of exciting different modes in another substance presupposes necessarily, in that other substance, the *foundation* of those modes. Thus in the case of all the *sensible qualities* of bodies, the *power of thinking* is beforehand in that being, wherein those qualities excite or occasion *different modes* of thinking.

It remains therefore that it must of necessity be a *real quality truly and properly inhering in the subject itself, the thinking substance,* there being no other *species* of *powers* or *qualities* left to which it can possibly be referred. And this indeed is of itself as evident by every man's experience as it can be rendered by any explication or proof whatsoever.

IX. No *real quality* can result from the *composition* of *different qualities,* so as to be a new quality in the same subject of a *different kind* or *species* from all and every one of the *component qualities.*

If it could, it would be a *creation of something out of nothing.* From compound *motions* can arise nothing but *motion;* from *magnitudes* nothing but *magnitude;* from *figure* nothing but *figure;* from *compositions of magnitude, figure,* and *motion* together nothing but *magnitude, figure,* and *motion;* from *mechanical powers* nothing but *mechanical powers;* from composition of *colors* nothing but *color,* which itself (as appears by microscopes) is still the *simple colors* of which it was compounded; from mixtures of *chemical liquors* nothing but *ferments* which are only mere *motions* of the particles in mixing, such motions as arise from the placing of *iron* and a *load-stone* near each other. *Gravity* is not a quality of matter arising from its texture or any other power in it, but merely an *endeavor* to *motion,* excited by some foreign force or power. *Magnetism* and *electricity* are not new qualities resulting from different and unknown powers, but merely emissions of certain streams of matter which produce certain determinate motions. Compositions of *colors* can never contribute to produce a *sound,* nor compositions of *magnitude* and *figure* to produce a *motion;* nor *necessary and determinate motions* to produce a *free and indeterminate power of self-motion;* nor any *mechanical powers* whatsoever to produce a *power not mechanical.* And the same must of necessity hold universally true of all qualities and powers whatsoever, whether known or unknown. Because otherwise, as has been before said, there would in the compound be something created out of nothing.

X. *Consciousness* therefore being a real quality (prop. VIII), and of a kind *specifically different* from all other qualities, whether known or unknown, which are themselves acknowledged to be *void of consciousness,* can never possibly result from any composition of such qualities.

This is as evident from the foregoing propositions, as that a *sound* cannot be the result of a mixture of *colors* and *smells,* nor *extension* the result of a composition of parts *unextended,* nor *solidity* the result of parts *not solid* — whatever other different qualities, known or unknown, those constituent parts may be supposed to be endued with.

XI. No individual *quality* can be *transferred* from one *subject* to another.

This is granted by all.

XII. The *spirits* and *particles* of the *brain,* being *loose* and in perpetual *flux,* cannot therefore be the seat of that *consciousness* by which a man not only remembers things done many years since, but also is conscious that *he himself,* the same *individual conscious being,* was the doer of them.

This follows evidently from the foregoing.

XIII. The *consciousness* that a man has at one and the same time is *one consciousness,* and not a *multitude of consciousnesses,* as the *solidity, motion,* or *color* of any piece of matter is a multitude of distinct *solidities, motions,* or *colors.*

This is granted by all who deny that the particles of the brain, which they suppose to constitute a conscious substance, are themselves each of them conscious.

XIV. *Consciousness* therefore cannot at all reside in the substance of the *brain,* or *spirits,* or in any other *material system* as its *subject,* but must be a quality of some *immaterial substance.*

This follows necessarily from the foregoing propositions compared together. For since every possible power of matter, whether known or unknown, must needs be either, first, a *real quality* of matter to which it is ascribed, and then it must inhere in the several distinct parts; or, secondly, a power of exciting or occasioning certain *modes* in some *other subject;* and then it is truly the quality not of the matter, but of that other subject; or, thirdly, a *mere abstract name* or *notion* of what is, properly speaking, no real quality at all, and inheres in no real subject at all. And *consciousness* is acknowledged to be none of these. It follows unavoidably that it must of necessity be a quality of some *immaterial substance.*

XV. Difficulties that arise afterwards concerning *other qualities* of that *immaterial substance,* as whether it be *extended* or *unextended,* do not at all affect the present argument.

For thus even abstract mathematical demonstrations as those concerning the *infinite divisibility of quality,* the *eternity of God,* and his *immensity,* have almost insuperable difficulties on the other side. And yet no man who understands those matters thinks that those difficulties do at all weaken the force, or diminish the certainty, of the demonstrations.

Anthony Collins

Reflections on Mr. Clarke's Second Defense of his Letter to Mr. Dodwell

——*Vimq; omnem eam, qua vel agamtus, vel sentiamus, in omnibus Corporibus vivus æqualiter esse fusam, nec separabilem esse a Corpore, quippe quæ nulla sit, nec quiquam, nisi corpus unum & simplex, ita figuratum ut temparatione naturæ vigeat & sentiat:* affirmat Dicærchus apud Cicer. Tusc. Quæst.

[——Neither in man nor in beast is there a spiritual or physical principle answering to the soul, and all the capacity we have of action or sensation is uniformly diffused in all living bodies and cannot be separated from the body, seeing that it has no separate existence and that there is nothing apart from one single body fashioned in such a way that its activity and power of sensation are due to the natural combination of the parts. This is what Dicaearchus affirmed according to Cicero in the *Tusculan Disputations.* Trans. J.E. King]

Nos autem animam corporalem & hic profitemur, & *in fuo volumine probamus, habentem proprium genus substantiaæ, soliditatis, per quam quid* & *sentire & pati possit.* Tertullian. de Refurrectione Carnis.

[I however both state here, and have proved in a treatise of its own, that the soul is corporal, having its own particular kind of substance and solidity by which it is capable both of perception and of suffering. Tertullian, *Concerning the Resurrection of the Body,* Trans. Ernest Evans.]

If the reader is not already tired with the continuance of this dispute concerning the *possibility of matter's thinking,* I will presume so far on his understanding and candor as (without endeavoring to lead him into my side of the question by making a previous judgment of Mr. *Clarke's Second Defense of his Argument, Made*

Use of in a Letter to Mr. Dodwell, *To Prove the Immateriality and Natural Immortality of the Soul*) to proceed directly to the question itself, after I have performed a piece of justice to Mr. *Clarke* and the reader by acknowledging that in my *Reply* to Mr. *Clarke*'s former *Defense* I did omit a line in citing his answer to my first objection; which, whether it was owing to *a fault in the press*, or to my negligence in transcribing, I cannot say. But I can assure the reader it was out of no design to give *a disadvantageous representation of his sense*, and I hope he will be induced to believe so when he considers that I made no manner of use of that *representation* to the disadvantage of his argument, and to excuse me in the same ingenious manner that Mr. *Clarke* has done.[1]

The question is whether a system of matter can have a power of thinking, or an individual consciousness, superadded to it, or flow from any modification of that system.

By the term *individual*, when applied to *consciousness*, both Mr. *Clarke* and I understand *one consciousness*, in opposition to a multitude of distinct *consciousnesses*.

By *a power of thinking*, I did understand on this occasion *actual thinking*, and not *a capacity of thinking*, "for else," as I said, "consciousness could not be properly employed, by Mr. *Clarke*, to signify the same thing with a power of thinking."[2] But to this state of the question Mr. *Clarke* excepts by saying *that he can see no reason for such a nicety of distinction for*, says he, *the thing to be proved being this, that a divisible substance is not capable of a power of thinking, what difference can it make whether by a power of thinking I understand actual thinking or a capacity of thinking? For* he *presumes, I will not deny but whatever is proved incapable of actual thinking is also proved incapable of a capacity of thinking, and whatever is proved incapable of a capacity of thinking is also proved incapable of actual thinking.*[3] And further to show the *needlessness* of distinguishing between *actual thinking* and *a capacity of thinking*, he says: *The reader may understand* the term *consciousness indifferently for either a capacity of thinking, or actual thinking, or the reflex act of thinking, because* his *argument proves universally that matter is neither capable of the reflex act, nor of the direct act, nor of the capacity of thinking.*[4]

1 Second Defense. [pp. 89-90 –ed.]

2 Reply. [p. 69 –ed.]

3 Second Defense. [p. 90 –ed.]

4 Second Defense. [p. 90 –ed.]

1. Now allowing this to be as Mr. *Clarke* represents it, what occasion was there for contending with me about the sense I fixed to the terms *power of thinking* and *consciousness?* All that could be hoped for by him in this dispute is, by his own account of the matter, as well attained by my understanding *a power of thinking* or *consciousness* in that sense wherein I understood those terms, as if either of them stood for three significations at once. For if his *argument proves universally that matter can neither have the direct act, nor the reflex act, nor the capacity of thinking;* and that *whatever is proved incapable of actual thinking is proved incapable of a capacity of thinking;* and, I may add likewise, and that whatever is proved incapable of *actual thinking* is proved incapable of the reflex act of thinking;[1] have I not then understood him in the sense that answered all the ends and purposes of his argument?

2. But there is still the less reason, if possible, to dispute with me about this matter, because he expressly says *the reader may understand* the term consciousness *indifferently in all or any* of the before-mentioned *significations.* So that I have taken but the same liberty he allows to every other *reader,* and until I am shown the difference between an answerer and a *reader* in this respect, I shall think myself justified by what Mr. *Clarke* allows to his *reader.* But that the reader may see the ground of his complaint against me, and that I may do Mr. *Clarke* justice, I will cite the whole sentence that he uses on this occasion, because it seems to me to contain one of the nicest distinctions that ever I met with. Says he, *the reader need not trouble himself with the nicety of distinction between a capacity of thinking, actual thinking, and the reflex act of thinking, but may understand consciousness indifferently in all or any of these significations.* Which is as much as to say that the reader need not understand consciousness indifferently in any of the before-mentioned significations, and yet may understand it indifferently in any of these significations. For I cannot see but that whoever understands *consciousness* in any one of those significations must use that *nicety of distinction* he complains of, whether he will or no. For by restraining consciousness to *any one* of those significations, he necessarily distinguishes that *one* from the other *two.* And therefore, I must own, I cannot see the least reason Mr. *Clarke* had to blame me for a *needless nicety of distinction,* when he allows me to understand consciousness

1 Second Defense. [p. 90 –ed.]

indifferently in three significations, one of which I did assign as my meaning or idea of that word.

3. Since then it is evident that I have understood him in a sense that answered all the ends and purposes of his argument, and in a sense wherein he allows his reader to understand him. He ought not to have supposed such a reason as he is pleased to assign for me, why I distinguish between actual thinking and a capacity of thinking, as he does when he says *that* he *cannot see any reason (unless it were to perplex the reader with a new question, whether the soul always actually thinks or not, which is wholly foreign to the matter at present in dispute) why I should affirm* "that consciousness could not be properly employed by Mr. *Clarke* to signify the same thing with a power of thinking, unless by a power of thinking be understood not capacity to think, but actual thinking." I say, he ought not to have assigned such a reason for me, for if I have understood him in one of those senses that he allows his reader to understand him in — and by consequence acknowledges that I do not *perplex* the reader with a new question by understanding *a power of thinking* to stand for *actual thinking,* but that I keep myself to the old question by understanding him in that manner — what ground could he have to imagine that I had any design to *perplex* the reader with a new question, but by either making the same question to be both new and old, or two different questions one and the same question? I shall not presume to enter so far into his thoughts, as to say that though he acknowledges his argument to be directed against the sense in which I understand *power of thinking* and *consciousness,* and that all that he requires from his argument equally follows from matter's being proved incapable of actual thinking, as if I understood him in any other sense that he can contend for. I say, I shall not presume to enter so far into his thoughts as to tell the reader that I can see no reason for his imagining that I had any design *to perplex him with a question foreign to the matter* (unless it be to *perplex* this dispute in that part where it is most necessary to be clear), but choose rather to demand a reason of his conduct when I cannot assign a good one for him. And that is what I think I had reason to expect from him if he means anything by attributing *candor and ingenuity to what I have written* besides mere compliment, whether I could have given a good reason or no for understanding consciousness to signify in this dispute *actual thinking,* and consequently for distinguishing between actual thinking and a capacity of thinking.

4. But to give Mr. *Clarke* and the reader full satisfaction on this head, I will show that the whole dispute turns upon that distinction, that my objections were entirely founded on that distinction, and that Mr. *Clarke*'s not attending to it has rendered all his answers foreign to the matter of my objections. Mr. *Clarke* had said *it is plain, unless matter were essentially conscious, no system of it in any possible composition or division can be an individual conscious being.*[1] Now upon my principles, and I suppose the principles of all those who say a divisible being may have a power of thinking, it is impossible to give any answer at all to this proposition, but by restraining the sense of the term *consciousness.* Because on supposition that consciousness stands at one and the same time for the direct act, for the reflex act, and for the capacity of thinking, what is meant by those words cited out of Mr. *Clarke*'s Letter to Mr. *Dodwell* will be allowed by me to be partly true and partly false. I grant the reasoning to be good thus far, that if matter be not made by God capable of thinking, or essentially conscious in that sense, *that no system of it in any possible composition or division can be an individual conscious being* — that is, no motion whatever can give matter a capacity of thinking — and only deny them to be true, understood after this manner, that unless all matter did actually think, or was essentially conscious in that sense, no system of it in any possible composition or division can actually think. So that what I maintain is in short this: that either matter was made originally capable of thinking, or may be made by God capable of thinking after its beginning to exist — and notwithstanding that no part of it may really or actually think, yet by virtue of that capacity some systems may by composition and division become subjects of thinking. All that I suppose arises new from composition and division is nothing else but a new operation or actual thinking, and therefore my principles led me to understand by a *power of thinking* actual thinking, and consequently to distinguish between actual thinking and a capacity of thinking. And had any end of truth been[2] served by further distinguishing, I had taken the same liberty to have spoken of *consciousness in the most strict and exact sense of the word, as it stands for the reflex act of thinking, by which I know that I think,* as I have now done in using it for *actual thinking.*

1 Letter to Mr. Dodwell. [This is a reference to Clarke's Letter to Dodwell (not published in this edition) but the passage is repeated in Collins' Letter to Dodwell. See p. 47 –ed.]

2 Deleting "to be" –ed.

5. As I could not make any objections to Mr. *Clarke*'s argument but by distinguishing between *actual thinking* and a *capacity of thinking,* so in fact my first objection is grounded on that distinction. I speak directly of *thinking* as an *operation*. And when I say "that matter of fact is so plain that a man cannot turn his eye but he will meet with material systems wherein there are individual powers which are not in every one, nor in any one, of the particles that compose them when taken apart and considered singly," and instance in a rose that produces in us the sensation of sweetness.[1] I plainly supposed the matter of which those material systems consisted essentially capable of those individual powers which are observable upon the different disposition of their parts, and likewise the matter of which a rose consists essentially capable of producing that sensation in us, and that it was from the composition of that matter of which it did consist into the form of a rose, whence the particular operation that causes our sensation arises.

Sect. 1. In order to prove that consciousness could not inhere in, or result from, a divisible substance, Mr. *Clarke* enumerated all the possible powers of matter under three heads.[2]

1. *Powers really inhering in the subject to which they are usually ascribed, such as magnitude and motion, which are sums or aggregates of powers of the same kind.*

2. *Modes produced in some other subject as, for instance, the sweetness and color of a rose, which are vulgarly looked upon as individual powers. But this,* says he, *is only a vulgar and gross error.*

3. *Certain effects or powers that do not properly reside in any subject at all, such as magnetism and electrical attractions.*

From whence it follows that, according to Mr. *Clarke,* no powers can inhere in matter, but such powers as magnitude and motion, which are only sums or aggregates of powers of the same kind. And therefore *if consciousness can inhere in a system of matter, it must necessarily be the sum or result of the consciousnesses of the*

1 Reply. [p. 67 –ed.]
2 1st Defense. [pp. 56-58 –ed.]

several parts. And so there would be as many distinct consciousnesses as there are particles of matter of which the system consists — which he supposes will be granted to be very absurd. Now in answer to his argument I said "that it was nothing else but *argumentum ad ignorantiam.* For by enumerating his three sorts of powers or qualities of matter, and showing that the two last are improperly called powers or qualities, he does suppose that a system of matter has, and can have, only powers of one sort or kind — such as magnitude and motion — which are only the sums and aggregates of powers of the same kind. Which, what else is it[1] to argue that because we know of no other powers in matter of a different kind from magnitude and motion, therefore it has, and can have, no other powers of a different kind?"

But Mr. *Clarke* says *if a disjunction be complete (as that in which he enumerates the several sorts of powers of which matter is capable, either is, or else* I *ought to have proved that another member could be added to it, to show that it was not), it contains in it all the possible particulars, as well the unknown as those that are ever so well known.*

1. It is very true, if a disjunction be complete, it must contain in it all possible particulars both known and unknown. But this amounts to no more than to say that if a disjunction be complete it is complete, and does by no means reach the question, which is how he can know that his disjunction is complete (if ranking all the true and proper powers of matter under one head can be called a disjunction) when he produces no proof that his heads are rightly distributed, and do contain under them all the possible powers of matter both known and unknown. And until he can prove that, he can never clear his argument from being *argumentum ad ignorantiam.* He therefore mistakes the objection of *argumentum ad ignorantiam,* when he says *that his disjunction either is complete, or else* I *ought to have proved that another member could be added to it to show that it was not.* For the nature of that objection does not oblige me to add another member to his disjunction, but obliges him to prove that another member cannot be added to his disjunction. For unless Mr. *Clarke* can prove it impossible for another member to be added to his disjunction, he can never know that another member cannot be added to it, and consequently an argument drawn from a disjunction which

1 Replacing "what is it else" –ed.

is not demonstrated to be complete is purely an *argumentum ad ignorantiam.* And to put me upon adding another member to it is to put me upon more than my objection obliges me to — nay is inconsistent with the nature of such an objection, and mixing things that are foreign together.

2. But I did not only tell him that his argument was an *argumentum ad ignorantiam,* which was sufficient to overthrow a precarious disjunction, but did instance in several powers of matter that did not fall in with his disjunction. I instanced particularly in the power of the eye to contribute to the act of seeing (for though I certainly think the eye to be the organ of seeing, as I do the nose of smelling, or the lungs of breathing, and I may add the brain of thinking, yet I attribute in my argument in this place no more to that system of matter called the eye, that I might not beg the question between us, than such undoubted matter of fact as I think no one will deny — *viz.* that by the disposition of its parts it is operated on in a peculiar manner by external objects, and that it does contribute by its own operation towards the act of seeing) as an operation of a system of matter that did not inhere in its parts in the same sense with magnitude and motion in body: "For divide and vary the parts of matter as much as you will, there will be magnitude and may be motion. But divide or vary the least part of the eye, and the power of contributing towards the act of vision is entirely at an end."[1]

But that I may explain myself more fully on this head, I shall observe that not only the power of the eye to contribute towards the act of seeing is a proof that there are powers in systems of matter that inhere not in the parts of those systems singly considered, but almost everything we see, feel, hear, taste or smell, may convince us of the existence of such powers. Does not a musical instrument, by being operated on in a peculiar manner, operate on us again and produce in us several agreeable sensations? And is not that *power or ability to be acted on by us, and to act on us,* peculiar to the modification of that body, and not the result of powers of the same kind, since there are parts of that system of matter absolutely necessary to the continuance of that power in them which produces our sensations? For as the strings of a violin are not sufficient of themselves, so neither are the remain-

1 Reply. [p. 72 –ed.]

ing parts of that instrument, to produce in us those harmonious sounds that are caused by the whole system of that matter being modified into that peculiar form.

What are particular figures in bodies, such as roundness or squareness, but qualities or powers in bodies that are not the sum of powers of the same kind? For divide a round body into what number of parts you please, and it will never be found to consist only of round parts, no more than a square or cubical body will be found to consist only of square of cubical parts, since a round body may by the motion or alteration of its parts become cubical, and a cubical body by the motion or alteration of its parts become round.

But Mr. *Clarke* says: *That seeing in the eye is not a real inherent quality, but merely situation of parts and pores* so *as to be the occasion of an effect wholly extrinsic to itself, an effect produced in some other substance by rays transmitted through the pores of the eye,* and *is one of those powers, etc., ranked under his third head of powers — viz. an effect that does not reside in any subject at all.*[1]

In this paragraph Mr. *Clarke* seems to confound his second and third heads together by making the power of the eye to see to be both *an effect produced in some other subject,* and *an effect residing in no subject at all,* at the same time. But I will show Mr. Clarke that it is neither the one nor the other. For what is *the transmission of rays* in a peculiar manner but an operation particular to the parts of the eye under such modification? And is there not then a peculiar motion of the eye whereby the soul is made capable of seeing objects transmitted, which operation or mode of motion entirely ceases upon the least alteration of the parts? Is not the whole being affected, and does it not act in a different manner from each of its parts singly considered, and from the whole system under another modification? Now it is that manner of acting peculiar to the structure of the eye that I call the *power of the eye* (which does not inhere in the parts of the eye in the same sense that it inheres in that whole eye) in the idea whereof is not only contained an effect wrought in another subject — *viz. actual seeing of the soul* — but an operation on the subject of seeing. As I suppose thinking not to be merely an effect wrought on another subject — *viz.* ideas and the images of things — but is likewise the action of the brain, or spirits of the brain, on those ideas

1 Second Defense. [p. 100 –ed.]

and images of things. And therefore, if the power of the eye to contribute towards seeing be a mode of motion peculiar to that system of matter, and motion be allowed truly and properly to inhere in the subject that moves, then the power of the eye to contribute towards seeing is neither a mode produced in another subject, nor an effect residing in no subject at all. But to this instance, and all other instances that I have mentioned before, it may be answered that the power to contribute towards seeing, and the power of a musical instrument to produce an harmonious sound, being really nothing else but an impression of a particular kind or mode of motion which those systems are capable of receiving from the particular dispositions of their parts, and the actions of other beings on them. And roundness or squareness being nothing else but modes of figures, the power of the eye, of a musical instrument, and the qualities of roundness and squareness are only the sums of the motions and figures of the parts, or sums of powers of the same kind, and consequently fall in with the powers of matter that Mr. *Clarke* ranked under the first head of distribution of the powers of matter, and are defective similitudes to prove the real existence of such powers as inhere in a system of matter without inhering in the parts of the system singly considered.

This, if I mistake not, comprehends the entire strength of all that can be said against my instances, and an answer to it will set this dispute in a clearer light than possibly it has hitherto been, and perhaps give Mr. *Clarke* particular satisfaction with relation to the inconclusiveness of his argument, by detecting what I conceive has particularly imposed upon him. In answer therefore to this objection, I own, since I undertook to give a proof drawn from matter of fact, that there are individual powers peculiar to systems of matter without belonging to each of their parts singly considered, I am obliged either to clear those instances I have given, or assign other instances, or else own that there are no known powers in matter, but what are the sums of powers of the same kind. And therefore to show that my instances are pertinent, I distinguish between *numerical powers* and *generical powers*. By *numerical powers* I understand such powers as motions and figures of the same species. The power of the eye to contribute towards seeing is a species of motion, and the roundness of a body is a species of figure. By *generical powers* I understand all the several species of *numerical powers* — as motion signifies all the various species of motion, and figure all the various species of figure. Now if the reader will be pleased to apply the foregoing distinction, he may see that the whole of the objection is founded on an '*equivoque* of' [equivocation on –ed.] the terms *powers of the same kind.* For if *powers of the same kind* are[1] understood *generically,* then I do agree that the known powers of matter are nothing else but the sums or powers of the same kind. That is, the figure and motion of a body consist of the figures and motions of the parts. But if the terms *powers of the same kind* be taken *numerically* (that is, as powers really exist), then there are powers inhering in systems of matter that are not the sums of powers of the same kind, as roundness of body is not the sum of the roundnesses of the parts, nor the power of a musical instrument to cause an harmonious sound, the sum of powers of the same kind in the parts singly considered. I shall now apply what I have said to consciousness, or a power of thinking, and to make myself the more intelligible will suppose consciousness (of whose nature I may be supposed ignorant) to be a mode of motion, and not a mode of some unknown power — and the rather, because I have to do with a gentleman that understands the rules of arguing too well to impute that to me as my opinion which I only take the liberty to suppose. If consciousness then be considered as a mode of motion, as roundness is a mode of figure, it will be so far from being true that if consciousness inheres in a system of matter it must be the sum of the consciousnesses of the parts, that it will be a contradiction to make [it –ed.] the sum of the consciousnesses of the parts, as it is a contradiction to make roundness to consist in the roundnesses of the parts. Though I would readily grant that were[2] consciousness a generical power like figure and motion, it would be likewise the sum and result of the consciousness of the several parts, and so there would be as many distinct consciousnesses as there are particles of matter of which the system consists — which I do allow to be very absurd. What I have now said I think sufficient to show that my instances to prove that there are powers in matter that are not the sums of powers of the same kind were rightly chosen, and consequently to show that consciousness, of whose nature we are ignorant, may inhere in a system of matter without being the

1 Replacing "be" –ed.

2 Replacing "was" –ed.

sum of the consciousnesses of the parts. Wherefore I take the liberty to conclude that besides such generical powers as motion, figure, etc., that Mr. *Clarke* only considers under his first head (which according to him contains all the true and proper powers of matter), there are numerical (or if Mr. *Clarke* pleases, individual) powers such as particular modes of motion, and particular modes of figure, in certain systems of matter, which he has omitted the consideration of. For had he considered *consciousness* as a mode of some power in matter, he could never have said *if consciousness could possibly be a quality inherent in a system of matter, it must likewise necessarily be the sum of the consciousnesses of the several parts* — but the contrary, if human consciousness be a mode of some generical power in matter, it must not be the sum of the consciousnesses of the parts.[1]

To make this matter still clearer, and answer all that I think can be alleged, I take the liberty to examine a passage relating to the argument that I am now upon in the *Historical and Critical Dictionary* of that learned and acute philosopher Mr. *Bayle,* a zealous asserter of the immateriality of the soul, who denied thinking could be a mode of matter. *Because,* he says, *all modes of which we have any knowledge are of such a nature that they never perish, but to make room for another mode of the same kind. There is no figure that is destroyed but by another figure, and no color but what makes room for another color. Therefore if we would reason from what we observe in matter, we ought to say that no thought ceases in matter but to make room for some other thought by which it is succeeded; divide* or *confound*[2] [mix indiscrimately –ed.] *this matter how you will.*[3] I am very far from denying, what is self-evident, that no mode ever ceases but to give place to another mode. And though it should be always to a mode of the same generical kind — as one color or figure is constantly succeeded by another — since all

1 1*st Defense.* [p. 25 –ed.]

2 The last clause in this sentence does not appear either in the original French (above) or in Popkin's translation in Appendix B. –ed.

3 Car toutes les modalités dont on a quelque connoissance sont d'une telle nature, qu'elles ne cessent que pour faire place à une autre modalité de même genre. Il n'y a point de figure qui soit détruite que par une autre Figure, ni point de couleur qui soit chasse par une autre couleur. Ainsi pour bien raisonner l'on doit dire qu'il n'y a point de sentiment qui soit chassé de la Substance que par l'introduction de quelque autre Sentiment. p. 1044. [This is the original French text that Collins is translating above. –ed.]

matter must necessarily exist under some figure and appear under some color to the eyes of animals, yet it is no good consequence that every mode must unavoidably be succeeded by a mode of the same numerical species — as that round or blue must be succeeded by round or blue — which would entirely destroy all change or succession of modes whatever, and so deprive the universe of all motion or diversity. Now if thought be supposed a species of motion, then it never ceases indeed but to make room for some other motion (the particles of all bodies being in perpetual action, as well as under some figure or color). But it follows not that the succeeding motion must always be a thought for the reasons and examples already alleged, no more than that the motion of a going clock existed in the several parts of it before, or continues after, they are separated. Now that human consciousness or thinking is a mode of some generical power in matter will, in my opinion, seem evident to every man that consults his own experience, and suffers it not to be contradicted or confounded by unintelligible distinctions or sophistry. Thinking or human consciousness begins, continues, and ends — or has generation, succession, and corruption — like all other modes of matter, as, like them, it is divided and determined, simple or compounded, and so on. But if the soul or principle of thinking be undivided, how can it think successively, divide, abstract, combine or ampliate, retain or revive impressions in the memory? And how can it be capable, partly or wholly, to forget anything? All which *phenomena* are naturally conceived, and may be commodiously explained, by the springs and movements, and receptacles, by the vigor, perfection, disorder or decay of a bodily organ — but not by anything indivisible.

Does not experience further convince us that our ordinary habits, no less than all our actions, are corporeal — those of contemplating and meditating, as well as those of singing and dancing? Are we not frequently as much tired by the one, as by the other? Which could never be if contemplation and meditation were immaterial. The reaction of our thoughts and words on one another does manifestly prove the corporeity of both, the word being no sooner spoken than the idea is excited, and the revived idea bringing its name immediately into our remembrance. If we forget the one or the other, it betokens some defect in the organ, as it is visible in children and old people — the fibers of whose nerves, and the consistence of whose brains, are ordinarily too moist and remiss in the one, as they are too dry and rigid in the other. Nor does want of memory, or slowness of conception, appear in persons of a middle age but from some assignable cause that discomposes the organ. Human thinking being therefore a mode of matter, all parts of matter may be supposed capable of producing it — not necessarily indeed, and at all times no more than any other modes, but only under a convenient structure and disposition.

Upon the principles I have now more fully explained, I think I might leave it to the intelligent reader, or to Mr. *Clarke* himself, to solve the remaining difficulties that he urges. But to show my willingness to give satisfaction to those who are of the opinion that[1] I should not otherwise pay respect enough to a man of his ability, I proceed to consider whatever I conceive affects the bottom of the cause between us.

I had said "that to suppose a power arising from matter without belonging to the parts of which the whole consists, is not to suppose a universal to exist, but a particular power existing to which several particular powers contribute — as every man is a particular man, though various powers are necessary to constitute him of that species."[2]

To this Mr. *Clarke* answers *that if that whole or result, which* I *call a particular power, be entirely and specifically different from all and every one of the particular powers contributing to it — as thinking is from all the particles not indued with thought* — I *shall find, if* I *consider carefully, that it is as certain as any arithmetical demonstration that such a particular power is a whole bigger than all its parts.* To show the want of force in this answer, let us apply it to roundness. For if it concludes against thinking's arising out of particles not singly endued with thinking, it will equally conclude against the possibility of the existence of roundness in body which no more consists of several roundnesses (since in a round body of an inch diameter, it is impossible that any one particle the surface should be round as it is needless that any other should be so, and therefore probable in many cases that not one particle of a round body is round in particular) — no more, I say, than thinking or consciousness does of several consciousnesses, and is as specifically different from other figures as consciousness is from a circular motion. *If the whole or result, which I call a particular*

1 Replacing "who are opinion" –ed.

2 Reply. [p. 71 –ed.]

power, be specifically different from all and every one of the particular powers contributing to it — as roundness *is from all the particles not endued with* roundness — I *shall find, if* I *consider it carefully, that it is as certain as any arithmetical demonstration that such a particular power is a whole bigger than all its parts.* But in behalf of roundness as well as thinking, I answer that it is so far from being as certain as an arithmetical demonstration that such a particular power is a whole bigger than all its parts, that it is an arithmetical demonstration that such a particular power as roundness is but just equal to all parts of which that roundness consists. For what more goes to the composition of roundness than the conjunction of several particles not singly endued with roundness? And agreeably to the supposition I lately made, what more goes to the power of thinking than the conjunction of several particles, not each endued with that species of motion called thinking?

2. But to proceed a step further, supposing we could not account for the beginning of consciousness or roundness from the various composition of matter, yet I cannot see what reason there is to exclude even created beings from superadding powers to matter that are not always existing in matter. If matter is not essentially active, as I presume Mr. *Clarke* contends it is not, I would ask, upon the supposition of some parts of it being at absolute rest, whether finite material beings in motion were not sufficient of themselves to put them into motion though they had no motion before? Was not matter's capacity of motion sufficient to make it move as soon as it was impelled by another being? In like manner, a capacity to think may be sufficient to cause us to think though we are sometimes without thinking, as a capacity to think of a triangle is ground enough to make us think upon it whenever that figure is placed before our eyes though we never have as yet thought upon it at all. And this I take to be the case of operations of all kinds in finite beings — *viz.* that it is so far from being a repugnancy to suppose them to have a beginning of their existence, that if we don't suppose a beginning of operations we must destroy all change or succession whatever, and so entirely deprive the universe of all diversity.

It is urged by Mr. *Clarke that to annex consciousness to* so *flux a substance as the brain or the spirits in it, is a very great absurdity. For if the parts of the brain or spirits be (as they certainly are) in perpetual flux and change, it will follow that consciousness by which* I *not only remember that certain things were done many years since, but also am conscious that they were done by the very same individual conscious being who now remembers them* — *it will follow,* he says, *that the consciousness is transferred from one subject to another. That is to say, that it is a real quality which subsists without inhering in any subject at all.*[1] In the examination of this argument I think something will appear quite contrary to what Mr. *Clarke* imagines — that it is so far from being absurd to annex human consciousness to so flux a substance as the brain, that it will rather be absurd to annex it to any other substance but so flux a one as the brain. For if we utterly forget, or cease to be conscious of, having done many things in the former parts of our lives which we certainly did, as much as any of those things which we are conscious that we have done; and if in fact we do by degrees forget everything which we do not revive by frequent recollection, and by again and again imprinting our decaying ideas; and if there be in a determinate time a partial or total flux of particles in our brains; what can better account for our total forgetfulness of some things, our partial forgetfulness of others, than to suppose the substance of our brain in a constant flux? And what can better show that consciousness is not transferred from one subject to another, than our forgetting totally or partially according to the brain's being more or less in a flux? But I will suppose that I am conscious to have done some things, without having one particle of the brain the same that I had when I did those things, how then can I be conscious that I did them, without allowing consciousness to be transferred from one subject to another? This I think contains the strength of Mr. *Clarke*'s objection. In answer to which, I will suppose myself conscious at forty of having been carried to a market or fair at five years old, without any particles of matter about me the same which I had at that age. Now in order to retain the consciousness of that action, it is necessary to revive the idea of it before any considerable flux of particles (otherwise I must totally lose the memory of it, as I do several things done in my childhood), and by reviving the idea of that action I imprint afresh the consciousness of having done that action — by which the brain has as lively an impression of consciousness (though it be not entirely composed of the same particles) as it had the day after I did the action, or as it has of a triangle or any other new idea not before imprinted on it. Consciousness of having

1 Second Defense [p. 96 –ed.]

done that action is an idea imprinted on the brain by recollecting or bringing into view our ideas before they are quite worn out — which idea continues in me not only the memory of the action itself, but that I did it. And if there is every now and then a recollection of a past action, Mr. *Clarke* may, by what I have said, conceive a man may be conscious of things done by him, though he has not one particle of matter the same that he had at the doing of those things, without *consciousness being transferred from one subject to another* in any absurd sense of those words.

[1. –ed.] I did incidentally in my *Reply* to Mr. *Clarke*'s first *Defense,* whither I refer the reader for the occasion, make this supposition: "as what seemed matter of fact to me, that the matter of which an egg consists does entirely constitute the young one, and that the action of sensation began under a particular disposition of the parts by motion, without the addition of an immaterial and immortal soul." Which, Mr. *Clarke* says, *is in every part contrary to all the discoveries in anatomy, and to all true philosophy. For,* so *far* is *it from being true that the matter of the egg, by any particular disposition of its parts by motion, is formed into, or constitutes, the young one, that it does not constitute it at all, not* so *much as the body of it, but only serves it for nourishment and growth — it being as impossible that the organized*[1] *body of a chicken should by the power of any mechanical motions be formed out of the unorganized matter of an egg, as that the sun, moon, and stars should by mere mechanism rise out of a chaos.*

In answer to which I aver that my supposition is so far from being contrary to all the discoveries in anatomy, and to all true philosophy, that if Mr. *Clarke* has given a just account of all those discoveries in anatomy and philosophy in this paragraph, it is agreeable to them all — except his saying *that the organized body of the animal is no part of the matter of the egg.* And as for that discovery *made in anatomy by microscopical observations,* I take it to be *not only removed backwards from the search and common notions even of the most inquisitive men,* but contrary to such undoubted matter of fact, that I will venture to insist on it in opposition to all the discoveries in anatomy Mr. *Clarke* is acquainted with. For if by our eyes we can perceive the organized body of the animal to be part of the matter of the egg, no microscopical observation can destroy

1 The original has "unorganized," which makes no sense here. Collins refers to the "organized body" just below. –ed.

such matter of fact. Microscopical observations may help us to discover the existence of some things, the beauty and contrivance of others, which by our mere organs we are unable to do — but can never make us see nothing where we do see something.

I nowhere deny the organized body of the animal to have been formed long before it is comprehended in the shell. All that I affirm is that when the organized body is comprehended within the shell, it then becomes part of the matter of the egg. And I continue to suppose that sensation does not begin in the animal until some of the other parts of the egg become parts of the animal by motion, or *by serving it for nourishment and growth.* Though I must, at the same time, confess that I see no absurdity in supposing the organized body of the animal to be formed by mechanical motions out of such matter, as the unorganized parts of the egg, if they may be called *unorganized.* Those parts are not indeed legs, wings, eyes, etc., and so are not organized in that sense. But yet they are so disposed or organized as to contribute by their motion towards something orderly and regular, and to become parts of the leg or the eye of an animal. I conceive, no matter in the present state of the universe, can be compared to a chaos. From whence I grant no regular work can be produced by mere mechanism, but all is disposed by the power of God in a state of regularity. And as there was no contradiction for the organized body of the animal to be first formed by matter regularly moved, nor any[1] contradiction for other parts of matter to be joined to that body by a regular motion, so it is no more a contradiction to suppose such a union of parts to begin in an egg, whereby the body of an animal may be formed, than it was for such a union of parts to begin a thousand years before, or than it is that those parts should grow in the manner they do by the addition of other particles to them. Mr. *Clarke* adds, *and that sensation should begin under a particular disposition of the parts is still more impossible, because it is supposing something to come out of that in which it never was.* Sensation is by me supposed to be in the parts of the animal, as roundness is in the parts which compose a round body — each part has as much of sensation, singly considered, as each part of a round body has of roundness — and when the parts are duly disposed, whole thinking is performed, as whole roundness exists by the conjunction of parts.

---

1 Replacing "no" –ed.

2. But supposing sensation did not exist in the parts antecedent to their union, as motion does not in those parts of matter that are at absolute rest, why may not the one have actual sensation by virtue of an antecedent capacity to have sensation without having always actual sensation, as well as matter at absolute rest may have actual motion by virtue of an antecedent capacity to have motion without being always in actual motion?

I did indeed think it absurd to *recur to the addition of an immaterial and immortal soul* to solve the phenomenon of sensations in animals, because I cannot conceive it possible for all the numerous sensible creatures which microscopical observations do discover to us to exist in all parts of the universe — even in our own bodies, and the liquors that we drink — to be proper subjects for eternal rewards and punishments. Mr. *Clarke* goes on, *let it be so* (that is, let it be absurd to have recourse to the addition of an immaterial and immortal soul to account for sensation in animals), he *can as easily suppose, if* I *must needs have an hypothesis, that the immaterial* and immortal soul *was not added afterward, but was in it from the time that the seminal principle itself of the organized body was framed.*[1] I am against all mere hypotheses, and was, particularly in that place Mr. *Clarke* refers to, contending against an opinion that I take to be a mere hypothesis. And though I did not expressly mention that hypothesis which Mr. *Clarke* is pleased to suppose for me, yet I conceive that that hypothesis is as much excluded by my supposing that an animal consists only of mere matter, as if I had directly mentioned it. And therefore I wonder that Mr. *Clarke* could imagine that one of those hypotheses should content me any more than the other, or that I have any fondness at all for any hypotheses. I satisfy myself with observing matter of fact, and believe what I see, until subsequent matter of fact convinces me of the first false appearance of things, and then I correct my first opinion from the second appearance. Micrography [here, the use of microscopes –ed.] and astronomy do help us to settle several important facts which, without their assistance, we should be apt to mistake. But as for any suppositions to account for any matters of fact of effects that we observe, I deny them all — unless it involves a contradiction not to make such suppositions, and I will allow Mr. *Clarke* to assign one or twenty unknown beings in

1 2nd Defense. [p. 99 –ed.]

every animal [only –ed.] when it is a contradiction not to suppose one or twenty. But until that time I think it not proper to go beyond my eyesight, nor, as I see nothing but matter in animals, to believe there is anything but matter in them.

One thing more under this head I think myself obliged to take notice of: Mr. *Clarke* had said, *that gravitation* is *the effect of the continued and regular operation of some other Being on matter.*[1] Upon which I said "that it does not appear but that matter gravitates by virtue of powers originally placed in it by God, and is now left to itself to act by those original powers. And it is as conceivable that matter should act by virtue of those powers, as that an immaterial Being should put it into motion, or continue it in motion."[2] This *opinion of mine Mr.* Clarke *thinks is a great mistake in my philosophy. For when a stone that was at rest does of itself, upon its support being removed, begin to fall downwards, what* is *it that causes the stone to begin* to *move? Is it possible to be an effect without a cause? Is it impelled without an impeller? Or can a law or a power — that is to say, a mere abstract name, or a complex notion, and not any real being — impel a stone and cause* it to *begin to move?*[3]

1. The question is not, whether *any real being* moves a stone that was at rest when it begins to fall downwards upon its support being removed, but whether *another being,* or a being distinct from matter, does continually impel it, either immediately or mediately (for I deny not the necessity of a being impelling another, in order to cause that mode of motion called *gravitation*). And therefore Mr. *Clarke* changes the question when he introduces some *real being* as necessary to impel a stone, or cause it to begin to move upon its support being removed, instead of what he first affirmed, *that gravitation is the effect of the continued and regular operation of some other Being on matter.* And consequently his questions — *what is it causes the stone to move? Is it possible to be an effect without a cause? Is it impelled without an impeller? Or can a law or power — that is to say, an abstract name, or complex notion, and not any real being — impel a stone, or cause it to move?* — reach not the question of the necessity of the regular and continued operation of an immaterial being on matter, in order to cause that mode of motion called gravitation.

---

1 1st Defense. [p. 57 –ed.]

2 Reply. [p. 75 –ed.]

3 2nd Defense. [p. 103 –ed.]

2. As I did not exclude the impulse of other bodies contiguous to the body gravitating, but only the continued and regular operation of an immaterial Being on it, from being a constant cause of gravitation, so I do not think the mere impulse of the surrounding bodies to be the sole cause of that motion. And to speak my own opinion, it seems matter of fact to me that the external figure and internal configuration of the parts of matter are those powers in matter by which it receives that peculiar mode of motion called gravitation from the circumambient impelling bodies. For drop a pound of lead, in the form of a bullet, from the top of a tower, and it descends in a very quick space to ground. Vary the external figure of the bullet by beating it out broad with a hammer, and its tendency downwards decreases. Vary the configuration of its parts by fire, and it will ascend instead of descending. The same action of the circumambient bodies producing these three different effect by this three-fold disposition of the selfsame quantity of lead, so that matter's determination seems purely owing to the causes and powers I have assigned. And I have often admired that gravitation should be esteemed a matter of such difficulty among philosophers. For when once motion is supposed, and that all matter is in constant motion, and perpetually striking one part against another — as I think nobody doubts — one part of matter must be determined one way and another part another way. And gravitation being one mode of motion — *viz.* a tendency towards a center (whether it be the whole vortex, or only of our earth, or the particular center of that peculiar motion which depends upon the sphere of its activity) — some parts of matter must as necessarily gravitate, as others have different motions. Nay, properly speaking, there is no motion whatever but is gravitation respectively. For whatever ascends with respect to us descends with respect to other bodies, and whatever descends with respect to us ascends with respect to others, so that if there is any motion in the universe, there must be gravitation.

3. When therefore I said "It does not appear but that matter gravitates by virtue of powers originally placed in it by God, and that it is as conceivable that matter should act by virtue of those powers, as that immaterial being should put matter into motion, or continue it in motion,"[1] I did not lay it down as my opinion

1 Reply. [p. 75 –ed.]

that matter did act without a direct impulse from matter, but supposed it as intelligible that matter might act without impulse by powers placed in it by God, as that an immaterial being should move matter without being able to impel it by contact. And whenever Mr. *Clarke* gives me an idea how an immaterial being can move matter, or in what place God can be conceived beginning a motion of gravity or levity in the universe when in the universe there is no up or down in reality (for to say that God acts respectively, shows but the pertinency of my question the more, since he must then be necessarily placed with respect to an assignable center), then I promise to give him an idea how matter should move by powers placed in it by God without the impulse of other bodies, or even *by* what Mr. *Clarke* calls *an abstract name* or a *complex notion*.

4. But was it my opinion that matter did act by virtue of powers placed in it by God without the impulse of matter, I think I have Mr. *Clarke* of my opinion when he says, *all matter consists of actually separate and distinct parts.*[1] For if it is actually divided *in infinitum*, it can never act by impulse, but must act by other powers, unless Mr. *Clarke* will say that it is an immaterial being that constantly and immediately moves every particle of matter. But whether I take Mr. *Clarke* right or no, the incomparable Sir *Isaac Newton* is of opinion that *several phenomena of nature may depend on certain forces whereby from causes (or powers) yet undiscovered the particles of bodies are mutually impelled against each other and cohere according to regular figures, or whereby they recede or are driven from one another — which forces* or powers *being yet unknown, the philosophers hitherto have attempted nature in vain.*[2]

Sect. 2. Besides answering directly to Mr. *Clarke*'s pretended demonstration, I did endeavor to show that if it proved the impossibility of matter's thinking, it would equally prove the impossi-

---

1 Letter to Mr. Dodwell. [p. 47 –ed.]

2 Suspicor ea omnia (viz. Phænomena Naturæ) ex viribus pendere posse, quibus Corporum particulæ per causas nondum cognitas vel in se mutuo impelluntur, & secundum figuras regulares cohærent, vel ab invicem fugantur & recedunt; quibus viribus ignotis Philosophi hactenus naturam frustra tentarunt, *Newtoni Præfation ad Philosophia Naturalis Principia Mathematica.* [This is the original Latin of Newton's Preface to *The Mathematical Principles of Natural Philosophy* that Collins translated in the text above. –ed.]

bility of an immaterial being's thinking, since Mr. *Clarke* did not exclude extension out of his idea of immaterial being. For, his argument being founded on the proof of this proposition, that divisibility and thinking cannot cohere or exist together in the same subject, and Mr. *Clarke* allowing *that there are particles of matter which are to any powers in nature indiscerptible,*[1] I observed "that if there may be matter which implies indivisibility by natural causes, no argument can be brought to prove the indivisibility of such particles of matter, but what will equally prove the divisibility of any finite extended being."[2] And consequently, either all matter is not divisible — and so, by Mr. *Clarke*'s principles, is not excluded from a possibility of thinking — or else an immaterial being is no more capable of thinking than a material one.

But Mr. *Clarke* answers *that such a difficulty is wide of the main question, for if the foregoing proof that matter is incapable of thinking cannot be shown to be defective, it necessarily follows that the soul must be an indiscerptible substance,* though extended.

[1.[3] –ed.] Though Mr. *Clarke*'s argument could not be shown to be defective; it does not follow that an extended being must be indiscerptible. For if I have as clear evidence of the divisibility of an immaterial being by the power of God as of a material one (as I contend we have, and have shown in my *Reply* whither I refer the reader), and if I have likewise clear evidence that a divisible being cannot think — as I am likewise supposed to have — what remains for us but darkness and confusion and skepticism under such a balance of evidence? A view of Mr. *Clarke*'s way of arguing against the possibility of matter's thinking, urged against the possibility of an immaterial being's thinking, will make it evident to the reader that there is no more ground from that argument to conclude against matter's thinking than against an immaterial being's thinking. And therefore as Mr. *Clarke* endeavors to show that matter cannot think, because by the Power of God it is divisible, so I who see no manner of difference between any other finite extended being and matter in that respect urge Mr. *Clarke*'s argument to prove that an immaterial being cannot

---

1 1st Defense. [pp. 59-60 –ed.]

2 Reply. [p. 82 –ed.]

3 Collins several times assumes that his readers will understand where the "1." should go, and thus leaves it out. Unfortunately, it is not obvious. This is my guess. –ed.

think. Thus, whatever is divisible by the power of God cannot, according to him, have a power of thinking. An immaterial being is extended, and consequently must be divisible by the power of God (if it be true that all matter is divisible because no argument can be brought to prove all matter divisible that will not prove all finite extended beings divisible), therefore an immaterial being cannot think. And if it be proved that an immaterial being cannot think, then it follows that the being which thinks in us must be material. If it is further objected, to weaken the force of the foregoing proof, that all material substance is likewise divisible, Mr. *Clarke*'s answer in behalf of immaterial substance will serve the case of material substances — and it may be said *that this difficulty is wide of the main question, for if the foregoing proof that immaterial being is incapable of thinking cannot be shown* to *be defective, it follows necessarily that the soul must be an indiscerptible material substance.*

2. But Mr. *Clarke* says *there are many demonstrations, even in abstract mathematics themselves, which no man who understands them can in the least doubt of the certainty of, which yet are attended with difficult consequences that cannot be perfectly cleared. The infinite divisibility of matter is an instance of this kind. Also the eternity of God and his immensity are attended with the like difficulties.*[1] In answer to this, I say that if there are any such demonstrations, from whence any contradictions or absurdities follow in our way of conceiving things, those absurdities and contradictions should affect a demonstration so far that I ought to suspend my assent. In our assent or dissent to propositions, we have no other ground of either than the perception of the agreement or disagreement of the ideas for which the terms in propositions stand. And if things make such an appearance to our understandings that we do *a priori* perceive, or imagine we perceive, demonstrative proof of the truth of a proposition — and perceive, or imagine that we perceive, absurdities and contradictions follow from that proposition which we imagined we perceived to be demonstrative — what have we but two repugnant demonstrations which ought to leave the mind in balance or suspense? For on which side can I suspect that my understanding fails me? There is no more reason to suspect that my understanding fails me when I think that I perceive an

1 2nd Defense. [p. 107 –ed.]

absurdity, contradiction, or disagreement of ideas, than when I think I perceive the agreement of ideas.

3. But I deny that there are any instances of this kind in nature, and particularly that the *infinite divisibility of matter, the eternity and immensity of God,* are such instances. And I desire Mr. *Clarke* to define those foregoing terms, and tell me what they stand[1] for in his mind. And if his meaning of those terms agree to the reality of things, instead of making real being of abstract notions, I require him to prove that any absurdity or contradiction follows either from the *infinite divisibility of matter, the eternity* or *immensity of God,* in our way of conceiving. And if he cannot, he has no ground from those instances to put human nature in such a state of skepticism and absurdity.

4. As to his urging again his instance of space,[2] which I readily own to be indiscerptible, to show the possibility of immaterial substance's being indiscerptible, though extended, I tell him again that space (which Mr. *Clarke* says is only *an abstract idea of immensity*) will by no means reach his purpose. For space is infinite, and not only infinite but, being incapable of being considered either as *acting or being acted on,* is no being or substance at all, and therefore its indivisibility cannot prove the possibility of a finite extended substance's being indivisible, but the contrary. For space is only indivisible by having those two before-mentioned qualities that make it differ from the immaterial being in question.

5. To show the difference between an immaterial and material substance as to their divisibility, Mr. *Clarke* says *the supposition of an immaterial substance's being by the power of God divided into parts — which, concerning matter, is allowed to be possible — may be denied to be possible, as being a supposition which destroys the essence of the substance itself.*[3]

What signifies the confession of some or all men that all matter is divisible, or Mr. *Clarke*'s denial that immaterial substance is divisible, to show a difference between an immaterial and material substance as to divisibility? Material substance is not upon that account proved divisible, nor immaterial substance indivisible. The divisibility or indivisibility of either

1 Replacing "shall stand" –ed.

2 2nd Defense. [p. 107 –ed.]

3 2nd Defense. [pp. 107-08 –ed.]

substance depends not upon such confession or denial. If it did, I might retort his argument upon him thus. That immaterial substance is by me confessed to be divisible, but may, concerning material thinking substance, be denied to be possible, *as being a supposition which destroys the substance itself.* For I have just as much reason to make that supposition concerning a material being *that cannot by natural causes be made smaller,* as he has concerning an immaterial being — that is, both suppositions are equally precarious.

But he had no reason at all to say that all matter was confessed to be divisible. Because I was so far from making any such general *confession,* that I did in my *Reply* deny all matter could be proved divisible by any argument that would not equally conclude for the divisibility of an immaterial being. And consequently, if those arguments were not sufficient to prove the divisibility of immaterial substance, neither would they, according to me, prove the divisibility of all material substance. And therefore I shall be so far from allowing all matter to be divisible, that whenever Mr. *Clarke* proves to me the necessary indivisibility of any finite extended substance, I will then deny that all matter can be proved to be divisible.

Sect. 3. I offered two arguments to show that the supposition of the immateriality of the soul was of no use to the ends and purposes of religion, were it capable of demonstration. For I said "unless a thinking immaterial substance can be proved naturally immortal, the soul cannot be proved naturally immortal," and I asked "of what use then is this argument to the ends and purposes of religion? For if we have no security that we must exist hereafter in a state of perception, as by only proving the natural immortality of the substance of the soul we have not, it can be of no use to influence our lives and actions."[1] From which passages it is plain that the question of this article was whether an immaterial being, or the substance of the soul, could be proved to be in a perpetual state of thinking. Or else, supposing that — though it could not by this argument be proved to be always in a state of perception — whether it was still of use to the ends and purposes of religion.

1 [Collins' –ed.] Letter to Mr. Dodwell. [p. 49 –ed.]

To prove the possibility of thinking as an action's ceasing in an immaterial being, I did in my *Reply* observe "that the soul has not only different passions at different times such as anger, love, etc., which are modifications that begin and have their period, but has qualities and powers such as seeing and hearing which by the defect of our organs plainly cease for a time." I likewise instanced in the motion of the soul from one place to another, which might be entirely owing to external and material causes.

And what answer has Mr. *Clarke* given to show the usefulness of his argument to the ends and purposes of religion, but by changing the terms of the question — and not only the terms themselves, but the meaning of those terms?[1] For instead of considering thinking as an *action,* he uses the terms *power of thinking* (by which I now find that he meant *capacity of thinking*), and, in his *Second Defense,* changes the term *motion* into *mobility,* and the powers of seeing and hearing urged on him to prove the possibility of thinking's ceasing in an immaterial being into a capacity of hearing and feeling. Whereby my argument is turned to quite another purpose than it was intended by me, and the reader is diverted from the true state of question. And Mr. *Clarke* himself, inconsistently with his censure of me for *nice distinguishing,* does distinguish between actual thinking and a capacity of thinking, actual motion and a capacity of motion, etc. But yet I should not have censured him for this, had he not really *perplexed* the reader with a new question. As I aver this question, *whether the soul must forever be capable of thinking,* to be, and to have, no relation to the question in dispute. For allowing the soul can never exist without a capacity to think, of what use is a proof that the soul must always have that *capacity* in order to influence men's actions, when notwithstanding that, the soul may no more exist in a state of perception, or rewards and punishments, than a man born blind sees colors, or a deaf man hears sounds?

What follows, being founded in this change of the question, needs no other answer than what I have already given.

Sect. 4. My last objection was "that if from the power of thinking we can prove the immateriality of the soul of man, and from its immateriality prove its natural immortality, and consequently its capacity of eternal happiness, the power of thinking must

1 1st Defense. [pp. 80-81 –ed.]

prove the immateriality of the souls of brutes, the immateriality of their souls must prove their natural immortality, and consequently their capacity of eternal happiness."[1]

To which Mr. *Clarke* answers *cannot God, if he pleases, cause them to perish at the dissolution of their bodies, or else annihilate them at any other time?*[2] Now by all the rules of answering, Mr. *Clarke* ought to have taken notice of the reply I made in the close of the objection itself to the answer he here gives me, and ought either to have confessed its force, or else showed the inconclusiveness thereof. But since he has thought fit to do otherwise, I take the liberty to repeat that part of my objection again that I esteem perfectly satisfactory to his answer, and which is as follows. "That if it be supposed that the Souls of Brutes may be sometime or other annihilated, then Mr. *Clarke*'s argument is not useful to the end for which it was intended, because mere natural immortality will then be no proof of the real immortality of the soul of man." But Mr. *Clarke* has a second answer: *cannot God,* says he, *dispose of them into states suitable to their particular natures, which yet may in no propriety be styled a capacity of eternal happiness as that of man is?* Mr. *Clarke* lays the stress in a wrong place. I meant no more by supposing brutes capable of eternal happiness as well as man but only a state wherein they enjoy constant agreeable perceptions, as Mr. *Clarke* may see if he considers the 144th page of my *Reply* [p. 86 –ed.], and had no design to compare the several degrees of happiness among created beings in the next world. But since Mr. *Clarke* acknowledges all the numerous sensible creatures to be subjects of eternal rewards, I ask him whether mites, fleas, lice, oysters, rats and mice, may be punished eternally, as well as enjoy eternal rewards? If he answers that they must only enjoy eternal rewards, then he elevates brutes above men, and places them in a much more eligible condition. If he answers that they are subjects both of eternal rewards and punishments, I ask for what it is that eternal rewards are bestowed on some animals, and eternal punishments bestowed on others? If they are to have eternal rewards or punishments, they must have them either according as they act agreeable or disagreeably to some rules of action — and then they must be allowed to be moral agents, and consequently to have all the powers in them which men have,

1 *Reply.* [p. 84 –ed.]

2 2nd Defense. [p. 108 –ed.]

that are necessary to make their actions esteemed *moral* — or else they must be punished or rewarded, that those who have received injuries in this life may be compensated in the next, and those who have been prosperous in the rapine and slaughter of their fellow animals may be punished, whereby there may be a perfect equality in God's dealing with them, agreeably to what Mr. *Arnaud* relates in *Réflexions sur le Sytème du P. Malebranche*: *Quand on leur demandoit* (that is, some *Jews* that maintained brutes were proper subjects of eternal rewards and punishments) *quelle justice il y avoit* dans *la mort des bêtes, quelle péché elles avoient commis,* & *pourquoi Dieu vouloit, puis que sa providence s'étendoit à tout, qu'un rat innocent fut déchiré par un chat, Ils répondoient, que Dieu l'avoit ainsi ordonné, mais qu'il recompenseroi ce rat dans le siècle à venir.* [Mr. Arnauld relates in *Reflections on the System of Father Malebranche*: that when some Jews that maintained animals were proper subjects of eternal rewards and punishments were asked ... What justice would there be in the death of animals, what sin have they committed, and, since his providence extends to all, why would God wish that an innocent rat should be tortured by a cat, they responded that such has God ordained, but he would reward the rat in the world to come. –ed.]

From these and some other consequences flowing from the foregoing argument, we have so strange a view of the state of man that I conceive there can be no greater service to religion than to show the uselessness of that argument to the ends and purposes of religion. Especially since there are such solid arguments for a future state from topics that can neither be answered by infidels, nor loaded with any absurd consequences.

Mr. *Clarke,* in the conclusion of his *Defense*, has summed up his argument in fifteen propositions which I now propose to consider, that my answer to him may be complete, though all that he advances in them is overthrown in the foregoing reflections.

His propositions are:

1. *Every system of matter consists of a multitude of distinct parts.*

This proposition, which he *thinks is granted by all,* is, I am sure, denied by a great many. However, I shall not at present enter into any debate with him concerning it, but continue to suppose it as I have hitherto done.

2. *Every real quality inheres in some subject.*

3. No *individual or single quality of one particle of matter can be the individual or single quality of another particle of matter.*

These two I grant.

4. *Every real simple quality that resides in any whole material system resides in all the parts of that system.*

5. *Every real compound quality that resides in any whole material system is a number of simple qualities residing in all the parts of that system — some in one part, some in another.*

These two propositions I shall not contend with him about, though he seems to me to confound *simple and compound qualities together.* For in his explication subjoined to his fourth proposition, as an example of what he means by a *simple quality* he instances in the *motion of a body which,* says he, *consists in the sum of the motions of its several parts.* And in his explication subjoined to his fifth proposition, as an example of what he means by *compound qualities* he says, *the simples blue and yellow make the compound color called green.* Now the motion of a clock is to me as much a *compound quality* as the color *green* is a *compound quality.* For the various motions of a clock — its circular, perpendicular, and other motions — are as specifically different from one another as blue and yellow are from one another. And therefore I confess that I have no clear ideas from Mr. *Clarke*'s explications to the terms *simple and compound.*

6. *Every real quality, simple or compound, that results from any whole material system, but does not reside in it — that is, neither in all its distinct parts, nor in all the parts of some portion of it — according to the explication of the two foregoing propositions, is the mode of some other substance, and not of that.*

This proposition I grant, on condition that instead of *other substance* be substituted the words *other subject.* For I grant sweetness does not reside in a sugar-loaf — that is, *neither in all the distinct parts, nor in all the parts of some portion of a sugar-loaf, but is produced in another* subject (and not in another *substance*) as all other sensations or modes of thinking are. Which subject I contend is material.

7. *Every power, simple or compound, that results from any whole material system, but does not reside in it — that is, in all its parts, in the manner before explained — nor yet resides in any other substance as its subject, is no real quality at all, but must be either itself a real substance (which seems unintelligible), or else it is nothing else but merely an abstract name, as all universals are.*

8. *Consciousness is neither a mere abstract name (such as the powers mentioned in prop. 7), nor a power of exciting or occasioning different modes in a foreign substance (such as are the sensible qualities of bodies, prop. 6), but a real quality truly and properly inhering in the subject itself, the thinking substance.*

Before I answer to this proposition, it is necessary to be very precise in unraveling what seems to be very much perplexed in it. Mr. *Clarke* confounds two things that ought to be separated — *viz. the power of exciting modes in a foreign subject,* and the modes that are excited — when he says *sensible qualities in bodies* are *powers of exciting modes in another subject.* Whereas sweetness, sounds, etc., which are vulgarly termed *sensible qualities in bodies,* are only ideas, sensations, or modes of thinking in us, and exist not at all in those bodies of which they are said to be sensible qualities — and therefore the powers in bodies must be something very different from those qualities, as different as a cause is from an effect, and (that I may proceed with the greater clearness) — I will suppose those powers to excite modes in another subject to be peculiar modes of motion in certain systems of matter.

Having thus distinguished, I shall answer to this proposition in each of the foregoing senses.

1. I do agree that consciousness is neither a mere abstract name (such as are the powers mentioned in prop. 7), nor does it exist in the brain — as sweetness is vulgarly supposed to do in a rose, and as all sensible qualities in bodies are supposed to do — but is a real quality truly and properly inhering in the subject itself, the brain — as modes of motion do in some bodies, and roundness does in others.

2. I do agree, again, that consciousness is not a mere abstract name, but is a power of the brain answering to the powers in matter

that produce sensations in us. For as those powers or modes of motion are peculiar to certain systems of matter, and are not the sums of powers of the same numerical kind, so neither is consciousness the sum of powers of the same numerical kind. And as those systems of matter do by peculiar modes of motion produce ideas in us, so we by the power of thinking can enlarge or abstract ideas — that is, modify them, or cause changes in them, as well as external sensible things can cause modes or changes in us. And therefore consciousness answers, or may be likened to, those powers in some systems of matter that are occasions of modes in another subject, and is at the same time a quality as much inhering in matter as the motion of a clock does in the parts of a clock, or as roundness or any other particular or individual figure in a body.

9. *No real quality can result from the composition of different qualities, so as to be a new quality in the same subject of a different kind or species from all and every one of the component qualities.*

According to Mr. *Clarke*'s explication of this proposition, I allow this likewise to be true. For *from motion nothing but motion can arise, and from figure nothing but figure.* But this reaches not the case of numerical powers, and particularly reaches not the case of consciousness. A real numerical power, as I suppose consciousness to be, and such as roundness is, may result from the composition of different qualities, as roundness does from different species of figures, and is consequently a new quality in the same subject of a different kind or species from all the component qualities considered together. But motion, being a generical power, does, I agree, consist of the motions of the parts, as figure does of the figures of the parts. And did consciousness answer to figure and motion, that would likewise consist of the consciousness of the parts.

10. *Consciousness therefore being a real quality* (prop. 8.), *and of a kind specifically different from all other qualities, whether known or unknown, which are themselves acknowledged to be void of consciousness, can never possibly result from any composition of such qualities.*

Though consciousness be a real quality, and different from all other qualities, whether known or unknown, which are themselves acknowledged to be void of consciousness, it can or may result from such qualities as, singly considered, are void of consciousness. Roundness is a real quality specifically different from other qualities void of roundness, and yet may be the result of composition of such qualities. But in Mr. *Clarke*'s sense of real qualities, I allow this proposition to be true. But then it reaches not the case of consciousness, which I deny to be a generical power, but affirm to be only a mode of a generical power.

11. *No individual quality can be transferred from one subject to another.*

This proposition I allow to be true. The quality of a subject can only be the quality of that subject wherein it exists, and not of another subject. The motion of a system of matter can only be the motion of that system. The consciousness of any being can only be the consciousness of that particular being. And I further observe that the motion of a system of matter one day can never be the motion of the same numerical system the next day, nor the consciousness of yesterday be the same numerical consciousness that I have today, let the being that is conscious in me be divisible or indivisible. The same individual quality can no more be transferred to the same *individual subject* that was formerly the subject of it, than it can be transferred to another subject.

12. *The spirits and particles of the brain, being loose and in a perpetual flux, cannot therefore be the seat of that consciousness by which a man not only remembers things done many years since, but also is conscious that he himself, the same individual being, was the doer of them.*

Though the spirits or particles of the brain cannot, by being in a perpetual flux, be the seat of that consciousness by which I know myself today to be the same individual conscious being that I was a year ago (for I deny that we have any consciousness at all that we continue the same individual being at different times), yet if it be not absurd for matter to think, matter must at the same time know that it thinks, or be conscious of its thinking. And if it can know at this instant that it thinks, I can see no reason why it may not remember tomorrow what it thinks of today, though some particles will be then wanting which it has at present. And if it can remember at all, then the memory of things may be continued even after we have lost all the particles of matter that we had at the time of the doing them, by continual intermediate repeating, or imprinting afresh our ideas before they are quite lost or worn out. And it is thus as intelligible to me that the memory of things should be preserved by a being in a flux, as by a being that is not so. For the individual consciousness today can neither in an individual or divisible being be the individual consciousness tomorrow — that consciousness is a perfectly distinct action in both beings from the preceding consciousness the day before. And whenever Mr. *Clarke* accounts for an indivisible being's remembrance of an action or thought, I promise to account for memory in a divisible being.

13. *The consciousness that a man has at one and the same time is one consciousness and not a multitude of distinct consciousness, as* [*the* –ed.] *solidity, motion, or color of any piece of matter is a multitude of distinct solidities, motions, or colors.*

14. *Consciousness cannot at all reside in the brain or spirits, or in any other material system as its subject, but must be a quality of some immaterial substance.*

Taking consciousness for a numerical power, either as answering to roundness in a body, or to a motion peculiar to a system of matter, this proposition by no means follows from those foregoing. For if consciousness be a numerical power, then it answers to never a one of the heads under which he ranks the powers of matter. For it neither answers to an effect residing in no subject at all (if there is any such thing in nature, which I utterly deny there is), nor does it answer to sweetness, or any other sensible qualities existing in bodies external to us (for they are only modes of thinking or perception in us, and exist not at all in those external bodies). Nor, lastly, is it a power which answers to figure and motion, which I agree consist only in the figures and motions of the parts, but agrees or answers to modes of figure and motion. From all which it is plain that all Mr. *Clarke*'s propositions are founded on his considering consciousness to be something else than what I contend it is. And so, though he may demonstrate the impossibility of matter's being conscious in his sense of the term consciousness, yet I deny that he has said one word to prove the impossibility of matter's thinking in the sense for which the term consciousness stands with me — and I suppose with all those that contend for the possibility of matter's thinking or being conscious. So that his demonstration may be granted by me without affecting the question between us, since it relates to a chimera or idea of his own framing. And thus endless demonstrations may be made without understanding things as they really exist, or any truth besides the relations of chimerical ideas. For I grant his demonstration to be good, if consciousness be considered either as a generical power like motion and figure, or as answering to the sweetness of a rose (which is a sensation or mode of thinking in us), or as an effect residing in no substance at all — then consciousness cannot inhere in a system of matter, and his demonstration reaches no farther. But consciousness answering to never a one of these powers, in demonstrating that consciousness in his sense cannot inhere in a system of matter, he has no more reached the question than if he had talked of anything else in the world. For his usage of the term consciousness does not make him one jot nearer the question, than if he had used a different term, or a term that no one would suspect stood for the thing really signified by the term *consciousness*.

15. *Difficulties that arise afterwards concerning other qualities of that immaterial substance, as whether it be extended or unextended, do not at all affect the present argument.*

How far the difficulty of making immaterial being extended affects Mr. Clarke's argument, I refer the reader to page 220, etc., of my *Reflections*.[1] And as for the difficulty of making it *unextended*, I will speak to that whenever Mr. Clarke defines the terms *unextended* and *being*, that I may see what they stand for when joined together. And then I will show how far considering immaterial being to be an unextended being affects his argument, as I have shown how far considering immaterial being to be an extended being affects it.

Thus I have gone through Mr. *Clarke*'s propositions, and shown wherein they fail to clear the point that he ought to have aimed at. And I conclude with this further observation, that he has not drawn up one proposition to show that his argument is of any use to the ends and purposes of religion, allowing it to be

1 pp. 136-40ff of this edition. –ed.

ever so true and just. And therefore, for proof that it is of no use to that end, I refer the reader to the 225th and the subsequent pages of the foregoing *Reflections* [p. 141ff –ed.]

Samuel Clarke

A Third Defense of an Argument

Made Use of in a Letter to Mr. Dodwell, To Prove the Immateriality and Natural Immortality of the Soul. In a Letter to the Author of the Reflections on Mr. Clarke's Second Defense, etc.

> *Arguments* seldom work on men of wit and learning, when they have once engaged themselves in a contrary opinion. Mr. Hobbes.[1]

> We have as much reason to be satisfied with our notion of *immaterial spirit,* as with our notion of *body,* and the existence of the one, as well as the other. For it being no more a contradiction that *thinking* should exist separate and independent from *solidity,* than it is a contradiction that *solidity should exist* separate and independent from *thinking,* they being both but *simple ideas,* independent one from another. And having as clear and distinct ideas in us of *thinking,* as of *solidity,* I know not why we may not as well allow a *thinking thing without solidity* — that is, *immaterial* — to exist, as a *solid thing without thinking* — that is, *matter* — to exist. Mr. Locke's Essay, Book II, *ch.* 23, *sect.* 32.

Sir,

In my last reply I persuaded myself I had set the question between us in so clear a light that there would have been no need of any new debate, or of giving our readers any further trouble in this matter. But seeing you have found out a seemingly new *distinction* by which you still endeavor to evade the force of the argument, and, though your evasion seems to me indeed extremely slight, yet seeing you have thought fit to insist upon it in such a manner — as

1 This epigraph is from *The English Works of Thomas Hobbes of Malmsbury,* ed. Sir William Molesworth (London: John Bohn, 1841), vol. 5, No. XXXVIII, Postcript, p. 435.

if you yourself really believed there was some strength and weight in it — I shall endeavor to gratify the sincere desire you profess to have of discovering the truth, by showing briefly the weakness and inconclusiveness of what you have advanced in your *Reflections.*

In order to prove that *thinking* cannot possibly be a quality or power of *matter,* I said that all the qualities or powers, which either are in matter, whether they be known or unknown, or are vulgarly ascribed to it, must of necessity be either:

1st, real qualities, truly and properly inhering in the subject to which they are ascribed, such as are *magnitude* and *motion* in matter. These are always the sums or aggregates of powers or qualities of *the same kind,* inhering distinctly in the several parts of the material subject. Which not being true of *thinking,* it is manifest that *thinking* cannot be a power or quality of *this sort,* inhering in a system of matter.

Or, *2dly,* qualities not really inhering in the subject to which they are usually ascribed, but being indeed modes excited and residing in some other subject, such as are *colors, sounds,* and all those which are commonly called the sensible qualities of matter. These do not exist at all in that subject to which they are usually ascribed, but in some other subject. And this also not being applicable to *thinking,* it is manifest therefore that *thinking* cannot be a power or quality of *this kind* in a material subject.

Or, *3dly,* qualities not really inhering in any subject at all, but being mere abstract names, or external denominations, to express certain complex ideas framed in our imaginations, or certain general extrinsic and relative effects produced upon particular systems of matter by foreign agents or certain dispositions of the particular systems of matter requisite towards the producing of those effects. Such as are *magnetism, electricity, attraction, reflexibility, refrangibility,* and the like. These have no real existence by way of *proper inhering* in any subject. Which likewise since it cannot be said of *thinking,* it is manifest that *thinking* cannot be a power or quality in a material system, of *this kind* neither.

You grant that *thinking,* for the reasons I urged, cannot be a power or quality of any of these kinds. But you *distinguish* upon the first sort, and allege:[1]

That there are some real qualities truly and properly inhering in the subject to which they are ascribed, which yet are not,

1 Reflections. [pp. 125-27 –ed.]

like magnitude and motion, sums or aggregates of powers or qualities of the *same kind,* inhering distinctly in the several parts of the subject. And that therefore *thinking,* though it be not an aggregate of powers of the *same kind,* may yet nevertheless be a real quality inhering in matter.

That numerical powers, or *particular and individual modes,* are such real inherent qualities, residing in a system of matter, without inhering distinctly in its several parts. In contradistinction to *generical powers,* such as *magnitude and motion,* which you acknowledge to be the sums of magnitudes and motions of the several parts.

That, for instance, the *power of the eye to contribute to the act of seeing,* the power of a *clock* to show the hour of the day, the power of a *musical instrument* to produce in us harmonious sounds, the particular *figures* in bodies such as *roundness* or *squareness,* and particular or individual *modes of motion,* are such *numerical powers* not at all resulting from any powers of the *same kind* inhering in the parts of the system. And that *thinking* therefore, in like manner, not being an aggregate of powers of the *same kind,* may yet inhere in a system of matter as one of these *numerical* or *individual modes* of some *generical power.*

That, upon this supposition of *thinking* being a *numerical mode* of some *generical power* of matter, it may be conceived that *as the roundness of a body is not the sum of the roundnesses of the parts,* nor the *squareness* of a body the sum of the *squarenesses* of the parts, nor *the power of a musical instrument to cause an harmonious sound the sum of powers of the same kind in the parts singly considered,* nor any particular *mode of motion* the sum of the same *modes of motion* in all the several parts, so the *consciousness* that *inheres in a system of matter* may yet *not be the sum of the consciousnesses of the parts.*

That the argument therefore drawn from *consciousness* not being made up of *several consciousnesses,* concludes no more against the possibility of its residing in a system of matter, than the like argument would *conclude against the possibility of the existence of* roundness, *or any other* numerical mode, *in a body.*

For *roundness no more consists of several roundnesses, than thinking or consciousness does of several consciousnesses.*

And *roundness is as specifically different from other figures* of which it may be composed, *as consciousness is from a circular motion.*

So that *sensation* may be conceived to be *in the parts of an animal's* body, just *as roundness is in the parts that compose a round body. Each part has as much of sensation, singly considered, as each part of a round body, has of roundness. And when the parts are duly disposed, whole thinking is performed, as whole roundness exists by the conjunction of parts.*

For *consciousness, being supposed to be a real numerical power, such as roundness is, may result from the composition of different qualities, as roundness does from different species of figure. And is consequently a new quality in the same subject, of a different kind or species from all the component qualities considered together.*

Wherefore, *though consciousness be a real quality, and different from all other qualities, whether known or unknown, which are themselves acknowledged to be void of consciousness, yet it may result from such qualities as singly considered are void of consciousness.* In like manner as roundness is a real *quality specifically different from other qualities void of roundness, and yet may be the result or composition of such qualities.*

That consciousness may be considered particularly as an individual *mode* or *species of motion.*

For as nothing more *goes to the composition of roundness than the conjunction of several particles not singly endued with roundness,* so upon *this supposition*, nothing more needs *go to the power of thinking than the conjunction of several particles not each endued with that species of motion called thinking.*

This, if I understand you right, is the sum and full strength of what you have urged in your *Reflections*.

And to this, I answer as follows.

It is absolutely impossible, and an evident contradiction, that any real quality should truly and properly inhere in a system of matter without being the sum or aggregate of a number of powers or qualities residing distinctly in the several parts of the system, and being always of the *same kind* with the whole that results from them. For, as the *substance itself* of a system of matter is nothing but the sum of its parts existing distinctly and independently from each other, and the whole cannot but be of the *same kind* with the parts that constitute it, so no *power* or *quality of the substance* can be anything else but the sum or aggregate of the powers of the several parts, and that sum or aggregate, without a creation of something out of nothing, cannot but be of the *same kind* with the powers that constitute it. If the parts of the substance be *similar*, then the system itself is a *uniform* or *homogeneous* substance. If the parts be *dissimilar,* then the substance is *difform* or *heterogeneous,* but still always of the *same kind* or *kinds* with the parts that compose it. In like manner, if the powers of the several parts of the system be *similar,* the power of the whole will be a *simple* and *uniform* power. If the powers of the several parts be *dissimilar,* the power of the whole will be a *compound difform* power, but still always necessarily of the *same kind* or *kinds* with the powers of which it is compounded. Since therefore you acknowledge *thinking* to be a power not composed of a multitude of *thinkings.* And it is evident (as shall in the sequel be made [to –ed.] fully appear) that no powers void of thinking can be of the *same kind* with the power of thinking, so as to be parts of it, and that from a composition of them the power of thinking may arise. It follows that *thinking* is not a power made up at all of parts, and consequently that it cannot reside in a substance that consists of distinct and independent parts, such as all matter is confessed to be.

From the clear explication of which whole argument, and to vindicate the notion from all the objections and pretended instances you have brought to the contrary, it is to be observed that the terms, *kind,* and *species,* and *of the same kind* or *species,* are very ambiguous terms, and used in a great variety of significations. Though among men who seek truth, and endeavor to express themselves with the greatest clearness; they [who –ed.] can, and are willing to understand each other's meaning, they [i.e. these terms] do not often cause any considerable mistakes.

For example, it is an evident truth that *all circles of four feet diameter* are of *one and the same kind* or *species,* and this is what the logicians call *species specialissima.* It is true in another sense that *all circles whatever* are of the *same species;* in another sense that *all curvilinear figures* are of the *same species;* in another that *all plain figures both straight-lined and curvilinear,* as opposed to solids, are of the *same species;* and in another that *all figures whatsoever, whether plain or solid,* are of the *same kind* or *species* — as contradistinguished from motion or thinking, or from anything else of a totally different kind.

This is what they call the *genus generalius* [most general genus –ed.]. And beyond this, it is neither *true* nor *good sense,* nor can it in any manner be said, that *figure* and *motion,* or *figure* and *color,* or *figure* and *thought,* are of the *same kind,* because there is nothing common in their ideas by which they can be ranked or compared together — save only as they are all comprehended perhaps under the mere abstract name of *quality* in general.

In like manner, *all squares of two feet diameter* are *specifically* different from *all squares of one foot diameter,* but not in the same sense, nor so much, as both are from *parallelograms.* And *all parallelograms* differ *specifically* from *all squares,* but not so as both do from *triangles.* And *all triangles* differ *specifically* from *all quadrilateral figures,* but not so as both do from *spheres* or *cylinders.* And *spheres* or *cylinders* differ *specifically* from all straight-lined figures, but not so as they and all other figures differ from *motion,* or from a *taste* or a *sound,* or as *figure* or *motion* does from a *thought.* Which makes it appear by the bye, with what truth and sense you affirm, that *roundness is as specifically different from all other figures as consciousness is from a circular motion.* That is, that a *circle* differs from an *ellipsis* (suppose) or from a *parabola,* not only as much as it differs from a *cube,* but even as much as it differs from the *reason of a man.* Or, as logicians would express it, that the *species specialior* [more specific species –ed.] differs as much from the *species* next and immediately superior to it as it does from the *genus generalissimum* — and not only so, but as it does also from anything that is not so much as included even in *that genus.*

Again, *all light blue colors* differ *specifically* from *all dark blue colours,* but not so as both do from *yellow* or *scarlet.* And *scarlet* differs *specifically* from *blue,* but not so as both do from the *sound of a trumpet.*

Now to apply this to our present question. When I affirm that every real power or quality inhering in a system of matter, must of necessity be the sum or aggregate of powers *of the same kind* residing distinctly in the several parts of that system, it is manifest that by this term *of the same kind* is not to be understood the *species specialissima* [most specific species –ed.], but some of the *species generaliores* [more general species –ed.]. For example, when I say the *magnitude* of a *cubic foot* of gold is the sum or aggregate of the *magnitudes* of its parts, I do not mean to say that it is an aggregate of *cubic feet,* but of other *magnitudes* which constitute a cubic foot, and which are of *the same kind* with it in the sense that *all magnitudes* are of the *same kind,* and may be parts one of another. But *magnitude* and *motion,* or *magnitude* and *figure,* are not in any sense *of the same kind,* and cannot be parts one of another. Neither can *figure* or *motion* be a *piece* of a *thought.*

In like manner, when I say the number *twenty* is made up of parts *of the same kind* with the whole, it is evident I do not mean that it is made up of *twenties,* but of other *numbers* which are *of the same kind* with it in the sense that *all numbers* are of *the same kind,* and may be parts one of another. But *number* and *sound,* or *number* and *color,* are not in any sense *of the same kind,* and cannot be parts one of another. Neither can *number* or *figure, motion* or *magnitude,* be a *piece* of a *thought.*

Again, when I say *roundness,* or *globosity,* or any other figure of a body, must needs be the sum of qualities *of the same kind* inhering in the several parts, it is plain I do not mean to affirm that *globosity* is made up of *globosities* — any more than the number *twenty* is made up of *twenties,* or the *motion of a cubic foot* of matter made up of the *motions of cubic feet* — but that a *whole round figure* must necessarily be made up of *pieces of roundness* which are all of the *same kind* with it — just as the *numbers* which are parts of *twenty* are of the *same kind* with the whole, and the *motions* of the particles of a cubic foot of matter which are parts of the motion of the whole are of the *same kind* with the whole motion. But *figure,* and whatever is not *figure,* are not in any sense *of the same kind.* Neither can anything that is *void of figure* be part of any *figure* whatsoever, nor anything that is *void* of *curvity* in particular be part of a *round circumference,* nor anything that is void of that *particular degree of curvity* which makes a circle of a certain determinate diameter be part of the *circumference of that circle,* nor anything that is *void of thinking* be a part or constituent of a *thought.*

From hence it clearly appears that your distinction of *generical* and *numerical* powers is of no service to your cause. For those powers which you call *numerical* must as necessarily be aggregates of powers of *the same kind* as those which you call *generical.* It is as evident that the *round figure* of a *globe* [its *superficial figure*] is the sum of the *convex surfaces* of its outward parts, and its *solid figure* the sum of all its *solid particles taken together* — considered like so many *concentric shells,* or any other figures which can be constituent parts of the solid content of a globe — as it is that the *motion* of a globe is the sum of the *motions* of its parts. And the *convex outsides* of its outward parts, and the *concentric roundnesses* of its inward parts, are as much *of the same kind* with the *whole roundness* or the *whole globosity* of which they are pieces, as the several distinct *motions* or *magnitudes* of its parts are of the *same kind* with the *whole motion* or *magnitude* which they constitute. For why is not a *semicircle* or the *arc of a quadrant* of the *same kind* with the circumference of a *circle,* and *concentric round figures* or any other *figures* which can be *constituent* parts of the solid content of a globe of *the same kind* with the figure of the *globe,* as much as the *motion* or *magnitude* of *half a foot cube* of matter is of the *same kind* with the *motion* or *magnitude* of the *whole foot cube?*

In reality, no other power but *numerical* powers can properly in the present question come under consideration at all. For *generical* powers, considered as such, are nothing but universals, having no being but in the imagination considering and comparing several particulars. In the individuals themselves, wherein alone powers really exist, they are not *general.* They are only made *general* by the considering and comparing together of particulars — which comparison has no existence but in the idea. And consequently *general* or *generical powers,* having no real existence in things without us, have really neither parts nor whole, nor can properly come at all under consideration in the present question. It is not *motion* or *figure* in *general,* that is made up of motions and figures, but it is the *individual numerical motion* or *figure* of a body that is made up of the motions or figures of its parts. The *numerical mode of motion* of the whole is always the sum of the *numerical modes of motion* of the parts. The *numerical mode of superficial figure* of the whole is the sum of the *numerical modes of figure* of the *outsides* of its *superficial* parts. And the *numerical mode of solid figure* of the whole is the sum of the *numerical modes of solid figure* of all the parts taken together. In like manner, if *thinking* could inhere in a system of matter, it would not be *thinking* in *general,* but always some particular *numerical thought* that would be the result of the *thinkings of the several parts.*

If you will reply that by *generical* powers you do not mean *general* powers, or *universals,* which have no real existence (though when you reckon *figure* among your *generical* powers in opposition to any *particular figure* as *roundness,* your words cannot easily bear any other than this absurd sense) — if, I say, you will reply that by *generical* powers you do not mean *general* powers, but only such *sorts* of *particular* powers as *are* sums or aggregates of powers of the *same kind,* in opposition to such other *particular* powers or qualities as *are not* sums or aggregates of powers of the *same kind,* I answer that there is no such distinction in nature.

But all powers or qualities whatever that inhere in systems of matter, whether they be such as you instance in for generical, or such as you instance in for *numerical* powers, are equally and alike sums or aggregates of powers *of the same kind.* For if by this term *of the same kind* or *species* you understand the *species specialissima,* in that sense neither the one sort of qualities, nor the other, nor any wholes in the world, are aggregates of parts *of the same kind.* It being no more true that the *magnitude* or *motion* (which you call the *generical* qualities) of a *foot cube* of matter are made up of *cubic feet magnitudes,* or *cubic feet motions,* than it is true that the *roundness* (which you call the *numerical* quality) of a *globe* is made up of the *like roundnesses.* But if by the term *of the same kind* be understood (as common sense requires, and as I before explained) the *species generalior,* then both the one sort of qualities, and the other, and all wholes in the world, are aggregates of parts *of the same kind.* It being equally true and evident that the *round figure* of a globe (the *numerical* quality) is as to its *surface* made up of *pieces of surfaces spherically and concentrically convex,* and as to its *solid content* made up of *concentric round figures,* or of *shells spherically and concentrically convex.* Which, being pieces of the whole spherical surface or of the whole spherical solid content, are respectively *of the same kind* with it, as that the *magnitude* of a *foot cube* of matter (the *generical* quality) is made up of *inches cube,* or of any *other magnitudes* which, being pieces of a foot cube, are *of the same kind* with it.

When therefore you say *if powers of the same kind be understood* generically, *then* you *do agree that the known powers of matter are nothing else but the sums of powers of the same kind. That is, the figure and motion of a body* [the *magnitude* and *motion* you should more properly have instanced in] *consist of the figures and motions* [*the magnitudes* and *motions*] *of the parts. But if the terms powers of the same kind be taken* numerically *(that is, as powers really exist), then there are powers inhering in systems of matter that are not the sums of powers of the same kind as the roundness of a body is not the sum of the roundnesses of the parts,* your·distinction is evidently very groundless. Because in the same sense that *the roundness of a body is not the sum of the* like roundnesses of the parts (for of *other* roundnesses, as of innumerable *concentric roundnesses,* and of the *convex outsides* of its minute external particles, it may be and always is the sum) — in the same sense, I say, that *the roundness of a body* is not *the sum of the* [like] *roundness of the parts,* in that same sense it is true also that *neither* does *the magnitude nor motion of a body consist of the* [like] *magnitudes nor motions of the parts.* And on the contrary, in the same sense that it is true that the *magnitude and motion of a body* does *consist of* [not the *same,* but the *different*] *magnitudes and motions of the parts,* in that same sense it is true likewise that the *numerical round figure of a body* — that is, the *round figure of its surface* — is the sum of the *roundnesses* — that is, of the *round* or *convex outsides* — of its *superficial* parts, and its *solid figure* is the sum of all its solid parts taken together — which, as I before said, may be considered as so many *concentric shells* or any other figures that can be *constituent* parts of the solid content of a globe.

And when you say, it is *a contradiction to make consciousness the sum of the consciousnesses of the parts, as it is a contradiction to make roundness to consist in the roundnesses of the parts. Though you would readily grant that were*[1] *consciousness a generical power like figure and motion, it would be likewise the sum and result of the consciousnesses of the several parts, and so there would be as many distinct consciousnesses as there are particles of matter of which the system consists — which you do allow to be very absurd.* And again, *if human consciousness be a* mode *of some generical power in matter, it must not be the sum of the consciousnesses of the parts.* And, *did consciousness answer to figure and motion* [the generical powers], *that would likewise consist of the consciousnesses of the parts.* And again *consciousness may result from such qualities, as singly considered are void of consciousness,* in like manner as *roundness is a real quality specifically different from other qualities void of roundness, and yet may be the result or composition of such qualities.* And, *nor is consciousness a power which answers to figure and motion* [the generical powers], *which you agree consist only in the figures and motions of the parts, but it agrees or answers to* [numerical] *modes of figure and motion.* All this is only amusing your reader with insignificant words. For *1st, consciousness* (as I shall hereafter have occasion more particularly to observe) is truly a *more generical* power than either *figure* or *motion*. For *figure* contains under it nothing but the modes of *figure,* and *motion* nothing but the modes of *motion.* But *consciousness,* comprehending under it all the modes of *thinking,* contains in itself the ideas of all the modes of *figure,* and the ideas of all the modes of *motion,* and infinite *other ideas* besides. *Consciousness* therefore being a

1 Replacing "was" –ed.

generical power not *like*, but infinitely *more* so than, *figure* and *motion*, must be (according to your own confession) *the sum and result of the consciousnesses of the several parts. And so there would be as many distinct consciousnesses as there are particles of matter of which the system consists — which* you *do allow to be very absurd.* But *2dly*, let us endeavor to imagine *consciousness* to be not a *generical* but a *numerical* power or quality, such as *roundness* is, and see what will follow from thence. It cannot be conceived that *consciousness in general* is a *numerical* power, any more than *figure in general*, or *roundness in general*. But, as the *individual roundness* of a *globe* is a *numerical* quality of that *individual globe*, so you can only say that the *individual consciousness*, which I find in myself at any particular moment of time, is a *numerical* mode of some power inhering in that system of matter which constitutes my brain. Now as the *individual roundness* of a *globe* is not indeed made up of a number of the *like whole roundnesses* (even as the number *a hundred* is not made up of *hundreds*, nor the *magnitude of a foot cube* made up of *feet cube*, nor any *whole* whatever made up of a number of the *like wholes*), but yet must needs be made up of *such figures* as are *parts of roundness* — nay parts endued with that *particular numerical degree of curvity or roundness* — and cannot be made up of *straight lines*, nor of any *figures* which are *not pieces of roundness*, or *not pieces* endued with that *particular determinate degree of curvity or roundness*. So the *individual consciousness* that I find in myself at any particular moment of time (supposing it to be a quality inhering in a system of matter) must be made up, though not indeed of a number of the *very same consciousnesses*, yet of such powers as are as much *of the same kind* with that *numerical consciousness* as *arcs of circles* are of *the same kind* with the *whole circular circumference*, or *pieces of surfaces spherically and concentrically convex* are of the *same kind* with the whole *spherical surface* composed of them all: That is, it must be made up of *different* consciousnesses indeed, but still *consciousnesses* only, and not *motions* or *figures*, or anything else; any more than the *roundness of a circle* can be made up of *straight lines*, or of *colors*, or *sounds*, or anything else besides *pieces of circular roundness*, or than the *surface of a sphere* can be made up of anything else than *little surfaces having every one of them the very same spherical and concentric convexity*, or that an *extended* or *solid* substance can be made up of any other ingredients than such as are themselves *pieces* of *extended* or *solid substance*. It is by no means true, which you affirm, that *roundness* is *a new quality, of a different* kind *or* species *from all the component qualities considered together,* or that *it may be the result or composition of qualities void of roundness,* since it cannot be affirmed of any part of the *arc of a circle* that it is wholly *void of circularity,* as a *straight line* is. And in like manner, it is by no means possible that *consciousness may result from such qualities as singly considered are void of* [all kind of] *consciousness,* as *motion* or *figure* is. Nay further, *every part* of the circumference of a circle is not only *not wholly void of roundness,* but has really *as much roundness* or *curvity* (as much in *degree,* though not so much of it in *quantity*) as the *whole* circle itself has. For the same reason as *one circle* has *as much roundness* as *twenty,* or *one inch cube* of boiling water *as much heat* [in degree] as *twenty,* or *one foot square* of a white surface *as much whiteness* as *twenty.* And therefore *consciousness* in like manner, if it were[1] a quality answering to, or that could be compared with, the roundness of a circle, must consist of parts every one of which would have *as much consciousness* [in degree] as the whole.

From the same principles may easily be shown the absurdity of all the rest that you have advanced — upon your favorite instance of ROUNDNESS.

You say that the argument drawn from consciousness' not being made up of several consciousness[es –ed.] concludes no more against the possibility of its residing in a system of matter, than the like argument would *conclude against the possibility of the existence of roundness in body which no more consists of several roundnesses than thinking or consciousness does of several consciousnesses, and* is *as specifically different from other figures as consciousness* is *from a circular motion.* But I think I have shown that the instances are not alike, and that *roundness* does not consist of qualities so different from *roundness,* as you suppose *consciousness* to be made up of qualities different from *consciousness.* That is, that the *roundness of the whole circumference of a circle* is not so specifically different from the *convexity of little arcs* of which it consists, or the *roundness of a whole globe* from the *little spherically and concentrically convex pieces of surfaces* of which it is composed, as *consciousness* is from a *circular motion,* or from *motion in a square,* or *any motion at all,* or *any other thing whatever that* is *wholly void of consciousness.* For *roundness* can subsist of nothing but *pieces of roundness* that differ

1 Replacing "was" –ed.

from it *specifically* only in the very lowest sense of the word *specifically.* Or, rather, they do not differ from it at all *specifically,* but *in magnitude* only, as the *part* from the *whole* — it being hardly good sense, to say that the *number twenty* differs *specifically* from the *number ten,* or that 360 degrees, or 60 degrees, differ *specifically* from 20 degrees, or from 20 seconds, or from any other part of *one and the same arc,* every *part* of which has necessarily (as I before said) just as much roundness or curvity [in degree] as the *whole* arc or *whole* circle itself has. But *thinking,* if it be made up of qualities *utterly void of thought* as *motions, figures,* and the like, must consist of qualities *generically* different from itself in the highest sense of the word *generically* — they being under no common *genus,* and having no similitude, nothing common one with another in their ideas, and consequently cannot with any sense be compared at all one with another, or be compounded one of another, any more than *circles* and *straight lines,* or *colors* and *sounds, numbers* and *tastes, figures* and *motions,* or any things whose ideas have nothing common or alike betwixt them.

Again, you allege *in behalf of roundness as well as thinking, that it is so far from being as certain as an arithmetical demonstration that such a particular power is a whole bigger than all its parts, that it is an arithmetical demonstration that such a particular power as roundness is, is but just equal to all the parts of which that roundness consists. For what more goes to the composition of roundness, than the conjunction of several particles not singly endued with roundness? And, what more goes to the power of thinking, than the conjunction of several particles not each endued with thinking?* But here also your comparison is nothing to the purpose. For when you ask *what more goes to the composition of roundness than the conjunction of several particles not singly endued with roundness?* If by *not singly endued with roundness* you mean *not singly endued with* [the same whole] *roundness,* then your assertion is no more than this, that the *parts of roundness* are not a number of the same *wholes,* or that the several *pieces* of the *circumference of a circle* are not so many *whole* [same] *circumferences.* And then I answer neither would the *parts of thinking* (if it inhered in a system of matter) be so many *whole* [the same] *thoughts*. But if you mean that a round figure is a composition of particles *not singly endued* with [any parts of] *roundness,* any [curvity] *at all,* then your assertion is directly false, and such a *roundness* would be a *whole* bigger than *all its parts,* just as I said *consciousness* would be if it was made up of motions or any other qualities *void of consciousness.* If you imagined *thinking* to be made up of innumerable different *consciousnesses,* as the *roundness of a circumference of a circle* is made up of innumerable *convex arcs* which are *pieces of roundness,* then indeed, and then only, your comparison would be good. But to suppose *thinking* made up of powers *utterly void of consciousness* is like supposing the *circumference of a circle* to be made up of *straight lines utterly void of convexity* (or rather like supposing it to be made up of *sounds* or *colors,* or whatever else can be imagined even still more remote from the idea of *roundness*), and this is evidently making a *whole* bigger than *all its parts,* that is, containing something different from, something over and above, something more than all its parts taken together. Nay, such a whole the sum of whose parts neither make up the whole itself, nor any part of it — which is a plain contradiction. It is evident that no *whole* can possibly differ from *all its parts* in anything else, but only in the abstract name, the mere external denomination of its being a *whole* — which is nothing at all in the thing itself, but merely a manner of conception, a conjunction of ideas in the imagination of the person that beholds or thinks upon it. *Thinking,* if it was the quality of a system of matter — that is, the *sum* or *whole* of the powers of its parts — must differ from the distinct powers of those parts no otherwise than as the idea of the roundness of a *circle* differs from the idea of the roundness of *two semicircles* (or of *four quadrants*) *joined together,* or as the idea of *twice six* differs from the idea of the number *twelve.* If therefore *thinking* was, as you suppose, a composition or result of several powers, and those powers such as were themselves *utterly void of consciousness, thinking* would be either a *mere outward denomination* and nothing at all really in the thinking substance itself — just as *a dozen* is only a mere name, and nothing at all differing really in the thing itself from *twelve units,* which is what you will not affirm — or else it must unavoidably be a *whole* bigger than *all its parts* — that is, containing *all its parts,* and *thinking* besides, just as the *curve circumference of a circle* would contain *more* of curvity in it than *all its parts taken together* if it could be composed of lines that had none of them singly any *curvity at all,* or a *cube* would be *bigger* than *all its parts* if it were made up of parts that had none of them singly any *magnitude at all.*

[If upon this you will forsake your first instance and, seeking still for new similitudes, allege that a *square* figure (suppose) may consist of parts that are none of them singly endued with anything like squareness, I answer that the *squareness* of the figure of a body is a mere *external denomination, a mere relative comparing together* in the imagination the *bounds of a surface, the situation of four straight lines with respect one to another*, and has not properly any real existence in things themselves, so as *consciousness* is acknowledged to have in the thinking substance. The like may be said concerning all other qualities whose essence consists merely in the *relative comparing the situation* or other *respects of the parts of a body one towards another*, such kind of qualities having really no *proper numerical* existence, save only in the idea. And roundness itself, being considered in the same manner, might *this way likewise* afford a just answer to your argument drawn from thence.]

Lastly, you affirm that *sensation is in the parts of an animal, as roundness is in the parts which compose a round body — each part has as much of sensation, singly considered, as each part of a round body has a roundness — and when the parts are duly disposed, whole thinking is performed, as whole roundness exists by the conjunction of parts.* But from what has been already said, I presume it is evident enough that *senseless figure* or *motion* cannot be *so* a *part of sensation* or a *piece of thought,* as a *semicircle* or *quadrant* is a *piece of a circle.* To affirm that it can — *viz.* that figure or motion *wholly void of sense* can be *so* a *part of sensation* — is plainly (as I have before shown) the very same thing as if you should affirm that a line *wholly void of curvity* could be *so* a *piece of the circumference of a circle* as the *arc of a quadrant* is, or that something that has *no solidity* and *no extension* might yet be a constituent part of an *extended* and of a *solid* substance.

I have shown that no part of the circumference of a circle is wholly void of roundness. If therefore *sensation is* (according to your assertion) *in the parts of an animal, as roundness is in the parts that compose a round body,* and *each part has as much of sensation, singly considered, as each part of a round body has of roundness,* it will follow, not (as you intended) that *sensation* can arise from a conjunction of particles *utterly void of sense* (for the *circumference of a circle* cannot be made by a conjunction of *lines,* or the *superficies of a sphere* by a conjunction of *surfaces, utterly void of curvity*), but, on the contrary, it will follow that *some degree of sensation* is really in *every part* of the animal, singly considered, as *some degree of curvity* is necessarily in *every part* of the *circumference of a circle,* or of the *surface of a sphere.* And so you run unavoidably into that confessedly *absurd* notion that there are *as many distinct consciousnesses as there are particles of matter of which the* thinking *system consists.*

I am afraid our readers are sufficiently tired with ROUNDNESS. The other instances you allege to prove that a quality or power inhering in a system of matter needs not be the result of powers of qualities *of the same kind* residing in the parts of the system, are still less to your purpose. For it is very evident concerning those, and all other possible instances, that they never are, nor can be, anything else but the sums of powers or qualities *of the same particular uniform kind* with the whole, when that whole is *simple and homogeneous,* or *of the same general kind* with it when it is *complex and heterogeneous.* Which since you acknowledge cannot be the case of *thinking,* it will follow that *thinking* cannot be a power or quality residing in a system of matter.

The *power of a clock* to show the hour of the day is not indeed a result from the *like individual powers* residing in the several parts, any more than the number *a thousand* is the result of a composition of *thousands,* or *any whole* a composition of a multitude of the *same wholes.* But, as the number *a thousand* is the sum of a great many *numbers,* but cannot with any sense be imagined to be a composition of *sounds* or *colors,* so the *numerical power of a clock,* being itself nothing but *motion* and *figure,* cannot be the result of any other powers in the parts, but such as are themselves singly *of the same kind* in the manner before explained — namely, *motions* and *figures.* And in like manner *my present numerical consciousness,* if it were at all a quality inhering in a system of matter, though it need not indeed be the sum of a multitude of the *like individual thoughts* inhering in the several distinct parts of the system, yet it must be the sum of *such* powers in the parts, as would themselves singly be of *the same kind* — namely, *consciousnesses* or *thoughts.* It being equally, and for the very same reason, impossible that my *consciousness* should be the result of such powers in the parts of my brain as are *toto genere* [in total nature –ed.] different from *thinking,* and have nothing in their ideas common with it or alike to it (such as are *figure* and *motion,* and all other powers which are *void of* consciousness) as that the fore-mentioned number *a thousand,* should be a composition of *sounds* or *colors,* or of anything else but *numbers.*

The *power of a musical instrument to produce harmonious sounds,* is not indeed a result from the *like individual powers* residing in the several parts of the instrument, any more than the *circumference of a circle* is made up of a number of the *like whole circumferences.* But, as the *circumference of a circle* is the sum of a multitude of *convex arcs of like curvity,* but cannot be an aggregate of *straight lines,* or of *cubic bodies,* or of *arcs of unlike curvity,* so the *harmony* produced by a musical instrument, being itself in the mind that perceives it nothing but *sound,* and in the instrument and in the air and in the organs of sensation nothing but a *motion of parts,* cannot be the result or composition of any other powers but what are themselves singly *of the same kind* in the several subjects respectively — namely in the mind that perceives them *sounds* likewise, and in the instrument itself and in the air and in the organs of sensation *motions of the parts.* And in like manner *consciousness,* if it were a power inhering in a system of matter, could not be the result of any other powers in the parts, but *some sorts of consciousness,* for the very same reason as the *circumference of a circle* cannot (as was before said) be an aggregate of *straight lines,* or of *cubic bodies,* nor an *harmonious sound* a composition of *colors,* or of anything else beside *sounds.*

The *power of the eye* to see is nothing else but such a power, as is in the *object glasses* of telescopes, of *transmitting* and *refracting* rays of light, so as to paint the image of the object in the bottom of the eye. And this is evidently nothing but the sum of powers *of the same kind* — namely, powers of *transmitting* and *refracting* of rays, residing distinctly in the several parts of the *eye* or of the *glass.* Every part of the eye *transmits* and *refracts* rays, and those rays paint several parts of the image. And the *whole image* differs no otherwise from *all its parts,* nor that which you call the *numerical powers of the whole eye* from the *single powers of all its parts,* than the idea of *a dozen* differs from the idea of *twelve units:* Which, if it be as great a difference, as is between the idea of *consciousness* and the idea of a *circular* or *any other motion,* I will confess I have lost my understanding.

But there is still a further peculiar unhappiness in your choosing to instance in the *power of the eye* to *contribute* to *the act of seeing,* as a *numerical power* of a *system of matter,* that does *not inhere in the parts* of that system, and in your affirming that upon *dividing or varying the least part of the eye, the power of contributing towards the act of vision is entirely at an end.* For so far is this from being true (excepting only *accidentally* upon account of the softness and fluidity of the matter of the eye) that, on the contrary, not only *every part* of the eye (as I now said) *transmits* and *refracts* rays in order to paint at the bottom the several parts of the image of the object (and the power of the *whole eye* is nothing more than the *sum* of those *transmissions* and *refractions*), but moreover even *every part* of the eye has the same power as the *whole* (differing only in *degree*) of painting at the bottom the *whole image* of the object. For as each half of a broken object glass of a telescope, or any piece of it that retains the polish on both surfaces, will represent distinctly the whole object only with less brightness and luminousness than the whole glass would do, so each part of the eye paints every part of the whole object. And if half of the eye, or almost the whole eye, be covered, so that you look only through a pinhole placed on the right side, or on the left side, or upon the middle of the pupil, still the whole object is seen distinctly even by that very small part of the eye, and consequently the power of the eye is the same both in the *whole* and in *every part.*

And the same that has been said concerning these several instances you choose to insist upon, may with very little variation be said likewise concerning all other powers whatsoever that do, or can, reside in any system of matter. The right explication of the nature of which powers shows even your own instances to be so many unanswerable arguments against the assertion you brought them to support.

This, I presume, may be sufficient to prove against you in the *general* that every power or quality residing in any system of matter must of necessity be the sum or aggregate of powers *of the same kind* residing distinctly in the several parts of the system. And consequently, that whatever power is not an aggregate of such powers, as you confess *consciousness* or *thinking* is not, cannot be at all a power or quality of matter.

Not without some unwillingness you seem at last to determine in *particular* what sort of generical power in matter you imagine *thinking* to be a numerical mode of. You *suppose consciousness to be a mode of motion.* You speak of *thought as a species of motion.* And you conceive it a proper expression to mention a certain *species of motion, called thinking.*

You desire indeed it may not be *imputed to you as your opinion,* since you *only take the liberty to suppose it.* But this will not serve you for an evasion, when the absurdity of the notion is proved upon you. For you declare it as your positive *opinion, that human consciousness or thinking* is *a mode of* some *generical power in matter.* What that generical power is, you will not positively determine, but you *suppose* it to be *motion.* Now I presume you *suppose* that which you judge the most probable, and which you think will best serve your purpose in explaining the nature of *thinking.* I shall prove presently that nothing can be more absurd than to suppose *thinking* to be a *mode of motion.* The same arguments will prove no less strongly that it is not possible for *thinking* to be a *mode of figure,* or of any other *known* property of matter, and also that it is not possible for it to be a *mode* of any *unknown* power of matter which in the general is *void of thinking.* Because every *unknown* power which is *void of thinking* is as different from *thinking,* as *motion* itself is, or *figure,* or any other *known* power. For the same reason that a *smell* or a *taste,* or any other *known* or *unknown* quality which is *not a color,* must of necessity be as different from *blue* or *scarlet* as *the sound of a trumpet* is. When therefore I have shown the absurdity of your *supposition* that *thinking* is a *mode of motion,* I shall likewise have shown the absurdity of your *declared opinion* that *human consciousness or thinking is a mode of* some *generical power in matter.*

Now to prove the absurdity of supposing *consciousness* to be a *mode of motion,* I offer the following arguments.

1. Every *mode* of any *power* or *quality* is nothing else but *that power* or *quality* of which it is a *mode,* understood with some particular limitation. That is to say, it is nothing but a *particular instance* of that *general power* or *quality,* nothing but the *general power* or *quality* considered under this or that *particular modification. Blue* and *red,* and all other *modes* of *color,* are nothing but several particular *colors,* and can contain nothing in their idea, beyond the *genus* of *color. Acute* and *grave,* and all other *modes* of *sound,* are nothing but several particular *sounds,* and can contain nothing in their idea beyond the *genus* of *sound. Circular* and *triangular,* and all other *modes* of *figure,* are nothing but several particular *figures,* and can contain nothing in their idea beyond the *genus* of *figure.* In like manner all *modes* of *motion* are nothing else but *merely* particular *motions,* and cannot contain anything in their idea beyond the *genus* of *motion.* Now if *simple ideas* be the foundation of all our knowledge, and *clear and distinct perception* of the *agreement or disagreement* of those ideas be the best and greatest *criterion* of truth that our faculties enable us to attain to, then it is as evident as any truth in the world that *consciousness*

cannot possibly be a *mode of motion*. For I have as *clear and distinct a perception* that the idea of *consciousness* contains something in it besides and beyond the *genus* of *motion*, as I have that it contains something in it beyond the *genus* of *figure*. The idea of *consciousness* is as totally and *generically* different from the idea of a *circular motion*, or an *elliptical motion*, or any other *mode of motion* whatsoever, as it is from the idea of a *circle* or a *cube*, or any other *mode of figure* whatsoever. I have therefore exactly the same *intuitive certainty* that *consciousness* cannot be a *mode of motion* as I have that a *circle* or a *cube* is not a *thought*, or that an *acute sound* is not a *purple color*, or that any one thing in the world is not another, whose idea is the remotest and most different from it that can be imagined. To suppose *consciousness* to be a *mode of motion* is really a greater absurdity (if possible) than it would be to suppose *roundness* to be a property of a *square*, because the idea of *local motion* and the idea of *thinking*, having *no common genus*, nothing wherein they agree or can be compared together, are evidently *more different* one from another than the ideas of *any two plain figures* can be which have a *common genus*. And your question *what more goes to the power of* thinking *than the conjunction of several particles not each endued with that species of* motion *called* thinking? is truly more ridiculous than if a man should ask *what more goes to the making up of a* scarlet color *than the conjunction of several particles not each endued with that species of* sound *called* scarlet? Because no two sensible qualities are in their ideas so different one from another as the idea of *consciousness* is from the idea of *local motion*.

Local motion can have no other effect upon any system of matter than only producing in it a different *juxtaposition* of parts. To which to ascribe thinking, Mr. *Locke* himself, who had no prejudice against the possibility of matter's thinking, acknowledges it is very absurd. *To suppose*,[1] says he, *the eternal thinking being* [or any finite thinking being] *to be nothing else but a composition of particles of matter, each whereof* is *incogitative*, is *to ascribe all the wisdom and knowledge of that eternal being* [or the wisdom and knowledge, and all the powers of the finite thinking being] *only to the juxtaposition of parts. Than which nothing can be more absurd. For unthinking particles of matter, however put together, can have*

1 Book IV, Ch. 10 & 16. [of Locke's *Essay Concerning Human Understanding* –ed.]

nothing thereby added to them but a new relation of position, which it is impossible should give thought and knowledge to them.

2. If *thinking* was any *mode or species of motion,* it would follow that *all motion* would be some *degree* or *kind* of *thinking.* For *motion* in the thing moved, excepting only the difference of *degrees* of its swiftness or slowness, is a *similar quality,* and has no variety in it. All its different *determinations,* or those which you call its *modes* and *species,* being *nothing really* in the *body itself* that is moved but *mere abstract notions* or *external denominations,* conceived *only in our imagination.* For, moving with one determination or with another — from north to south, or from south to north — is *merely* relative, and not really a different thing in the body moved, that one of those motions should be *consciousness,* the other not. In like manner *circular motion,* or *motion in any other figure,* is not anything really and truly inhering in the body itself, different from motion in a *straight line.* For the determination of any body that *moves in a circle,* is nothing else at any given point of time but a determination to *move in a certain straight line,* and at another given point of time to *move in another straight line,* and so on. So that there is no such thing as a *circular motion* of any particle of matter, coexistent at once, but all motion is, strictly and properly speaking, a similar and uniform quality — *viz.* a body's *going on* according to its determination, which determination is always in a straight line and causes the body to go on actually in a straight line where it meets with no resistance; and where it meets with resistance by intervals, there to go on into new straight lines successively into which it is diverted by such resistance; and where it meets with continual resistance, there to go on in a curve[d –ed.] line into which it is continually diverted. And every such *curvilinear motion,* whether *circular,* or of *any other species whatsoever,* is but the idea of a number of successive motions of a body, never existent together — a pure *ens rationis* [mental being –ed.], or operation of the mind, which considering past motion and future, and recollecting *the whole* by the memory and fancy, calls *that whole* sometimes by one denomination and sometimes by another.[1] How then can any of those *modes of motion* be the *efficient of thought,* or (according to your supposition) be themselves *thought,* when

1 See Bishop of Norwich's Sermon on Immortality of the Soul, p. 9, and Dr. Bentley's Sermon II at Boyle's Lecture, p. 55.

they are evidently nothing but the *effect and product* of it — *viz.* ideas framed merely by the imagination and memory?

And the same that has been said concerning the *modes of motion* of a *single body* may easily be applied to the *modes of motion* of *any number of bodies* in any *system* or *composition* whatsoever. It being very evident that if the *progression* of *one particle* of matter *directly in a straight line* be not *consciousness* or *thought,* the *like progression* of *twenty particles* at the same time *in straight lines* cannot be *consciousness* either. The position of those lines with respect one to another, which determines the particular *modes of motion* of the whole system, being merely *imaginary, relative,* and *comparative* — a figment only in the mind or imagination, and not anything really existing in the bodies themselves at any one and the same moment of time.

In like manner the *impulse* also, or *beating of one particle of matter against another,* is a thing similar and in all cases alike, differing in nothing but in the *degrees* or quantity of the force. And therefore must always and in all cases, if ever in any case at all, be some *degree* of *thought.* From whence it would follow that there must be as many several incoherent *consciousnesses* as there are particles of the brain or spirits, or of any other matter in any system that ever dash one against another — which is what you are not willing to affirm.

3. If *consciousness* were a *mode* or *species of motion,* then *motion* would be the *more generical* power, containing *thinking* under it, as (in the language of logicians) the *genus* does the *species.* But, on the contrary, it is evident (as I before observed) that *thinking* (though simple and not compounded of parts) is, in the sense we are now speaking of, a power infinitely *more generical* than either *motion* or *figure,* or any other *power of matter,* and consequently cannot be a *mode* or *species* of any of them. There are as many *ideas of figure* as there are *figures,* and as many *ideas of motion* as there are *modes of motion,* and as many *ideas of other things* as there are *other things* in the world that *can be thought upon.* And all these *ideas* are modes and sorts, or kinds, of *thinking.* Now if *thinking* is a power more various, more extensive, more *generical,* than *motion,* it is manifest it cannot be a *mode* or *species* of *motion,* as *roundness* is a *mode* or *species* of *figure.* If *thinking* is a power *more generical* than *figure,* or *motion,* or any other *power of matter,* if it is a power as universal as all things taken together that can be thought upon, it is certainly a *generical* power in the *highest*

degree, and consequently (if it be at all a *power of matter*) it will oblige you to run into the *absurdity* you declare you would avoid. For, by your own confession, you *would grant readily that were*[1] *consciousness a generical power like figure and motion* (*like* figure and motion it is not, but infinitely *more generical* than either of them), *it would be likewise the sum and result of the consciousnesses of the several parts, and so there would be as many distinct consciousnesses as there are particles of matter of which the system consists — which you do allow to be very absurd.*

As *figure* is the *genus* of all *the species of figure,* so the *idea of figure* is the *genus* of *all the ideas of all the species of figures.* And so the *idea of motion* is the *genus* of *all the ideas of all the species of motions,* and the *idea of color* is the *genus* of *the ideas of all the species of colors,* and the *idea of sound* is the *genus* of *the ideas of all the species of sounds,* and the *idea of an animal* is the *genus* of *the ideas of all the species of animals.* The general ideas of *figure, motion, color, sound, animal,* etc., are *generical* powers of the mind — and *thinking* is the *genus generalius* of all those powers. With what sense then can it be said to be one of the *lower species,* or a *numerical mode,* of one of those powers?

4. *If it was the motion* of the parts of a corporeal system *on which its thinking depends, all the thoughts there must be unavoidably accidental and limited, because each one of the particles that by motion cause thought, being in itself without any thought, cannot regulate its own motions, much less be regulated by the thought of the whole, since that thought of the whole is not the cause of motion (for then it must be antecedent to it, and so without it) but the consequence of it. Whereby freedom, power, choice, and all rational and wise thinking or acting, will be quite taken away. So that such a thinking being would be no better nor wiser than pure blind matter, since to resolve all into the accidental unguided motions of blind matter, or into thought depending on unguided motions of blind matter, is the same thing. Not to mention the narrowness of such thoughts and knowledge that must depend on the motion of such parts. But there needs no enumeration of any more absurdities and impossibilities in this hypothesis (however full of them it be) than that before-mentioned, since, let this thinking system be all or a part of the matter of the universe, it is impossible that any one particle should either know its own, or the motion of any other particle, or the whole know the motion of every particular, and*

---

1 Replacing "was" –ed.

so regulate its own thoughts or motions, or indeed have any thought resulting from such motion. This argument is Mr. Locke's own words (Book IV, ch. 10, sect. 17) to which I cannot but suppose you will give some deference.

5. If *thinking* was a *mode* or *species* of *motion*, then in like manner as it is a proper expression to say that *circularity* is one *species* of *figure*, and *squareness* a second, and *cubicalness* a third, and *ellipticalness* a fourth, so it would be proper also to say that *circular motion* is one *species* of *motion*, and *motion in a square* a second, and *motion in an ellipsis* a third, and *thinking* or *consciousness* a fourth — and I appeal to the common sense of all mankind whether I may not add with exactly the same reason that a *tree* is a fifth, and a *syllogism* a sixth, and *personality* a seventh, etc.

[If to this you will reply that you do not mean, as you say, that any *particular motion* is itself *thought*, but that *thought* may be the *result* of some *particular motion*, I answer in the words of Mr. *Hobbes* that no *result* of motion can ever be anything else but *mere motion* still.[1] (With a different juxtaposition of parts perhaps; of which before.) And consequently all the foregoing arguments hold equally good against one notion as against the other.]

Some of these absurdities are so very gross, and yet such obvious consequences of your notion, that it can hardly be imagined you should have overlooked them. And indeed you do at last endeavor to obviate them in a *very effectual manner.* In such a manner by which you may, whenever you please, answer all the arguments upon any question in the world, and remove out of your way not only any *demonstration,* but even *intuitive knowledge* itself. You tell me that I imagine *consciousness to be something else than what* you *contend it is;* that *the term of consciousness stands with* you *in* another *sense* than with me; that with you it signifies a *numerical power answering to roundness in a body, or to a motion peculiar to a system of matter,* but that with me *it relates to a chimera or idea of* my *own framing.*

Now to this I reply in the words of Mr. *Locke* (Book IV, ch. I, sect. 4) *a man infallibly knows, as soon as ever he has them in his mind, that the ideas he calls* white *and* round *are the very ideas they are, and that they are not other ideas which he calls* red *or* square.

1 Motus nihil generat præter motum. *Lev.* ch. I. [Clarke gives the original Latin from Book I of Hobbes' *Leviathan,* which he had translated above. –ed.]

I think I know infallibly, as soon as ever I have it in my mind, that the idea I call *consciousness, perception* or *thinking,* is the very idea it is, and that it is not another idea which I call *circular motion,* or *elliptical motion,* or *motion in a square,* or the *motion of a watch or of any other machine.* And I appeal to what every man finds in his own mind, whether my account of *consciousness* or yours, which makes it to be merely a *mode of motion,* be the more *chimerical* idea.

Simple ideas cannot be defined nor described. When any dispute is carried so far as to terminate in questioning the idea *itself,* there is nothing then left but to appeal to the idea which every man has in his own mind. If I affirm that this paper is *white,* and you will contend that it is *red,* we cannot confute one another by arguments, but must appeal to the judgment of the world. If a man will tell me that by a *scarlet color* he does not mean that chimerical idea which I frame in my own mind and call by that name, but that he means thereby only a certain *numerical mode of sound,* I know not how he can be confuted, but by appealing to every man's own ideas. The *idea of consciousness* which I have in my mind appears to me an idea which I think I clearly and distinctly perceive to be altogether as different from the *idea of any possible numerical mode of figure or motion,* as my idea of *scarlet color* is different from my idea of *the sound of a trumpet.* If any other person thinks his idea of *consciousness* to be the same with his idea of a *circular motion,* or of any *other numerical mode of motion* I conceive there is nothing more to be done, but to permit him to have the pleasure of continuing to think so as long as he pleases.

The sum is this. I affirm that *thinking* cannot possibly be a mere *mode of motion,* because the idea of *thinking* and the idea of *motion or any of its modes,* have not the least likeness or affinity between them. This, you say, proves nothing, because my idea of *thinking* is a mere chimera, but your idea of it is the same as your idea of some *numerical mode of motion.* I reply, if this proves nothing, then neither can any argument in the world ever prove anything. For, suppose the thing in dispute be whether *a square is a circle,* or whether *blueness* is a *taste.* I contend this cannot possibly be, because my idea of *a square* includes in it nothing of that *roundness* which is my idea of *a circle,* and my idea of *blueness* includes in it nothing like *that sensation* which is my idea of a *taste.* May not another person answer that this proves nothing? Because my idea of a *square,* or of *blueness,* is a mere chimera, but his idea of a *square* is the same as his idea of a *round figure,* and his idea of *blueness* the same as his idea of some certain *taste.*

To conclude. In reviewing this whole matter, I can hardly persuade myself but that you have mistaken your own argument. Some ingenious persons[1] in the present age have indeed undertaken to maintain that God, by the immediate exercise of his omnipotence, may make matter think — notwithstanding it be impossible that *thinking* should result naturally, from any composition or division of the original properties of matter. I suppose they meant that to matter disposed in a certain manner, and put into some particular modes of motion, omnipotence could *superadd* the power of *thinking.* I think the argument drawn from the divisibility of matter proves that matter is not a subject capable of such *superaddition.* And if it be not, then recurring to the divine omnipotence for the making out of impossibility is not *magnifying,* but *destroying,* the power of God — as indeed all contradictory apprehensions concerning any of his perfections are really and in event destructive of our whole notion of God, and have no other effect than to give profane men an occasion of scoffing at religion. However, that assertion had the appearance (though a very false one) of being founded in a certain modest apprehension concerning the inconceivable extent of the divine power. But that any *mode of motion* should be (not a previous disposition or qualification, towards capacitating matter for the addition of such a power, but that it should be) *thinking itself,* when all the matter supposed to be in that motion is acknowledged otherwise to be *void of thought,* this is such an extravagant absurdity as may justly cause wonder how it should ever enter into the heart of any rational man — especially in an age wherein philosophical knowledge has received so considerable improvements.

Having thus particularly answered the argument wherein you placed your main strength, it remains that I take notice of some incidents in your *Reflections,* wherein I think you have either greatly misrepresented me, or give very disadvantageous representations of your own philosophy.

In the question *whether a system of matter can have a* power of thinking, *or an* individual consciousness, *superadded to it, or flowing*

1 Clarke certainly had Locke in mind here. What others he was thinking of is not clear. –ed.

from any modification of that system, you said you understood by a *power of thinking* only *actual thinking*, and not a *capacity of thinking*.

I replied there was no need of making any such distinction, because my argument was of equal force in whatever sense the term *consciousness* was understood — whether to signify the *capacity of thinking*, or *actual thinking*, or the reflex act of being *conscious that I think*.

Upon this, you make a long expostulation *what occasion* I had *for contending with* you *about the sense* you *fixed to the terms*. I did not *contend* much about it. But the *occasion* of saying what I did was because in all questions the greater latitude of signification the terms may be allowed to be understood in, without making any alteration in the strength of the proof, the clearer and stronger such proof always is, and the less perplexity, or room for quibbling, remains in the question itself.

You ask *have* you *not understood* me *in a sense that answered all the ends and purposes of* my *argument?* My argument was indeed conclusive in the sense you understood me in. But I had no reason to approve of your confining me to that sense only, when the argument was equally conclusive in any other sense the reader might happen to understand the terms in.

You say you *have taken but the same liberty* I *allow to every other reader*. But, if I mistake not, there is some difference between allowing the reader to take the term *consciousness* in which of the three fore-mentioned senses he pleases, and allowing you to confine it to one of those senses, exclusive of the others. I affirmed that *the reader needs not trouble himself with the nicety of distinction between a capacity of thinking, actual thinking, and the reflex act of thinking, but may understand consciousness indifferently in all or any of these significations*.

This sentence, you think, *contains one of the nicest distinctions that ever* you *met with*, being *as much as to say that the reader* need *not understand consciousness indifferently in any of the before-mentioned significations, and yet* may *understand it indifferently in any of these significations*. But where is the *niceness* (the *ridiculousness* I suppose you mean) of saying that the reader *may* take a word in a sense which yet he is not under a *necessity* of taking it in, but *may* likewise take it in some other sense if he pleases?

You add *for* you *cannot see but that whoever understands consciousness in any one of those significations* must use *that nicety of distinction* I *complain of, whether he will or no. For by* restraining *consciousness to any one of those significations, he necessarily distinguishes that one from the other two. And* that *therefore* you *must needs own,* you *cannot see the least reason* I *had to blame* you *for a needless distinction, when* I *allow* you *to understand consciousness indifferently in three significations, one of which* you did *assign as* your *meaning or idea of that word.* But, if you please to look once again, I suppose you will *be able to see,* that there is no absolute necessity for *him that understands consciousness in any one of those fore-mentioned significations, to* restrain *it to that one signification* as you desired to do.

Lastly, you allege that *the whole dispute turns upon the* present *distinction* of the significations of the word *consciousness.* And to prove that it does so, you cite a sentence out of my letter to Mr. *Dodwell,* wherein the word *conscious* cannot be understood in any other sense than to signify *actual thinking.* It is true, in that sentence the word was so used. And in the very same sentence it was also used otherwise. Now, because in that passage which you made *the occasion* of our present debate, I once used the word in such a manner as that the nature of the thing accidentally confined it to that signification — though in the more emphatic part of the very same sentence, it was used in a larger sense — does this prove that *the whole dispute* now *turns upon* any distinction of the signification of that word? You might as well have said it proves the remotest thing in the world from our present question. The sentence itself was this, *it is plain, unless matter were essentially conscious, ... no system of it in any possible composition or division can be an individual conscious being.* My meaning was that, unless matter were essentially *conscious* — that is, unless it were essentially endued with *actual thinking* — it might be proved from its divisibility that no system of it in any possible composition or division could ever be an individual *conscious* being — that is, could ever either *actually think* or attain a *capacity of thinking.* How does it follow now from hence that because in the former part of this sentence the word *conscious* happens to signify only *actual thinking,* therefore in the question [whether *consciousness can inhere in a system of matter*] the word *consciousness* may not be understood at large to signify either *actual thinking,* or a *capacity of thinking?* Between which, after all, there is no great difference at the bottom.

Upon the whole, why you should be displeased with me for allowing the terms of the question to be understood in the greatest latitude, and for endeavoring to prove more than you expected — *viz.* that no system of matter could either have *actual thinking,* or so much as any *capacity of thinking* — I could not imagine. And why you made such a stir about a distinction which did, and still does, appear to me to be very needless, I could conceive no other cause, but only that you might *perplex* the question.

Thus I have given you the *reason* you *demanded of my conduct* in this matter. I do not *demand* of *you,* but leave it to your discretion to choose whether you will give any *reason* of *yours* or no. For (if you will give me leave to use your own expression) *I cannot assign a good one for you.*

You ask *if the soul or principle of thinking be undivided, how can it think successively, divide, abstract, combine or ampliate, retain or revive impressions in the memory? And how can it be capable, partly or wholly to forget anything?* And the *corporeity* of the soul, you think, is further proved experimentally, from our being *tired with contemplating,* as much as with *singing and dancing;* from the *reaction of our thoughts* or of our ideas *and words* mutually exciting each other; and from the *forgetfulness* of *children and old people* upon any *cause that discomposes the organ.*

To this I answer. The reason why the soul or principle of thinking, though itself *undivided,* yet thinks successively, divides, abstracts, combines or ampliates, retains or revives impressions in the memory, or partly or wholly forgets things, is because *the whole soul* thinks successively, divides, abstracts, combines or ampliates, retains or revives impressions in the memory, or party or wholly forgets things. And none of these phenomena can be explained by the various acts of the *various parts of a bodily organ* alone.

Our being *tired with contemplation,* the mutual *reaction of our ideas and words,* our *forgetfulness* that follows upon certain *defects* or *discomposures* of the brain, etc., do not prove that the *soul itself* is a *bodily organ,* but only that it *acts upon,* and is *acted upon by,* bodily organs, and is assisted by them as instruments in its operations. Experience shows us that the *sight* is bettered by good telescopes, and the *hearing* by instruments of conveying sounds, but not that those instruments therefore *hear* or *see;* that all *sensation* is bettered by good organs of sense, but not that the organs themselves are *sensible;* that *imagination* and *memory* depend on the brain, but not that the brain *imagines* or *remembers.* The organs of the senses are entirely distinct from one another, but the thing which perceives by those different organs is one and the same thing — one thinking being which every man calls *himself*. And this one thinking being has not some powers in some parts and other powers in other parts, some actions in some parts and other actions in other parts, but all its powers are the powers of the whole, and all its actions are the actions of the whole. The whole thinking substance sees both the whole object and every part of it. The same whole substance hears every sound, smells every odor, tastes every sapour, and feels everything that touches any part of the body. Every imagination, every volition, and every thought is the imagination, will, and thought, of that whole thinking substance which I call *myself*. And if this one substance (which we usually stile the *soul* or *mind*) has no parts that can *act* separately, it may as well be conceived to have none that can exist separately, and so to be absolutely indivisible.

I alleged that it is *absurd to annex consciousness to so flux a substance as the brain or spirits because, if such a substance could be the seat of that consciousness by which a man not only remembers things done many years since, but also is conscious that he himself, the same individual being, was the doer of them, it would follow that consciousness could be transferred from one subject to another — that is, that a quality could subsist without inhering in any subject at all — which all rational men allow to be impossible.* To this you reply that *in order to retain the consciousness of an action, it is necessary to revive the idea of it before any considerable flux of particles, and by reviving the idea of that action I imprint afresh the consciousness of having done that action — by which the brain has as lively an impression of consciousness (though it be not entirely composed of the same particles) as it had the day after it did the action, or as it has of a triangle or any other new idea not before imprinted on it. Consciousness of having done that action is an idea imprinted on the brain by recollecting or bringing into view our ideas before they are quite worn out — which idea continues in me not only the memory of the action itself, but that I did it. And if there is every now and then a recollection of a past action,* it may hereby be *conceived* that *a man may be conscious of things done by him, though he has not one particle of matter the same that he had at the doing of those things, without consciousness being transferred from one subject to another in any absurd sense of those words.* And again, *if* matter *can know at this instant that it thinks,* you can *see no reason why it may not remember tomorrow what it thinks of today, though some particles will be then wanting which it has at present. And if it can remember at all, then the memory of things may be continued even after we have lost all the particles of matter that we had at the doing them, by continual intermediate repeating or imprinting afresh our ideas before they are quite lost or worn out.* But the fallacy of this reply is very evident. For to affirm that *new matter* perpetually added to a fleeting system may, by repeated impressions add recollections of ideas, participate [in –ed.] and have communicated to it a *memory* of what was formerly done by the *whole system,* is not explaining or proving, but begging the question by assuming an *impossible* hypothesis. But supposing it were *possible* that the *memory* in general of such or such an action having been done might be preserved in the manner you suppose, yet it is a manifest contradiction that the *consciousness* of its being done by *me,* by *my own individual self* in particular, should continue in me after my whole substance is changed unless *consciousness* could be transferred from one subject to another in the absurdist sense of those words. For to suppose that one substance should be *conscious* of an action's having been done by itself, which really was not done by it but by another substance, is as plainly supposing an individual quality to be transferred from one subject to another, in the most absurd sense, as it is plain that *consciousness* is a *real individual quality,* and different from bare *general memory.*

If therefore you will answer (which is the only possible seeming evasion in this case) that that which we call *consciousness* is not a *fixed individual numerical quality* like the numerical figure or motion of a solid body, but a *fleeting transferable mode or power* like the roundness or the mode of motion of circles upon the face of a running stream, and that the *person* may still be the same by a continual superaddition of the *like consciousness,* notwithstanding the whole *substance* be changed: Then I say you make *individual personality* to be a mere *external imaginary denomination* and nothing at all in reality, just as a *ship* is called the *same ship* after the whole substance is changed by frequent repairs, or a *river* is called the *same river* though the water of it be every day new. The *name* of the ship is the same, but the *ship itself* is not at all the same, and the continued *name* of the river signifies water running in the same channel, but not at all the *same water.* So, if a man at forty years of age has nothing of the same substance in him, neither material nor immaterial, that he had at twenty, he may be called the *same person* by a mere *external imaginary denomination,* in such a sense as a *statue* may be called the *same statue* after its whole substance has been changed by piecemeal. But he cannot be *really and truly* the *same person* unless the *same individual numerical consciousness* can be transferred from one subject to another. For the continued addition or exciting of a *like consciousness* in the new acquired parts, after the manner you suppose, is nothing but a deception and delusion under the form of memory — a making the man to seem to himself to be conscious of having done that which really was not done by him, but by another. And such a consciousness in a man whose substance is wholly changed can no more make it just and equitable for such a man to be punished for an action done by another substance, than the addition of the like consciousness (by the power of God) to two or more new created men, or to any number of men now living, by giving a like modification to the motion of the spirits in the brain of each of them respectively, could make them all to be one and the same individual person, at the same time that they remain several and distinct persons, or make it just and reasonable for all and every one of them to be punished for one and the same individual action done by one only, or perhaps by none of them at all.

Mr. *Locke* himself, in the very place where he contends that *consciousness* makes the *same individual person,* notwithstanding that the *whole substance* be supposed to be changed, acknowledges expressly (Book II, ch. 27, sect. 13) that such a continuation of the *same consciousness* in a fleeting substance would be *a representing that to the mind to have been, which really never was, a representing to one intellectual substance as done by itself what it never did, and was perhaps done by some other agent — a representation without reality of matter of fact, as several representations in dreams are — a transferring by a fatal error from one to another, that consciousness which draws reward or punishment with it; a making two* [or two hundred] *thinking substances to be but one* [individual] *person;* and *leaves it to be considered how far this may be an argument against those who would place thinking in a system of fleeting animal spirits.*[1]

To say here that God's *justice and goodness* will not permit him to put any such inevitable deceit upon men, is nothing to the purpose. For, if it be but *naturally possible* for him to do that

1 It is remarkable that the phrase beginning "a making" to "person" is not to be found in any edition of Locke's text. Clarke is reading the Reduplication argument into Locke! –ed.

which, upon supposition of the truth of your notion, will be a *plain contradiction,* this is a certain demonstration that your notion is false. And I think it is a *contradiction plain enough* to say that God's impressing permanently upon a thousand men's minds, after the manner of the representation of a dream, the like consciousness with that which I find in my own mind, would make every one of them to be not persons *like* me, but the *same individual person* with myself. According to such reasoning as this, accidents need not have any necessary dependence on their substance, and the same individual substance may as well be conceived to exist in a thousand places at once under like accidents, as the same *individuating* accidents or qualities can inhere in a thousand different substances at once. By which same subtlety (as believing *too much* and *too little* have commonly the luck to meet together, like things moving two contrary ways in the same circle), all the absurdities in the doctrine of *transubstantiation* may easily be reconciled.

You *deny that we have any consciousness at all that we continue the same individual being at different times.* If so, it can be to no great purpose for us to dispute about anything. For, before you receive my reply, you may happen possibly to be entirely changed into another substance, and the next time you write may deny that you have any consciousness at all that you continue the same individual being who wrote this remarkable sentence. But to the assertion, I answer either consciousness proves a man to be the same individual being at different times, or else it is a mere deceit and delusion, and, by being added in like manner to other substances, might (as I said) make a hundred other men with equal justice liable to the same punishment with himself for any one individual action done by him. But of this, more when I come to speak of the usefulness and importance of the present argument to the ends and purposes of religion.

You affirmed, that *the matter of which an egg consists does entirely constitute the young one, and that the action of sensation began under a particular disposition of the parts by motion.* To this I answered that *so far is it from being true that the matter of the egg, by any particular disposition of its parts by motion, is formed into, or entirely constitutes, the young one, that (according to the best discoveries by microscopes and in anatomy) it does not constitute it at all, not* so *much as the body of it, but only serves it for nourishment and growth.* You reply, *if by* our eyes *we can perceive the organized body of the animal to be* part of the matter *of the egg, no microscopical observation can destroy such matter of fact,* and ... *make us see nothing where we do see something.* Now I am very sorry, sir, to find you in a serious and important question descend to so extremely mean and trifling a quibble. For, this is exactly the same thing as if you should say that *by your eyes* you can perceive an enclosed worm to be *part of the matter* of the nut it feeds on, or that *by your eyes* you can perceive a man to be *part of the matter* of the house he dwells in.

I called *gravitation* the *effect of the continued and regular operation of some other being on matter.* You replied that *it does not appear but that matter gravitates by virtue of powers originally placed in it by God, and is now left to itself to act by those original powers.* To this I answered that a *law or power — that is to say, a mere abstract name or complex notion, which is no real being — cannot impel a stone and cause it to begin to move.* You reply again that you *deny not the necessity of a being impelling another, in order to cause that mode of motion called gravitation,* that you suppose it to be caused by the *impulse of other bodies,* and *to speak your own opinion, it seems matter of fact to you that the external figure and internal configuration of the parts of matter are those powers in matter by which it receives that peculiar mode of motion called gravitation from the circumambient impelling bodies.* I did imagine, sir, when I expressed myself with such brevity in my first answer, you had been so well acquainted with natural philosophy as not to be ignorant that it has been demonstrated even mathematically that gravitation cannot arise from the *configuration and texture of the parts of matter,* and from the *circumambient impelling bodies.* Because if it did, it would not be proportionable to the quantity of matter, or the solid content of all bodies, without any regard to their superficial proportion — as we find by experience it is, seeing all bodies of all textures, and all configurations of parts, and all varieties of superficial proportion [a bullet, or a feather, or a piece of leaf-gold, or a sheet of paper] descend in *vacuo* with equal swiftness.[1] And if *material impulse* be not the cause of gravity, then some being that is *not material* (for *laws* or *powers* are nothing but mere empty words) must of necessity be allowed to be the cause of it. But it seems you are, notwithstanding the force even of demonstration itself, still of opinion that gravitation is *purely owing* to the

1 See the incomparable Sir Isaac Newton's *Principia* throughout; and the *Quæries* at the end of the Latin edition of his *Opticks.*

outward figure and inward configuration of the parts of matter, and the impulse of circumambient bodies. For *drop a pound of lead, in the form of a bullet, from the top of a tower, and it descends in a very quick space to the ground. Vary the external figure of the bullet by beating it broad with a hammer, and its tendency downward decreases. Vary the configuration of its parts by fire, and it will ascend instead of descending.* Certainly the reader cannot but be greatly surprised to meet with such philosophy as this in *our present age.* For what has all this to do with *gravitation?* Or with the cause of bodies *tending downwards?* Has a *pound* of lead in the form of a bullet a greater *tendency downward* than under any other form because the air making less resistance to it when in that form suffers it to fall more swiftly? Or when it is beaten out into a *thin plate,* which is still of a *pound weight,* does its *tendency downward decrease* because the air making greater resistance to it when under that new form its superficies is enlarged suffers it now to fall but slowly? You might by the same philosophy, and exactly with the same truth, affirm that a *hundred-pound-weight,* so long as you support it with your hands, has lost its *tendency downward* because it does not descend. But, I presume experience will easily convince you of the contrary. In like manner, when *lead,* being evaporated by fire, *ascends* in the air *instead of descending* because it is carried upward by the motion of the air which ascends being rarefied with heat, is therefore its *tendency downwards decreased?* You might exactly with the same reason have affirmed that a *pound of lead* in one *scale of a balance* loses its *tendency downwards* whenever a greater weight in the opposite scale forces it to *ascend instead of descending.* The truth is plainly this. As a pound of *wood,* during the time of its ascending from the bottom of a pail of water towards the top, is as much a pound-weight added to the weight of the whole water as a pound of *lead* is that lies still at the bottom. And consequently the *tendency* of the wood *downwards* is always the very same, whether it be *ascending* in water or *descending* in the air. So your *bullet,* whether it falls swiftly in the form of a *bullet,* or slowly in the form of a *thin plate,* or falls not at all while it is *supported in your hand,* or on the contrary ascends in the form of *fume* (in which case, *it* is in the air exactly what *wood* is in the water) still its *tendency downward* — that is, its gravitation — continues always the same, without any the least *decrease* or *increase* — which is the direct contradictory of your assertion. As *in vacuo* all bodies, of all figures, and all textures whatsoever, actually descend with equal swiftness, so in the open air, and everywhere else, their *tendency downwards* — that is, their gravitation — whether they ascend or descend, whether they fall swiftly or slowly, or not at all, continues always invariably the same, and cannot be *increased* or *decreased* by any change whatsoever of their *external figure,* or of the *internal configuration of their parts,* or of the *circumambient impelling bodies.* Gravitation therefore cannot possibly arise from the *external figure,* nor *internal configuration of the parts of matter,* nor from the *circumambient impelling bodies,* since by no alteration of any or all of these things, can the gravitation of any body be in the least *increased* or *diminished.* And consequently gravitation is quite another thing than you seem to have at all thought of when you *spoke your opinion* about what *seemed matter of fact to you,* and talked of the *decrease* of a bullet's *tendency downward* upon the variation of its figure.

[Whoever will explain *gravity,* which by experience is always proportionable to the *solid content* of bodies, must assign such a cause as can act upon bodies in proportion to their *solid content,* without any regard to their *superficial* proportion — that is to say, such a cause as can reach and penetrate to the very center of every solid particle of matter. Which I suppose you will hardly affirm your *circumambient bodies,* how subtle soever, are capable of doing.]

And not content to have erred so very grossly in the first foundation of all natural philosophy, you could not forebear professing further that you *have often admired that gravitation should be esteemed a matter of such difficulty among philosophers,* and that you think it to be so evident and necessary an effect of *matter in constant motion perpetually striking one part against another* that you wonder every body should not see it. I suppose the rest of the world will no less *admire* at *you* for imagining that by so slight an *admiration* you could at once set aside all the propositions in that most excellent book before-mentioned,[1] wherein it is made [to –ed.] appear by strictly mathematical demonstrations, drawn from the laws of motion now agreed on by mathematicians and established by experiments, and from the phenomena of the heavenly bodies, that the present operations of nature, depending

1 *Prinçipia Philosophiæ Mathematica.* [Newton's *The Mathematical Principles of Natural Philosophy* –ed.]

upon gravitation, cannot possibly be mechanical effects of *matter in constant motion perpetually striking one part against another.*

Not much unlike to this, was Mr. *Hobbes'* fancying that he had confuted all the propositions in *Euclid* by *admiring* at *Euclid*'s definitions of lines and surfaces. And all men ever since, that understand the first elements of geometry, have *admired* at *him* for fancying so.

But that which follows is still the most wonderful of all. You say *whether* you *take Mr.* Clarke *right or no, the incomparable Sir* Isaac Newton (in the Preface of his *Principia*) *is of opinion "that several phenomena of nature may depend on certain* forces *or* powers *whereby from causes yet undiscovered the particles of bodies are mutually impelled against each other, ... or recede and are driven from one another — which* forces *or* powers *being yet unknown, the philosophers hitherto have attempted nature in vain."* Now, to insinuate to your reader by such a citation that this great man is of your opinion in the present question — when, on the contrary, the very sentence you cite, was spoken by him (as appears from the words immediately preceding those you have cited) not concerning *gravitation,* but concerning other more particular phenomena of nature, in *express contradistinction* to those of *gravitation;* and when in that whole book, from one end to the other, he is professedly confuting and showing the absolute impossibility of your notion of gravitation; and when he has elsewhere in express words declared that by the terms *forces* and *powers* he does not mean (as you did by *powers originally placed in matter by God*) to signify the *efficient cause* of certain determinate motions of matter, but only to express the *action* itself by which the effect is regularly produced, without determining the immediate *agent* or *cause* of that action[1] — after all this, I say, to insinuate to your reader, by the citation of a piece of a single sentence, that that great man is of your opinion is (to use your own expressions once more) such a *conduct* as the world may justly *demand a reason of* from yourself, for *I cannot assign a good one for you.*

Lastly, as you declare it to be your opinion that gravitation is caused by *material impulse,* so you think it impossible that it should be owing to any *immaterial cause.* And you believe it to be *as intelligible that matter might act without impulse by* powers

1 *Optic,* pag. 323.

placed in it by God, as that an immaterial being *should move* matter *without being able to impel it by contact.*

This belief of yours is founded wholly upon the supposition that there is nothing in the world but *tangible* substance — which opinion you give no reason for, and therefore it is a *mere prejudice.* But further, I presume you will hardly deny but *God* himself is an *immaterial being,* and that *he* can move matter though he does not *impel it by contact.* Other *immaterial beings* therefore, though they do not *impel matter by contact,* yet it does not from thence follow that they cannot move it at all because; from *God's* moving it, it is manifest that there are other ways of moving it besides that of *impelling by contact.* But *powers* or *laws* are not real beings. They are nothing but mere words or notions, and can neither act in any sense, nor move matter either with contact or without it. I conceive an ordinary reader may be able to discern the difference between affirming that an *immaterial substance* — a real being, though not hard and solid — may move matter, and affirming that a *law* or *power* — a mere word or term of art, which is really nothing, and has not truly any being or existence, save only in the imagination — can cause matter to move.

Upon the whole, all that you have advanced in these sections about *gravitation* is such marvelous reasoning to be made use of in the present age, after so many great discoveries founded upon experience, and even mathematical demonstration, that though I have no cause at all to be displeased with you for arguing in such a manner, yet I believe your readers cannot but think you might very well have forborne going out of your way to give so very disadvantageous a representation of your own philosophy.

I have been the longer upon this head because the true theory of *gravitation,* as it has been made out by that excellent person whom you just now so unfortunately cited, does in its obvious and necessary consequences more entirely subvert the very foundations of all possible hypotheses wherewith *materialists* would undertake to explain the phenomena of nature *mechanically* — by the mere powers of matter and motion — than any discovery in natural and experimental philosophy that has ever yet been made in any age. Showing the *matter* of the universe to take up almost an infinitely small and inconsiderable part of that space, which you suppose to be filled with it, bearing in truth far less proportion to it than a tennis ball does to the body of the earth; and consequently, that the great phenomena of nature cannot possibly depend upon any *mechanical* powers of matter and motion, but must be produced by the force and action of some higher principle;[1] and so leading us, even with mathematical certainty, to *immaterial powers,* and finally to the author of all power, the *great creator and governor of the world.*

I affirmed that *there are many demonstrations, even in abstract mathematics themselves, which no man who understands them can in the least doubt of the certainty of, which yet are attended with difficult consequences that cannot be perfectly cleared.* As, for instance, those concerning *the infinite divisibility of quantity and the eternity and immensity of God.* In answer to this you say that *if* there are any such demonstrations, from whence any *contradictions or absurdities* follow in our way of conceiving things, etc. And again: *absurdity, contradictions* &. And again: *absurdities, contradictions* or *disagreement of ideas* &. And again, you *require* me *to prove* that any *absurdity or contradiction* follows either from the infinite divisibility of matter, or from the eternity or immensity of God, in our way of conceiving — and if I cannot, I have no ground, *you say,* from those instances to put human nature in such a state of *skepticism and absurdity.* Now, *by all the rules of answering* (to use your own expression), you ought not to have changed my words *difficult consequences that cannot be perfectly cleared* into *absurdity, contradictions, and disagreements of ideas,* because *absurdities, contradictions, and disagreements of ideas* are things just as different from *difficult consequences* of demonstrated truths *which cannot be perfectly cleared* as *light* is from *darkness. Absurdities, contradictions, and disagreements of ideas* are things *already perfectly cleared* — that is, things proved with *perfect clearness* to be false and impossible — but *difficulties* that *cannot be perfectly cleared* may attend things either *possibly* or *certainly* true. *Absurdities, contradictions, and disagreements of ideas* do with as *perfect clearness* prove a thing to be *false* as a *positive demonstration* proves a thing to be *true.* And therefore it is absolutely impossible that they can both be applied to the same thing — even just as impossible as that the same thing should at the same time be both *true* and *false.* But *difficult consequences that cannot perfectly be cleared* may be, and very often are, found to attend things which are demonstrated to be true. The reason is because *difficulties that cannot perfectly be cleared* do

1 See Sir Isaac Newton's *Optics,* pages 314 & 346, Lat. Edit. [That is, Clarke's Latin translation of the *Optics* –ed.]

not (like *absurdities and contradictions*) arise from a *perception of the disagreement of ideas,* but barely from the *defect* or *imperfectness of the ideas themselves.* Our *reason* is able to *apprehend* clearly the demonstration of the certainty of the existence of some things, where the *imagination* is not able to *comprehend* the ideas of the things themselves. This is plainly the case of the *infinite divisibility of quantity,* of *infinity and eternity* in general, of the *actions of immaterial substances upon matter,* and of many other things. Here therefore I have just cause (if I may use your own expression once again) to *demand a reason of your conduct,* and to complain that you have greatly departed from that fairness for which your former papers were justly commended.

And you can still the more hardly be excused in this matter, because you knew I had before expressed myself very particularly and fully concerning the same thing, in a book which you yourself cite upon another occasion, in the very next page to that wherein you accuse me wrongfully. My words were these (*Demonstration of the Being and Attributes of God,* p. 11) [Clarke, 1998, pp. 8-9 –ed.] "Since in all questions concerning the nature and perfections of God, or concerning anything to which the idea of eternity or infinity is joined, though we can indeed demonstrate certain propositions to be true, yet it is impossible for us to comprehend or frame any adequate or complete ideas of the manner how the things so demonstrated can be. Therefore, when once any proposition is clearly demonstrated to be true, it ought not to disturb us that there be perhaps perplexing objections on the other side which, for want of adequate ideas of the manner of the existence of the things demonstrated, are not easy to be answered. Indeed, were it possible there should be any proposition which could equally be *demonstrated* on both sides of the question, or which could on both sides be *reduced to imply a contradiction* [*as some have too inconsiderately* asserted], this it must be confessed would alter the case. Upon this absurd supposition, all difference of true and false, all thinking and reasoning, and the use of all our faculties, would be entirely at an end. But when to demonstration on the one side there are opposed, on the other, only objections raised from our want of having adequate ideas of the things themselves, this ought not to be esteemed a real difficulty. It is positively and clearly demonstrable that something has been from *eternity.* All the objections therefore raised against the *eternity* of anything, grounded merely on our want of having an adequate idea of *eternity,* ought to be looked upon as of no real solidity. Thus in other the like instances, it is demonstrable, for example, that something must be actually *infinite.* All the metaphysical difficulties therefore which arise usually from applying the measures and relations of things finite to what is infinite, and from supposing *finites* to be [aliquot (some, several –ed.)] parts of *infinity*[1] — when indeed they are not properly so, but only as mathematical points to quantity which have no proportion at all [and from imagining all *infinites* to be *equal,* when in things disparate they manifestly are not so; an *infinite* line being not only *not equal to,* but *infinitely less* than, an *infinite surface;* and an *infinite surface* than *space infinite in all dimensions*] — ought to be esteemed vain and of no force. Again, it is in like manner demonstrable that quantity is infinitely divisible. All the objections therefore raised [by supposing the *sums total of all infinites* to be *equal,* when in disparate parts they manifestly are not so, and] by comparing the imaginary *equality or inequality of the number* of the parts of unequal quantities — whose parts have really *no number at all,* they all having parts *without number* — ought to be looked upon as weak and altogether inconclusive, etc."

Concerning the *questions* whether immaterial substances be extended or not, *and* whether, upon supposition of their being extended, they may not nevertheless be of such a nature as not to consist of parts which (like the parts of matter) are themselves every one of them complete distinct beings separable and wholly independent of each other — *also,* whether from the immateriality of the souls of brutes, it follows that they must of necessity be put into an eternal state of rewards and punishments — concerning these questions, I say, I have nothing further to add, but only that I think all you have advanced upon these heads in your *Reflections* has been already clearly obviated in my former papers, to which therefore I refer the reader, who, I fear, is already too much tired with repetitions.

In the last place, you challenge me to show that my argument is *of any use to the ends and purpose of religion.* That it is of the *greatest use* will I suppose easily be granted, if it be evident that the notion I am arguing against is utterly destructive of religion.

1 "y" replacing "e" –ed.

And in what respects it is so, I shall give you an instance or two to consider of, and so conclude.

1st then, if the *mind* of man were nothing but a certain *system of matter,* and *thinking* nothing but a certain *mode of motion* in that system, it would follow that, since every *determination* of motion depends *necessarily* upon the *impulse* that causes it, therefore every *thought* in a man's mind must likewise be *necessary* and depending wholly upon external causes, and there could be no such thing in us as *liberty* or a power of *self-determination.*[1] Now what *ends and purposes of religion* mere clocks and watches are capable of serving needs no long and nice consideration.

2dly, if *thinking* in a *man* be nothing but a *mode of motion,* or *of any other quality of matter,* it will be but too natural a consequence to conceive that it may be only the same thing in all *other rational beings* likewise, and even in God himself. And what a notion of *God* this would give us is not difficult to imagine. A friend of yours has given us a very broad hint, whither this tends, when he tells us that *the greatest freedom or liberty we can conceive to belong to* ANY BEING is such as he there largely explains to be no liberty at all, but absolute necessity, such as the motion of a watch or clock is determined by.[2]

3dly, if the *soul* be nothing but a *system of matter,* and *thinking* nothing but a *mode of motion,* or *of some other power of matter,* the doctrine of the *resurrection* (as I before observed) will be inconceivable and incredible, and the justice of future rewards and punishments impossible to be made out. The notion of the soul's *immateriality* evidently facilitates the belief of a *resurrection* and of a future retribution by securing a principle of *personal individuality,* upon which the justice of all reward or punishment is entirely grounded. But if *thinking* be in reality nothing but a *power* or *mode* which, inhering in a loose and fleeting system of matter, perishes utterly at the dissolution of the body, then the restoring the power of *thinking* to the same body *at the resurrection* will not be a raising again of the *same individual person,*

---

1 See above, p. 173.

2 *Essay concerning the Use of Reason in Propositions, the Evidence Whereof Depends Upon Human Testimony,* pag. 47. [The "friend" Clarke is referring to is Anthony Collins himself! He had published this book anonymously in 1707 and Clarke had discovered that Collins was its author. Clarke is making the point that, in Collins' view, God has no free will. –ed.]

but it will be as truly a *creation* of a *new person* as the addition of the like power of *thinking* to a new body *now* would be the *creation* of a *new man*. For as God's superadding *now* to a new parcel of matter the like *consciousness* with what I at this time find in myself would not make that new parcel of matter to be the *same individual person with me*, but only *another person like me*, so his superadding that *consciousness* at the *resurrection* to the same particles of dust of which my body was formerly composed will not be a *restoration* of the *same person*, but a creation of a *new one* like me. For the sameness of the senseless particles of dust, it is evident from the flux nature of the substance of our bodies, is not that which *now* makes me to be the same person, and therefore cannot be that which will *then* make me to be so. If my present *consciousness* be nothing but a *mode of motion* in the fleeting particles of my brain or spirits, this *consciousness* will be as utterly destroyed at the dissolution of my body as if the very substance of my body were[1] annihilated. And it would be just as possible for the *same individual person* to be *created again* after an *absolute annihilation*, as to be *restored again* after such a *dissolution*. But now, if the *same person* after *annihilation* could, by restoring of the same *consciousness*, be created again, he might as possibly be created again by addition of the same *consciousness* to new matter, even before annihilation of the first. From whence it would follow that two, or two hundred, several persons might all, by a superaddition of the like *consciousness*, be *one and the same individual person*, at the same time that they remain *several and distinct persons* — it being as easy for God to add *my consciousness* to the new formed matter of one or of one hundred bodies at this *present time*, as to the dust of my present body at the *time of the* resurrection. And no reason can be given why it would not be as just at any time to punish for my faults a new created man, to whom *my consciousness* is by the power of God superadded, as to punish that person who at the *resurrection* shall by the same power be new made out of the dust of my body with the same *consciousness* superadded — it being allowed that *then*, as well as *now*, it is not the sameness of the particles of dust that makes the *same person*. But if it was, yet that would make no difference in this matter. For the particles of dust which, in the course of twenty years, have successively been part of the substance of my body are

1 Replacing "was" –ed.

enough in quantity to form several bodies, and if the addition of a like consciousness with what I now find in myself to one of those bodies at the resurrection will make *it* to be the same *individual person* with *me,* the addition of the like consciousness to twenty of them would consequently make every one of them to be (not persons *like* me, but) the same *individual person* with *me,* and with *each other likewise.* Which is the greatest absurdity in the world — an absurdity equal (as I before said) to that of *transubstantiation.* This inexplicable confusion, wherewith your doctrine perplexes the notion of *personal identity* upon which identity the justice of all reward or punishment manifestly depends, makes the *resurrection,* in your way of arguing, to be inconceivable and impossible. And consequently your doctrine (which supposes the body to be the whole man) is destructive of religion, leaving no room for reward or punishment but in the present life only, and consequently giving men liberty to do everything for their present pleasure or advantage that can be done with a good color, and without being obnoxious to human laws — which is the greatest mischief that can possibly befall mankind. But if the soul be, as we believe, a *permanent indivisible immaterial substance,* then all these difficulties vanish of themselves.

It is here to be observed that all the absurd consequences which I have now (in considering of what use my argument is to *religion*) shown to follow from your doctrine with respect to the *resurrection,* do equally follow from it (as has been before proved) even *without respect to the resurrection.* For as it is absurd to suppose (which you must do in your scheme) that at *the resurrection* the *same individual person* can be restored merely by the addition of a *like* consciousness with that which utterly perishes at the dissolution of the body to the dust of the same body when recollected again — as this, I say, is plainly absurd — because in the same manner twenty other men formed out of the same dust (of which there is quantity enough belonging to every person that has lived any number of years) may also by an addition of the like consciousness become every one of them *that one same individual person,* at the same time that they remain so many several and distinct persons — so, without regard to any future resurrection, there is the very same absurdity in supposing (as you do) that a man *at this present time,* though he has none of the same substance belonging to him, may yet, merely by a like modification of the motion of his spirits, continue to be *the same individual person he was* twenty years since. There is, I say, the very same absurdity in this supposition as in the former, because there is no difference between supposing that any number of new bodies at the resurrection *coexistently,* or any number of different men now living *contemporarily,* or any number of different bodies *succeeding* one another in one continued form by a perpetual uninterrupted flux of particles (which is the thing you contend for) can be *one and the same individual person* merely by a *like* modification of the figures and motions of their parts respectively, without having anything at all *the same* in them.

To the *propositions* I laid down at the conclusion of my former reply, you have objected nothing but what (I think) is already clearly answered in the foregoing pages.

Anthony Collins

An Answer to Mr. Clarke's Third Defense of his Letter to Mr. Dodwell

——Neque decipitur ratio neque decipit unquam.
Manilius.

[——For neither does our system deceive or is ever deceived.
Manilius, *Astronomia,* G.P. Goold trans.]

When I consider that the question between Mr. *Clarke* and me is concerning the force of an *Argument Made Use of in* his *Letter* to *Mr.* Dodwell to *Prove the Immateriality and Natural Immortality of the Soul;* and that, out of four objections insisted on in my *Reflections* against that argument, he has dropped the consideration of *three;* and in answer to the fourth is so far from showing *that if consciousness did inhere in a system of matter, it must consist of the consciousnesses of the parts* (which was the absurdity that, by his argument, he labored to fix on those who judged it possible for consciousness to inhere in a system of matter), that, on the contrary, he has only endeavored to prove, against my parallel instance of roundness, that it must consist of several pieces of roundness, or tendencies towards roundness; and consequently can only infer, *that if consciousness did, in like manner with Roundness, inhere in a system of matter, it must consist of several tendencies towards consciousness* — I freely acknowledge that I cannot tell how to justify myself to any reader (except Mr. *Clarke* himself) in not appealing to him, or in presuming that he had any need of my assistance to find out Mr. *Clarke*'s apparent desertion of his argument. But some incidental points to that in hand, of great importance to be cleared, having crept into our dispute, I hope the further continuance of this debate will not be unacceptable to lovers of truth, and that upon account they will pardon a review of the controversy between us.

There are few disputes of any consequence but the *rule* by which they ought to be determined is both appealed to, and called in question. When reason is on our side, we cheerfully submit to its dictates, and expect that others should do so too. But when we are not able to answer difficulties alleged against our *schemes,* then we contend that reason is weak, and from its supposed weakness infer that our inability to clear up difficulties and answer objections ought not to hinder our assent to *them.*

Mr. *Clarke* has thought fit to pursue this method of proceeding with me, and therefore I cannot but esteem it a necessary preliminary to this debate to examine what he says on this head, and thereby endeavor to fix a standard or measure by which all that we say must be tried. For to what purpose is disputing and reasoning about the truth and falsehood or propositions, when by any doubt or scruple concerning the measure whereby we judge of truth and falsehood, truth and falsehood either become names without any signification at all, or else signify different things in different men's minds?

It is demonstrable, according to Mr. *Clarke,* that matter is incapable of thinking because it is divisible by *the power of God.*[1] From whence he concludes that thinking must reside in an immaterial being, in the Idea whereof Extension is contained — which is in effect to say that thinking can and cannot reside in a divisible being. For what other argument can be made use of to prove all matter divisible by the power of God but what is drawn from the consideration of its extension? And if matter as an extended being is divisible, all extended beings must be divisible, and consequently must be incapable of thinking, unless Mr. *Clarke* will say that a divisible being is both capable and incapable of thinking.

To clear his argument from this manifest contradiction, he has recourse to the following distinction (by which a man may be enabled to believe everything, and reason about nothing), that it is absurd to suppose matter indivisible by the power of God, but to suppose an extended unsolid substance indivisible by the power of God is only a *difficult consequence that cannot be perfectly cleared.*[2] And to make this distinction intelligible, he urges *that difficult consequences that cannot be perfectly cleared do not (like absurdities and contradictions) arise from the perceptions of the disagreement of ideas, but barely from the defect and imperfectness of*

1 1st Defense. [p. 60 –ed.]

2 2nd Defense. [p. 59 –ed.]

the ideas themselves,[1] which is as much as to say, that difficulties which cannot be perfectly cleared do not arise from the perception of the disagreement of ideas, but from the perception of the disagreement of ideas. For what is a difficulty which cannot be *cleared* (or *perfectly cleared,* for I know no difference) by reason of *defective ideas* but a difficulty which arises from the perception of the disagreement of those ideas? If he means that there is a difference between a difficulty which arises from the perception of the disagreement of perfect or adequate ideas, and a difficulty that arises from the perception of disagreement of imperfect or inadequate ideas, I answer that there is no manner of ground for such a distinction — or, if there was any ground for that *distinction,* it is not to his purpose, as will evidently appear if we do but consider what we mean by adequate and inadequate ideas.

By an adequate or perfect idea I understand an idea which *perfectly represents the archetype the mind supposes it taken from* — as, for instance, *all complex ideas of modes,* such as fear, courage, etc., *which being voluntary collections of simple ideas that the Mind puts together, without reference to any real archetypes existing anywhere, are adequate ideas because they, not being intended for copies of things really existing but for archetypes made by the mind, cannot but represent themselves.*[2]

By an inadequate idea I understand an idea which does not perfectly represent that archetype the mind supposes it taken from — as, for instance, if I put into my idea of gold only its *color* and *weight,* it is evident they represent not the archetype my idea is taken from, but only imperfectly or inadequately. And thus, for ought we know to the contrary, all the ideas we have that we refer to real existences may be inadequate, for we can never be certain that we contain in our idea all the whole plenitude of essence, properties, and affections, that reside in any being whatever.

What I have said, if I mistake not, comprehends the entire sense of the distinction of adequate and inadequate ideas. I know Mr. *Locke* accounts simple Ideas adequate, but I cannot see on what ground but what destroys the distinction of adequate and inadequate ideas, and does in reality make all ideas adequate. For if, as he says, simple ideas are adequate *because, being nothing but the effects of certain powers in things ordained by God to produce*

1 3d Defense. [pp. 189-90 –ed.]

2 Mr. Locke's *Essay of Human Understanding.* B. 2, ch. 31.

such sensation in us, they cannot but be correspondent and adequate to those powers, then every idea whatever may be adequate in that sense that is formed with care. For we ought not to use a word to signify any idea whatever, but so far as the idea goes it ought to correspond to the archetype it is referred to. As, for instance, if I should put into my idea of man *solid substance, life, sense, spontaneous motion, and a faculty of reasoning,* it is plain all this agrees to man, how inadequate so ever a representation it is of him, and is as much correspondent and adequate to the subject it is taken from as any simple idea is to the power that occasions it. For simple ideas, by means of organs of different perfection, cannot be precisely alike in different men, and consequently must in many men, if not in all, be imperfect and inadequate, if considered with relation to the whole power that occasions them, though they are adequate and correspondent to a power in nature, so far as they go and were designed to be. Now, if all ideas, as referred to things existing, are really imperfect and inadequate, and if with relation to things existing there is no other test of truth but the perception of the agreement or disagreement of ideas, then, if Mr. *Clarke* denies not all knowledge that relates to things existing, he cannot distinguish between difficulties that arise from the perception of the disagreement of inadequate ideas, and difficulties that arise from the perception of the disagreement of adequate ideas. And if he allows that difficulties which arise from the perception of the disagreement of inadequate ideas are absurdities and contradictions, he gives up his distinction. So that he must either destroy all knowledge or science relating to things existing, or else own that there is no difference between difficulties that arise from the perception of the disagreement of adequate ideas, and difficulties that arise from the perception of the disagreement of inadequate ideas.

2. But to vindicate human knowledge, and show further the groundlessness of Mr. *Clarke*'s distinction, I observe that though we can never be sure that we have adequate ideas of anything that exists, yet we have as much reason to think that our inadequate ideas agree to the reality of things, as adequate ideas do to the archetypes they are referred to — and consequently have no reason but to conclude that inadequate ideas can be as well compared together, and as right judgment formed from their comparison, as from the comparison of adequate ideas. For suppose I see something in a mist near the size and shape of an

ordinary man which, though I see not distinctly enough to know whether it be a statue or a man, yet I may certainly know it not to be a *steeple* by perceiving the disagreement between the idea of a *steeple* and the figure I see — as I know a moral or abstract mathematical proposition to be false by perceiving the disagreement of the ideas of which it is made up. Wherefore, since we can as well know, or be certain, by the perception of the agreement or disagreement of inadequate ideas as of adequate ideas, the difficulties that arise from the perception of the disagreement of both adequate and inadequate ideas must be equally contradictions, and consequently there is no ground for Mr. *Clarke*'s distinction.

3. Was not a difficulty that arises from the perception of the disagreement of inadequate ideas as much an absurdity as a difficulty that arises from the perception of the disagreement of adequate ideas, we could not discourse at all with certainty of the principal objects of religion — *God and his attributes.* The ideas we fix to the terms *God and his attributes* are no doubt inadequate ideas, if any of our ideas are inadequate and yet in religious discourses we argue from the justice, veracity, goodness, holiness and wisdom of God, and say that such and such things must be because they follow from the supposition of those attributes, and that such and such things cannot be because they are inconsistent with them — that is, such and such things agree or disagree to our ideas of the justice, veracity, holiness, goodness and wisdom of God. As, for instance, we say it is inconsistent with his justice to punish eternally a man who obeys his laws, and to reward a man who disobeys them, and, on the other side, that it is agreeable to his justice to reward a man that obeys his laws, and to punish a man that disobeys them. Mr. *Clarke* himself argues that moral and immoral actions *must be attended with rewards and punishments, because the same reasons that prove God himself to be necessarily just and good, and the rules of justice, equity, and goodness, to be his unalterable will, law, and command to all created beings, prove also that he cannot but be pleased with and approve such creatures as imitate and obey him by observing those rules, and be displeased with such as act contrary thereto, and consequently cannot but some way or other make a suitable difference in his dealings with them.* But *since the condition of men in this present state* is *such that the natural order of things in this world is in event manifestly perverted, and virtue and goodness are visibly prevented in great measure from obtaining their*

proper and due effects, in establishing men's happiness proportionable to their behavior and practice. — Therefore, *it is certain that there must be a future state of existence* for men *as that, by an exact distribution of rewards and punishments therein, all the present disorders and inequalities will be set right, and the whole scheme of providence which, to us who judge of it by only one small portion of it, seems now* so *inexplicable and confused.*[1]

Now on what is this argument founded but on Mr. *Clarke*'s inadequate idea of the justice of God? And wherein does its strength lie (if it has any) but in his perception of the disagreement of the visible disorders and inequalities in this world with his inadequate idea of the justice of God, without the necessary supposition of a future state to set right those disorders and inequalities? Wherefore, since Mr. *Clarke* thinks he argues with *certainty* for a future state, and since he argues only from a defective or inadequate idea, and since there can be no arguing in the case but from the agreement or disagreement of such ideas as we have, it follows that Mr. *Clarke* must allow that certainty can be attained as well where our ideas are inadequate or imperfect, as where they are adequate or perfect. That is, the perception of the agreement or disagreement of such ideas as we have, whether perfect or imperfect, adequate or inadequate, is the true and only criterion of truth — unless Mr. *Clarke* will deny the force of his own argument for a future state, or say that we have an adequate idea of the attributes of God.

4. But supposing there was a just ground to distinguish between our knowledge that relates to things existing, and our knowledge that relates to ideas of the mind which have no archetypes beyond their own existence — so that in one case there is not the same degree of certainty as in the other — yet Mr. *Clarke* has no reason here to oppose them to one another, because his argument for the immateriality of the soul is, and can be, only founded on the sole comparison of the inadequate ideas of matter, spirit, and thinking. And therefore an objection or difficulty founded on the disagreement of those imperfect or inadequate ideas is as much a demonstration of the falsehood of a proposition that involves such a difficulty, as the agreement of inadequate ideas is a demonstration of the truth of a proposition

1 [Clarke's Boyle –ed.] Lectures, [in *Works*, II. *A Discourse*, pp. 641-42 –ed.]

made up of such ideas. And consequently, whether there is or is not any just ground for Mr. *Clarke*'s distinction, it serves not his purpose in the least.

5. But perhaps the reader may, from the writings of the papists for transubstantiation, and from the writings of some Protestants against the *Socinian heresy,* ask whether there are not in some questions demonstrations on both sides, and consequently that the perception of the agreement or disagreement of ideas is not the criterion or test of truth. In answer to which I freely declare it to be my opinion that whatever can be demonstrated can be *perfectly cleared* from all objections and difficulties, and that any person that understands a demonstration, and the objections made against it, is capable of solving them, and that all the difficulties that may be urged against the *immensity and eternity of God, which* Mr. *Clarke* says *cannot be clearly answered,* are to be clearly answered.[1] And, in order to answer them clearly, I would only require these equitable conditions of him — that he would define the terms *immensity, eternity, immaterial being,* etc., and show that his definitions agree to the things existing that they refer to.

He proceeds: *Our reason,* says he, *is able to apprehend clearly the demonstration of the certainty of some things, where the imagination is not able to comprehend the ideas of the things themselves.*[2] That is, if I understand him right, we can apprehend clearly, suppose, that an immaterial being exists, or that something exists correspondent to the idea we fix to the terms *immaterial being,* without being able to comprehend entirely all that exists in the being our idea refers to. And what then? How does it follow from hence that there is any difference between difficulties that arise from the perception of the disagreement of adequate ideas, and difficulties that arise from the perception of the disagreement of inadequate ideas? Cannot I, though I know but in part the archetype to which my idea of immaterial being refers, have a just idea of immaterial being as far as my idea goes? And if it be so, why should I not be able to answer all objections against the existence of that which I clearly apprehend does exist? Nay, what other method can there be taken in the use of such words as *immaterial being, infinity, immensity,* etc., but to make them stand

---

1 2d Defense. [pp. 106-07 –ed.]

2 3d Defense. [p. 190 –ed.]

for intelligible and consistent ideas, which have a conformity to things that really exist? And why intelligible and consistent ideas should not be capable of being cleared from all difficulty I shall then be able to conceive when I can see no difference between *intelligible* and *unintelligible, consistent* and *inconsistent.*

By what has been said, the intelligent reader may be satisfied that when I understood *difficulties that cannot be perfectly cleared* to signify *contradictions and absurdities,* I *did not depart from that fairness for which* Mr. *Clarke* says my former papers were justly commended.[1] *And I am not without some hopes that Mr. Clarke* may contradict himself once more in my favor, since in his *Third Defense* he is pleased to contradict what he said in his *Second Defense* — for he there accused me of *unfairness* and now acquits me of it.[2]

I proceed now to the question concerning the possibility of matter's being conscious and, as I have shown that finite extension in an immaterial being implies divisibility as well as in a material being,[3] and which consequently, according to Mr. *Clarke,* must be a subject equally incapable of thinking with material being, so I shall endeavor to reconcile Mr. *Clarke* to himself by showing that his argument drawn from the divisibility (or, which is all one, the extension) of matter is inconclusive. His argument is as follows, *that all the qualities or powers which either are in matter, whether they be known or unknown, or are vulgarly ascribed to it, must of necessity be either:*[4]

1. *Real qualities truly and properly inhering in the subject to which they are ascribed, such as magnitude and motion in matter. These,* says he, *are always the sums or aggregates of powers of the same kind inhering distinctly in the several parts of the material subject. And could consciousness in like manner be a quality really inherent in a system of matter, it must likewise be the sum and result of the consciousnesses of the several parts. And so there would be as many distinct consciousnesses as there are particles of matter of which the system consists.*

Or, 2. *Qualities not really inhering in the subject to which they are usually ascribed, but being indeed modes excited and residing in*

1 3d Defense. [p. 190 –ed.]
2 2d Defense. [p. 103. –ed.]
3 Reflections. [pp. 136-37 –ed.]
4 3d Defense. [p. 152 –ed.]

some other subject — such as are colors, sounds, and all those which are commonly called sensible qualities of matter. These do not exist at all in that subject to which they are usually ascribed, but in some other subject. And this also not being applicable to thinking, it is manifest therefore that thinking cannot be a power or quality of this kind in a material subject.

Or, 3. *Such qualities as magnetism, electricity, attraction, reflexibility, refrangibility, and the like. These have no real existence by way of proper inhering in any subject, which likewise since it cannot be said of consciousness, it is manifest that consciousness cannot be a power or quality in a material system of this kind either.*

In answer to which argument, the substance of one objection that I urged was that his enumeration was imperfect because he omitted the consideration of the modes of those kinds of powers mentioned in the first branch of his division, and that consciousness being, according to me, a mode of one of those kinds of powers, it is impossible his argument should conclude against consciousness' inhering in a system of matter when that quality that agrees with consciousness is not named in his enumeration. As, for instance, consciousness being with me a power or quality in matter answering to a mode of motion or figure — such as the peculiar motion of a clock, or roundness — the consideration of consciousness as such a quality or power shows that his argument is perfectly foreign to the question. For if consciousness be considered like roundness or any mode of figure, or like a mode of motion in an animal or clock, it is manifest, 1*st,* that it has a real and proper inherence, and is not an effect residing in no substance at all, and consequently answers not to *magnetism, electricity,* etc. 2*dly,* that it has a real inherence in the subject of which it is said to be a quality, and consequently answers not to color and sound, which exist not in the substance to which they are ascribed. And, 3*dly,* that as it inheres truly and properly in matter, so it is not of the same extent, nor does it answer to figure, magnitude, and motion. For roundness inheres in a system of matter without being the sum of the roundnesses of the parts. And the like may be said of the peculiar and individual modes of motion in a clock, or an animal — that they inhere not distinctly in each of the distinct parts. I did not take upon me to determine of what kind of power thinking or consciousness was a mode, but for greater clearness in arguing I did take the liberty to speak of it as a mode of motion.

Now, if it be considered as a mode of motion — that is, if it consists of ten thousand distinct motions — it is as impossible that whole consciousness should exist in each of the distinct parts of a system of matter, as that whole roundness should exist in each part of a circle, or that the individual motion of an animal or clock should exist in each of their distinct parts. Wherefore it is evident that the strength of his argument lies in considering consciousness as standing for an idea inconsistent with its being a power of matter that follows *from the division or composition* of matter, as he proposed to consider it in his *Letter to Mr.* Dodwell. *And* therefore his demonstration was granted by me as not affecting the question he proposed to prove, since it related solely to a chimera or idea that he was pleased to suppose, without any ground, I was obliged to rank consciousness under.[1]

Mr. *Clarke,* to show that his argument is conclusive against the possibility of matter's thinking, lays down this proposition as what he proposes to *explain* and *vindicate:* that *it is absolutely impossible, and an evident contradiction, that any real quality should truly and properly inhere in a system of matter without being the sum or aggregate of a number of powers and qualities residing distinctly in the several parts of the system, and being always of the same kind with the whole that results from them.*[2]

In answer to this, I humbly conceive that Mr. *Clarke* ought to have laid down a conclusion clearly contradictory to me, and not have expressed himself in such a manner that I can agree to what he says consistently with maintaining the force of my objection. As, for instance, I do allow that no quality can reside in a system of matter, but what *must be always* in a certain sense *of the same kind with the whole that results from the parts.* For when roundness or any other individual figure inheres in a system of matter, the parts must be so far *of the same kind* as to have a tendency to that individual figure of which they are a part. And in that sense I have always allowed consciousness to consist of *powers of the same kind.*[3] For if consciousness inheres in a system of matter, it must necessarily be allowed that the

1 *If the reader could doubt of my meaning in my* Reflections, *he may consider what I say as the explication of it, and then he will see that what Mr.* Clarke *advances needs no particular answer.* [pp. 148-49 –ed.]

2 3d Defense. [p. 154 –ed.]

3 Collins' Letter to Mr. Dodwell — perhaps p. 49; Collins does not explicitly start talking about "powers of the same kind" until his Reply. –ed.

distinct beings in that system contribute towards thinking — as the pieces of a circle do towards a circle, or as all the parts of a system of matter contribute towards the system — unless a man will say that consciousness inheres in a divisible substance, and does not inhere in it at the same time. Wherefore his proposition to be vindicated is obscure. And I desire the reader to observe that no proposition can be truly contradictory to what I affirm, unless it affirms that every quality that inheres in a system of matter must inhere wholly in each part of it — that is, that in a round figure every particle must be round. For unless he affirms and proves *that*, which is so manifestly against experience, he will never contradict me, or be able to show that consciousness must necessarily (if it inheres in a system of matter) consist of several distinct consciousnesses.

To vindicate his conclusion, Mr. *Clarke* premises a discourse of the various uses of the terms *powers of the same kind.*[1] To which, that I may not disoblige him by taking no notice of it, I answer that when terms are defined, and instances agreeing to those definitions given — whereby all doubtfulness about one another's meaning is in the most effectual manner excluded — I cannot see of what use it is to enumerate the various senses that *logicians* give to the same terms, especially since I have the authority of the schools (as Mr. *Clarke* represents them) for my use of those terms.[2] Though, had I understood them in a sense not to be justified from their authority, my mistake had only been in the meaning of two or three *English* words which was a matter of no great consequence when the words were defined. Wherefore I proceed to the defense of his argument.

He says, *when he affirms that roundness, or globosity, must needs be the sum of qualities of the same kind, he does not mean that globosity is made up of globosities, but that a whole round figure must necessarily be made up of pieces of roundness which are all of the same kind with roundness. For nothing that is void of figure can be part of any figure whatsoever, nor any thing that is void of curvity in particular be part of a round circumference, nor any thing that is void of that particular degree of curvity which makes a circle of a certain determinate diameter be part of the circumference of that circle.* And

1 3d Defense. [p. 155ff –ed.]

2 3d Defense. [p. 156 for the reference to the logicians. I can find no explicit reference by Clarke to the Schools, but see p. 156 "That is what they call ..."

to prove that roundness consists of pieces of roundness, or *powers of the same kind* in that sense *with roundness,* he spends near twenty pages. All which, for ought I know, may be a vindication of the *conclusion* he laid down, and that I cited, but concerns not his argument in the least. For what Mr. *Clarke* endeavored to prove against those who judged it possible for matter to think was that no power could inhere in a system of matter without being the sum of powers of the same kind, and consequently that if thinking, or consciousness, did inhere in a system of matter, there must be as many distinct consciousnesses as there are parts in that system. And to show how inconclusive that was, I produced roundness (and I might have produced almost all the modes of motion and figure that can exist) as an instance that a power might inhere in a system of matter without being the sum of powers of the same kind — that is, that roundness might inhere in a system of matter without making as many roundnesses as there are parts in that system, and consequently that consciousness, if it inhered in a system of matter in like manner with roundness, could not consist of the consciousnesses of the parts. Now, how does it follow *that if consciousness inheres in a system of matter, it must consist of the consciousnesses of the parts* — or, in that sense, of *powers of the same kind* — because, in another sense, roundness, which I made parallel to consciousness, consists of *powers of the same kind* — viz. of *figures* and *curvities?* For it is readily allowed by me that roundness consists of pieces of roundness which by being all figures are of the same kind with roundness considered as a figure, and by being little curves or arches are likewise of the same kind with roundness considered as a curve. And in that sense I allow consciousness to consist of powers of the same kind. For that, according to me, consists of parts which have a tendency to thinking or consciousness, as roundness does of parts that have a tendency to roundness. And yet for all that, neither roundness nor consciousness consists of *powers of the same kind* in the sense of Mr. *Clarke*'s argument. For, unless in a round figure each part must be wholly round, and in a conscious system of matter each part be wholly conscious — and in that sense consist of *powers of the same kind* — not one step can be taken in defense of Mr. *Clarke*'s argument. Nay, what he has advanced is so far from defending it, that it evidently demonstrates the falsehood of it. For if roundness does consist of parts, none of which can possibly be round (as Mr. *Clarke* evidently shows it must, by proving that roundness must consist only of pieces of roundness), and that are only powers of the same kind with roundness — by being all figures, and by consisting of parts that have a nearer affinity to roundness than straight lines — it is a demonstration that there may be powers in matter which are not the sums of powers of the same kind — in that sense which shows the inconclusiveness of his argument. For when it is proved that roundness consists of parts, none of which can possibly be round, there is a full and perfect instance to show that consciousness may inhere in a system of matter without each of the parts being distinctly conscious. So that, as far as I can see, the force of Mr. *Clarke*'s *Defense* lies in understanding the terms *powers of the same kind* in a different sense from what he did at first, and in a sense that evidently shows his argument has no force. However, he is capable of making the same conclusion in words that he did at first — *viz. that no power can inhere in a system of matter without being the sum of powers of the same kind,* and that, I will allow him, is artful enough to impose on readers that are willing to be satisfied on his[1] side of the question.

But let us see how he applies all that he says, for twenty pages together, to prove *roundness must consist of powers of the same kind* (in the sense he now contends for, and that I allow to be true), to the question *that if consciousness does inhere in a system of matter, it must consist of the distinct consciousnesses of the parts.*

I can find nothing to that question but in these words, *that the individual roundness of a globe* is *not made up of a number of the like whole roundnesses* (and, I add, nor is it made up of any number of roundnesses or any round parts at all), *but yet must needs be made up of such figures as are parts of roundness — nay parts induced with that particular numerical degree of roundness — and cannot be made up of straight lines, nor of any figures which are not pieces endued with that particular degree of roundness. So that an individual consciousness (supposing it to inhere in a system of matter) must be made up, though not of the very same consciousnesses, yet of such powers as are of the very same kind with that numerical consciousness as the arcs of a circle are of the same kind with the whole circumference.... That is, it must be made up of different consciousnesses indeed, but still consciousnesses only.* All which, I humbly conceive, amounts to this much: that though roundness consists of parts or pieces of roundness (none

1 Replacing "this" –ed.

of which can possibly be round), yet if consciousness inheres in a system of matter in like manner with roundness (that is, consists of parts, none of which can possibly be conscious), there must be as many distinct consciousnesses as there are parts. Which is in effect to say, if consciousness inheres in like manner in a system of matter with roundness, it inheres in a different manner from roundness. Or, in other words, if consciousness, by inhering in a system of matter, does not consist of the consciousnesses of the parts, it does consist of the consciousnesses of the parts.

This is the stress of his demonstration, which I think I may submit to the intelligent reader without any reply — first, because it visibly confutes itself, and, secondly, because on this occasion I have a mind to show complaisance to Mr. *Clarke* in letting him have the satisfaction to see his *demonstration* stand in its full force without any attack from me. For when I consider that it can deceive no reader but himself, and that by a citation from Mr. *Hobbes* in his title-page he is of opinion *that arguments seldom work on men of wit and learning when they have once engaged themselves in a contrary opinion,* I think it would be a piece of ill nature to disturb his particular satisfaction in the force of his argument.

But there is one thing more which I think it necessary to inform the reader, with relation to my instance of *roundness,* and that is that I made use of it to no other purpose than to give the reader an idea how consciousness might inhere in a system of matter, without consisting of the consciousnesses of the parts. And that purpose I think it fully answers. But whether in other respects consciousness answers to roundness concerns not me. Nay, I profess that I think it differs from roundness, and all other modes of figure, in many respects. And therefore I am not answerable for any disagreement between roundness and consciousness, provided they agree in consisting of parts none of which are distinctly round or distinctly conscious.

I did urge several other instances of modes to my purpose (for indeed almost every mode in matter is to my purpose), but I choose rather to remit their defense to the consideration of the reader — who may, from the principles already advanced, easily solve Mr. *Clarke*'s objections — than spend more words to show the inconclusiveness of his argument, when I think enough has been said already.

Wherefore I proceed to the consideration of the remaining parts of Mr. *Clarke*'s *Defense.*

That I might let the reader more clearly into the force of my objection to Mr. *Clarke*'s argument, and make myself more intelligible, I did *suppose consciousness (of whose nature I was ignorant) to be a mode of motion, and not a mode of some unknown power — and the rather because* I thought *I had to do with a gentleman that understood the rules of arguing too well to impute that to me as my opinion which I only took the liberty to suppose.*[1] But Mr. *Clarke,* not taking to himself my character of an ingenious adversary, will make me accountable for the *absurdity of the notion of thinking's being* really *a mode of motion,*[2] though he might as well have made me accountable for the *absurdity of the notion* of thinking's being really a mode of figure, because I likened thinking to roundness as much as I did to a mode of motion — but, without any design by either to assert it as my opinion that thinking was either a mode of motion or a mode of figure, having no design then to enquire into the nature of thinking. Wherefore I am concerned to vindicate my *supposition* no farther than the nature of my objection required, which was only to assign such an instance of a power in matter that did not consist of powers of the same kind in such a sense as destroyed the force of Mr. *Clarke*'s argument. And therefore, should the absurdity of the notion of thinking's being *really* a mode of motion be proved, yet the absurdity of my *supposition* would not in the least be proved. I use the supposition of thinking's being a mode of motion to no other end but to express my meaning intelligibly how thinking may inhere in a system of matter without being the sum of the distinct thinkings of the parts. And if my supposition serves that purpose, it is nothing to me let the absurdity of supposing thinking to be really a mode of motion be as great as he pleases. Therefore when Mr. *Clarke* proposes *to prove* against me, by the *arguments* contained between page 270 and page 279, vol. 8 [pp. 169-74 –ed.], *the absurdity of supposing consciousness to be a mode of motion* (meaning the supposition that *consciousness* is really *a mode of motion*), he changes the question in dispute, under an appearance in words of confuting my *supposition* — whereas my *supposition* is no more touched on in those arguments, than the most foreign question in the world. However, that Mr. *Clarke* may be kept a little more in countenance for his labors here, than for the pains

1 Reflections. [p. 125 –ed.]

2 3d Defense. [p. 168 –ed.]

he has taken about *roundness,* I will so far transgress the rules of dispute as to consider whether he proves a proposition that was not in debate between us. And I hope the reader will be pleased to excuse me for the breach of the rules of disputation, for the sake of my complaisance to Mr. *Clarke.* The method I shall take shall be briefly to enquire into the nature of thinking, and then into the force of Mr. *Clarke*'s arguments to prove thinking cannot be a mode of motion.

1. As to the nature of thinking, I observe that thinking is an action that begins not in us until we are operated on by external material objects that act on us as by motion and contact — no more than a windmill begins to go until the air, or some other body, strikes against the sails. For we having no objects or ideas to think upon but what are ultimately founded on, and resolved into, the simple ideas of *sensation* and *reflection* (by the first of which we have all our ideas of sensible qualities in bodies external to us, and by the latter all our ideas of thinking, and its modes — *viz.* doubting, willing, knowing, etc.) cannot think first on the ideas of reflection, because we must think upon something before we can reflect or think upon thinking and its modes. And since that *something* cannot be thinking or any of its modes, it remains that we must first think on the simple ideas of sensation. And if we think on the simple ideas of sensation, it is matter of fact that we do not begin to think upon them until bodies operate upon us. And this is an evident agreement of human thinking with a power or affection of matter; whichever owes its existence to the motion or operation of some other body. What is *fire* but a power or affection of matter, beginning in matter perfectly free from that peculiar mode of motion, until by the application of matter in motion it is produced? And what are other powers or affections of matter such as bitter, sweet, sour, soft, hard, cold, all smells, tastes, sounds, etc., but peculiar modes of motion or figure that begin in particular systems of matter upon the action of other matter upon them?

Did we perceive ideas antecedent to the operation of matter on our senses, there might be some color to suppose human thinking not a power or affection of matter (since matter cannot be conceived from no action, or rest, to begin an action). But thinking following the motion of matter on our senses, we have just as much reason to conclude that it is a power or affection of matter occasioned by the action of matter, as we have to say that fire is a power or affection of matter, when it is produced by the rubbing of a wheel and its axle-tree. And I see not why it is not as necessary to introduce the hypothesis of an immaterial being into every material subject, to account for its wonderful operations, as for the operation of man or beast. I doubt not but that it is very possible to be part of the religion of the most learned country in *Europe* (if we can form any judgment what they may believe from what they do believe) to believe that repetitions of words in echoes are performed by an intelligent or immaterial being that mocks us, according to *Ovid*'s description of her, as a real being:

> *—Que nec reticere loquenti,*
> *Nec prior ipsa loqui didicit, resonabilis Echo.*
> *Corpus adhuc Echo, non vox erat; & tamen usum*
> *Garrula non alium nunc habet, oris habebat;*
> *Reddere de multis ut verba novissima posset*
> ——————————*in fine loquendi*
> *Ingeminat voces; auditaq; verba reportat.*

> [——who could neither refrain from speaking.
> Up to this time Echo had form and was not a voice alone;
> And ye though talkative, she had no other speech than now—
> Only the power out of many words to repeat the last she heard
> ——————————She merely repeats the concluding phrases of a speech and returns the words she hears.
> Ovid, *The Metamorphoses* Frank J. Miller trans.]

And then we should see as many learned treatises to show the inconsistency of such a regular repetition of articulate sounds in any being but an immaterial being (which is supposed only to have memory and reflection), as *Tertullian's*,[1] and some other ancient fathers, are to prove the soul material — and as any of the moderns are to prove the soul immaterial.

2. Human thinking has succession and parts, as all material actions have. For all our thoughts succeed one another, can be suspended in a point or continued in like manner with a mode of motion, and so are as much distinguishable into parts.

---

1 Tertullian's *Resurrection of the Body* argues for the materiality of the soul. See the epigraph at the beginning of *Reflections on Mr. Clarke's Second Defense*. –ed.

3. Thinking has its modes, such as doubting, willing, knowing, pleasure, pain, etc., just as particular powers of matter have their modes. Sound (which in the body to which it is attributed is nothing but a mode of motion) has modes of acute, grave, etc., which, with their several degrees, are capable of being varied *in infinitum.* And as sounds are swift or slow, regular or irregular, according to the different action of matter, so the soul thinks swiftly or slowly, regularly or irregularly, is drunk or sober, has pleasure or pain, according to the different motions produced in our bodies.

4. It is evident to me that God must be an immaterial being — that is, a proper immaterial being, a being without any of the properties of matter, without solidity, extension or motion, and that exists in no place — and not a being that has extension (and consequently exists in place, and has parts) according to Mr. *Clarke*'s ideas of immaterial being. Now thinking in God cannot be founded on any objects acting upon him. Nor is thinking in him supposed to be successive, or to consist of parts, or to have any modes because modes of thinking are distinct acts of thinking. But as his essence is eternal and immutable, without any the least variation or alteration, so his thinking is supposed to be one numerical individual act, comprehending all things, and all the possibilities of things at one view, and is as fixed, and permanent, and unvariable, and as much without succession and parts as his essence. So that if we can form any judgment of the nature of thinking in man from its perfect conformity with the powers of matter, and its entire and total disagreement with thinking in that only immaterial Being which we are satisfied exists, we may reasonably conclude human thinking a power or affection of matter.

If it be asked of what kind of power in matter thinking is a mode — is it a mode of motion, or a mode of some unknown power — to that I answer that I pretend not to know that secret, and therefore will only make these two observations.

1. That Mr. *Clarke* allows matter, or the *bodily organs,* to *act upon the soul.* Now matter cannot act upon an immaterial being by motion, because there can be no contact between a material and immaterial being by motion, because there can be no contact between a material and immaterial being. Wherefore by Mr. *Clarke*'s own principles, there must be a power in matter unknown to us, and of which we have no idea. And if there is a

power in matter, of which we have no idea, that power in matter may comprehend under it thinking and its modes, as figure does roundness, etc., and motion the several modes of motion, and their modes.

2. It is by many thought a difficulty to conceive how, by a mere preference of the mind, we can cause our left hand which was in motion to be at rest, and our right hand which was at rest to be in motion, and by a new will, choice, or preference (call it as you please) to put the left hand in motion and the right hand at rest — and so on, let our wills vary and change ever so often. But that difficulty is entirely at an end, if thinking in man be nothing but a mode of motion, or matter in motion. And it is then as conceivable that thinking should produce those motions, as that a spring or weight in a clock strike, or point to, the hour of the day.

But let us proceed to Mr. *Clarke*'s arguments to prove that *thinking cannot be a mode of motion in matter.*

His first argument is *that modes of motion are nothing else but particular motions, and cannot contain anything in their idea beyond the genus of motion....* And he *has as clear and distinct a perception that the idea of consciousness contains something in it besides and beyond the genus of motion, as* he *has that it contains in it something beyond the genus of figure....* He *has therefore exactly the same intuitive certainty that consciousness cannot be a mode of motion as he has that any one thing in the world is not another whose idea is the remotest and most different from it that can be imagined.*[1]

[1. –ed.] To which I answer that though we have an abstract idea of motion which, as it ought so I doubt not but it does, comprehend under it all the modes of motion that ever did or can exist, yet I deny that we have an idea of all the really existing, much less of all the possibly existing, modes of motion. We have ideas of the more simple modes of motion, such as a circular motion, or motion in a straight line. But when the motions are very complex, such as the mode of motion in a tree by which vegetation is performed, and the mode of motion in a man or animal by which life and sensation is continued, we have not a distinct conception of them in our minds. The only distinct conception that we have of such modes is that they have in them the genus of motion, and that they have succession and parts,

1 3d Defense. [pp. 169-70 –ed.]

and can be variously modified. Now as far as we know anything of the nature of thinking by what we find and feel in ourselves, *that* has likewise the genus of motion by arising from motion, by being varied by motion, and by its producing other motions distinct from itself — and has likewise succession and parts, and withal innumerable modifications. Wherefore, since no particular idea of human consciousness can be produced beyond the genus of motion, and that we have no particular ideas of the more complex modes of motion that exist, it is impossible for him to prove or know that one is not the other. For until he has a further idea of the nature of human thinking than what I have described, and a particular distinct idea of that complex mode of motion that exists in our animal spirits, he can no more know that one is not the other, than he can know whether two things agree or differ from one another — that he has no idea at all. Indeed a man may say that a wheel in motion does not think, or that a circular motion is not thinking, because we see not any of the effects of thinking follow from a circular motion — though I doubt not but (if the effects of thinking followed from a circular motion, as much as they do whenever that complex motion peculiar to the body of a man exists) that Mr. *Clarke* would have recourse to the *hypothesis of immaterial being,* and say that immaterial beings were added to all wheels on the production of every circular motion. But it is not possible for us to say that thinking does not consist in the peculiar motion of the spirits in the brain, until we have a particular idea of the motion of those spirits, and an idea of thinking as something distinct from a mode of motion, or as distinct from a power or affection of matter — of none of which has Mr. *Clarke* given us any ideas.

2. I have been the longer on this argument than was necessary because what I have offered will in a great measure serve to set this question in a true light — otherwise there needed nothing to be said to an argument which does only affirm the question in debate, and which can signify nothing to anybody that wants conviction. For as he only affirms *that he has an intuitive certainty that consciousness cannot be a mode of motion,* so a man may affirm against him that by a survey of the nature of human thinking, and the different effects of motion, he knows or perceives that human thinking is a mode of motion. And another may affirm with me that he is so far ignorant of the nature of human thinking as not to know whether it be a mode of motion or no. All

three prove alike, and have nothing else to do but to submit their several affirmations to the reader, but can never convince one another. Mr. *Clarke* has indeed affirmed the question that he has brought into dispute, in stronger words that I have produced from him, as *that it is a greater absurdity,* and *more ridiculous* than some evidently false and ridiculous propositions which he is pleased to produce as parallels to what he would make me affirm.[1] But I humbly conceive there is no more proof in such assertions than in the most modest and civil affirmations. However, I thought myself obliged to do him the justice, to produce what he says, that it may have its weight with the reader, because I ought to suppose he intended it for argument.

His second argument to prove that *thinking cannot be a mode of motion* is *if thinking was a mode or species of motion, it would follow that all motions would be a degree of thinking.*[2] To which, as well as to all that follows under this head, I think it sufficient to reply that matter is everywhere the same and all alike, but becomes fire, or water, or produces smells, tastes and sounds, etc., according as it is diversified by motion. And as it is supposed that motion can produce nothing but motion, so these differences in matter are nothing but peculiar modes of motion. Wherefore, if it be proper to say that every motion is a degree of fire, a degree of water, a degree of all the modes of smell, a degree of all the modes of sound, a degree of bitter and a degree of sweet, a degree of vegetation, and a degree of corruption — I do not in that sense allow that every motion is a degree of thought, if it be true that thinking is a mode of motion, as Mr. *Clarke* supposes it to be in this argument.

His third *argument* to prove *thinking cannot be a mode of motion* is *that if thinking was a mode of motion, then motion would be a more generical power* than thinking. Whereas, *on the contrary,* says he, *it is evident that thinking is a power infinitely more generical than either figure or motion, or any other power of matter. There are as many ideas of figure as there are figures, and there are as many ideas of motion as there are modes of motion, and as many ideas of other things as there are other things in the world that can be thought upon. And all these ideas are modes and sorts, or kinds, of thinking.*

1. When motion is said to be more *generical* than any particular species or mode of motion, and when figure is said to be more

---

1 3d Defense. [p. 170 –ed.]

2 3d Defense. [p. 171 –ed.]

generical than any particular mode of figure, I take the meaning of it to be that figure and motion are abstract ideas which comprehend under them all the particular modes of figure and motion that can possibly exist. So that wherever any particular figure or motion exists, it has a conformity to our abstract ideas of figure and motion, whereas a circular motion and squareness are abstract ideas, to which only a particular mode of motion and figure has a conformity. So that motion and figure are called more generical than any particular motion or figure, because their ideas are contained under them.

But when Mr. *Clarke* calls *thinking* in a man *a more generical power than motion and figure,* I am perfectly at a loss what he means. Does he mean that thinking is a power which does consist both of motions and figures? If he does mean so (and I know not what other sense, according to the meaning of the terms *more generical,* in this place to understand him in), then if it be proper language to call that an individual power which consists of all possible motions and all possible figures, what does Mr. *Clarke* do in affirming thinking to be *more generical than motion,* but make thinking a perfectly material action? For unless it comprehends under it all possible modes both of motion and figure, as motion and figure does all possible modes both of motion and figure (which thereby become *more generical* than any particular mode of figure and motion), he uses the term *generical* in one sense in one place, and in another sense in another place. Wherefore it follows from this argument that either thinking is, by consisting of figures and motions, a material action, or else that he uses the term *generical* fallaciously.

If he uses the term *generical* in one and the same sense in both places, and pretends it follows from his argument that thinking must, by being more generical than figure and motion, consist both of figures and motions, and so cannot consist of motion alone — and would thereby destroy the supposition *that thinking is a mode of motion* — I answer that when thinking is supposed to be a mode of motion in the animal spirits, the figure and structure of them, as well as the principal parts of a man, are included as necessary to constitute an act of thinking. For otherwise, neither the motion of thinking, nor the various motions in the body of a man, could be performed — no more than the mode of motion called vegetation could be performed in an oak without such an organic disposition of parts as is peculiar to that kind of tree called an oak.

If he uses the term *generical* fallaciously, *and not in the same sense that it is used when figure is said to be* more generical *than roundness,* but for thinking's containing in it ideas, etc. — that is, for being *more generical* than motion and figure, because we have ideas of motion and figure — his discourse is not to the point, and he might as well have used any other term in the world as the term *generical.* For if he means that the objects of *thinking are more generical* than motion *and* figure (as by affirming *that thinking contains in itself the ideas of all the modes of figure, and the ideas of all the modes of motion, and infinite other ideas besides,* and by what he says in this article, I am apt to think he does), then what he says is not to the question in dispute — which has no relation to the *genericalness* of the objects on which we think, but to the *genericalness* of thinking itself.

Indeed Mr. *Clarke* does help himself out as well as he can, by saying *that ideas of figure, etc., are modes and sorts, or kinds, of thinking.* But that, I conceive, is a clear mistake, and a confounding together the faculty and the object. I allow there can be no thinking without an idea or object, nor can there be any idea or object without thinking — for they are as relative ideas as father and son, and must therefore subsist together. But yet thinking, when roundness is the object, is no more the material idea we think on, nor that material idea — thinking — than the idea of *father* is the idea of *son,* or the idea of *son* the idea of *father.*

2. But let thinking in man be whatever Mr. *Clarke* pleases. Let it be a power in an extended substance that, according to him, consists but of one figure and one motion, and not of the figures and motions of the parts, and that is indivisible by the power of God, though one side cannot but be distinct from the other side. Does not that extended being of Mr. *Clarke*'s, with only one[1] figure and one motion, by means of that supposed power, perceive the ideas of figures and motions? And if one power can perceive, or have the idea of, another power, as by Mr. *Clarke*'s own supposition he must allow, I see no more reason against making figures, etc., the objects of a *mode of motion,* than against making them the objects of any other power that exists in a subject which has neither modes of motion, nor modes of figure contained in it.

1 Replacing "one only" –ed.

3. It must be allowed that every distinct thought is a particular mode of thinking, and so thinking must in us have a great number of modes. But yet for all that our thoughts are finite and limited. And notwithstanding Mr. *Clarke* affirms *that thinking* in man *contains in it the ideas of all the modes of figure, and the ideas of all modes of motion.*[1] Yet I take it to be a matter of fact that we comprehend only the more simple modes of motion and figure. And since our thoughts are all limited, in point of number, I see no reason from their variety necessarily to conclude that human thinking cannot be a mode of motion. For if we consider but the prodigious variety of sounds which are called distinct modes of sound, it is as easy to conceive that upon the supposition of thinking being a mode of motion, it should have the several modes that we are conscious it has, as that sound should have all the distinct innumerable modes which that has.

His fourth argument to prove *thinking cannot be a mode of motion* is a citation from Mr. Locke's *Essay of Human Understanding, which* he *cannot but suppose I will give some deference to.*[2] But why he should expect any deference from me to any man's words, any further than they carry evidence along with them — except those of the inspired writers — is as surprising to me as that Mr. *Locke* should be made choice of as a proper authority to submit to. However, since Mr. *Clarke* is so far mistaken in me as to think I would pay any more deference to Mr. *Locke* than I do to him, I will on this occasion freely declare it to be my opinion that I look on it to be contrary to the duty of a rational agent to pay any manner of deference in matters of opinion or speculation to any man, or number of men whatsoever — and that could I so far prostitute my conscience as to submit to any mere human authority, Mr. *Locke*'s would in all likelihood be last for my purpose. Because it would be much more for my ease, if not my profit, to submit to the decisions and determinations of those men that in every country have worldly preferments to bestow, than act the same low part out of so poor a prospect as I must see would follow from believing in so rational an author as Mr. *Locke*.

As to the passage itself, I refer the reader to it, who will see that it is so far from having any relation to the question that

---

1 3d Defense. [p. 172 –ed.]

2 3d Defense. [pp. 173-74. The remark about deference is at the end of the quotation from Locke. –ed.]

Mr. *Clarke* has been pleased to start — whether *human thinking be a mode of motion* — that its whole design is to prove that thinking in the deity cannot *depend on the motion of the parts of a corporeal system,* against such theists as affirm that *God is a certain system of matter,* and that *thinking is a certain motion of the parts* of that system.[1] And as the question is not the same, so some of the consequences that Mr. *Locke* draws from those principles affect only that really absurd supposition of thinking's being a mode of motion in God. For if it be a just inference *that all thoughts must be unavoidably accidental and limited* that depend *on motion* — as I think it is — it sufficiently proves the absurdity of those theists that Mr. *Locke* argues against, but is no manner of objection against those imaginary people that maintain thinking in man to be a mode of motion.

His fifth argument, as far as I can understand it, is that it is not *proper* to distinguish motions and figures into *modes* or *species of motion and figure,* and that a man may as well call a *syllogism* a mode or species of motion, as call any particular motion a mode or species of motion. And for this he appeals to the common sense of mankind. This argument has relation only to propriety of language, and therefore I can only say this to it. That I have distinct ideas of several motions, and distinct ideas of several figures, whereby I distinguish those motions and figures from one another as well as I can figure from motion. That some of these peculiar motions and figures have distinct names given to them, and consequently those motions and figures are as much ranked into kinds and sorts (though they may be never called kinds or sorts) as any things else in the world. For what do we mean by a kind or sort, but several particulars having a conformity to an abstract idea? So that if our abstract idea of roundness agrees to the figure of any number of beings, we do as necessarily call them all round, and reckon their figure a sort of figures, as we do a negro of the sort or species of men, by his answering or having a conformity to our abstract idea of man, though the term *species* or *sort* may not perhaps be made use of in one case as it is in the other. But after all, I cannot see what ground Mr. *Clarke* has to contest this language with me — who says so much about *figures differing specifically* from one another.

Thus I have gone through his arguments to prove that *thinking cannot be a mode of motion,* and will conclude what I have

1 B. 4. c. 10. §. 17. [of Locke's Essay; see Appendix A4c –ed.]

to say on this head with considering the apology he makes for my maintaining so absurd an opinion — though it be only an opinion he puts upon me, as he did, that I maintained *sweetness existed in a rose,* in a direct defiance of my words that were before him. He says *that in reviewing the matter* he *can hardly persuade* himself *but that* I *have mistaken my own argument.* And his reason is because *some ingenious persons have undertaken to maintain that God can make matter think* — which, it seems, though a *false* and *impossible* assertion, is not so *extravagant* an absurdity as mine. And therefore I presume he thinks I intend to follow, or should have followed, those *ingenious persons* — which is as much as to say I am more extravagantly absurd than others, therefore I have mistaken my own argument. I may as well say that Mr. *Clarke* has mistaken his own argument, because I think him more mistaken than *Descartes,* and some other *ingenious persons,* in making the soul *an extended being,* and yet indivisible by the power of god. Have not Mr. *Clarke* and I, and every man else, a liberty to judge and argue for ourselves? And though it be very possible for us all to argue in such a manner as will seem *extravagantly absurd* to some men or other, yet I humbly conceive that we ought not from thence to be charged with mistaking our own arguments. When a papist argues for *transubstantiation,* I cannot see how he can be charged with *mistaking his own argument,* because *some ingenious* divines of the church of *England* contend only for a real presence. If we look into the world, is there not evident proof that men professing learning are capable of believing and defending any absurdity in nature? Nay, are not almost all the *extravagant* opinions that abound in the world chiefly confined to those that profess philosophy and learning? For as *no living creature is subject to the privilege of absurdity but man only,* so the common people, by their incapacity for speculation, can enter no farther into the particular speculations of their country than, like the common soldiers of an army, by showing their courage and warmth *for they know not what.* Indeed we have had the happiness in *England* to have such rational parliaments and convocations that have established nothing but truth, yet an *Englishman* is thereby no more privileged from maintaining and believing any the most *extravagant* absurdity, than a man born in *Turkey, France,* or *Spain* — and that with the same degree of honesty and sincerity. Had I contradicted myself, I might be said to have *mistaken my own argument,* as Mr. *Clarke* may justly be said to have done in making an extended being, as such, divisible and indivisible at the same time. But to say I have mistaken my own argument, because I exceed another in absurdity, is such a *mistake,* and argues so little insight into the nature of man (so prone to error and absurdity), that I know not under what *kind* or *species* of mistakes to put it.

To prove the impossibility of matter's thinking, Mr. *Clarke* urged another argument, *viz. that it is absurd to annex consciousness to so flux a substance, as the brain or spirits because, if such a substance could be the seat of that consciousness by which a man not only remembers things done many years since, but also is conscious that he himself, the same individual being, was the doer of them, it would follow that consciousness could be transferred from one subject to another — that is, that a quality could subsist without inhering in any subject at all.*[1]

To which argument I answered that no man has the same numerical consciousness today that he had yesterday.[2] The consciousness he has today is a distinct numerical act from all past consciousness, and can be no more the same numerical individual consciousness with any of those past consciousnesses than the motion of a system of matter today can be the numerical individual motion it had yesterday.

That we are not conscious that we continue a moment the same individual numerical being. That we utterly forget or cease to remember a great many things done in the former part of our lives, which yet we as certainly did, as ever we did any of those things that we are conscious we did. That we do by degrees forget things partially, which we do not revive by frequent recollection. And that in order to retain the memory or consciousness of a past action, it is necessary to revive the idea of it, before any considerable flux of particles; and by reviving the idea, we have as perfect a memory or consciousness of having done that action (though the brain or spirits be not composed of the same numerical particles) as we had the day after we did the action; or as we have of a triangle, or any other new idea not before imprinted on the brain. And if there is every now and then a recollection of a past action, a man may be conscious of things done by him, though he has not one particle of matter, the same that he had at

1 2d Defense. [p. 96 –ed.]

2 Reflections. [pp. 147-48 –ed.]

the doing of those things, without *consciousness being transferred from one subject to another,* in any absurd sense of those words. And nothing can better account for a total forgetfulness of some things, and partial forgetfulness of others, than the supposition of consciousness' inhering in a substance, whose particles are in a constant flux.

But, Mr. *Clarke* says, *the fallacy of this reply* is *very evident. For to affirm that new matter perpetually added to a fleeting system may, by repeated impressions and recollections of ideas, participate* [*in* –ed.] *and have communicated to it a memory of what was formerly done by the whole system,* is *not explaining or proving, but begging the question, by assuming an impossible hypothesis.*[1]

Now as far as I understand anything of the nature of arguing, it was not my business, as a respondent, to *prove,* but *assign* an hypothesis. For assigning an hypothesis, provided that hypothesis be possible, is a full answer to an argument whereby the contrary is proposed to be demonstrated, because what is possible cannot be reduced to an absurdity. And this I have done in the words I have cited. But whether that hypothesis be possible or impossible, I leave to be determined by every man's reason, and whether it be not the real truth of the matter by every man's experience. This I am sure of, that Mr. *Clarke*'s calling it *an impossible hypothesis,* and, instead of saying a word to prove it impossible, immediately arguing on the supposition of its *possibility,* is begging the question, and supposing that which he was to prove. Whereas I was not to prove, but assign a supposition or hypothesis. The substance of what he adds, while he argues on the supposition of the possibility of my hypothesis relating to the question of personal identity, and justice of future rewards and punishments, shall be considered under another head.

I had urged that, though from the immateriality of the soul it did follow that the substance of the soul was naturally immortal or indivisible,[2] yet it would by no means follow that the soul, considered as an actually thinking being, was naturally immortal.[3] And unless the soul, as an immortal being, did perpetually think or perceive, or, as a thinking being, was naturally immortal, a future state of rewards and punishments could not be proved

1 3d Defense. [p. 181 –ed.]

2 Letter to Mr. Dodwell. [by Collins, p. 49 –ed.]

3 Reflections. [p. 141 –ed.]

from Mr. *Clarke*'s argument. And therefore it was of *no use to the ends and purposes of religion — that is, it was of no use to prove what it was designed for, viz. a future state of rewards and punishments.*

To this Mr. *Clarke* says *that he supposes it will be granted to be of the greatest use if it be evident that the notion he is arguing against* is *utterly destructive of religion.*[1]

Let *the notion he is arguing against* be *utterly destructive of religion,* it will not therefore follow that a proof of the immateriality of the soul is any proof of a future state of rewards and punishments. And if a future state of rewards and punishments does not follow from the supposition of the soul's immateriality, his argument is not of any *use* to that *end* for which it was intended, and no more proves a future state of rewards and punishments than any opinion or principle whose supposition is *utterly destructive of a future state.* For whatever *medium* does not prove a proposition, when the pretended use of that *medium* is to prove that proposition, that medium no more serves that *end* and purpose than the most absurd proposition in the world. Wherefore it is plain that his subsequent arguments, should they prove *my notion destructive of religion,* do not prove the usefulness of his own *argument,* and are no more to the question in dispute than his endeavors to prove roundness consists of *powers of the same kind,* and that *thinking* is not a *mode of motion.* But to pursue the complaisance with which I have treated him, I will consider what he says to prove *my notion destructive of religion.*

His first argument to prove my notion destructive of religion is *that if the mind of man were nothing but a certain system of matter, and thinking nothing but a certain mode of motion in that system, it would follow that, since every determination of motion depends necessarily upon the impulse that causes it, therefore every thought in a man's mind must be necessarily and depending wholly upon external causes, and there could be no such thing in us as liberty or a power of self-determination. Now what ends and purposes of religion mere clocks and watches are capable of serving needs no long and nice consideration.* To which I answer:

1. I nowhere affirm thinking to be a mode of motion in any system of matter, and therefore let his argument be ever so just and conclusive, it cannot prove my *notion destructive of religion.*

2. But supposing I had affirmed *the mind of man to be nothing*

1 3d Defense. [p. 191 –ed.]

but a certain system of matter, and that *thinking* is *a mode of motion in that system,* and that therefore there can be *no such thing in us as a power of self-determination* — no more than there is in *clocks or watches* — how does it follow *that my notion is destructive of religion?*

Men and clocks agree in being necessarily determined in all their actions — therefore, says he, they are alike incapable of religion. I might as well argue that, because an immaterial substance and a clock agree, according to Mr. *Clarke,* in being extended, therefore an immaterial substance is no more capable of religion than a clock. For what is it makes a man a proper subject of religion but his understanding? And what excludes a clock from being a proper subject of religion but the want of a human understanding? Both are necessarily determined in their actions. The one by the appearances of good and evil, and the other by a weight or a spring. But how does this agreement destroy man's capacity for religion? How does it appear that an intelligent agent that acts necessarily is not a proper subject of religion, because an unintelligent agent that acts necessarily is not? When Mr. *Clarke* proves that such an intelligent agent cannot be a proper subject of religion, I will allow him that man is no more a subject of religion than a clock — nay, I will go farther and allow that there can be no such thing as religion. For among all the speculations relating to the human mind, or any other intelligent beings, there seems to me nothing more evident than that there cannot exist in any intelligent being, nor do we enjoy any other liberty than, *a power to do as we will, and forbear as we will* — that is to say, if I have the will to stay in my chamber I have a power to stay there, and if I have the will to go out of my chamber I have a power to go out. Let my mind determine either way, I have still the power to act as I will, unless something happens to hinder me from acting as I will. If I am locked up fast, I have no longer my liberty in that respect, I have not then a power to do as I will. And if I am thrust out by violence, I am not at liberty in that respect, because I cannot forbear going out though I should will not going out. Whenever therefore the doing or forbearing any action, according to the determination of my will, is in my power, I am then always free and at liberty — that is, from any agent's hindering me from acting as I will, but not *free* from *necessity.* For when I will or prefer going abroad to staying at home, that act of volition or preference as much determines me to act according to that *preference,* if it is my power to go abroad, as locks and bars will hinder me from acting according to that preference. The only difference is that in one case I am necessitated to act as I will, and in the other case to act contrary to my will.

This seems to me to contain the whole idea of human *liberty.* Now if Mr. *Clarke* cannot assign another idea of *liberty* that is intelligible and consistent with itself, and that we can know to be true by comparing it with the actions of our minds, then, if he shows that a necessary agent cannot be a subject of religion, it will follow from his principles that man is not a subject of religion. And that he can have no consistent, intelligible, idea of *liberty,* besides what I have assigned, I think will be evident to any man that carefully considers the actions of intelligent beings, or endeavors to frame an idea of *liberty* that is distinct from *necessity.* Upon the best information I can get, I can put no other intelligible meaning on the terms *liberty,* or *self-determination,* for Mr. *Clarke*'s purpose, than a *power to will or choose differently under the same circumstances.* That is, though I will or prefer staying in my chamber to leaping out at the window, yet I could under those very circumstances, wherein I preferred staying in my chamber, have preferred leaping out the[1] window; which is as much as to say, I could have preferred what I did not prefer, though all the causes of preference continued. Now this to me is perfectly inconsistent. For whenever I prefer one thing to another, it is always on some motives or causes. And I find that I cannot but prefer what I do prefer, until different motives or causes produce another preference, choice, or will. And, particularly in the case before us, the consideration of the duty I owe to God and my country, the satisfaction I take in living, etc., are some of those causes that produce that will or preference. And therefore, to say I can prefer or will differently under the same circumstances is to say I can prefer what displeases me — than which nothing can be more inconsistent. I know the doctrine of *necessity* is too generally supposed to be irreligious and atheistical. And I must confess I cannot but wonder at it, considering that the predestinarians are so numerous in all the sects of Christians, and that it is established in so many *confessions of faith.* Among the reformed I think it cannot be doubted but there are more Calvinists than Arminians. And if the *Jansenists* in the Church of *Rome* are not

1 Replacing "at" –ed.

equal in number to their opposers, their writings show them to be the most acute and ingenious *persons* of that communion.[1] And if in the Church of *England,* its members incline to Arminianism,[2] yet it is affirmed by many that our articles are *Calvinistical,* and acknowledged by all that they were not designed to exclude a *Calvinistical* meaning — which is a sufficient ground to presume that the compilers were *Calvinists,* or at least they did not think *Calvinism* led to irreligion. I could produce many Divines of our Church that, in terms, teach the *doctrine of necessity* (for indeed it would be strange if some *Divines* did not maintain what seems so evidently the doctrine of the church), but I think it sufficient to name only Dr. *South* — whose penetration to know what is orthodox, can no more be called in question by any man that has looked into his writings than his zeal to be orthodox can be suspected, when it is considered that after declaring what he takes to be *the commonly received doctrine of the Church concerning the Blessed Trinity,* he *humbly submits* it to *the Church of* England.[3] And I look upon his authority alone to be sufficient to convince every impartial reader that a poor layman may hold the opinion of the necessity of all events as innocently as so reverend a Doctor of the Church, and take off from the force of Mr. *Clarke*'s imputation of irreligion on that principle, since the doctor has never met with any censure for asserting it. In his *first volume of sermons,* he says, *providence never shoots at rovers. There* is *an arrow that flies by night as well as by day, and God* is *the person that shoots it — who can take aim then as well as in the day. Things are not left in an equilibrium* to *hover under an indifference, whether they shall come* to *pass or not come to pass, but the whole train of events* is *laid beforehand, and all proceed by rule and limit of an antecedent decree. Nay, and sinful actions too are overruled* to *a certain issue — even that horrid villainy of the crucifixion of our Savior was not a thing left to the disposition of chance and uncertainty, but in* Acts ii. 23 *it is said of him* that he was delivered to the wicked hands of his murderers by the determinate counsel and foreknowledge of God. *For surely the son of God could not die by chance, nor the greatest thing that ever came* to *pass in nature be left* to *an indeterminate event. Those*

1 *Mr.* Arnaud, *Mr.* Paschal, *Mr.* Nichole, etc.

2 A sect that held free will views against Calvinistic determinism. –ed.

3 *Animadversions on Dr.* Sherlock's *Vindication of the Trinity,* p. 240.

that suspend the purposes of God, and the resolves of an eternal mind upon the actions of the creature, and make God first wait and expect what the creature will do (and then frame his decrees and counsels accordingly) forget that he is the first cause of all things, and discourse most unphilosophically, absurdly, and unsuitably to the nature of an infinite being, whose influence in every motion must set the first wheel a going. He must still be the first agent, and what he does he must will and intend to do before he does it, and what he wills and intends once he willed and intended from all eternity. It being grossly contrary to the very first notions we have of the infinite perfection of the divine nature, to state or suppose any new immanent act in God. The Stoics indeed held a fatality, and a fixed unalterable course of events, but then they held also that they fell out by a necessity emergent from and inherent in the things themselves, which God himself could not alter. So that they subjected God to the fatal chain of causes, whereas they should have resolved the necessity of all inferior events into the free determination of God, who executes necessarily that which he purposes freely.

In the foregoing words the learned doctor, in terms, asserts the *necessity of all inferior events,* and though he distinguishes between the Christian and Stoical necessity, yet that is only with relation to the cause of that necessity. A necessity founded on the will of God must as much destroy the *power of self-determination* in man, as if that necessity was founded on a chain of causes.

But let us suppose that the necessity of all actions was destructive of all religion by destroying the *power of self-determination.*[1] I desire Mr. *Clarke,* who maintains the *certainty of all events,* to show what different influence that supposed necessity of our actions can have on the *power of self-determination,* that the supposition of the *certainty of our actions* has not. If every action, and the least circumstance of it, be certain to exist before they do exist, can I possibly have a power to act contrary to such an action, or any circumstance of it, any more than I can contrary to an action that will necessarily exist? Now unless he can show such a difference between the certainty and necessity of all actions, whereby it may appear that the necessity of all actions destroys all *power of self-determination,* and the certainty of all actions does not, he must give up religion on his principles — or, if he quits them, he must own with me that religion is consistent with maintaining the necessity of all events.

1 [Clarke's Boyle –ed.] *Lectures,* Vol. 1. pp. 209-11. [Clarke, 1998 –ed.]

Besides, Mr. *Clarke* must suppose that God himself can have no other liberty but a *liberty to do or forebear according as he wills,* when he says *that the necessary and eternal different relations which different things bear to one another always and necessarily do determine the will of God,* and that *God is unalterably determined to do always what is best in the whole.*[1] For if the will of God is always necessarily and unalterably determined, how can he have a *power of self-determination,* as before explained. That is, how can he will differently under the same circumstances, and if his will be necessarily determined what other liberty can be attributed to the deity but a power to do all that he wills, and to forebear what he wills the forbearance of? The force of truth has produced these expressions from Mr. *Clarke,* and he is desired to reconcile them with his censure of the author *of the Essay of etc.* for asserting only the same opinion.[2] And not only so, but to reconcile the power of *self-determination* in man, with his principle of *God's will being necessarily determined.* For if he considers the matter, he will find that as God's will is necessarily determined by what is really best, so the human will must always be determined by what seems best, and that it is impossible to conceive but that every intelligent being that has a power of action must be thus determined — nay, that the perfection of intelligent beings, as distinguished from unintelligent beings, lies in being determined by appearing good and evil, and a power of acting pursuant to those appearances. What would man have? Or can he wish for more than to have a will, election and choice, and a power to do as he wills or chooses? Would he be able to choose or will pain, when he wills or chooses pleasure? Or would he, when he wills or chooses pleasure, be capable of acting contrary to his will? That is, would he be so miserable a being, as to be able to will pain under the notion of pain, or by acting contrary to his will or choice have all his actions involuntary? Both which must follow from a supposed power in man to will or choose differently under the same circumstances, and from a power to act contrary to what he wills. But, God be thanked, we are in a much better state. We are surrounded with objects which, so far as they seem preferable one to another, we do, and cannot help

1 [Clarke's Boyle –ed.] *Lectures,* Vol. 2. pp. 255-56. p. 128. [Clarke, *Works,* II. p. 90 –ed.]

2 3d Defense. [p. 192 –ed.]

willing or preferring. And while we will or prefer them, we cannot help acting agreeable to the will or preference, and nothing but violence offered to us can hinder us from acting agreeable to our wills — which compulsion or violence sure no one can desire. Indeed we are a little restrained in our liberty — if [for example –ed.] we will going to[1] the moon, or no further than the atmosphere, we are not at liberty to act as we will. For had we a liberty in all cases to act as we will, we should be omnipotent.

His next argument to prove *my notion destructive of religion* is *that the doctrine of the resurrection will be inconceivable and incredible, and justice of rewards and punishments impossible to be made out.*[2]

What he says to make out this point, being founded on the question of identity, it will not be amiss to state briefly my opinion before I consider his exceptions.

1. A particular substance I call the same substance that it was formerly, from its perfect agreement to that idea which I then supposed it correspondent to. As for instance, the identity of a material substance, at different times, lies in consisting of exactly the same numerical particles, to which no addition or subtraction has been made.

2. A particular mode (as, suppose, any particular mode of motion) not being capable of a continuation of existence — like *being* and *substance* — but perishing the moment it begins, its identity cannot consist in being the same numerical mode of motion at different times, but only in being that mode of motion that it was when it existed, and not another mode of motion. In like manner, any particular act of consciousness is incapable of the continuation of its existence, wherefore its identity can only consist in being that very numerical act of consciousness that it is.

3. The identity of an *oak, animal,* or *man,* consists in a participation of a continued life, under a particular organization of parts. An oak that contains several loads of timber is called the same oak with an oak that was an inch long an hundred years ago, by partaking thence-forward of a continued vegetable life, in a like continued organization of parts. And an animal or man is called the same animal or man at twenty years old that it was a quarter old, by partaking of a continued animal life, under a like continued organization of parts — let this vegetable and animal

1 Replacing "into" –ed.

2 3d Defense. [p. 192ff –ed.]

life in the oak, animal, or man, be united at different times, to ever so different particles of matter.

4. Besides these sorts of identity, there is a fourth, very different from these, which we signify by the word *self,* and sometimes call *personal identity.* Now to understand what it is that constitutes *self* or personal identity, let us consider to what ideas we apply the term *self.* If a man charges me with a murder done by somebody last night, of which I am not conscious, I deny that I did the action, and cannot possibly attribute it to my *self* because I am not conscious that I did it. Again, suppose me to be seized with a short frenzy of an hour, and during that time to kill a man, and then to return to my *self* without the least consciousness of what I have done. I can no more attribute that action to my *self,* than I could the former which I supposed done by another. The mad man and the sober man are really two as distinct persons as any two other men in the world, and will be so considered in a court of judicature, where want of consciousness can be proved. And it will be thought as unjust to punish the sober man for what the mad man did, as to punish one man for another's fault, though the man both sober and mad is the same man.

And lastly, should there be so strong a representation to my understanding of a murder done by me (which was really never done at all) so that I could not distinguish it in my mind from something *really* done by me, I can no more help attributing this to my *self,* than I can any other action which I really did, and was conscious of. So that it is evident that *self* or personal identity consists solely in consciousness, since when I distinguish my *self* from others, and when I attribute any past actions to my *self,* it is only by extending my consciousness to them. And further, to give the reader an idea of the nature of personal identity, let him consider that our limbs or flesh, while vitally united to [our –ed.] *thinking conscious self,* are part of ourselves, but when separated from us are no part of *self,* but that flesh which succeeds in the room of the flesh separated becomes as much a part of *self* as the separated piece of flesh was before.

The question then between Mr. *Clarke* and me is whether, upon supposition that personal identity consists in consciousness, and that consciousness is only a mode in a fleeting system of matter, the doctrine of the *resurrection will be incredible,* and *the justice of future rewards and punishments impossible to be made out.*

Mr. *Clarke* says *if thinking be in reality nothing but a mode, which inhering in a loose and fleeting system of matter, perishes utterly at the dissolution of the body, then the restoring the power of thinking to the same body at the resurrection, will not be a raising again of the same individual person, but it will be as truly a creation of a new person as the addition of the like power of thinking to a new body now would be the creation of a new man.*[1]

[1.[2] –ed.] To which I answer that if *personal identity* consists in consciousness, as before explained, and if consciousness be a mode in a fleeting system of matter, consciousness can perish no more at the dissolution of the body than it does every moment we cease to think, or be conscious. Suppose we were taken to pieces every night after we are asleep, and our parts put into the same form and order which they would have been in in the morning had we continued sleeping. I think it is not to be doubted but we should have the same consciousness or memory that we should have had in our natural state. Consciousness is no more created anew in one case than in the other. There is only a suspension of the operation of thinking. Therefore the restoring the power of thinking to the same (or, if you please, a different) body at the resurrection, with a memory or consciousness extending to past actions, will be a raising the same person, and not a creation of a new person *as adding the like power of thinking* to *a new body now would be the creation of a new man.* Because the identity of man, consisting in a participation of a continued *life* under a particular organization of parts, must be new created whenever such a *life* begins. Whereas, if personal identity consists in consciousness, or a memory extending to past actions, *that* will make anyone as much the same person that he was in this world as anyone is the same person here two days together. *That memory* or *consciousness* preserves him from being a *new person* (the essence whereof, *ex hypothesi,* consists in having a power of thinking that cannot be extended backwards).

2. But if Mr. *Clarke* means by the *same individual person,* in the paragraph I cited, the *same numerical being* with the *same individual numerical consciousness* at different times, as I suppose

1 3d Defense. [pp. 192-93 –ed.]

2 Collins several times assumes that his reader will know where the numbering of a section begins, and thus omits the "1." that would begin that section. Unfortunately, it is not obvious where the first number should go. This is my guess. –ed.

he does, since therein consists his notion of personal identity (as the reader may see, if he will read the places referred to in the margin),[1] I do allow that such an individual person cannot be raised at the resurrection. Nay, I think it is demonstrable that there can be no resurrection at all of the *same* person on that supposition. And thus I demonstrate it.

1. Being as being cannot be rewarded or suffer.

2. Being only as conscious or thinking can be rewarded or suffer.

3. Human thinking or consciousness consists of a number of particular acts of thinking or consciousness which, whether they reside in a fleeting or indivisible substance, can each of them have but one existence, and cannot possibly exist at different times as substances do, but perish the moment they begin.

4. Since it is not possible for those individual numerical acts of thinking or consciousness that are past to exist again, the same numerical being, with the same numerical individual consciousness, cannot exist at two different times, and consequently cannot possibly be rewarded or punished for an action done.

5. Therefore if personal identity consists in the same numerical being, with the same individual numerical consciousness, there can be no resurrection of the *same person* — nay, there can be no such thing as the *same person* at two different times.

So that, upon the whole, my notion of personal identity is so far from contradicting the doctrine of the resurrection, or making it *impossible or incredible,* that there can only be a resurrection of the *same person* on these principles — that present *consciousness* or memory *is nothing but a present representation of a past action,* and that *personal identity* consists only in having such a *consciousness* or memory. For on these suppositions, a particular consciousness or memory of past actions can begin at the resurrection as well as after a night's sleep. Whereas, if the *same numerical individual consciousness* that existed in this world is to exist at the resurrection, as Mr. *Clarke* maintains, he requires a condition in order to [have –ed.] a resurrection that implies a contradiction.

There seems to me but one objection more to my notion of *personal identity* that requires a solution, and that is as follows: *that if the addition of a like consciousness with what Mr.* Clarke *now finds in himself to any system of those particles of dust which, in the*

1 3d Defense. [pp. 192-93 –ed.]

course of twenty years, have successively been part of the substance of his body, and are enough to form several bodies at the resurrection, will constitute *the same person with himself— the addition of the like consciousness to all those systems would consequently make every one of them to be, not persons like* him, *but the same individual person with* him, *and with each other likewise. Which is the greatest absurdity in the world — an absurdity equal to transubstantiation.* It is making *them all to be one and the same individual person at the same time that they remain several and distinct persons.*[1]

1. To which objection I answer by asking him if these thinking beings can know themselves to be the same or different persons any other way but purely by consciousness? And I ask him whether each of them must not unavoidably think himself the *same person* with Mr. *Clarke?* If each conscious being cannot help thinking himself to be the same person with Mr. *Clarke,* it is past doubt that nothing can be meant by the term *self* but purely a present representation of past actions, or a consciousness extending itself to past actions, without regard to sameness or change of substance. Wherefore I do allow that each of those beings would be the *same person* with Mr. *Clarke* — that is, each of them would have a present representation of the past actions of Mr. *Clarke* (for that is what I understand, and what I think every man must unavoidably signify, by the term *self,* or by *sameness* of person). And if each thinking being is in that sense the *same person* with Mr. *Clarke,* and if sameness of person *or self* consists in having a present representation of a past action, and applying that action to a man's self, let there be ever so many thinking beings that have a present representation of a past action, they can all constitute but one and the same person. Because they all agree in, or have a present representation of, the same past action wherein *self* or personal identity consists — as my consisting of ever so great a bulk of matter, or ever so many distinct beings, does not constitute different persons, but constitutes what we call *self,* by the sympathy and concern I have for each part united to me, though I have a distinct act of sensation for each part that is at any time affected. I suppose Mr. *Clarke,* when he expects *any deference should be given* to an authority he cites against me,[2] will pay the same deference to the same authority that he expects

1 3d Defense. [pp. 193-94 –ed.]
2 3d Defense. [p. 182 –ed.]

I should. And therefore on this occasion I shall give him Mr. *Locke*'s own words, who says *it must be allowed that if the same consciousness can be transferred from one thinking substance to another* (as in a certain sense he evidently shows that it may), *it will be possible that two thinking substances may make but one person.*[1]

2. It is an article of Christian faith that the same numerical particles that are laid in the grave shall be raised at their resurrection. And since God almighty has made that necessary by the declaration of his will, the *same person* will at the resurrection only exist in those very numerical particles that were laid in the grave, by virtue of which personal identity or *self* will begin in the same manner at the resurrection as it does in morning when we awake from sleep. Besides, if God should cause to exist twenty present representations of the same past sinful actions in so many distinct beings, the consequent punishment would be twenty times as much as the sinful action deserved, and his justice required. Wherefore if God will not punish for punishment's sake — as to be sure he will not — there cannot be two distinct thinking beings with, each of them, a consciousness extended to the same past actions, and attributing them to themselves.

3. But supposing that each of these twenty distinct beings is the *same person* with Mr. *Clarke* (which, *ex hypothesi,* is true), and supposing further that they can be considered as distinct *persons* from one another (which yet is not the case, as the reader may see by what I have said before), yet I humbly conceive Mr. *Clarke* will not upon recollection say this is an absurdity equal to *transubstantiation,* but will rather choose to call it *a difficulty that cannot be perfectly cleared,* when he considers that it is one of the articles of our Christian faith to believe that two complete persons, singly considered — *viz.* the second person in the Trinity, and a human person — do constitute, by an hypostatical union [two natures, human and divine united in Christ –ed.], but one person.

4. But as to his own scheme, besides the absurdity of making the same *individual numerical consciousness* necessary to constitute the *same person,* I think there follows another absurdity from his making the same numerical being necessary to constitute *self,* or the *same person.* For how can he account for the resurrection on the following case? Suppose a man lives and believes

---

1 B. 2. c. 27. § 12. [of Locke –ed.]

as a good Christian ought to do for forty years, and then has a distemper in his body which obliterates all the ideas lodged in the numerical individual immaterial substance, so that on his recovery there remains no memory, no consciousness of any idea that he perceived for forty years past. And further, suppose this numerical individual immaterial substance to get ideas again as a young child does, and, until its separation from the body, leads a dissolute and debauched life. Here, on my principles, is the same being at different times — as much two persons as any two men in the world are two persons, or as the same man mad or sober is two persons. Now I ask him whether or no they are two distinct persons? If he answers they are two distinct persons, I ask him how one of them can be punished eternally, and the other eternally rewarded, on supposition that the same numerical individual substance is necessary to continue the *same person?* And if they are two persons, whether personal identity must not consist in consciousness alone, without any regard to its existing in the same or different substances? If he answers that they are not two persons, but one person, I ask him whether he can suppose this being rewardable or punishable? And what kind of consciousness it will have when it is either rewarded or punished? When he has answered these questions to himself, and will give himself the trouble to consider Mr. *Locke*'s chapter of *Identity* and *Diversity,* he will see that, let him frame what imaginary schemes of *personal identity* he pleases, if there lie not unanswerable objections against them all, except that of *personal identity consisting in consciousness,* yet at least that experience perfectly contradicts his notion of *personal identity* which consists in *an individual numerical being with the same numerical consciousness.* And when he sees the impossibility of the *same numerical consciousness* continuing a moment in a finite being, but that every moment's consciousness is a new action, and nothing but bringing the idea of a past action into view, he may perhaps see the needlessness of contesting whether *self* or *personal identity* must inhere in the same or different beings at different times. Because he may then as easily conceive that the *same consciousness* may exist in different beings at different times, as in the same numerical being at different times, and may have as clear an idea of *personal identity* continuing under the greatest change of substance — as he may have an idea of animal or human *identity* which, consisting in a continued life under a like continued organization of parts, cannot be destroyed by the greatest change or flux of particles imaginable. Though after all, was a flux of particles absolutely inconsistent with personal identity, God almighty could as easily preserve the most loose particles from a separation, as he can an immaterial or unextended being from annihilation.

As to what Mr. *Clarke* says about the injustice of punishment, on supposition that *personal identity* consists in consciousness, and that consciousness is a mode of motion in a system of matter, it is to no purpose to enter into that question until we are agreed on the ends and reasons of both temporal and eternal punishments — which he has not as yet assigned. And when he assigns what I take to be the true ends of punishment, both in this world and the next, it will be then time enough to show that they may all take place on my principles as they can on any principles whatsoever.

[1. –ed.] Being come to the conclusion of what I think fit to reply to Mr. *Clarke*'s *Third Defense* on the head of the possibility of matter's thinking, I will, out of a desire to have this argument put on its true foot, observe in this place that Mr. *Clarke* and I have only spoken of matter so far as [it –ed.] is knowable — *viz. as solid* — and the question between us has been, in effect, whether thinking can be an affection of solidity? And therefore should he have demonstrated with the greatest clearness the impossibility of all I have said (as I humbly conceive it is quite the contrary), yet, for all that, he cannot upon his principles prove that there are different kinds of substances in the world. For since he supposes *that we are utterly ignorant of the substance or essence of all things, and that there is no substance in the world of which we know anything further than only a certain number of its properties or attributes,* it is absolutely impossible for him to prove that there are two different substances in the world.[1] Because, having no idea of the *substance of matter,* nor of the *substance* of a *being distinct from matter,* it is impossible for him to know that the substance of one is not the substance of the other, or that there exists any other substances but the substance of matter.

He can only know a thing to be true either by intuition, or by perceiving the agreement or disagreement of ideas by the help of intermediate ideas.

1 [Clarke's Boyle –ed.] *Lectures,* vol. I. [Clarke, 1998, p. 30 –ed.]

He cannot know that the substance of matter and the substance of spirit, or being distinct from matter, are not the same by intuition, when he has no idea of either. For that would be to say that he perceived a difference when he perceived no difference at all.

Nor can he perceive or know that there is a difference between them by the help of an intermediate idea, because no intermediate idea can discover any agreement or disagreement of ideas but by being placed between two ideas. Now no intermediate idea can be placed between two ideas of things, when there is no idea of either, no subject of comparison. Suppose a brass farthing put into a box, and a ring into another box. How is it possible for a man that has no idea of either by any intermediate idea to know whether they differ from one another or no? And suppose one man should affirm to another, who has no ideas to the terms *three angles of a triangle and two right angles,* that three angles of a triangle are equal to two right ones. How is it possible for him to know their equality, by the help of any intermediate ideas, under that ignorance? Other angles can never show him the agreement of *he knows what* with *he knows not what* — no more than if he was showed the sun and the moon.

All that I can find said against this most evident demonstration by Mr. *Clarke,* to whom it has been objected, is *that from the demonstrable attributes of God, and from the known properties of matter, we have unanswerable reasons to convince us that their essences are entirely different, though we know not distinctly what those essences are. The attributes of God,* says he, *are that he is self-existent, eternal, infinite, intelligent, free, wise, etc. The known properties of matter are,* adds he, *that it* is *not self-existent, but dependent, finite, divisible, passive, unintelligent, etc.*[1] But by what intermediate idea does it appear that the substance of matter is not *self-existent,* but *dependent, finite, passive, divisible, unintelligent, etc.?* Nay, is it not supposed by our having no idea of the substance of matter, that we cannot possibly know whether it be *self-existent, dependent, finite, passive, divisible, unintelligent,* or no? How then can Mr. *Clarke,* on his own principles, know that the *substance* of matter is not *self-existent,* etc.? There is nothing in matter that appears to be *dependent, passive,* not *self-existent, finite,* etc., but

1 *Preface to the Second Volume of* [Clarke's Boyle –ed.] *Lectures.* [Clarke *Works,* p. 582 –ed.]

solidity and the affections thereof. The substance in which solidity inheres we have no idea of, and consequently cannot affirm of it that it is *finite, divisible,* or *unintelligent,* or *not self-existent.* So that it is evident that Mr. *Clarke,* and all those gentlemen who say we are entirely ignorant of the substances and essences of things, or have no idea at all of them, cannot take a step to prove that there are different substances in the world, without contradicting themselves, and supposing that they are not utterly ignorant, but that they have an idea of the substances and essences of things when, at the same time, they confess that they are utterly ignorant, or have no idea at all of the substances and essences of things.

Mr. *Locke* — who always speaks of a *substance* as something unknown, and of which we have no idea, whether it be applied to material or immaterial substances, but *a mere relative idea of a support* — might very justly argue *that from our not having any notion of the substance of spirit, we can no more conclude its non-existence, than we can for the same reason deny the existence of body. It being as rational,* says he, *to affirm there is no body because we cannot know its essence, as it is called, or have no idea of the substance of matter, as to say there is no spirit because we know not its essence, or have no idea of a spiritual substance.* For on the supposition of our having no idea of substance, and that substance is something distinct from what are usually called properties, it will be impossible for any *Spinozist* or Materialist to prove that there is no other substance in the universe but material substance. But then on the other side, it will be as impossible for such an Immaterialist to prove that there must necessarily be two kinds of substances, because by having no idea either of the substance of matter, or the substance of spirit, he cannot know but that the *substance of matter is the substance of spirit.* From what I have said, it is evident that Mr. *Clarke,* and those that are of his mind, cannot possibly, upon their own principles, prove the necessity of thinking's inhering in an immaterial being. For though they should prove that thinking cannot inhere in matter, because it is solid, and consequently divisible, yet that is no more than to say *that thinking cannot be an affection of solidity.* For that is what they must mean when they say *thinking cannot inhere in matter,* because, having no idea of the substance of matter, they only say thinking cannot inhere in that part of matter of which we have an idea. Wherefore, supposing Mr. *Clarke* to argue right *that thinking cannot inhere in matter* —

that is, cannot be an affection of solidity — it would by no means follow that it may be made an affection of, or be annexed to, that substance which is vested with solidity. For of that *substance* we are supposed to have no idea, and consequently cannot exclude it from a possibility of thinking — any more than a possibility of being solid.

Mr. *Locke,* to justify the consideration of *substance* as an unknown *support* in which properties inhere, says *a philosopher that says substance (or that which supports accidents) is something he knows not what, and a countryman that says the foundation of the great church at* Harlem *is supported by something he knows not what, and a child that stands in the dark on his mother's muff and says that he stands upon something he knows not what, in this respect talk exactly alike.*[1] Now I humbly conceive that they may not all talk exactly alike in this respect. For the countryman and child may have a clear abstract idea of solid being or matter, a species whereof the countryman may imagine the church at *Harlem,* and the child himself, supported by. Whereas the philosopher has no idea at all. For let the philosopher strip any part or piece of matter of solidity, and nothing conceivable remains, nothing in which solidity can inhere. For, as to that portion of space in which it existed, that could not be the substance in which it inhered, because that portion of space in which it existed was really distinct from the material substance, and accidental to it. For that portion of space exists immutably and perpetually in the same place (if I may so speak), though ever so many particular material substances are coextended to it, and then removed from it.

But as far as I can judge, all this talk of the essences of things being unknown is a perfect mistake, and nothing seems clearer to me than that the essence or substance of matter consists in solidity, and that the essence or substance of a being distinct from matter must consist in want of extension, and is truly defined an *unextended being.* For nothing can be conceived to be coextended with the parts of space (if I may so speak) but what is solid. And therefore to make immaterial being extended (as Mr. *Clarke* does) is to make immaterial being material, which indeed

1 *Letter to the Bp. Of W., p. 16.* [by Locke, a reference to Locke's long public correspondence with the Bishop of Worcester, Edward Stillingfleet. –ed.]

is but of a piece with his making an extended being indivisible, though he has no other reason to make all matter divisible but because it is extended.

As to what he has said against material impulse being the cause of *gravitation,* the whole is founded on this, that because a *bullet, a feather, and a piece of leaf-gold descend with equal swiftness in vacuo* (that is, in a vessel out of which the air is exhausted, according to Mr. *Boyle*'s definition of the term *vacuum* — in the like case, by which he *understands not a space wherein there* is *no body at all, but such as* is *either altogether, or almost totally devoid of air*),[1] therefore material impulse cannot be the cause of gravitation. I use the term *vacuum* in the aforesaid sense, because it is so far from being evident that all matter is exhausted (though it should be granted that there is no perfect *plenum* there) that there are experiments which prove that body remains there after the air is exhausted, and that does receive actual modifications by motion from bodies without the vessel. And if so, a bullet, a feather, and a piece of leaf-gold may descend *in vacuo,* as Mr. *Clarke* calls it, with equal swiftness, by virtue of the impulse of those parts of matter that are contiguous to them — as that lead under different forms ascends or descends according to the pressure of the circumambient air. And as to that external motion which is the cause of that mode of motion called *gravitation,* I think the experiment of several pieces of thread, tied to the inside parts of a hoop, all tending to a center upon a globe's being whirled round its axis in the middle of the hoop, and this further experiment of bodies not descending *in vacuo,* as Mr. *Clarke* calls it, with the same velocity at a greater distance as they do near the earth, evidently show that the motion of the earth is a proximate cause of the *gravitation* of bodies in our neighborhood, and do discover the cause of gravitation throughout the material universe. But however this be, unless Mr. *Clarke* proves that there is a real *vacuum* in nature — that is, that there are some portions of space without body — and unless he proves withal that there can be an entire portion of space in a vessel without any the least particle of matter — so that he may try whether bodies weigh or descend without the least contact from other bodies — he will not be able to prove that material impulse is not the cause of gravitation. And I may, in the mean while, say what I think, that

1 *New Experiments touching the Air,* 4 to, *p.* 10. [by Robert Boyle –ed.]

could any body be at first so situated as to be surrounded with nothing but pure space, there would be no beginning of motion, no weight, no gravitation in that body. This I humbly conceive is sufficient to obviate all he has advanced without proof under this article. For as to his treatment of me I pass it all by, except one particular and extraordinary liberty he has taken — *viz.* his saying that I *insinuate* to *my reader that Sir Isaac* Newton *is of my opinion in the present question,* and to that will say no more than assure the reader that it is a pure fiction.[1]

He says *that the great phenomena of nature* (and particularly that of gravitation) *cannot possibly depend upon any mechanical powers of matter and motion, but must be produced* (that is, constantly) *by the force and action of some higher Principle; and* so *leading us, even with mathematical certainty,* to *immaterial powers, and finally to the creator of the world.*

But the honorable *Robert Boyle* was of opinion *that it seems manifest enough that, whatsoever is done in the world, at least where the rational soul intervenes not, is really effected by corporeal causes and agents acting in a world so framed as ours is according to the laws settled by the omniscient author of things.* And, *that as it more recommends the skill of an engineer to contrive an elaborate engine, so as that there need nothing to reach his ends in it but the contrivance of parts devoid of understanding, than if it were necessary that ever and anon a discreet servant should be employed to concur notably to the operations of this or that part, or to hinder the engine from being out of order — so it more sets off the wisdom of God in the fabric of the universe that he can make so vast a machine perform all those many things which he designs it should, by the mere contrivance of brute matter managed by certain laws of motion, and upheld by his ordinary and general concourse, than if he employed from time to time an intelligent overseer to regulate and control the motion of the parts.*[2] And therefore, could it be proved that the *grand phenomena of nature* depended on the constant *force and action of* immaterial beings, it would, according to Mr. *Boyle,* argue a less degree of wisdom than if they *depended on the mechanical powers of matter and motion,* and consequently overturn the existence of an infinitely perfect being by not attributing to him the highest wisdom we can possibly conceive.

1 3d Defense. [p. 187 –ed.]

2 Boyle's *Inquiry into the Vulgar Notion of Nature*, p. 66, p. 7.

2. But let this matter be as it will, I conceive this argument of Mr. *Clarke*'s for the existence of God, or the *creator of things,* is as *obscure* and *defective* as he thinks *Descartes'* argument for[1] the idea of God is.[2] For the true question being *whether there has existed from all eternity one immaterial being of infinite perfections that created matter and everything else* ex nihilo, how does it follow that such a being exists from the mere supposition of the existence of two beings of different kinds? For it does not necessarily follow from that supposition that one must have created the other *ex nihilo,* and therefore other mediums are necessary to prove that point.

To infer a *creator* of one being or substance from the mere existence of two kinds of beings or substances is a reasoning nowhere extant in the old profane authors — who *had not so much as a word to signify the production of things* ex nihilo, and therein agreed with the *Jews* who (as the same author observes) everywhere apply the *Hebrew* word, which we render *creation,* to express *other actions and effects* than a production of matter *ex nihilo.*[3] The question, therefore, of a *creation ex nihilo* is a modern question, and consequently out of reverence to sacred and profane antiquity, it became Mr. *Clarke* not barely to suppose the mere existence of two beings of different kinds sufficient to demonstrate the creation of one of them *ex nihilo.*

3. Since, on occasion of the *Boylean* Lecture, the existence of God is often made a question (which otherwise would be with few any question at all), and since the gentlemen that preach that Lecture propose to prove the existence of God *by the rules of demonstrative argumentation* (and thereby give men a right to expect demonstration),[4] I shall, out of the inclination I have to see the foundation of all religion established on demonstration, and to gratify that *desire* which even *atheists* (as Mr. *Clarke* observes) *must of necessity own* they have to see a truth established that is so much *for the benefit and happiness of men* — for, says he, *on whatever hypothesis* they proceed, *nothing is so certain as that man, considered without the protection and conduct of a superior being, is in a far worse case than upon*

1 Replacing "from" –ed.

2 [Clarke's Boyle –ed.] *Lectures,* vol. I. [This may refer to a passage on pp. 14-15, Clarke, 1998 –ed.]

3 Burnetii Arch. Phil., p. 315.

4 [Clarke's Boyle –ed.] *Lect. Vol. I.* [Clarke, 1998, p. 7 –ed.]

the supposition of the being and government of God, and of men being under his peculiar conduct, protection, and favor (from whence it seems to follow that atheists, according to Mr. *Clarke,* even while they continue so, have no reason to fear anything for their disbelief) — I say, I shall conclude this debate with an essay showing a way how to demonstrate the *existence of God,* since demonstration is thought so necessary in the case, though I should think probability enough to determine any man. As far as I can judge of the opinions of *Strato, Xenophanes,* and some other ancient atheists — from a few sentences of theirs which yet remain — and of the opinions of the *sect* called the *Literati* [the Confucians –ed.] in *China* — from the accounts we have in the several voyages thither — and more particularly from Father *Gobien*'s Preface before his *Histoire de l'Edid de l'Empereur de la Chine en Faveur de la Religion Chrétienne* [Narrative of the Edicts of the Emperor of China in Favor of the Christian Religion –ed.], *vol.* 8 *par.* 1698, they seem all to me to agree with *Spinoza* (who, in his *Opera Posthuma,* has endeavored to reduce atheism into a system) that there is no other substance in the universe but matter — which *Spinoza* calls *God,* and *Strato, nature.* And this system is thus described by *Manilius,* Lib, I.

Omnia mortali mutantur lege creata.
Nec se cognoscant terræ vertentibus annis
Exutas. Variant faciem per sæcula gentes.
At manet incolumis mundus suaq; omnia servat,
Quæ nec longa dies auget, minuitq; senectus.
Nec motus puncto currit, cursusq; fatigat:
Idem semper erit, quoniam semper fuit Idem.
Non alium videre Patres, aliumve Nepotes
Aspicient. Deus est qui non mutatur in œvum.

[Everything born to a mortal existence is subject to change
Nor does the earth notice that despoiled by the passing years
It bears an appearance that varies through the ages
The firmament, however, conserving all its parts remains intact,
Neither increased with length of time nor diminished by old age,
It is neither the least bit warped by its motion, nor wearied by its speed; it will remain the same forever, for the same it has always been. No different heaven did our fathers see, no different heaven will our posterity behold. It is God, and changes not in time.
Manilus, *Astronomia,* G.P. Goold trans.]

Now to answer these atheists demonstratively, and on principles which will stand the test, I am so far of Mr. *Clarke*'s mind as to think that we ought to prove the creation of matter *ex nihilo* — or, which is all one, that matter is not a self-existent being. For if once matter be allowed to be a self-existent being, we Christians who believe but in one self-existing being, are obliged by our reasoning to allow matter all possible perfections, and to exclude everything else from being self-existent. Because it is from the idea of self-existence that we infer the perfections of God. Besides, should we admit two self-existent beings — *spirit* and *matter* — we could not then be able to prove but that there may be self-existent beings *in infinitum,* and a plurality of gods — which is as inconsistent with the being of God, or a creator, as the self-existence of matter. Wherefore it is evident that to avoid the two dangerous extremes of believing either that nothing exists but the material universe, or that beings of different kinds necessarily exist, we must not only know that beings of different kinds exist (which Mr. *Clarke* thinks sufficient to prove a creator), but we must have an idea how it is possible for matter not always to have existed. And then it will evidently follow that what we can conceive possible not always to have existed, cannot be a self-existing being, and consequently that there must be a God or a creator of matter.

Now the way to prove *that matter* is *not self-existent* — or, which is all one, *the creation of matter ex nihilo* [out of nothing –ed.] — is to form to ourselves an idea of the *creation of matter ex nihilo,* as we have an idea of the several powers of matter beginning to exist without any preceding existence. For unless we have an idea of the *creation of matter ex nihilo,* we must inevitably conclude matter a self-existent being. For what is a self-existing being but a being which we cannot but conceive existing? And what is the idea of *creation ex nihilo,* but an idea of the possibility of the existence of matter, or an idea how matter may begin to exist? As our idea of the creation of the powers of matter is an idea of the possibility of those powers beginning to exist, of which we have as clear a conception as we have that any powers of matter do really exist. Now to get an idea of creation, or a conception how matter might begin to exist, *we must* (as the incomparable Mr. *Locke* with great modesty expresses himself) *emancipate ourselves from vulgar notions, and raise our thoughts as far as they can reach to a closer contemplation of things, and then we may be able to aim at some dim and seeming conception how matter might at first be made, and begin to exist by the power of the eternal first being.*[1] But as he thought that *this would lead him too far from the notions on which the philosophy now in the world* is *built,* and that it *would not be pardonable to deviate* so *far from them,* so the small compass of this treatise, and the great labor of showing the falsehood of so many received prejudices and opinions as is necessary to give an idea of *creation ex nihilo,* must make it more pardonable in me (who own myself to be infinitely below him in abilities) if I omit for the present so useful a design, or should leave it entirely to some of those gentlemen that are appointed annually to preach at the Lecture founded by the honorable *Robert Boyle.*

Before I conclude, it may be expected that I should take some notice of the expressions of contempt used towards me in Mr. *Clarke*'s *Third Defense.* But to everything of that kind, I think it sufficient to say, first, to Mr. *Clarke* that I heartily forgive all such usage from whomever I receive it, and that I think myself in a particular manner obliged to forgive him. Because I sincerely believe he endeavored to be civil, and that he was as civil as he could be. And, secondly, as to my other readers, I will take the liberty to believe them so much philosophers as that, upon second thoughts, they will think *civility* the best answer and reproof. Notwithstanding that we have been[2] lately told, by a reverend author, that *good nature and good humor make* men *atheists and skeptics.*[3]

But there is one thing which I am very much surprised to find in Mr. *Clarke,* and of which I did not think him capable, and that is an insinuation that I *believe too little.*[4] For I did imagine that the *usage* he had had of the like kind,[5] would have given him an opportunity to consider that such reflections are capable of being made by anybody, and so derive no credit on their author, and that they can please no man of candor and ingenuity. However, I shall not make that return which such an insinuation does suggest and would justify, but instead thereof will give him on this occasion a testimony in his favor before I finally take my

1 *Essay of H. U. B. 4c.10. §.18.*

2 Replacing "are" –ed.

3 Edwards' *Preface to the Doctrines of Faith, Etc.,* p. 19.

4 3d Defense. [Perhaps p. 191 –ed.]

5 *In the Remarks on his Sermons, and* Defense *of those Remarks.*

leave of him — that I verily think he neither *believes too little,* nor *too much,* but that he is perfectly and exactly orthodox, and in all likelihood will continue so.

Samuel Clarke

A Fourth Defense of an Argument

Made Use of in a Letter to Mr. Dodwell, To Prove the Immateriality and Natural Immortality of the Soul. In a Letter to the Author of the Answer to Mr. Clarke's Third Defense, etc.

If we look into the world, is there not evident proof that men professing learning are capable of believing any absurdity in Nature?

Answer to Mr. Clarke's Third Defense

Sir,

Of repeating the same things over and over again, there is no end. The thing I proposed to prove is, I think, so fully made out in my foregoing *Defenses* that I might safely leave the whole matter to the intelligent and impartial reader, without any further enlargement. Your last answer is little more than a renewing of your former assertions, sometimes in the same, and sometimes in different words — as if you thought all that I had advanced to the contrary was entirely wide of the question. Whether that be the case or no, I am very willing the world should judge. And therefore, in reply to your perpetual repetitions, I shall not transcribe my former papers, but only refer to them as occasion shall offer, and desire they may fairly be compared together. And, as I go along, shall endeavor to point out to you some of the chief misrepresentations and fallacies you appear to be guilty of. And where you offer[1] any argument that seems new in any part of it, [I –ed.] shall consider it in its place.

You begin with charging me that *out of four objections insisted on in your Reflections, I have dropped the consideration of three.*

Whether this be true or no, they who please to compare the papers may find I am not sensible that I have passed over any of

1 Deleting "at" –ed.

your objections, or any part of any of them, unanswered. Only where you have repeated the same things again (as for instance in that poor objection drawn from our *ignorance of the manner how God will dispose of the souls of brutes*), instead of repeating my answers, I have only referred to them as they stood in my former Defenses — which is ultimately appealing to the judgment of the intelligent reader. And for this complaint, I shall give you more frequent occasions hereafter.

And in answer to your *fourth objection,* you say I *am* so *far from showing* (as I ought to have done) *that if* consciousness did inhere in a system of matter, it must consist of the *consciousness* of the parts, *that on the contrary* I *have only endeavored to prove that as roundness must consist of several* pieces *of roundness, or* tendencies *towards roundness,* so if consciousness did, in like manner with roundness, inhere in a system of matter, it must consist of several *tendencies* towards consciousness. And this you call an *apparent desertion of* my *argument.*

Now, to this I reply that *consisting of the consciousness of the parts,* and *consisting of several* tendencies *towards consciousness,* is the very same thing. For as nothing that is not *curved* can have any *tendency* towards *curvity,* as nothing that is not [a –ed.] *color* can have a *tendency* towards *color,* as nothing that is not [a –ed.] *sound* have any *tendency* towards *sound,* so nothing that is not *consciousness* can have any *tendency* towards *consciousness.* Differences indeed, and degrees, there may be of the distinctness of *consciousness* and vigor of *thinking,* as there are different degrees of the *curvity of a line,* different degrees of the *brightness of a color,* and different degrees of the *clearness of a sound.* But, as it is plainly impossible that any *color* should have any *tendency towards being any* sound, *or that any* figure *should have any* tendency *towards* being any *motion,* so it is likewise ridiculous to imagine that any *motion,* or any other quality of matter void of consciousness, should have any *tendency* towards being *consciousness.*

Besides, the curvities of the several little arcs that constitute the circumference of a circle are not properly *tendencies* towards *roundness* (for a *part* has no more *tendency* to the *whole* by *composition* than the *whole* has a *tendency* to its *part* by *division*), but they are themselves, being taken together, the whole circle, or the *roundness* itself. So that *roundness* is not a new real quality, resulting from the curvities of the several parts, but only a *name* of the *whole,* a *mere external denomination.*[1] Even in the same manner as the twelve units that constitute the number *a dozen* are not properly so many *tendencies* towards *a dozen* (as towards any *real* new thing or quality), but are themselves, being taken together, the number *a dozen* — which name is nothing but a *mere term,* an *external denomination of the whole,* and nothing at all really in the things numbered. *Consciousness* therefore, in like manner, if it was nothing but the *sum* of those motions or modes of motion which you call *tendencies* towards consciousness, would not be a distinct quality really inhering in the thinking substance (as every man feels by experiencing, and you yourself grant that it is), but it would be a mere *word,* or *term of art* — nothing but a *name,* or *external denomination,* such as are those qualities which I ranked under the third sort.

Wherefore, when you confess that *the parts* (of roundness, suppose) *must be* so *far of the same kind as to have a* tendency *to that individual figure of which they are a part. And* that *in that sense* you *have always allowed consciousness to consist of powers of the same kind, because if consciousness inheres in a system of matter, it must necessarily be allowed that the distinct beings in that system contribute towards thinking, as the pieces of a circle do towards a circle, or as all the parts of a system of matter contribute towards the system.* And again, that what is said in the *Third Defense* may, *for ought* you *know, be a vindication of the conclusion before recited* (viz. *that if consciousness did inhere in a system of matter,* it *must consist of several* tendencies *towards consciousness*). And again, you *do, in that sense, allow consciousness to consist of powers of the same kind. For, according to you, it consists of parts which have a* tendency *to thinking or consciousness, as roundness does of parts that have a* tendency *to roundness.* In all these passages you directly give up the question. For those modes of motion (or of any other quality of matter) which you call *tendencies to consciousness* either are themselves *consciousnesses and thoughts,* or not. If they be, then, as the whole curvity of a circle is made up of the curvities of the several little parts or arcs of which it is composed, so *whole consciousness or thinking* will likewise be made up of several *partial consciousnesses or thoughts.* Which is giving up the question with one hand. Or, if they be not, then, as the roundness of a circle, so far as it differs from the curvities of the little arcs of which it is composed, is

1 See *Third Defense.* [p. 164 –ed.]

nothing but a *bare name* of a *whole,* a *mere external denomination,* so *consciousness,* as far as it differs from those constituent modes that are *no consciousnesses,* will be only a *name of a whole,* a *mere external denomination,* and nothing at all really in the thinking substance itself. Which is giving up the question with the other hand.

You represent me all along speaking as if my whole argument was founded upon the supposition that *in the idea of an immaterial being extension is contained* — that *extended being of Mr.* Clarke*'s.* You *think him mistaken in making the soul an extended being — in making an extended being, as such, etc.* An *immaterial substance and a clock agree, according to Mr.* Clarke, *in being extended*: and, *to make immaterial being extended, as Mr.* Clarke *does.*

This is neither doing me, nor your readers, justice. For my argument is not at all founded upon any supposition either of immaterial substance being extended or unextended. That which I undertook to prove was that matter (all whose solid parts are so many distinct, separable, independent, unconnected beings), could not be a subject capable of individual consciousness. And that therefore consciousness must have some other subject to reside in. Whether that other subject be extended or unextended (whatever you may suppose my opinion to be, upon other grounds), the present argument determines not, but leaves every reader at liberty [to –ed.] judge as he shall find reason. Only I affirmed *by the bye,* for argument's sake, that I thought the difficulties arising from the supposition of immaterial substance being extended were not greater, but rather less, than those which arise from the supposition of its being unextended. See *Second Defense.*

It is here also further to be observed, incidentally, that when you ask *what other argument can be made use of to prove all matter divisible by the power of God, but what is drawn from the consideration of its extension;* and affirm that *if matter, as an extended being,* is *divisible, all extended beings must be divisible;* and that I have *no other reason to make all matter divisible but because it is extended;* and when you mention the *divisibility,* add by way of explication *or (which is all one) the extension, of matter;*[1] you seem to forget that you yourself expressly allowed *space,* though

1 Answer to the 3d Defense. [p. 151 –ed.]

extended, to be absolutely indiscerptible[1] — and therefore, you yourself make matter divisible, not barely *as extended being,* but as *finitely* extended — and that I gave still another reason for styling matter divisible. *Viz.* God's having by his own will and good pleasure created it such a substance, all whose solid parts we find by experience to be so many distinct beings, loose, independent one from another, and unconnected — that is, having no essential connection one with another, nor any dependence one upon another for their existence, as the parts of *space* evidently have, even separate from the consideration of its being absolutely infinite, and as the parts of *time* have (for as much as every *moment,* coexisting with all the parts of space, is yet both *indivisible* in itself, and *inseparable* from the other parts of *duration*), and as the parts, improperly so called, of immaterial substances may have, for anything that can ever be proved to the contrary, on supposition of their being extended.[2] But all this is beside the main argument, which (as I have said) does not necessarily imply any such supposition.

In like manner, when you make a long and pompous discourse about *adequate and inadequate ideas,* and about *difficulties that cannot be perfectly cleared* (that is, which cannot be cleared *wholly,* but yet may *in great part,* and enough to satisfy any reasonable person — though, it seems, you *know no* such *difference*),[3] when, I say, you talk about these things as of great necessity to be premised, and as if you would have the reader think the whole argument depended upon the right stating of them — whereas, in reality, they have no relation at all to the argument, but were started only upon the occasion of that foreign and incidental question concerning the *extension of immaterial substances* — in all this matter, you have by no means made a right representation of things.

However, as to the distinction itself between *absurdities,* or *contradictions,* and *difficulties that cannot perfectly be cleared,* I desire only that what I have said upon this head (*3d Defense*) may be compared with what you have said upon it (*Answer*). And whether then I had not reason (notwithstanding the amusement

---

1 *Reply to* First *Defense* and *Reflections on* [*the* –ed.] *Second* Defense. [p. 83 and p. 139 respectively –ed.]

2 *First Defense* and *Second Defense.* [p. 16 and pp. 59-60 respectively –ed.]

3 *Answer to 3d Defense.* [pp. 198-204, particularly p. 199 –ed.]

of 7 or 8 pages about *difficulties arising from the perception of the disagreement of perfect or adequate ideas, and difficulties arising from the perception of the disagreement of imperfect or inadequate ideas;* when, on the contrary, I had expressly said that the difficulties I meant did not arise from the perception of *any disagreement of ideas at all,* but merely from our having in our *imagination* either *no ideas,* or such very imperfect ones, as cannot well be compared together, of things whose existence or certainty we can nevertheless demonstrably prove by *reason,* and apprehend many of their properties by the *understanding,* which everyone that understands the first elements of mathematics, knows to be the case of *all sorts of infinites* and of *some finites* — whether, I say, I had not good reason) for the distinction I made, I am willing anyone who pleases to compare the books should judge.

You ask what is a difficulty which cannot be perfectly cleared by reason of defective ideas, but a difficulty which arises from the perception of the disagreement of those ideas? I answer it is a difficulty arising not from the perception of any disagreement of ideas, but from the want or defectiveness of ideas in the imagination, which therefore we cannot compare so as to imagine distinctly how they agree, though we can by our reason and understanding demonstrate it is impossible they should disagree. This is plainly the case in most questions concerning *eternity, immensity,* etc.

You declare yourself of another opinion, and that you think *whatever can be demonstrated can be perfectly* cleared *from all objections and difficulties, and that all the difficulties that may be urged against the immensity and eternity of God, etc., which Mr.* Clarke *says cannot be clearly answered, are to be clearly answered. And, in order to answer him clearly, you would only required these equitable conditions of him — that he would define the terms, immensity, eternity, immaterial being, etc.* It is a pleasant instance of an *equitable condition,* that you desire me give a definition — that is, to express the idea of things whereof I contend we have no ideas, or very imperfect ones (seeing we can only give negative descriptions of them) though we have certain demonstrations of their existence. And it is no less remarkable that notwithstanding all this stir about the *perception of the agreement* or *disagreement of ideas,* yet you yourself, when you come to discourse more particularly concerning the nature of thinking, talk of a *power of matter unknown* to us, and of which we have *no ideas* — of which nevertheless you venture to affirm that it may *comprehend under it thinking and its modes,* as *figure does roundness.* But — to pass this over — since it is your declared opinion that all the sorts of difficulties now mentioned may be *clearly* answered, I cannot but think you would very much oblige the world in answering them *clearly.* And I will offer you a fair opportunity of doing it, by reconciling, if you please, the two following accounts together — or else by maintaining either of them, and answering *clearly* the objection and difficulties contained in the other.

It is evident to me that God must be an immaterial being — that is, a proper immaterial being, a being without any of the properties of matter, without solidity, extension or motion, and that exists in no place — and not a being that has extension, and consequently exists in place and has parts.... thinking in God cannot be founded on any objects acting upon him. Nor can thinking in him be SUCCESSIVE, *or consist of parts, nor can his thinking have any* MODES *because modes of thinking are* DISTINCT ACTS *of thinking. But as his essence is eternal and immutable, without any the least variation or alteration, so his thinking is one numerical* INDIVIDUAL *act, comprehending all things, and all the possibilities of things, at one view, and is as fixed and permanent and unvariable, and as much without* SUCCESSION *and parts as his essence. (Answer to Mr. Clarke's Third Defense.)*

The next absurdity charged on the attribute of eternity is how God should coexist with all the differences of time, and yet there can be no SUCCESSION *in his being. This I own to be as absurd as ——, and that there is a manifest contradiction in this notion or conception. For if by* succession *in God's being is understood (and I know not what other sense to put upon it) coexisting with all the differences of time, then the difficulty* is *how to conceive God to coexist with all the parts of time, and yet not to coexist with all the differences of time. Now I acknowledge I cannot do this. But, in behalf of God's eternity, I beg leave to plead that if God does coexist with the differences of time, then he does coexist with the differences of time, and it by no means can be said that he does not coexist with all the differences of time.*[1] *... To say*

1 *Note:* All that is here argued concerning God's coexisting with the differences of *time*, may in the very same manner be applied to his coexisting with the different parts of *place* or *extension*.

God exists all at once, is *to say that he actually exists in time past, present, and to come — that is, that time past* is *not past, and that time to come* is *come, and was always come. But to give some satisfaction to those who think it an imperfection for God to coexist with the several parts' of time, I desire it may be considered that if God operates at different times, and takes up the space of six days in the creation of the world, redeems mankind* 4000 *years after, and will judge men in a time not yet come, then he operates not all at once. And if he operates not all at once, then he exists not all at once. For if he existed all at once, there could be no distinction of time in his operations. Past, present, and to come, must be attributed to the being that operates, as well as to its operations, because operations at different times suppose* succession *in the nature of things, and existing all at once supposes* no succession. *And consequently, if there is a* succession *in the nature of things, there* is *no such thing in nature as existing all at once. Now if there* is *no imperfection in supposing that God acts at different times, as there is not, what imperfection can there be in supposing that he does not exist now at the time of the general judgment, any more than that he is not now judging the world?* (*Essay Concerning the Use of Reason, Etc.*, p. 53, 54.)

This difficulty you must by no means pass over unsatisfied, because the author of the Essay here cited is believed to be a person whose reasoning you cannot slight.[1]

But to *proceed now* (as you say) *to the question* itself. My argument, you pretend, is inconclusive, because, in my enumeration of the possible qualities of matter, individual modes of figure, motion, and other qualities (such as are the *roundness of a circle,* the *individual mode of motion of a clock,* and, in your opinion, *consciousness or thinking*) are omitted, not being reducible to any of the three heads there mentioned.

I answer, *whole roundness* (as you call it) — that is, the name of the sum of the curvities of the arcs that constitute a circle — and the *whole mode of motion of a clock* — that is, the name of the sum of a certain number of motions — and *consciousness or thinking* — that is, as you suppose, the name of the sum of *ten thousand distinct motions,* or of a number of any other qualities

1 Again, Collins is the author of the *Essay* and so it is his own reasoning that he cannot slight. –ed.

void of consciousness — do all plainly belong to the *third* sort of qualities I mentioned — that is, they are all plainly nothing but bare *names of wholes,* mere *external denominations,* so far as their idea is different from that of their constituent parts, and are nothing at all really in the things themselves.[1] Which, whether it can possibly be the true notion of consciousness — making it nothing at all really in the thinking substance itself, but a mere empty and foreign name — I leave every man to judge from his own experience.

For my contending that *thinking* was not such a bare external *name* of a number of qualities, but itself a *real distinct quality* in the thinking substance, you before called my idea of *thinking a mere chimera of my own framing* (though I believe no man can help being conscious of the like *chimera* in himself), and now you repeat it again.[2] In answer to which, I refer you to what has been already said (*3d Defense*), and to what you will presently give me occasion to add further upon this head.

You *allow that no quality can reside in a system of matter, but what must be always* in a certain sense *of the same kind with the whole that results from the parts* (that is to say, *of the same kind with itself,* but I suppose you mean *of the same kind with its constituent parts*),[3] namely, that *the parts must be so far of the same kind as to have a* tendency, etc. *And* that *in that sense,* you *have always allowed consciousness to consist of powers of the same kind.*

But I have proved at large in my *Third Defense* that *motions* (or any other qualities void of consciousness) can be *in no sense* of the same kind with consciousness.[4] And I have shown *just now* that they cannot possibly in any sense have any *tendency* towards it, any more than *colors* or modes of color can have any tendency to *sound* or *smell.*[5]

The distinct beings in a system of matter contribute, you say, *towards thinking, as the pieces of a circle do towards a circle.*[6]

---

1 See 3*d Defense.* [pp. 163-64 –ed.]

2 *Reflect. on 2d Defense.* [p. 149 –ed.] Answer *to 3d Defense.* [p. 206 –ed.]

3 Answer. [p. 206–ed.]

4 *3d Defense. passim.* [For the claim see p. 168 –ed.]

5 See above, pp. 250-54.

6 Answer. [p. 207 –ed.]

That they cannot do so, and that there is no analogy, no similitude in the least, between the things you compare together, I have shown at large in my *Third Defense* — particularly, p. 248, ff., vol. 8 [p. 161ff –ed.], to which I refer you and the reader.

You allege that, in order *to contradict you, it must be affirmed that every quality that inheres in a system of matter must inhere* wholly *in each part of it;* that *roundness* is *an instance, that a power may inhere in a system of matter, without being the sum of powers of the same kind* — that is, *of whole roundnesses;* that *it is as impossible that* whole *consciousness should exist in each of the distinct parts of a system of matter, as that* whole *roundness should exist in each part of a circle;* and that, *unless in a round figure each part must be* wholly *round, and in a conscious system of matter each part must be* wholly *conscious, and* in that sense *consist of powers of the same kind — not one step can be taken in defense of Mr.* Clarke's *argument.*

To all this, I think I have already given a clear and distinct answer. *Third Defense.*

In representing part of which answer, you make it amount to this ridiculous proposition: that *though roundness consists of parts, none of which can possibly be round, yet, if consciousness inheres in a system of matter in like manner with roundness — that is, if it consists of parts, none of which can possibly be conscious — there must be as many consciousnesses as there are parts.* Whereas the plain strength and sum of the argument was this: that *as roundness consists of parts, none of which can indeed be the* whole *roundness, but yet every one of them must of necessity be* pieces *of roundness, so consciousness, if it inhered in matter in like manner with roundness, must likewise consist of parts, none of which could indeed be the* whole *consciousness, but yet every one of them must of necessity bear the same* analogy *to the whole consciousness, as the curvity of a semicircle bears to the curvity of two semicircles, or the curvity of one quadrant to the curvity of four quadrants.* And whether such parts can be *wholly* void of consciousness, because they have not in them singly the *whole* consciousness — any more than the arcs of a circle can be *wholly* void of curvity or roundness, because they have not in them singly the *whole* curvity or roundness — I leave to yourself to judge. Herein therefore you are guilty of a very great misrepresentation, in charging me with a contradiction which arises only from *your own* ludicrous interpretation of *my* words. For if you absurdly, and in defiance of the most perspicuous expressions, put *your contrary sense* upon *my* words, what wonder then is it if they become contradictory to *my own evident meaning?*

What you repeat (*Answer to Third Defense*) concerning your using it as a *supposition* only, and not declaring it your *opinion*, that *thinking* may be a mode of *motion*, I only desire the reader would be pleased to compare with what I offered (*Third Defense*). And, if in your *supposition* you pitched upon the likeliest quality of matter you could find to make thinking a mode of, and I prove the absurdity and impossibility of thinking's being a mode of that quality — and, at the same time, made it evident that the same arguments proved equally the absurdity and impossibility of thinking's being a mode of *any other* quality or power of matter whatsoever[1] — and yet you declared it positively to be your *opinion* that thinking was a mode of some power in matter,[2] I presume, your denying yourself to be accountable for the absurdity I charged you with, and complaining of my *disingenuity* in charging it upon you (or, as you are pleased to express yourself in *putting it upon you*), will not be looked upon as of any weight until you can answer the *argument* by which I prove it to be justly chargeable upon you — which argument you have not taken the least notice of, as I might reasonably have expected an *ingenuous adversary* would have done.

You proceed to offer some considerations, concerning the *nature of thinking*, from whence to deduce arguments to prove that it is merely an *affection of matter*.[3]

The sum of your first argument is this. The mind is operated upon by matter, and sensations are excited in it by the operation of matter, and all our senses depend on material organs. Matter likewise is operated upon by matter, and motions are excited in it by the contact and impulse of matter. Therefore, the mind is matter, and thinking a mere affection of matter. This argument, I think, deserves no answer. Yet the reader may, if he pleases, consult upon this head the *Third Defense*.

I shall only observe here, by the bye, that, whereas you say: *seeing thinking follows the motion of matter in our senses, we have just as much reason to conclude that it is a power or affection of matter occasioned by the action of matter, as we have to say that fire is a power*

1 *3d Defense*. [p. 168 –ed.]

2 *Reflections on 2d Defense*. [p. 127 –ed.]

3 *Answer*. [p. 212ff –ed.]

or affection of matter, when it is produced by rubbing of a wheel and axle-tree: it is evident, on the contrary, that we have all the reason in the world to conclude there is no similitude between these two things. Because fire, as it exists in the matter itself (separate from the sensations it excites in our minds), is confessedly nothing but mere motion. But thinking cannot possibly be mere motion, as I have abundantly proved in my *Third Defense,*[1] and will still further appear when I come to consider, in their proper place, the exceptions you have made to the proofs there urged.

Your second argument is this. Human thinking has succession and parts. Material actions likewise have succession and parts. Therefore, human thinking is a material action. This argument also, I think, deserves no answer.

Your third argument is. Thinking has its modes. Qualities of matter have likewise their modes. Therefore, thinking is a quality of matter. This is just as if I should argue: sound has its modes; color has likewise its modes; therefore, sound is a color. Or thus: spirit has existence; matter also has existence; therefore, spirit is matter. That I have not in the least misrepresented your sense in these argument, *I* appeal to whoever pleases to compare our papers together.

Your fourth argument is this. Thinking, in God, who is an immaterial being, is without any succession, modes, and distinct acts. Thinking in man has, on the contrary, succession, modes, and distinct acts — as the powers of matter have. Therefore thinking, in man, is a power or quality of matter.

In this also there is no consequence, though the premises were true. But, that thinking, in God, is without *succession,* I know not whether you will continue to affirm, or not,[2] when you have considered and compared together the two different accounts of this matter which I just now transcribed, and shall have resolved which of them you will adhere to by answering clearly the objections contained in the other.

In the mean time I cannot but take notice that you use a very strange expression, when you say *it is evident to you that God must*

1 *3d Defense.* [pp. 169-74 –ed.]

2 See above, pp. 255-56.

be an immaterial being — that is, a proper immaterial being, a being without any of the properties of matter, without solidity, extension or motion, and that exists in no place — that is, in other words, *which exists not at all.* For, if he exists at all, it is certain he exists in *every place.* I should not have made this remark, but that I am sure you are no friend to unintelligible distinctions, and words that have no signification, and that you will be ashamed to give me the Shoolmen's answer that God exists in every *Ubi* [place –ed.], but not in any *place* — that is, that in *Latin* he exists *everywhere,* but in *English nowhere.* And yet, unless you give either this answer or a better (for it is a thing of too great importance to be passed over without any answer at all), it cannot be helped, but your words will signify what it is not possible to suppose you could mean.

Nor is it a less wonderful expression, when you affirm that *thinking in God cannot be successive, nor have any modes or distinct acts of thinking, but that it is one numerical individual act, fixed, and permanent, and unvariable, and without succession,* etc. That is to say, that God cannot vary his will, nor diversify his works, nor act successively, nor govern the world, nor indeed have any *power* to *will* or *do* anything at all. I do not *charge* you with consequences, but I affirm they *are* too plain consequences of what you profess.

You observe that I allow *matter to act upon the soul* — which, since it cannot do by *contact,* it must be a *power whereof we have no idea* — and if there be in matter any such *power whereof we have no idea,* why may it not as well be capable of *thinking?*

I answer, the power by which matter acts upon the soul is not a *real quality* inhering in matter, as *motion* inheres in it, and as *thinking* inheres in the thinking substance, but it is only a power or occasion of exciting certain *modes* or *sensations* in another substance. Which power is one of those qualities I ranked under the *second* sort,[1] and there is no analogy at all between a subject's being itself capable of sensation, and its being the occasion of certain sensations being excited in another subject.

However, as to the thing itself, there is no more difficulty in conceiving how *matter* may act upon *immaterial substance,* than in conceiving how it acts upon *material substance.* When a globe, suppose, of a foot diameter, in motion, strikes upon a globe of

1 3*d Defense.* [p. 152 –ed.]

a foot diameter, at rest, tell me how *matter* acts upon *matter,* by *contact* — why the quiescent globe makes a *certain determinate* degree of resistance, why it *does not* make an infinitely great resistance, or why it *does* make any resistance at all. And when light is reflected and refracted by bodies, which it never touches; nay, at a distance from them evident to sense; and, in some circumstances, the nearer the medium, whose surface it reflects from, approaches to a vacuum, the greater and stronger the reflection is (of which there are convincing[1] experiments published to the world). Or when matter acts, by the cause of gravitation, upon other matter, in proportion, not to the bigness of the superficies [surface area –ed.], but to the quantity of the solid matter itself — that is, acts upon the very centers of the original solid parts of matter (of which, mathematicians know there are demonstrations extant). Tell me how, in these cases, *matter* acts upon *matter, without contact,* and I will undertake to tell you, how matter acts upon *immaterial substance.*

It is worthy of remark that, both here and elsewhere,[2] you seem willing to allow that power in matter, whereof you contend thinking to be a mode, is a power you *pretend not to know* — a power *unknown to us,* and *of which we have no idea, no distinct conception* in our minds, and which you *know not* whether it *be motion or no.*[3] Whatever it be, I have shown that the same arguments hold equally against thinking's being a mode of that unknown power, as against its being a mode of motion. But that which I would here remark is this. If *it is absolutely impossible* (as you elsewhere affirm[4]) *to prove that there are two different substances in the world, because we have not ideas of them,* how can we know there is any such unknown *power* in matter, without having an *idea* of it? And if it can be known that there is a *quality* in matter, of which we have *no idea,* why can it not as well be known that there is a *substance* in the world of which we have *no idea?* If there be (as you say) *no other test of truth but the perception of the agreement or disagreement of ideas,* how can we affirm anything concerning a *quality* of which we have *no idea?* If *difficulties which cannot be perfectly cleared* are (according to you) *contradictions and absurdities,* why is this important difficulty

1 Replacing "convictive" –ed.
2 Answer. [p. 211 –ed.]
3 See above.
4 Answer. [p. 238 –ed.]

left *uncleared?* Again, if it be true (as you affirm in another place) that *unless we have an idea of the creation of matter out of nothing, we must inevitably conclude matter a self-existent being,* how comes it not to be as evident that, unless we have an *idea* of the formation of a thought out of such qualities of matter as we have *no idea* of, we must inevitably conclude that matter cannot think? And that, unless we *have ideas* of those qualities which we *have no ideas of,* there can be no such qualities in matter? But all this is only upon your *own suppositions.* For the *unknown quality* you make *me* to ascribe to matter, in order to enable it to act upon immaterial substance, is not (as I just now showed[1]) a real *inherent quality,* but only a *power* or *occasion* of exciting *modes in another subject.*

You observe further that, if the soul be an immaterial substance, it is *a great difficulty to conceive how, by a mere preference of the mind,* we can move our hand, and cause it to rest again, when we will. Whereas, *if thinking be nothing but a mode of motion, or matter in motion, that difficulty is entirely at an end,* there being then nothing in it harder to be understood than how the hand of *a clock* is moved by the *weights or spring.*[2]

It is very true, if there be *no liberty of will at all,* then all the difficulties concerning the *manner* of it are *entirely at an end.* Thus *Descartes* put an end to all the *difficulties* concerning the *knowledge and perception of brutes,* by denying that they have any such thing as *sense, knowledge, or perception* at all. And if *you* had deprived your *human machines,* as he did his brutal ones, of all *sense and perception,* all *knowledge and understanding,* as well as all *liberty of will,* some further *difficulties* still concerning the nature of *thinking* and *perception* in general would have been also *entirely* at an end. And thus, if I should say I could *entirely put an end* to all the difficulties about *Optics* by supposing that men have *no eyes at all,* I should likewise say very true. But who would thank me for the notable discovery, I cannot tell.

And yet there is a difficulty even upon your own supposition, greater than you seem to be aware of. For by what *impulse,* by what *preference,* by what *power,* that matter *first and originally began* to move — which you suppose impels both the *weights of a clock,* and the *thinking materials in a man* — is just *as difficult*

1 See above, p. 261.

2 Answer. [p. 215 –ed.]

to conceive as how, by *a mere preference of the mind,* without any external impulse, we can cause our *hands* to *move.*[1]

You go on in the next place to consider my arguments against the possibility of thinking's being a mode of motion.

To my first — *viz. that modes of motion are nothing but particular motions, and cannot contain anything in their idea beyond the genus of motion;* and that *therefore we have the same intuitive certainty that consciousness cannot be a mode of motion, as we have that any one thing* is *not another, whose idea is the most remote from it that is possible* — you reply that *we have no idea of all the possible modes of motion;* that though *we have* indeed *ideas of the more simple modes of motion,* yet of the *very complex* ones *we have no distinct conception in our minds;* that therefore we *can no more prove or know that* thinking *is not one* of these more complex modes of motion *than* we *can know whether two things agree or differ from one another, that* we *have no idea of at all;* that *it is not possible for us to say that thinking does not consist in the peculiar motion of the spirits in the brain, until we have a particular idea of the motion of those spirits, and an idea of thinking as something distinct from a mode of motion;* that *thinking has the genus of motion, by arising from motion, by being varied by motion, by producing other motions, by having succession and parts, and innumerable modifications;* that *no idea of human consciousness can be produced beyond the genus of motion;* that *saying we have an intuitive certainty that consciousness cannot be a mode of motion, is only affirming the question in debate, which can signify nothing to any body that wants conviction, etc.*[2]

Now in all this, you have at last plainly declared the πρώτον ψεύδος [the first or primary error –ed.] of your whole hypothesis — namely, that you intend to make *thinking* not a *real quality,* but a *mere empty name* or *external denomination, such* as I at first ranked under the third head.[3] For the most complex modes of motion possible, whatever *name* we call them by, are still nothing but motions, and the *name* we give them is nothing but a *mere external denomination. Thinking* therefore, according to you, being only a *very complex mode of motion* [or *of any other quality of*

1 See *Boyle's Lecture, for the Year* 1704, *p. 96, etc., 2d Edit., p. 122. etc.,* 1*st Ed.* [Likely pp. 18-19, Clarke, 1998 –ed.]

2 Answer. [pp. 215-16 –ed.]

3 3*d Defense.* [Perhaps p. 152. –ed.]

matter] is likewise nothing but a *mere external name or denomination* of that mode. Which notion of yours, concerning thinking, is certainly a mere *chimera*, and a very absurd one.[1]

Every man has within himself the *idea* (or, in your language, the *chimera*) *of consciousness*,[2] which, though he cannot *produce* (as you absurdly require) — that is, cannot *define*, nor *describe*, any more than you can describe your idea of any *color* or *sound* — yet he as certainly knows it not to be any complex *mode of motion*, as you know your idea of *color* not to be any complex mode of *sound*.[3] Which intuitive certainty, if it be only a bare *affirming the question in debate* in one case, *and can signify nothing to anybody that wants conviction*, it is so in the other likewise. And then there is an end of all human knowledge, and no man can pretend to know any one thing not to be any other.

Thinking has indeed *succession and modes*, and many other things in common with *motion* — and so has *everything* with *everything*. The thing I affirmed was not that *thinking* has *no property* that motion has, but that it has something in its idea which motion has not — that it has something *beyond*, and *totally different from*, the genus of motion. And this, I still affirm, every man has an *intuitive* certainty of: which *intuition* you yourself allow to be one way (*Answer*) and, I add, it is of all others the most infallible way of knowing a thing to be true.[4]

We cannot indeed frame in our minds distinct *images* of the more complex modes of motion, as we can of the more simple ones.[5] But are we not, nevertheless, equally certain that they[6] are all alike *imaginable*, though our *narrow imaginations* cannot comprehend them? And that, if we could represent them to our imaginations, they would all appear as remote from the idea of *thinking*, as any one of them does? Because we cannot comprehend in our imagination a distinct conception of a *vast number in arithmetic*, as we can of a *small one*, do we not therefore know but that a *vast number* may possibly prove so different from a small one, as to turn into a *plant* or an *animal?* Because we cannot form

---

1 *Answer to* 3*d Defense.* [Perhaps p. 205 –ed.]
2 See above. [p. 257 –ed.]
3 *Answer to* 3*d Defense.* [p. 215 –ed.]
4 See *Third Defense.* [p. 169 –ed.]
5 *Answer.* [p. 215 –ed.]
6 Deleting the second "they" –ed.

in our minds an *image* of a space *ten thousand millions of miles* square, as we can of *ten foot* square, are we not therefore sure but that the great space may possibly be something whose true idea shall have no similitude, no relation to extension? If I should plead in favor of *motion's* being a mode of *figure* (as you do for *thinking's* being a mode of *motion*) — that, *though we have indeed ideas of the more simple modes of* figure, *yet of the very complex ones we have no distinct conception in our minds;* and that therefore, though we are sure indeed that a *triangle* or a *square* is not a *motion,* yet we *can no more prove or know that* motion *is not one of the more complex modes of* figure, *than we can know whether two things agree or differ from one another, that we have no idea of at all* — if I should argue thus, I say, I know well what mathematicians would argue concerning me. And I can guess what answer I should deserve, if I should tell the world further that *it is not possible for us to say that* color *does not consist in a peculiar* mixture of ten thousand various sounds, *till we have a particular distinct idea of the result of the mixture of those ten thousand sounds.* I may call *scarlet-color,* if I please, a very complex mode of *sound;* and who shall confute me, by *producing* the *particular distinct idea* of the result of a *peculiar* mixture of ten thousand sounds? And you may call *thinking,* if you please, a very complex mode of *motion.* Yet neither of them will, by either of our confidence in giving things *names,* be ever the nearer becoming such in reality. This I think, clearly shows your notion to be something more than a *difficulty that cannot be perfectly cleared* — that is (according to you), something more than *an absurdity and contradiction.* But I will be content to look upon it as being but barely *contradictory and absurd.*

To my second argument — *viz. that, if thinking was a mode or species of motion, it would follow that all motion would be a degree of thinking* — you reply that you *do allow that every motion is a degree of thought, in that sense wherein it* is *proper to say that every motion is a degree of fire, etc.* That is, you *allow* every motion to be as much a degree of the *sensation itself* — of *heat,* for instance, or of any other *sensation* or *thought* arising in the *mind* — as it is a degree of that *mode* of *motion* in *matter* which excites in us such or such a particular sensation. You *allow* even[1] the slowest motion of a *needle* to be as much and as properly a degree of *pain,* as it is a

1 Replacing "every" –ed.

degree of *that motion* which causes it to prick the skin. You *allow* every motion of a particle of air to be as truly a degree of the *thought and reason* of a man, as it is a degree of that *mode of motion* which, striking the ear, excites in us the sensation of *sound*. You must by the same reason have *allowed,* if it had been desired of you, that a *straight line* is as much a piece of a *motion* as it is a piece of the *figure of a triangle*. But I accept contentedly what you *do allow,* and I do not desire to be *allowed* any more.

To my third argument — *viz. that if thinking was a mode of motion, then motion would be a more generical power than thinking; whereas on the contrary, etc.* — your reply is so uncertain and obscure, that it is hard to know what to make of it. The strength of the argument, which you pretend you cannot understand, was plainly this: that *no particular mode of any power can contain under it so great a variety of modes as the superior power itself does, for the same reason that quadrilateral figure, which is a mode of figure, cannot contain under it so great a variety of modes as figure in general does. And that therefore, if thinking was a particular mode of motion, there could not possibly be* so *many modes of thinking as there are of motion. But now, on the contrary, it is evident there are more modes of thinking than there are of motion, because every mode of motion has a mode of thinking* [*an idea*] *answering to it, and there are innumerable other modes of thinking besides. Thinking therefore cannot possibly be a mode of motion.* [And *the same argument holds against the possibility of its being a mode of any other power of matter whatsoever.*] This is in short the sum of that argument, which, you say, *you are perfectly at a loss to know what it means. To know what it means,* I believe every man, except yourself, is very able. But to *know what to answer to it,* you might well be *perfectly at a loss.* Instead of answering it, therefore, you were resolved to be even with me for offering you an argument you could not understand, and would needs say something in opposition to it which you were sure neither *I* nor *any body else* could understand — namely, that *ideas* are not *modes,* but *objects* of *thinking.* However, this being manifestly absurd, you contradict yourself again in the next page, and say *it must be allowed that every distinct thought,* [that is, every *idea*] *is a particular* mode *of thinking, and* so *thinking must in us have a great number of modes. But yet, for all that,* you say, *our thoughts are finite and limited,* and *we comprehend only the more simple modes of motion and figure;* and, *since our thoughts are all limited in point of number, you see no reason from their variety necessary* to *conclude that human thinking cannot be a mode of motion.* You seem resolved indeed not to *see the reason.* But the reason is visible enough, and will force any man to see it that does not shut his eyes — *viz.* that there being more variety of *modes of thinking* than there is of *modes of motion,* and all the *modes of motion* (though we cannot actually attend to them, because their number is infinite) answering only to *one species* of the *modes of thinking* (which modes of thinking, under that *one species,* are likewise infinite in number), it is plainly, and for the very same reason, as impossible that *thinking* should be any one of the infinite number of the *modes of motion,* as that *figure in general* should be any one of the infinite number of the *modes of quadrilateral figure.*

You add: *if we consider but the prodigious variety of sounds which are called distinct modes of sound, it is as easy to conceive, that upon supposition of thinking being a mode of motion, it should have the several modes that we are conscious it has, as that sound should have all the distinct innumerable modes which that has.* But from what has been said, it is evident that, as all the modes of *sound,* though infinite in number, yet bear no proportion to the infinite variety of the modes of infinite other things put all together, so the infinite modes of *motion,* and their correspondent ideas, bear no proportion to the infinite variety of infinite other modes of thinking. And that therefore *thinking,* with its infinite variety of modes, can no more possibly be a *mode of motion,* though the *modes of motion* be allowed to be capable of infinite variation, than *colors,* or *smells,* or any other thing that has no similitude to these, can any of the infinite number of the modes of *sound.*

My fourth argument was drawn from the *authority,* and from the *reasoning* of Mr. *Locke.*

The *authority,* you profess to despise.

To the *reasoning,* you answer that Mr. *Locke*'s *whole design, in the passage* I cited, was not to prove *that* human *thinking cannot be a mode of motion,* but that *thinking in the* deity cannot *depend on the motion of the parts of a corporeal system;* and that, *as the question is not the same, so some of the consequences that Mr.* Locke *draws from those principles affect only that really absurd supposition of thinking's being a mode of motion in God.*

I reply: it is very true that Mr. *Locke* indeed is not there proving that *thinking in man,* but that *thinking in God* cannot be a *mode of motion,* and that *some* of the consequences he there draws do indeed affect only the latter question, and not the former. But, if the *reasoning* he uses be as strong in one case as in the other, and the *consequences* I made use of from him were only such as affect both questions alike (for which I appeal to every reader),[1] it was by no means consistent with ingenuity and candor for you to endeavor to impose upon readers with so weak an answer.

To my last argument (which also you seem unwilling to *understand)* — *viz.* that *if thinking was a mode or species of motion, then in like manner as it* is *a proper expression to say that circularity is one species of figure, and squareness a second, and cubicalness a third, and ellipticalness a fourth,* so *it would be proper also to say that circular motion is one species of motion, and motion in a square a second, and motion in an ellipsis a third, and thinking or consciousness a fourth* (which consequence, I think, is abundantly absurd) — you reply, by quibbling upon the word *proper:* that the argument has relation only to *propriety of language,* and that you see not what ground I have to *contest this language* with you.[2] Whereas the question was not whether it was *proper* with respect to the *language,* but with respect to the *sense* — that is, whether it was *true* according to your hypothesis, and a *just and necessary consequence* from it to say that *thinking* differs no otherwise from *circular motion* than *circular motion* does from *elliptical motion,* or from *motion in a square.* And this, it seems (as you are indeed this time very liberal in your concessions), you are willing to grant, and I am well contented with the concession.

Upon the question *whether individual personality can be preserved by a continual transferring of consciousness from one parcel of matter to another in so flux a substance as the brain or spirits,* you repeat what you had before advanced in your *Reflections.*[3] In answer to which, I shall not repeat, but only desire the reader to compare what I offered in my *Third Defense,* pp. 288, 289, and 302, 303, *vol.* 8 [pp. 180–81 and 192–95 in this edition –ed.]. And I shall here make only some brief incidental observations on what seems new in your reply.

1 See *Third Defense.* [p. 173 –ed.]
2 *Answer.* [p. 221 –ed.]
3 *Answer.* [p. 223 –ed.]

In the first place, you disown none of the absurd consequences I charged on your hypothesis.[1] You deny not but *one substance may be conscious of an action's having been done by itself which really was not done by it, but by another substance;*[2] you make *individual personality to be a mere external imaginary denomination, and all self-consciousness a mere dream and delusion; you own that one man may possibly be two persons, and two or two hundred men one person — that is, not persons exactly like one another, but all really and truly one and the same individual person, at the same time that they continue so many distinct, intelligent, rational men.*[3] These absurdities, I say, you have not denied to be unavoidable consequences of your hypothesis, nor have you done anything towards clearing them from being absurdities, but instead thereof have only offered some loose objections against what I propose under this head.

You say you *are sure* that my *calling* your *hypothesis* an *impossible* one, *and, instead of saying a word to prove it impossible, immediately arguing on the supposition of its possibility, is begging the question, and supposing what I was to prove.* The particular hypothesis here referred to (*viz. that memory may be preserved in a fleeting substance by continually repeating the ideas, and imprinting them afresh upon new particles of matter perpetually succeeding in the room of those that pass away*) was, I said, an impossible hypothesis; and an impossible hypothesis it will always appear to be until you can find out some new hypothesis by which to make it intelligible how it is possible that new ideas printed upon new particles should be a *memory* of old ideas printed upon old particles. But I did not enlarge upon this, because, supposing the *possibility* of it, yet it would avail nothing towards your main purpose, the question being, not whether the *memory* in general of such or such an action's having been done might possibly be preserved in the manner you suppose, but whether the *consciousness* of its being done by *me*, by *my own individual self* in particular, could in this manner be continued. Now how it was in me a *begging of the question* to argue that, even on supposition of the possibility of the hypothesis now mentioned, yet it would nevertheless be impossible for you from thence to make out the conclusion you were to prove, I confess I understand not. Neither do I understand how

1 See *Third Defense*. [pp. 180-83 –ed.]

2 *Answer*. [p. 224 –ed.]

3 Compare 3*d Defense*, and *Answer*. [Cf. pp. 180-83 with pp. 234-35 –ed.]

you can prevail upon yourself to dispute in such a manner.

A man, you say, who, during *a short frenzy, kills* another, *and then returns to himself, without the least consciousness of what he has done, cannot attribute that action to himself,* and therefore *the mad man and the sober man are really two as distinct persons as any two other men in the world, and will be so considered in a court of judicature.* Extraordinary reasoning indeed! Because in a *figurative* sense a man, when he is mad, is said *not to be himself,* and in a *forensic* sense is looked upon as not answerable for his *own actions,* therefore in the *natural and philosophical* sense also *his actions* are not *his own actions,* but *another person's,* and the *same man* is *really two distinct persons!*

You add: *should there be* so *strong a representation to my understanding of a murder done by me (which was really never done at all)* so *that I could not distinguish it in my mind from something really done by me, I can no more help attributing this to myself, etc.* It is true, I could not *help* it indeed — but it would be (as Mr. *Locke* well expresses it) a *fatal error,* and not (as you would have it) a making me to be really the person I am not.[1] *So that it is evident* (you go on) *that self or personal identity consists solely in consciousness,*[2] though a false one — that is, it consists in a *false representation,* in *a dream,* as Mr. *Locke* well expresses it again. And so all mankind, it seems, are nothing but a dream. Unless rather your opinion itself be a dream, as, I presume, it will be found to be by every man whose reason is wake.

The restoring, you say, *the power of thinking to the same or to a different body at the resurrection, with a memory or consciousness extending to past actions, will be a raising the same person, and not creation of a new one.* If so, then the restoring the like power of thinking to twenty different bodies with false memory (a dream), or a consciousness extending to imaginary past actions, will be a making them all (as I said, and as you expressly allow) to be, not persons like one another, but one and the same individual person, at the same time that they continue different, intelligent, rational men. That is to say, if twenty of your clocks happen to go exactly alike, they are no more twenty clocks, but one and the same individual clock.

Your distinction, between *raising the same person* and *creating*

1 See *Third Defense.* [p. 182 –ed.]

2 *Answer.* [p. 232 –ed.]

a new one, is a distinction without any the least difference. For the *memory or consciousness extending to past actions,* which you suppose makes the *same person* in the one case, does exactly as well make the same person in the other case. It being evidently as easy for God to add an imaginary *consciousness extending to past actions that never were* to a new created body *now,*[1] as to add an imaginary *consciousness extending to past actions that were done by one body* to another body at the *Resurrection.* So that from your opinion it unavoidably follows that I may now, at this present time, as possibly be created anew, and have another *self, existing* at the same time with me, by God's adding to *the understanding* of a new-made body so *strong a representation* of my past actions, that that other my-self *could not distinguish them in his mind from things really done by him* (as you express yourself in a like case).[2] This, I say, is exactly as possible, in your hypothesis, as it is for me to be raised again at the Resurrection.

Your argument, by which you endeavor to retort upon me that, according to my notion of individual personality, there can be no Resurrection, nor any such thing as personal identity at all, is founded upon a fallacious representation — as if, by the *same individual numerical consciousness,* I understood the *same individual numerical act of thinking.* Whereas the *individual numerical consciousness,* which identifies the person, is that perception by which the person is sensible that his *past acts of thinking* were his *own thoughts* and not *another's.* Which *perception,* in the same continued being, is a *true memory,* and can be *true* in that one numerical being only. But in your fleeting being, it would be a *false memory,* a *mere delusion,* and might be impressed on any number of beings at one and the same time. All which, distinct, intelligent, rational beings, because they happened to be in the same *dream,* you would affirm to be one and the same individual person. And, for the same reason, if twenty pieces of money happen to be stamped with so like an impression that they could not be distinguished one from another, you must affirm them all to be one and the same *individual shilling,* notwithstanding their being different *pieces of silver.*

Having granted that if *ever* so *many thinking beings* have — not *one and the same numerical consciousness,* as by your comparison

1 See Answer. [p. 233 –ed.]
2 See *Answer.* [p. 232 –ed.]

of a *vast bulk of senseless matter* being added to a man's body, you would very artfully insinuate, in contradiction to the whole course of your argument and most express concessions, but — having granted, I say, and contended, that if *ever* so *many distinct thinking beings* have within themselves a like *consciousness,* or a like *present representation of past actions,* they *can all constitute but one and the same person,* you ask me whether each of these distinct thinking beings must not unavoidably *think* himself the *same person* that did the action, and the *same person* that everyone of the rest will likewise distinctly think himself to be? I answer as before. They must indeed *unavoidably think* so, but in so doing, they must also *unavoidably be mistaken.*[1] And so, according to your notion, we are all *unavoidably we know not who,* and do but *fancy and dream* ourselves to be the persons we think we are, and write and read about *we know not whom nor what.*

To your taking refuge in the *justice* of God, I have already answered that the question is not whether God *will* do an absurd thing, but whether in the nature of things it be possible to be done.[2] And whereas you allege that *if God should cause to exist twenty present representation of the same past sinful actions in* so *many distinct beings, the consequent punishment would be twenty times as much as the sinful actions deserved and his justice required,* and that therefore God *will not* do any such thing, I reply the difficulty does not lie there.[3] Because the punishment due to the single person's sinful actions might be divided proportionably among the twenty distinct intelligent beings — which, in your way, are one and the same individual person, and so, *according to you,* there would be no injustice done, because the punishment would not be more that the offenses deserved. And yet it is manifest that, *in reality,* nineteen at least of these twenty distinct intelligent beings would be punished unjustly, how small a proportion so ever they bear of the punishment, because they would be punished for what they had never been guilty of at all — however, by a false *consciousness,* they might *imagine* themselves to have *done* what they *never did.*

The case you put, of a person living well for some years, and afterwards forgetting that he had done so, and then living for

1 See above. [p. 271 –ed.]
2 *3d Defense.* [p. 182 –ed.]
3 *Answer.* [p. 236 –ed.]

the future in all manner of debauchery, is so far from being an *absurdity,* as you call it, upon my notion of personal identity, that, on the contrary, there is no manner of difficulty in it. The man is not *two persons, as much as any two men in the world are two persons* (which you declare he must be, in consequence of *your* principles — a consequence sufficient to have convinced almost any man of the falsity of the principles from which he sees and owns such an absurdity to follow). But he is, I confess (as you add in the next words), *as much two persons* as *the same man mad and sober is two persons* — that is, he is *not at all two persons,* but plainly *one and the same person* — and shall justly be punished as his iniquities deserve.

You urge that my argument is no more useful to the ends *of religion* than yours, because, *unless the soul, as an immaterial being, did perpetually think, a proof of the immateriality of the soul* would not necessarily *prove a future state of rewards and punishments.* And upon this you are pleased to make yourself merry in a very needless manner. Now what connection there is between the soul's *immateriality* and its *perpetual thinking* has been considered elsewhere. In this place it may be sufficient to add that whether the *immateriality and immortality* of the soul necessarily infers its perpetual actual thinking, or not, yet *my* argument is evidently *useful* to religion, by proving at least the *possibility,* and *great probability,* of a future state of rewards and punishments. And *yours* is evidently *destructive* of religion, by making a future state of rewards and punishments not only *improbable,* but *impossible* — seeing it infers (as I have at large shown) an absolute *impossibility* of a *resurrection of the same person;* and if a resurrection were possible, yet, by introducing such an absolute and fatal *necessity* of all human actions, as Mr. *Hobbes* and *Spinoza* formerly attempted to establish by the same *numerical* argument (though from your *thinking in the same way,* I would not conclude you all to be the same *individual* person), it manifestly makes all future *reward unreasonable,* and all *punishment unjust.* Of which more immediately.

My first argument to prove your notion destructive of religion was that *by inferring the necessity of all human actions, it makes men to be subjects no more capable of religion than clocks and watches are.*

To this you reply, first, that *thinking's being a mode of motion in any system of matter* (which is the supposition I refer to, that destroys all liberty of will) is *nowhere affirmed by you.*[1] But this is a mere quibble, as I have shown at large. (*Third Defense,* pp. 270, 271, pp. 168-69 this edition. And above, pp. 407, 408, *vol. 8*, p. 259 this edition.)

In the next place, therefore, you answer seriously that *men and clocks agreeing in being necessarily determined in all their actions does no more prove them to be alike incapable of religion, than an immaterial substance and a clock's agreeing in being extended, proves them to be alike incapable of religion.*[2] Had I not seen it, I could not have believed that either you or any reasonable man could have given such an answer. *Necessity,* if men and clocks agree in it, must make them both alike incapable of religion, because *necessity* is the very thing that makes any being incapable of religion. But *extension,* supposing immaterial substance and clocks to agree in that, would not make them both alike incapable of religion, because *extension* is not the thing that makes any being incapable of religion.

Necessity, you *must reply,* is not the thing that makes any being incapable of religion. What is it then that incapacitates for religion? *Want of understanding,* you say.[3] For *what excludes a clock from being a proper subject of religion, but the want of a human understanding?* And *what is it that makes a man a proper subject of religion, but his understanding?* I answer, it is not *understanding,* but *will,* that makes a man capable of religion, and it is not *want of understanding,* but *want of will and of power of acting freely,* that makes a clock incapable of religion. For, supposing a clock to have the understanding of a man, yet if, for all that understanding, it continued to be moved by the weights as necessarily as it is now, it is manifest it would then have no more power of doing *good* or *evil* than it has now, and the only difference would be that it would then know and understand itself to be incapable of religion, whereas now it is incapable of religion without understanding or being sensible that it is so.

And to make it appear that *necessity* in an intelligent, as well as an unintelligent, being incapacitates for religion, and that there can be no religion without *freedom of will,* I offer only the following

1 Answer *to 3d Defense.* [p. 226 –ed.]

2 See above. p. 226.

3 Answer. [p. 226 –ed.]

argument. *Religion* supposes a *future state of rewards and punishments,* and a *future state of rewards and punishments* supposes that God is *pleased* and *displeased* with the different actions of men, and God's manifesting his *displeasure* towards certain persons by *punishing* them finally supposes that such *punishment* is *just,* and that the persons *deserved* it. For *God cannot err.* Now, if men, with all their *understandings,* were under the same *necessity* in all their actions — as a clock is in its motions — then, though you would unreasonably imagine perhaps it might serve *some designs* of human government to *pull* and *draw,* to *drive* and *push,* such necessary agents with the *screws* and *springs* of *rewards* and *punishments* — as men govern their clocks by the addition and subtraction of weights — yet neither from the hands of *God* or *men* could the good or evil actions of such intelligent machines *deserve* either reward or punishment; nor could there possibly be any *justice* in God's final distribution of rewards and punishments; nor is there any reason why any man should *reproach* himself, or be *blamed* by others (even by those who would be so unreasonable as to *punish* the machine), for any profaneness, impiety, or wickedness whatsoever — for murdering a man, for instance, with his sword when his hand was moved *necessarily* to do it by the action of subtle matter upon his brain and spirits, any more than if he had done it by another man's *forcibly* using his hand and sword. Neither is it possible that God should be *pleased* or *angry* with any man for doing what he could not avoid doing, any more than a man can be *angry* with his clock for going wrong, even supposing the machine endued with understanding enough to feel and be sensible that its weights necessitated it to do so. The notion therefore you maintain, of men's actions being all *necessary,* is totally destructive of religion.

Until you can give a *clear* answer to this argument, you stand obliged by promise to *allow that man is no more a subject of religion, than a clock — nay, to go further, and allow that there can be no such thing as religion.* Though, I hope, you will be better than your word, and own rather that there is no such thing as *necessity.*

Before we dismiss this argument, you will expect I should answer the two questions you put to me *ad hominem.* Though indeed you have no reason to expect it, because you knew (but, for reasons best known to yourself, took not the least notice of it) that they were both of them *directly* and *clearly* answered in the places from whence you had them.

First, you *desire* Mr. Clarke, *who maintains* (you say) *the* certainty of all events, *to show what different influence the supposed* necessity *of our actions can have on the* power of self-determination, *that the supposition of the* certainty of our actions *has not.* I answer, your supposed *necessity* is directly contradictory to the *power of self-determination,* and therefore manifestly inconsistent with it, but the *certainty* I speak of in the place you cite,[1] has no inconsistency at all with the *power of self-determination,* because it means (as is there largely explained) only that *mere futurity,* which you yourself must confess all actions had while they were *yet future,* even upon supposition of the *power of self-determination.* For you can *suppose,* what you will *not grant,* a *power of self-determination.* And, I presume, you cannot deny but every *past* action *had,* and every *future* action *has* a *futurity* (which is all that was meant by *certainty of event* in the place referred to), notwithstanding that supposed *power of self-determination.*

Secondly, you ask, *if* (as Mr. *Clarke* affirms) the necessary and eternal different relations, which different things bear to one another, always and *necessarily* do determine the will of God, *and* God is *unalterably* determined to do always what is best in the whole, then *how can he have a power of self-determination?*[2] I answer, the *necessity* there spoken of is only a *moral* necessity — which, as to the effects, may be depended upon with infallible certainty (*viz.* that a *wise* being *will* not act *foolishly,* and a *good* being *will* not do *evil*) — but, as to the *thing itself,* it is in the *natural and philosophical* sense (of which we are now treating) *no necessity at all,* but *mere self-determination.* As is at large explained in the book you refer to.[3] Which, if you would have *taken to yourself the character of an ingenuous adversary,* certainly you ought to have taken some notice of.[4] For *when terms are defined, and instances agreeing to those definitions given, whereby all doubtfulness about one another's meaning is in the most effectual manner excluded,* to cite an author's words, notwithstanding this, and apply them to a sense directly contrary to what the author largely and expressly

---

1 *Boyle*'s Lect., Vol. I., 1st Ed., *p.* 215, 216. 2d Edit., *p.* 169, 170. [pp. 74-75, Clarke, 1998 –ed.]

2 *Boyle*'s Lect., Vol. I, 1st Ed., *p.* 256 *and* 128. 2d Edit., *p.* 200 *and* 101. [Perhaps pp. 54 and 84, Clarke, 1998 –ed.]

3 *Ibid.*, Vol. I, 1st Ed., *p.* 140, 237, 243, etc., 247, etc. 2d Edit., *p.* 110, 111, 115, 190, etc.

4 *Answer to 3d Defense.* Ibid. [p. 230 or perhaps p. 207 –ed.]

explains he intends they should be taken in, is no fair way of managing a controversy.

My second argument to prove your notion *destructive of religion* was drawn from the consideration of the nature of *personal identity,* and of the *resurrection of the same person.* To which all the reply you have made has been considered already.[1]

To your argument that, *if we have no idea of the substance of matter and of the substance of spirit, it is impossible to prove that one is not the other,*[2] it might be sufficient to answer that an unprejudiced person would be apt to think it as easy to prove that there is a substance in the world of which we have *no idea,* totally different from the *substance of matter,* as that there should be a *quality* in matter of which we have *no idea,* totally different from all the known *qualities of matter.* But to pass this over, I affirm that from our knowledge of any being's having certain properties incompatible with the *essential properties* of matter, we may certainly infer that the substance of that being and the substance of matter are not the same, though we have no idea of the substances themselves. We have no idea of *infinity,*[3] and yet every mathematician can demonstrate concerning many infinites that one is not another, and in some the exact proportion between one and another, without having an idea of either. And to *yourself,* you say, *it is evident that God must be an* immaterial *being,* because he is *without any of the properties of matter.* (I hope you mean the *peculiar* properties of matter, otherwise *existence* will be one of its properties, as much as any of those you mention.) The most *essential properties* of matter we know are, I think, *impenetrability, divisibility,* and that which mathematician's call its *vis inertiae* [inertial power –ed.]. If you will say that, though these properties belong indeed universally to all the matter we have any knowledge of, yet, for ought we know, there may be other matter which wants these properties, and so these properties may possibly not be *essential,* but only *accidental* to matter. Then, I say, you either mean nothing at all by the word *matter,* or else you mean by it the same as you do by the word *substance,* and then your affirming God to be *immaterial* will be as much as affirming him to have *no existence.* And, as to the *thinking substance* in man, when you shall declare that by the *thinking system of matter*

1 *3d Defense.* [pp. 180-84 –ed.]

2 Answer. [pp. 238-39 –ed.]

3 Replacing e with y. –ed.

in the brain you mean a system of such matter as has no *impenetrability,* no *divisibility,* and no *vis inertiæ,* we shall then dispute upon a new foot.

In the mean time, *nothing seems clearer* to you *at present than that the essence or substance of matter consists in solidity,* and that to be *solid* is to be *coextended with the parts of space.* If so, then the *omnipresent God* cannot co-exist with all the parts of space without being *material.* And I desire you would be pleased, in your next, to answer the difficulties objected against your notion of *God's immateriality,* as they are expressed in the passage I before cited out of the *Essay Concerning the Use of Human Reason,* substituting only the words [*coexist with all the different parts of space*] all along instead of the words [*coexist with all the differences of time*], and [*immensity*] instead of [*eternity*].[1] And this I insist on the rather, and desire it the more earnestly, because (as I before observed) it is generally believed that that Essay {was} written by a person with whose *reasoning* (for we are not to give any deference to authority) you are thoroughly acquainted.

As to what I said against material impulse being the cause of gravitation, the *whole,* you say, *is founded on this, that because a bullet, a feather, and a piece of leaf-gold descend with equal swiftness in vacuo, therefore material impulse cannot be the cause of gravitation.* Whereas, on the contrary, this was only an incidental instance, to show by a gross and vulgar experiment (what mathematicians know are proofs enough of in nature) that gravity is exactly proportionable to the quantity of *solid* matter contained in bodies, and not at all to the quantity of their *superficies.* This proportion it is, that evidently shows gravitation not to be caused by material impulse. And unless you could have found an hypothesis, whereby either the quantity of *solid* matter in bodies, and the quantity of their *superficies,* could be made one and the same, or, upon mechanical principles, bodies could, by *superficial* contact, receive impulses proportional to the quantity of *solid* matter contained in them, you would much more advantageously to yourself have acknowledged the first palpable error, than by a heap of things beside the purpose have endeavored to amuse only such readers as want skill in mathematics.

1 See above. [See pp. 255-56 –ed.]

My saying that you endeavor to insinuate to your reader that that excellent person, Sir *Isaac Newton,* was of your opinion in the present question, you *assure the reader is a pure fiction.* But I hope you will take it in good part, that I was so complaisant to you as to imagine that you were not yourself so sensible of the *needlessness* of your citation out of his book, as you now acknowledge that you were.

You tell us, *if we have not an idea of the creation of matter out of nothing, we must inevitably conclude matter a self-existent being.* I answer, by the same argument it follows, on the contrary, that *if we have not an idea of the self-existence of matter* — that is, that every distinct particle of matter in the universe, is a necessary, independent, self-existent being — we must inevitably *conclude matter to be a created being.* And by a better argument it follows, *if we have an idea of the possibility of the non-existence of matter* — that is, *if we have an idea that space can (without a contradiction) exist without matter in it* — *we must inevitably conclude matter not be a necessarily existing, but a created being.* In like manner, by the same argument with yours, it follows that, *if we have not an idea* (as you own we have not) *of the inherence of thinking in matter, we must inevitably conclude it to inhere in something immaterial.* And by a better argument it follows, *if we see a disagreement of ideas in supposing thinking to inhere in matter, we must inevitably conclude it to inhere in immaterial substance.*

What the rest of your loose and uncertain discourse about *creation* and *self-existence* tends to, I do not well understand. Only, I am sure, it is foreign to our present question. Yet two things there are in it which, I think, deserve to be remarked incidentally.

The first is that from these words of mine — *on whatever hypothesis they* (that is, atheists) *proceed, nothing is* so *certain, as that man, considered without the protection and conduct of a superior being, is in a far worse case than upon the supposition of the being and government of God, and of men's being under his peculiar conduct, protection, and favor* — you most uncandidly infer that *atheists, according to Mr.* Clarke, *even while they continue so, have no reason to fear anything for their disbelief.*

The second is this, that *to gratify that desire which even atheists have to see a truth established so much for the benefit of men, you shall conclude this debate* (you say) *with an essay showing a way how to demonstrate the existence of God* — viz. *by proving the creation of matter out of nothing.* And this you do, by *omitting for the present so useful a design, and leaving it entirely to some of those gentlemen that are appointed annually to preach at the Lecture founded by the Honorable* Robert Boyle.

Instead of concluding therefore, as you promised, with *an essay showing a way how to demonstrate the existence of God,* you almost in the same breath repent of so noble an undertaking, and end your discourse with a pretended *compliment* to *me,* that you *will give me upon this occasion a testimony in my favor* — viz. *that you verily think I neither believe too little, nor too much, but am perfectly and exactly orthodox, and in all likelihood will continue so.* And considering *we have had (you say) the happiness* in England *to have such rational Parliaments and Convocations, that have established nothing but truth,* I should have taken this as a testimony very much in my favor indeed, had you not elsewhere dropped some expressions concerning *prostituting conscience* so *far as to submit to any mere human authority, and to the decisions and determinations of those men that in every country have worldly preferments to bestow.* Which yet since you make no application of, neither shall I. Only, in return for your *favor,* I shall, instead of giving any testimony concerning you, conclude with most hearty wishes, that you would be very careful, while you are disputing about *metaphysics,* not to oppose the interest of *true religion and virtue,* without which nothing is truly valuable or praiseworthy among men.

Appendix A: Before the Correspondence

1. From Henry More, *The Immortality of the Soul* (1662)

[The Cambridge Platonist Henry More (1614-87) probably knew Isaac Newton, and More's view of space may have influenced Newton's account of absolute space. In *The Immortality of the Soul*, More sets forth a rather baroque theory of an extended soul. In the section selected here, he argues that the soul is extended, penetrable, and indiscerptible, while matter is extended, impenetrable, and discerptible. While Samuel Clarke's account of the soul is much less detailed than More's, the distinction between an extended but indiscerptible soul and extended but discerptible matter is at the very heart of Clarke's position in the Clarke-Collins Correspondence. Anthony Collins argues that if the soul is extended it ought to be discerptible. If this were so, the asymmetry between mind and matter would disappear and with it Clarke's argument against the possibility of matter thinking. *The Immortality of the Soul* was first published in 1659 and then included in More's *A Collection of Several Philosophical Writings* (1662). This selection is reproduced from Volume 2 of the two-volume Garland reprint of More's *A Collection of Several Philosophical Writings* (1978).]

AXIOM IX

There are some properties, powers and operations, immediately appertaining to a thing, of which no reasons can be given, nor ought to be demanded, nor the way or manner of the cohesion of the attribute with the subject can by any means be fancied or imagined.

10. The evidence of this axiom appears from the former. For if the *naked substance* of a Thing be so utterly unconceivable, there can be nothing apprehended there to be a connection between it and its first properties. Such is *actual divisibility* and *impenetrability* in *matter*. By *actual divisibility* I understand *discerptibility*, gross tearing or cutting one part from another. These are *immediate*

properties of matter; but why they should be there, rather then in any other subject, no man can pretend to give, or with any credit ask, the reason. For *immediate attributes* are indemonstrable, otherwise they would not be *immediate*.

11. So the *immediate properties* of a *spirit* or immaterial substance are *penetrability* and *indiscerpibility*. The necessary cohesion of which Attributes with the Subject is as little demonstrable as the former. For supposing that, which I cannot but assert, to be evidently true, That there is no substance but it has in some sort or other the three dimensions; this substance, which we call *matter*, might as well have been *penetrable* as *impenetrable*, and yet have been substance: But now that it does so certainly and irresistibly keep one part of it self from *penetrating* another, it is so, we know not why. For there is no necessary connection discernible between *substance* with *three dimensions*, and *impenetrability*. For what some allege, that it implies a contradiction, that *extended* substance should run one part into another; for so part of the *extension*, and consequently of the *substance*, would be lost; this, I say, (if nearly looked into) is of no force. For the substance is no more lost in this case, than when a string is doubled and redoubled, or a piece of wax reduced from a long figure to a round: The dimension of *longitude* is in some part lost, but without detriment to the *substance* of the wax. In like manner when one part of an *extended* substance runs into another, something both of *longitude*, *latitude* and *profundity* may be lost, and yet all the *substance* there still; as well as *longitude* lost in the other case without any loss of the *substance*.

And as what was lost in *longitude* was gotten in *latitude* or *profundity* before; so what is lost here in all or any two of the dimensions, is kept safe in essential *spifsitude*: For so I will call this *mode* or *property of a substance*, that is able to receive one part of it self into another. Which *fourth mode* is as easy and familiar to my understanding, as that of the *three dimensions* to my sense or phansy. For I mean nothing else by *spifsitude*, but the redoubling or contracting of substance into less space then it does sometimes occupy. And analogous to this is the lying of two substances of several kinds in the same place at once.

To both these may be applied the terms of *reduplication and saturation*: The former, when essence or substance is but once redoubled into it self or into another; the latter, when so oft, that it will not easily admit any thing more. And that more *extensions* then one may be commensurate, at the same time, to the same place, is plain, in that motion is coextended with the subject wherein it is, and both with space. And *motion* is not nothing; wherefore two things may be commensurate to one space at once.

12. Now then extended *substance* (and all substances are extended) being of it self indifferent to *penetrability* or *impenetrability*, and we finding one kind of substance so *impenetrable*, that one part will not enter at all into another, which with as much reason we might expect to find so irresistibly united one part with another that nothing in the world could dissever them (For this *indiscerptibility* has as good a connection with substance as impenetrability has, they neither falling under the cognizance of reason or demonstration, but being *immediate* attributes of such a subject. For a man can no more argue from the extension of substance, that it is discerptible, then that it is *penetrable*; there being as good a capacity in *extension* for *penetration* as *discerption*) I conceive, I say, from hence we may as easily admit that *some substance* may be of it self *indiscerptible*, as well as others *impenetrable*; and that as there is one kind of *substance*, which of its own nature is *impenetrable* and *discerptible*, so there may be another *indiscerptible* and *penetrable*. Neither of which a man can give any other account of, than that they have the immediate properties of such a subject.

2. From Ralph Cudworth, *The True Intellectual System of the Universe* (1678)

[The Cambridge Platonist Ralph Cudworth (1617-88) was a colleague of Henry More at Cambridge and connected certain forms of ancient materialism with atheism. As Sarah Hutton notes in her *Stanford Encyclopedia of Philosophy* article on the Cambridge Platonists: "... Cudworth identifies four schools of atheistic philosophy, each of which is a type of materialism — Hylozoic atheism which attributes life to matter, Hylopathian atheism, which attributes all to matter, Cosmo-plastic atheism which makes the world-soul the highest numen. Each of these ancient brands of atheism has its latter-day manifestations in philosophers such as Hobbes (an example of a Hylopathian atheist) and Spinoza (a latter-day Hylozoist)" (Hutton, 2008). Cudworth advocates the dualism of the "ancient physiologers" and sees Cartesian dualism as a revival of that ancient view. As some of the views of Anthony Collins are similar to those that Cudworth rejected and some of Clarke's arguments are similar to Cudworth's reasons for rejecting materialism, it is useful to consider selections from that vast work. Cudworth also uses the term "consciousness" in a significant philosophical context for the first time — in the refutation of materialism. This selection is taken from the Friedrich Fromman Verlag reprint of *The True Intellectual System of the Universe* (1964), and the page numbers refer to that edition, should the reader want to place the selections back in their context.]

[Cudworth's articulation of the Homogeneity Principle]

Pp. 758-60

In the next place, should we be so liberal, as to grant to the atomic atheists, *motion without a cause*, or permit Strato and the Hylozoick atheists to attribute to matter a self-moving power, yet do we affirm that this matter and motion both together, could not possibly produce any new real entity, which was not before; matter as such efficiently causing nothing, and motion only changing the modifications of matter as figure, place, site, and disposition of parts. Wherefore if matter as such, have no animal sense and conscious understanding essentially belonging to it, (which no atheists as yet have had the impudence to assert) then can no motion or modification of matter, no contexture of atoms, possibly beget sense and understanding, soul and mind; because this would be to bring something out of nothing in the impossible sense, or to suppose something to be made by itself, without a cause. Which may serve also for a confutation of those imperfect and spurious theists who will not allow to God almighty (whether supposed by them to be corporeal or incorporeal) a power of making anything, but only out of pre-existent matter, by the new modifying thereof: as a carpenter makes a house out of pre-existing timber and stone, and a tailor out of pre-existing cloth. For since animal life and understanding are not by them supposed to belong at all to matter as such, and since they cannot result from any modifications or contextures thereof, it would plainly follow from hence, that God could not possibly make animals, or produce sense and understanding, souls and minds, which nevertheless these theists suppose him to have done; and therefore ought in reason to acknowledge him, not only to be the maker of a new modification of matter, (and one who built the world only as a carpenter does a house) but also of real entities distinct from the same.

And this was the very doctrine (as we have already declared) of the most ancient atomic physiologers; not that everything whatsoever might be made out of pre-existent matter; but on the contrary, that in all natural generations that there is no real entity produced out of matter; and consequently that souls and minds being not mere modifications of matter in respect of magnitude, figure, size and motion could never be produced out of it, because they must then of necessity, come from nothing; that is, be made either by themselves, without a cause, or without a sufficient cause.

* * * * *

[Cudworth argues that life and cognition cannot be considered as modes of matter.]

Which is all one as if they should say, that all things whatsoever besides matter, being but accidents thereof, being generated out of it and corruptible into it, without the production of any real entity out of nothing, or the reduction of any into nothing, so long as the substance of matter, which is the only real entity, remains the same. Wherefore though life, sense and understanding, all souls and minds, be generated out of matter, yet does it not follow from thence that therefore there is any real entity made or produced, because these are nothing but accidents or modifications of matter. This was the subterfuge of the old Hylopathian atheists.

Now it is indeed true that whatever is in the universe is either substance or accident, and that accidents of any substance may be generated and corrupted without the producing any real entity out of nothing; for as much as the substance remains entirely the same. But the atheists, taking it for granted that there is no such substance besides body or matter, do thereby falsely suppose that which is really incorporeal substance, or else the attributes, properties or modes thereof to be the mere accidents of matter and consequently conclude that these to be generable out of it without the production of any real entities out of nothing. We say, therefore, that it does not at all follow, because the same numerical matter (as for example a piece of wax) may be successively made spherical, cubical, cylindrical, or any other figure; and the same man may successively stand, sit, kneel and walk; both without the production of anything out of nothing; or because a heap of stones, bricks, mortar and timber lying altogether disorderly and confusedly may be made into a stately palace and that without the miraculous creation of any new entity out of nothing; that therefore the same may be affirmed likewise of everything else, besides the bare substance of matter, as namely life and understanding, soul and mind, that though there is no such thing in matter itself yet the production of them out of matter would be no production of something out of nothing. One ground of this mistake has been from men not considering what the accidents of substance are, and indeed that they are nothing but modes thereof. Now a mode is such a thing as cannot possibly be conceived without that thing whereof it is a mode; as standing, sitting, kneeling and walking cannot be conceived without a body organized, and therefore are but modes thereof. But life and cogitation may be clearly apprehended without body, nor anything of extension, nor indeed can a thought be conceived to be of such a length, breadth and thickness or to be hewed or sliced out into many pieces, all of which laid together, as so many small chips thereof, would make up again, the entireness of that whole thought. From whence it ought to be concluded that cogitation is no accident of or mode of matter or bulky extension but a mode or attribute of another substance really distinct from matter, wholly incorporeal. There is indeed nothing else clearly conceivable by us in body or bulky extension but only more or less magnitude of parts, figure, size, motion or rest, and all the different bodies that are in the whole world, are but several combinations of syllables made up of one of these few letters. But no magnitude, figure, size and motion can possibly spell or compound life and sense, cogitation and understanding, as the syllables thereof; and therefore to suppose these generated out of matter is plainly to suppose some real entity to be brought out of nothing, of something to be made without a cause, which is impossible.

[Cudworth denies that life and understanding are emergent properties — and gives an argument against the Hylozoic atheists similar to the one later advanced by Clarke in the Clarke-Collins correspondence.]

Pp. 838-40

But we shall now make it evident, that in both these Atheistic Corporealisms, (agreeing in these two things, that body is the only substance, and that the principles of body are not vital) there is an absolute impossibility; not only as Aristotle objects, they suppose no active principle; but also because their bringing of life and understanding (being real entities) out of dead and senseless matter is also bringing something out of nothing. And indeed the atomic atheist, is here of the two rather the more absurd and unreasonable, for as much as he discarding all real qualities, and that for this very reason, because nothing can come out of nothing, does himself notwithstanding, produce life, sense and understanding (unquestionable realities) out of mere magnitude, figure, sizes, and motion; that is, indeed, out of nothing. Wherefore, there being an absolute impossibility, of both these atheistic hypotheses, neither of which is able to save the phenomena of life and understanding) from that confessed principle of theirs, that matter as such, hath no life or understanding belonging to it, it follows unavoidably, that there must be some other substance besides body or matter, which is essentially vital and intellectual ... Because all things cannot possibly have a peregrine, adventitious and borrowed life, but something in the universe, must needs have life naturally and originally. All life cannot be merely accidental, generable and corruptible, producible out of nothing and reducible to nothing again, but there must of Necessity be, some substantial life, which point (that all life is not a mere accident, but that there is life substantial) hath of late with much reason and judgment, insisted upon, and urged by the writer *Of the Life of Nature*. Neither must there be only, such a substantial life, as is naturally immortal for the future, but also such as is eternal, and was never made; all other minds and lives whatsoever, (none of which could possibly be generated out of matter) being derived from this eternal unmade fountain of life and understanding.

Which thing, the Hylozoick Atheists being well aware of; namely, that there must of Necessity be, both substantial and eternal unmade life; but supposing also matter to be the only substance;

thought themselves necessitated, to attribute to all matter as such, life and understanding, though not animalish and conscious, but natural only: they conceiving, that from the modifications thereof alone by organization, all other animalish life, not only the sensitive in brutes, but the rational in men was derived. But this hylozoick atheism, thus bringing all conscious and reflexive life or animality, out of a supposed senseless stupid and unconscious life of nature, in matter, and that merely from a different accidental modification thereof, or contexture of parts, does again plainly bring something out of nothing, which is an absolute impossibility. Moreover, this hylozoick atheism, was long since and in the first emersion thereof solidly confuted by the atomic atheists, after this manner; if matter as such had life, perception and understanding belonging to it, then of necessity must every atom or smallish particle thereof, be a distinct percipient by itself; from whence it will follow, that there could not possibly be, any such men and animals as now are, compounded out of them, but every man and animal, would be a heap of innumerable percipients, and have innumerable perceptions and intellections; whereas it is plain, that there is but one life and understanding, one soul or mind, one perceiver or thinker in every one. And to say, that these innumerable particles of matter, do all confederate together; that is to make every man and animal, to be a multitude or commonwealth of percipients and persons as it were clubbing together; is a thing so absurd and ridiculous, that one would wonder, the Hylozoists should not choose, to recant that their fundamental error, of the life of matter, than seek shelter and sanctuary for the same, under such a Proteus. For though voluntary agents and persons, may many of them, resign up their wills to one, and by that means, have all but as it were one artificial will, yet can they not possibly resign up their sense and understanding too, so as to have all but one artificial life, sense and understanding: much less could this be done by senseless atoms, or particles of matter supposed, to be devoid of all consciousness or animality.

★★★★★

[Cudworth enumerates the errors of atheistic materialists concerning life and matter.]

Pp. 848-50

We shall in this place only add; that as the atheists can no way salve the phenomenon of motion, so can they much less that of cogitation, or life and understanding. To make which yet the more evident, we shall briefly represent a system or catalogue of the many atheistic hallucinations or delirations concerning it. As first, that senseless matter being the only substance, and all else but accidental modifications thereof; life and mind are all mere accidental things, generable and corruptible, producible out of nothing, and reducible to nothing again; and that there is no substantial life or mind anywhere, in opposition to which, we have before proved, that there must of necessity be some substantial life, and that human souls being lives substantial, and not mere accidental modifications of matter, they are consequently in their own nature immortal, since no substance of itself ever vanishes into nothing.

Again the Democriticks, and other atheists conclude that life and mind are no simple and primitive natures, but secondary and compounded things; they resulting from certain concretions and contextures of matter, and either the commixtures and contemporations of qualities, or else the combinations of those simple elements of magnitude, figure, site, and motion; so being made up, of that which hath nothing of life or mind in it. For as flesh is not made out of fleshy particles, nor bone out of bony (as Anaxagoras of old dreamed), so may life as they conceive, be as well made out of lifeless principles, and mind out of that which has no mind or understanding at all in it: just as syllables pronouncable, do result from combinations of letters, some of which are mutes and cannot by themselves be pronounced at all, other but semivocal. And from hence do these atheists infer, that there could be no eternal unmade life or mind, nor any that is immortal or incorruptible; since upon the dissolution of that compages or contexture of matter from whence they result, they must needs vanish into nothing. Wherefore according to them, there hath probably, sometime heretofore been no life or understanding at all in the universe, and there may possibly be none again. From whence the conclusion is that mind or understanding is no God or Principle in the universe, it being essentially factitous, native and corruptible ... mortal from mortal things: as also that the souls of men cannot subsist separately after death, and walk up and down in airy bodies; no more than the form of a house or tree, after the dissolution thereof can subsist by itself separately, or appear in some other body. But all this foolery of atheists has already been confuted, we having before shown that life and understanding are active powers, vigours and perfections that could never possibly result from mere passive bulk or dead and senseless matter, however modified and compounded; because nothing can come effectively from nothing. Neither is there any consequence at all in this, that flesh is not made out of fleshy principles, nor bone out of bony, red out of red things, nor green out of green; therefore life and understanding may as well be compounded, out of things dead and senseless: because there are no syllables or complexions, as the others are, nor can either the qualities of heat and cold, moist and dry; or else magnitude, figures, sites and motions, however combined together, as letters spell them out, and make them up; but they are simple and primitive things. And accordingly it has been proved, that there are or must of necessity be, some eternal unmade life and mind: for though there be no necessity that there should be any eternal unmade red or green, because red or green may be made out of things not red or green, they and all other corporeal qualities (so called) being but several contextures of matter, or combinations of magnitude, figures, sites and motions, causing those several fancies in us, and though there be no necessity that there should be eternal motion, because if there was once no motion in matter, but all bodies rested, yet might motion have been produced by a self-moving or self active principle; and lastly though there be no necessity that there should be eternal or unmade matter or body either, because had there been once no body at all, yet might it be made or produced by a perfect omnipotent incorporeal being. Nevertheless, there is an absolute necessity that there should be eternal unmade life and mind, because were there once no life nor mind at all, these could never have been produced out of matter altogether lifeless and mindless. And though the form of a house cannot possibly exist separately from matter and substance thereof, it being a mere accidental thing, resulting from such a compages of stone, timber and mortar, yet are human souls and minds, no such accidental forms of compounded matter, but active substantial things, that may therefore subsist separately from these bodies, and enliven other bodies of a different contexture. And however some that are no atheists are over prone to conceive, *life, sense, cogitation* and *consciousness* in brutes, to be generated out of dead, senseless and unthinking matter, then can no philosophy hinder, but that all might have been so.

3. From Pierre Bayle, "Dicaearchus," *Historical and Critical Dictionary* (1696), trans. Richard Popkin

[In notes C and L of the article "Dicaearchus" in his *Historical and Critical Dictionary,* Pierre Bayle (1657-1706) brings up a materialistic view of the soul in note C, which he then refutes to his own satisfaction. Then in note L he explains an anonymous objection to his refutation. Scholars have determined that the anonymous objector was John Toland (1670-1722), later a friend or at least acquaintance of Anthony Collins. Toland's objection is very similar to the position that Collins takes in the Clarke-Collins correspondence and Bayle's response is remarkably similar to Clarke's position in the correspondence. Clearly, as noted in the introduction to this volume, Collins was attempting to answer both Clarke and Bayle in his *Reflections on Mr. Clarke's Second Defense.* In the introduction I explain what Bayle had to say in note C (see pp. 28-29). What follows is the portion of note L in which Bayle states Toland's objection and replies to it.]

Selections from Note L in the article "Dicaearchus"

L. (*A person ... has sent me some objections that I am going to examine ... on the subject of his views ... of the nature of the soul.*) The author of these objections begins by unfolding the system of our philosopher. He claims that Dicaearchus meant that living bodies differ from non-living ones only in the shape and arrangement of their parts. He compares this theory with that of Descartes in the following manner. If a dog differs from a stone, it is not because a dog consists of a body and a soul, and the stone of a body only. It is solely because the dog is so composed of parts put together that they make a machine, while the arrangement of the parts of the stone do not. This is Descartes' view. This presentation is very helpful for understanding the theory of Dicaearchus. We only have to suppose that he extended to all living things what the Cartesians said only with regard to beasts. We need only suppose that he reduced man to the condition of a machine. From this will follow that the human soul is not distinct from the body, but that it is only a construction, a mechanical disposition of several parts of matter. Assuming this is supposed, the author of the objection claims that I do not really undermine the system of Dicaearchus because I have not shown that the difficulty

I advanced cannot be overcome. I maintained that Dicaearchus either did not know what he was saying or he was obliged to say that the power he said the soul consisted in always accompanied the body. The answer is made that he only had to maintain that it [this power] always accompanied the living body. It is added that had I always jointed together the two terms "body" and "living" my conclusion could have been completely accepted by Dicaearchus and would have done no damage to his system. It is claimed, therefore, that he can deny that, if the soul is a power of living bodies, then it follows that it exists in cadavers. For if the soul consists only of the mechanical arrangement of certain bodies as he supposes, it obviously follows that it ought to cease, as soon as the machine no longer exists. Thus, the answer goes on, a Cartesian would reply to those who might assert that, according to this hypothesis, the souls of beasts exist even after the beasts have been killed. "You are wrong," he would answer, "for since I suppose that it consists only of a certain disposition of organs, I ought to suppose necessarily that it perishes as soon as the disposition has been destroyed." The author of the objection supposes "that it has never been proved against the Cartesians that the power of feeling does not cease in dead bodies, and that the parts of living bodies each carry away with them their life and soul when they decay." It is certain that this conclusion has not been raised against the Cartesians. But this is due to the fact that they do not attribute any sensation to the souls of beasts: for if they did then the same difficulties I raised against Dicaearchus, would apply to them, and they would also be obliged to find an answer. Lastly, the objection is raised against me concerning the remarks I made to the effect that all modalities known to us only cease by being replaced by other modalities of the same kind. From this it follows that a body that had sensation on some occasion would never cease having it. The objection that is raised against me is that it has little to do with Dicaearchus, for "he attributed life to matter only after it possessed the modification necessary to make it a living body, that is, the various arrangements of its parts. I had, therefore, no right to make him hold that there was life in any of the parts of matter after its dissolution, although before and after it was a living body it really was a body but not a living body." This is the conclusion of the author of the objection. Note that he is not trying to defend Dicaearchus' doctrine itself. He recognized both its falsity and its impiety. He only wanted to show that I was wrong in accusing Dicaearchus of inconsistency, and that the system does not fall apart just because the philosopher has not admitted sensation and imperishable life to be in bodies that have once been alive.

You can clearly see here the entire state of the question. It is solely to determine whether a philosopher who believes that there are bodies that think, and bodies that do not, reasons logically. I maintain that he does not: and that whoever once admits, for example, that a collection of bones and nerves feels and reasons ought to maintain, on pain of being declared guilty of not knowing what he is talking about, that every other assemblage of matter thinks, and that the thought which existed in such a collection exists in other modifications of the disunited parts after the collection has been dissipated. I shall not repeat the proofs I have already given of this, nor is it necessary that I add any new strength to them, for the author of the objections has not attacked them. He has only observed that Dicaearchus does not have to be troubled about the matter, since he has asserted only that matter begins to live after a certain arrangement of its parts. But, it is here, principally, that I would want to accuse him of not knowing what he is saying. He did not understand by life, simply, breathing, eating, walking: he understood it to include all the operations of man, the actions of the five senses, imagination, reflection, reasoning, and the like. I maintain that something is being supposed that has hitherto been inconceivable to all mankind, if one supposes that the arrangements of the organs of the human body alone make a substance that has never thought to become a thinking one. All that the arrangement of the organs can accomplish is reducible, as in the case of a clock, to various different kinds of local motion. The difference can only consist in the greater or lesser degree of motion. But just as the arrangement of several wheels that make up a clock would be of no use in producing the effects of the machine, if each wheel being placed in a certain way, did not actually possess an impenetrable extension, a necessary cause of motion as soon as it is pushed with a certain degree of force; so I also say that the arrangement of the organs of the human body would be of no use to produce thought, if each organ before being put in its place were not actually endowed with the ability to think. Now this capacity is quite different from impenetrable extension for all that you can do with this extension, by pulling it, hitting it, pushing it, in every way imaginable, is a change of situation whose whole nature and essence you fully conceive without having need to suppose any sensation in it, and even if you deny that there is any sensation in it. There have been some great geniuses who have been a little too *halfhearted in believing* the distinction between the soul of man and the body. But up to now no one I know has dared to say that he conceived clearly that, in order to make a substance pass from the absence of all thought to actual thought, it sufficed to move it[1] so that this change of situation would be, for example, a feeling of joy, an affirmation, an idea of moral virtue, and so forth. And even if some people should boast that they clearly conceived this, they do not deserve to be believed. They ought to be shown the passage of Aristotle that I cited in another place.[2] Would it not be an absurdity to maintain that there are two kinds of color, one which is the object of sight and nothing more, the other the object of sight, and smell also? It is still more absurd to maintain that there are two kinds of roundness, one consisting merely in the parts of a body's circumference being equidistant from the center; and the other kind, being, beside this, also an act whereby the round body perceives that it exists and sees several other bodies around it. The same absurdity occurs in maintaining that there are two kinds of circular motion, one of which is only the change of situation on a line whose parts are equidistant from the center, the other that, besides this, is an act of love of God, a fear, a hope and so forth. What I have said of roundness with regard to vision may be applied to all sorts of figures with regard to all sorts of thoughts; and what I have said about circular motion is not less forceful with regard to all the other lines along which a body can move either slowly or quickly. And thus we ought to conclude that thought is distinct from all modifications of body of which we have any knowledge since it is distinct from all figure and all change of situation. But as this

1 Note that the peripatetics, in attributing thought to beasts, do not give matter this property but ascribe it to a substantial form, which according to them is neither matter nor body, and which is produced anew in matter without being composed of matter. Thus, they agree that matter never acquires either sensation or knowledge.

2 See above, article "Arriga," remark C and footnote 8.... [Bayle makes reference to a passage in which Aristotle formulates the law of non-contradiction. –ed.]

is not the question here, let us content ourselves with concluding that Dicaearchus ought to have admitted that thought is in every kind of matter; for otherwise it would be absurd to claim that if several veins, several arteries, and the like, were placed together like the parts of a machine, this would produce the sensation of color, taste, sound, smell, cold, heat, love, affection, negation, and so forth.

4. From John Locke, *An Essay Concerning Human Understanding*, 2nd ed. (1692)

[As noted in the introduction to this volume, John Locke's (1635-1705) monumental *An Essay Concerning Human Understanding* contributed in a variety of ways to the views of Samuel Clarke and Anthony Collins expressed in their correspondence of 1707-08. The selections below include much of Chapter XXVII, "Of Identity and Diversity," from Book II of the *Essay* (added to the second edition in 1692) because consciousness is central to the discussion of personal identity in the chapter and both Clarke and Collins adopt much of what Locke says about consciousness. Apart from making his theory of personal identity a materialist theory, Collins adopts Locke's account of personal identity without change. Clarke's account of consciousness is different in important respects. Like Cudworth, he holds that consciousness must belong to an immaterial soul, while Locke's view is that it could belong to any kind of substance, material or immaterial, simple or compounded. It looks like Clarke's reading (or misreading) of section 13 of this chapter gave rise to his powerful reduplication argument against both Collins' and Locke's theories of personal identity. Section 4 of this chapter may have inspired Collins' account of organization as the origin of emergent properties. The passages from John Locke's *An Essay Concerning Human Understanding* are from *The Works of John Locke in Nine Volumes* (London: Rivington, 1824), 12th ed., vol. 1.]

a. From Book II, Chapter XXVII, "Of Identity and Diversity"

1. *Wherein identity consists.* Another occasion the mind often takes of comparing, is the very being of things, when, considering anything as existing at any determined time and place, we compare it with itself existing at another time, and thereon form

the ideas of identity and diversity. When we see anything to be in any place in any instant of time, we are sure (be it what it will) that it is that very thing, and not another which at that same time exists in another place, how like and undistinguishable soever it may be in all other respects: and in this consists identity, when the ideas it is attributed to vary not at all from what they were that moment wherein we consider their former existence, and to which we compare the present. For we never finding, nor conceiving it possible, that two things of the same kind should exist in the same place at the same time, we rightly conclude, that, whatever exists anywhere at any time, excludes all of the same kind, and is there itself alone. When therefore we demand whether anything be the same or no, it refers always to something that existed such a time in such a place, which it was certain, at that instant, was the same with itself, and no other. From whence it follows, that one thing cannot have two beginnings of existence, nor two things one beginning; it being impossible for two things of the same kind to be or exist in the same instant, in the very same place; or one and the same thing in different places. That, therefore, that had one beginning, is the same thing; and that which had a different beginning in time and place from that, is not the same, but diverse. That which has made the difficulty about this relation has been the little care and attention used in having precise notions of the things to which it is attributed.

2. *Identity of substances.* We have the ideas but of three sorts of substances:

1. God.
2. Finite intelligences.
3. Bodies.

First, God is without beginning, eternal, unalterable, and everywhere, and therefore concerning his identity there can be no doubt.

Secondly, Finite spirits having had each its determinate time and place of beginning to exist, the relation to that time and place will always determine to each of them its identity, as long as it exists.

Thirdly, The same will hold of every particle of matter, to which no addition or subtraction of matter being made, it is the same. For, though these three sorts of substances, as we term them, do not exclude one another out of the same place, yet we cannot conceive but that they must necessarily each of them exclude any of the same kind out of the same place: or else the notions and names of identity and diversity would be in vain, and there could be no such distinctions of substances, or anything else one from another. For example: could two bodies be in the same place at the same time; then those two parcels of matter must be one and the same, take them great or little; nay, all bodies must be one and the same. For, by the same reason that two particles of matter may be in one place, all bodies may be in one place: which, when it can be supposed, takes away the distinction of identity and diversity of one and more, and renders it ridiculous. But it being a contradiction that two or more should be one, identity and diversity are relations and ways of comparing well founded, and of use to the understanding.

Identity of modes and relations. All other things being but modes or relations ultimately terminated in substances, the identity and diversity of each particular existence of them too will be by the same way determined: only as to things whose existence is in succession, such as are the actions of finite beings, v.g. motion and thought, both which consist in a continued train of succession, concerning their diversity there can be no question: because each perishing the moment it begins, they cannot exist in different times, or in different places, as permanent beings can at different times exist in distant places; and therefore no motion or thought, considered as at different times, can be the same, each part thereof having a different beginning of existence.

3. *Principium Individuationis.* From what has been said, it is easy to discover what is so much inquired after, the *principium individuationis*; and that, it is plain, is existence itself; which determines a being of any sort to a particular time and place, incommunicable to two beings of the same kind. This, though it seems easier to conceive in simple substances or modes; yet, when reflected on, is not more difficult in compound ones, if care be taken to what it is applied: v.g. let us suppose an atom, i.e. a continued body under one immutable superficies, existing in a determined time and place; it is evident, that, considered in any instant of its existence, it is in that instant the same with itself. For, being at that instant what it is, and nothing else, it is the same, and so must continue as long as its existence is continued;

for so long it will be the same, and no other. In like manner, if two or more atoms be joined together into the same mass, every one of those atoms will be the same, by the foregoing rule: and whilst they exist united together, the mass, consisting of the same atoms, must be the same mass, or the same body, let the parts be ever so differently jumbled. But if one of these atoms be taken away, or one new one added, it is no longer the same mass or the same body. In the state of living creatures, their identity depends not on a mass of the same particles, but on something else. For in them the variation of great parcels of matter alters not the identity: an oak growing from a plant to a great tree, and then lopped, is still the same oak; and a colt grown up to a horse, sometimes fat, sometimes lean, is all the while the same horse: though, in both these cases, there may be a manifest change of the parts; so that truly they are not either of them the same masses of matter, though they be truly one of them the same oak, and the other the same horse. The reason whereof is, that, in these two cases — a mass of matter and a living body — identity is not applied to the same thing.

4. *Identity of vegetables.* We must therefore consider wherein an oak differs from a mass of matter, and that seems to me to be in this, that the one is only the cohesion of particles of matter any how united, the other such a disposition of them as constitutes the parts of an oak; and such an organization of those parts as is fit to receive and distribute nourishment, so as to continue and frame the wood, bark, and leaves, &c., of an oak, in which consists the vegetable life. That being then one plant which has such an organization of parts in one coherent body, partaking of one common life, it continues to be the same plant as long as it partakes of the same life, though that life be communicated to new particles of matter vitally united to the living plant, in a like continued organization conformable to that sort of plants. For this organization, being at any one instant in any one collection of matter, is in that particular concrete distinguished from all other, and is that individual life, which existing constantly from that moment both forwards and backwards, in the same continuity of insensibly succeeding parts united to the living body of the plant, it has that identity which makes the same plant, and all the parts of it, parts of the same plant, during all the time that they exist united in that continued organization, which is fit to convey that common life to all the parts so united.

5. *Identity of animals.* The case is not so much different in brutes but that any one may hence see what makes an animal and continues it the same. Something we have like this in machines, and may serve to illustrate it. For example, what is a watch? It is plain it is nothing but a fit organization or construction of parts to a certain end, which, when a sufficient force is added to it, it is capable to attain. If we would suppose this machine one continued body, all whose organized parts were repaired, increased, or diminished by a constant addition or separation of insensible parts, with one common life, we should have something very much like the body of an animal; with this difference, That, in an animal the fitness of the organization, and the motion wherein life consists, begin together, the motion coming from within; but in machines the force coming sensibly from without, is often away when the organ is in order, and well fitted to receive it.

6. *The identity of man.* This also shows wherein the identity of the same man consists; viz. in nothing but a participation of the same continued life, by constantly fleeting particles of matter, in succession vitally united to the same organized body. He that shall place the identity of man in anything else, but, like that of other animals, in one fitly organized body, taken in any one instant, and from thence continued, under one organization of life, in several successively fleeting particles of matter united to it, will find it hard to make an embryo, one of years, mad and sober, the same man, by any supposition, that will not make it possible for Seth, Ismael, Socrates, Pilate, St. Austin, and Caesar Borgia,[1] to be the same man. For if the identity of soul alone makes the same man; and there be nothing in the nature of matter why the same individual spirit may not be united to different bodies, it will be possible that those men, living in distant ages, and of different tempers, may have been the same man: which way of speaking must be from a very strange use of the word man, applied to an idea out of which body and shape are excluded. And that way of speaking would agree

---

1 Seth was the third son of Adam and Eve and brother of Cain and Abel; Ismael was the son of Abraham and Agar; Socrates (468-399 BCE) was a Classical Greek Athenian philosopher; Pilate is presumably Pontius Pilate, best known as the judge at the trial of Jesus; St. Austin, presumably St. Augustine (354-430 CE), became Bishop of Hippo, and Caesar Borgia (1476-1507), son of Pope Alexander VI, was an Italian nobleman, politician, and cardinal. –ed.

yet worse with the notions of those philosophers who allow of transmigration, and are of opinion that the souls of men may, for their miscarriages, be detruded into the bodies of beasts, as fit habitations, with organs suited to the satisfaction of their brutal inclinations. But yet I think nobody, could he be sure that the soul of Heliogabalus[1] were in one of his hogs, would yet say that hog were a man or Heliogabalus.

7. *Idea of identity suited to the idea it is applied to.* It is not therefore unity of substance that comprehends all sorts of identity, or will determine it in every case; but to conceive and judge of it aright, we must consider what idea the word it is applied to stands for: it being one thing to be the same substance, another the same man, and a third the same person, if person, man, and substance, are three names standing for three different ideas; — for such as is the idea belonging to that name, such must be the identity; which, if it had been a little more carefully attended to, would possibly have prevented a great deal of that confusion which often occurs about this matter, with no small seeming difficulties, especially concerning personal identity, which therefore we shall in the next place a little consider.

8. *Same man.* An animal is a living organized body; and consequently the same animal, as we have observed, is the same continued life communicated to different particles of matter, as they happen successively to be united to that organized living body. And whatever is talked of other definitions, ingenious observation puts it past doubt, that the idea in our minds, of which the sound "man" in our mouths is the sign, is nothing else but of an animal of such a certain form. Since I think I may be confident, that, whoever should see a creature of his own shape or make, though it had no more reason all its life than a cat or a parrot, would call him still a man; or whoever should hear a cat or a parrot discourse, reason, and philosophize, would call or think it nothing but a cat or a parrot; and say, the one was a dull irrational man, and the other a very intelligent rational parrot.

* * * * *

1 Heliogabalus was a Roman emperor (218-222) infamous for his licentious behavior. –ed.

For I presume it is not the idea of a thinking or rational being alone that makes the idea of a man in most people's sense: but of a body, so and so shaped, joined to it: and if that be the idea of a man, the same successive body not shifted all at once, must, as well as the same immaterial spirit, go to the making of the same man.

9. *Personal identity.* This being premised, to find wherein personal identity consists, we must consider what person stands for; — which, I think, is a thinking intelligent being, that has reason and reflection, and can consider itself as itself, the same thinking thing, in different times and places; which it does only by that consciousness which is inseparable from thinking, and, as it seems to me, essential to it: it being impossible for any one to perceive without perceiving that he does perceive. When we see, hear, smell, taste, feel, meditate, or will anything, we know that we do so. Thus it is always as to our present sensations and perceptions: and by this every one is to himself that which he calls self: — it not being considered, in this case, whether the same self be continued in the same or divers substances. For, since consciousness always accompanies thinking, and it is that which makes every one to be what he calls self, and thereby distinguishes himself from all other thinking things, in this alone consists personal identity, i.e. the sameness of a rational being: and as far as this consciousness can be extended backwards to any past action or thought, so far reaches the identity of that person; it is the same self now it was then; and it is by the same self with this present one that now reflects on it, that that action was done.

10. *Consciousness makes personal identity.* But it is further inquired, whether it be the same identical substance. This few would think they had reason to doubt of, if these perceptions, with their consciousness, always remained present in the mind, whereby the same thinking thing would be always consciously present, and, as would be thought, evidently the same to itself. But that which seems to make the difficulty is this, that this consciousness being interrupted always by forgetfulness, there being no moment of our lives wherein we have the whole train of all our past actions before our eyes in one view, but even the best memories losing the sight of one part whilst they are viewing another; and we sometimes, and that the greatest part of our lives, not reflecting on our past selves, being intent on

our present thoughts, and in sound sleep having no thoughts at all, or at least none with that consciousness which remarks our waking thoughts, — I say, in all these cases, our consciousness being interrupted, and we losing the sight of our past selves, doubts are raised whether we are the same thinking thing, i.e. the same substance or no. Which, however reasonable or unreasonable, concerns not personal identity at all. The question being what makes the same person; and not whether it be the same identical substance, which always thinks in the same person, which, in this case, matters not at all: different substances, by the same consciousness (where they do partake in it) being united into one person, as well as different bodies by the same life are united into one animal, whose identity is preserved in that change of substances by the unity of one continued life. For, it being the same consciousness that makes a man be himself to himself, personal identity depends on that only, whether it be annexed solely to one individual substance, or can be continued in a succession of several substances. For as far as any intelligent being can repeat the idea of any past action with the same consciousness it had of it at first, and with the same consciousness it has of any present action; so far it is the same personal self. For it is by the consciousness it has of its present thoughts and actions, that it is self to itself now, and so will be the same self, as far as the same consciousness can extend to actions past or to come, and would be by distance of time, or change of substance, no more two persons, than a man be two men by wearing other clothes to-day than he did yesterday, with a long or a short sleep between: the same consciousness uniting those distant actions into the same person, whatever substances contributed to their production.

11. *Personal identity in change of substance.* That this is so, we have some kind of evidence in our very bodies, all whose particles, whilst vitally united to this same thinking conscious self, so that we feel when they are touched, and are affected by, and conscious of good or harm that happens to them, as a part of ourselves; i.e. of our thinking conscious self. Thus, the limbs of his body are to every one a part of himself; he sympathizes and is concerned for them. Cut off a hand, and thereby separate it from that consciousness he had of its heat, cold, and other affections, and it is then no longer a part of that which is himself, any more than the remotest part of matter. Thus, we see the sub-

stance whereof personal self consisted at one time may be varied at another, without the change of personal identity; there being no question about the same person, though the limbs which but now were a part of it, be cut off.

12. *Personality in change of substance.* But the question is, Whether if the same substance which thinks be changed, it can be the same person; or, remaining the same, it can be different persons? And to this I answer: First, This can be no question at all to those who place thought in a purely material animal constitution, void of an immaterial substance. For, whether their supposition be true or no, it is plain they conceive personal identity preserved in something else than identity of substance; as animal identity is preserved in identity of life, and not of substance. And therefore those who place thinking in an immaterial substance only, before they can come to deal with these men, must show why personal identity cannot be preserved in the change of immaterial substances, or variety of particular immaterial substances, as well as animal identity is preserved in the change of material substances, or variety of particular bodies: unless they will say, it is one immaterial spirit that makes the same life in brutes, as it is one immaterial spirit that makes the same person in men; which the Cartesians at least will not admit, for fear of making brutes thinking things too.

13. *Whether in change of thinking substances there can be one person.* But next, as to the first part of the question, Whether, if the same thinking substance (supposing immaterial substances only to think) be changed, it can be the same person? I answer, that cannot be resolved but by those who know what kind of substances they are that do think; and whether the consciousness of past actions can be transferred from one thinking substance to another. I grant were the same consciousness the same individual action it could not: but it being a present representation of a past action, why it may not be possible, that that may be represented to the mind to have been which really never was, will remain to be shown. And therefore how far the consciousness of past actions is annexed to any individual agent, so that another cannot possibly have it, will be hard for us to determine, till we know what kind of action it is that cannot be done without a reflex act of perception accompanying it, and how performed by thinking substances, who cannot think without being conscious of it. But that which we call the same consciousness, not being

the same individual act, why one intellectual substance may not have represented to it, as done by itself, what it never did, and was perhaps done by some other agent — why, I say, such a representation may not possibly be without reality of matter of fact, as well as several representations in dreams are, which yet whilst dreaming we take for true — will be difficult to conclude from the nature of things. And that it never is so, will by us, till we have clearer views of the nature of thinking substances, be best resolved into the goodness of God; who, as far as the happiness or misery of any of his sensible creatures is concerned in it, will not, by a fatal error of theirs, transfer from one to another that consciousness which draws reward or punishment with it. How far this may be an argument against those who would place thinking in a system of fleeting animal spirits, I leave to be considered. But yet, to return to the question before us, it must be allowed, that, if the same consciousness (which, as has been shown, is quite a different thing from the same numerical figure or motion in body) can be transferred from one thinking substance to another, it will be possible that two thinking substances may make but one person. For the same consciousness being preserved, whether in the same or different substances, the personal identity is preserved.

14. *Whether, the same immaterial substance remaining, there can be two persons.* As to the second part of the question, Whether the same immaterial substance remaining, there may be two distinct persons; which question seems to me to be built on this, — Whether the same immaterial being, being conscious of the action of its past duration, may be wholly stripped of all the consciousness of its past existence, and lose it beyond the power of ever retrieving it again: and so as it were beginning a new account from a new period, have a consciousness that cannot reach beyond this new state. All those who hold pre-existence are evidently of this mind; since they allow the soul to have no remaining consciousness of what it did in that pre-existent state, either wholly separate from body, or informing any other body; and if they should not, it is plain experience would be against them. So that personal identity, reaching no further than consciousness reaches, a pre-existent spirit not having continued so many ages in a state of silence, must needs make different persons. Suppose a Christian Platonist or a Pythagorean should, upon God's having ended all his works of creation the seventh

day, think his soul hath existed ever since; and should imagine it has revolved in several human bodies; as I once met with one, who was persuaded his had been the soul of Socrates (how reasonably I will not dispute; this I know, that in the post he filled, which was no inconsiderable one, he passed for a very rational man, and the press has shown that he wanted not parts or learning;) — would any one say, that he, being not conscious of any of Socrates' actions or thoughts, could be the same person with Socrates? Let any one reflect upon himself, and conclude that he has in himself an immaterial spirit, which is that which thinks in him, and, in the constant change of his body keeps him the same: and is that which he calls himself: let him also suppose it to be the same soul that was in Nestor or Thersites,[1] at the siege of Troy, (for souls being, as far as we know anything of them, in their nature indifferent to any parcel of matter, the supposition has no apparent absurdity in it), which it may have been, as well as it is now the soul of any other man: but he now having no consciousness of any of the actions either of Nestor or Thersites, does or can he conceive himself the same person with either of them? Can he be concerned in either of their actions? attribute them to himself, or think them his own, more than the actions of any other men that ever existed? So that this consciousness, not reaching to any of the actions of either of those men, he is no more one self with either of them than if the soul or immaterial spirit that now informs him had been created, and began to exist, when it began to inform his present body; though it were never so true, that the same spirit that informed Nestor's or Thersites' body were numerically the same that now informs his. For this would no more make him the same person with Nestor, than if some of the particles of matter that were once a part of Nestor were now a part of this man; the same immaterial substance, without the same consciousness, no more making the same person, by being united to any body, than the same particle of matter, without consciousness, united to any body, makes the same person. But let him once find himself conscious of any of the actions of Nestor, he then finds himself the same person with Nestor.

1 Nestor was the wise advisor of Agamemnon and Achilles in the *Iliad*, while Thersites is a common soldier, dull-witted, vulgar and who verbally abuses Agamemnon and Achilles. –ed.

15. *The body, as well as the soul, goes to the making of a man.* And thus may we be able, without any difficulty, to conceive the same person at the resurrection, though in a body not exactly in make or parts the same which he had here, — the same consciousness going along with the soul that inhabits it. But yet the soul alone, in the change of bodies, would scarce to any one but to him that makes the soul the man, be enough to make the same man. For should the soul of a prince, carrying with it the consciousness of the prince's past life, enter and inform the body of a cobbler, as soon as deserted by his own soul, every one sees he would be the same person with the prince, accountable only for the prince's actions: but who would say it was the same man? The body too goes to the making the man, and would, I guess, to everybody determine the man in this case, wherein the soul, with all its princely thoughts about it, would not make another man: but he would be the same cobbler to every one besides himself. I know that, in the ordinary way of speaking, the same person, and the same man, stand for one and the same thing. And indeed every one will always have a liberty to speak as he pleases, and to apply what articulate sounds to what ideas he thinks fit, and change them as often as he pleases. But yet, when we will inquire what makes the same spirit, man, or person, we must fix the ideas of spirit, man, or person in our minds; and having resolved with ourselves what we mean by them, it will not be hard to determine, in either of them, or the like, when it is the same, and when not.

16. *Consciousness alone unites actions into the same person.* But though the same immaterial substance or soul does not alone, wherever it be, and in whatsoever state, make the same man; yet it is plain, consciousness, as far as ever it can be extended — should it be to ages past — unites existences and actions very remote in time into the same person, as well as it does the existences and actions of the immediately preceding moment: so that whatever has the consciousness of present and past actions, is the same person to whom they both belong. Had I the same consciousness that I saw the ark and Noah's flood, as that I saw an overflowing of the Thames last winter, or as that I write now, I could no more doubt that I who write this now, that saw the Thames overflowed last winter, and that viewed the flood at the general deluge, was the same self, — place that self in what substance you please — than that I who write this am the same myself now whilst I write

(whether I consist of all the same substance, material or immaterial, or no) that I was yesterday. For as to this point of being the same self, it matters not whether this present self be made up of the same or other substances — I being as much concerned, and as justly accountable for any action that was done a thousand years since, appropriated to me now by this self-consciousness, as I am for what I did the last moment.

17. *Self depends on consciousness, not on substance.* Self is that conscious thinking thing, — whatever substance made up of, (whether spiritual or material, simple or compounded, it matters not) — which is sensible or conscious of pleasure and pain, capable of happiness or misery, and so is concerned for itself, as far as that consciousness extends. Thus every one finds that, whilst comprehended under that consciousness, the little finger is as much a part of himself as what is most so. Upon separation of this little finger, should this consciousness go along with the little finger, and leave the rest of the body, it is evident the little finger would be the person, the same person; and self then would have nothing to do with the rest of the body. As in this case it is the consciousness that goes along with the substance, when one part is separate from another, which makes the same person, and constitutes this inseparable self: so it is in reference to substances remote in time. That with which the consciousness of this present thinking thing can join itself, makes the same person, and is one self with it, and with nothing else; and so attributes to itself, and owns all the actions of that thing, as its own, as far as that consciousness reaches, and no further; as every one who reflects will perceive.

18. *Persons, not substances, the objects of reward and punishment.* In this personal identity is founded all the right and justice of reward and punishment; happiness and misery being that for which every one is concerned for himself, and not mattering what becomes of any substance, not joined to, or affected with that consciousness. For, as it is evident in the instance I gave but now, if the consciousness went along with the little finger when it was cut off, that would be the same self which was concerned for the whole body yesterday, as making part of itself, whose actions then it cannot but admit as its own now. Though, if the same body should still live, and immediately from the separation of the little finger have its own peculiar consciousness, whereof the little finger knew nothing, it would not at all be concerned for it,

as a part of itself, or could own any of its actions, or have any of them imputed to him.

* * * * *

20. *Absolute oblivion separates what is thus forgotten from the person, but not from the man.* But yet possibly it will still be objected, — Suppose I wholly lose the memory of some parts of my life, beyond a possibility of retrieving them, so that perhaps I shall never be conscious of them again; yet am I not the same person that did those actions, had those thoughts that I once was conscious of, though I have now forgot them? To which I answer, that we must here take notice what the word I is applied to; which, in this case, is the man only. And the same man being presumed to be the same person, I is easily here supposed to stand also for the same person. But if it be possible for the same man to have distinct incommunicable consciousness at different times, it is past doubt the same man would at different times make different persons; which, we see, is the sense of mankind in the solemnest declaration of their opinions, human laws not punishing the mad man for the sober man's actions, nor the sober man for what the mad man did, — thereby making them two persons: which is somewhat explained by our way of speaking in English when we say such an one is "not himself," or is "beside himself"; in which phrases it is insinuated, as if those who now, or at least first used them, thought that self was changed; the selfsame person was no longer in that man.

* * * * *

22. *But is not a man drunk and sober the same person?* Why else is he punished for the fact he commits when drunk, though he be never afterwards conscious of it? Just as much the same person as a man that walks, and does other things in his sleep, is the same person, and is answerable for any mischief he shall do in it. Human laws punish both, with a justice suitable to their way of knowledge; — because, in these cases, they cannot distinguish certainly what is real, what counterfeit: and so the ignorance in drunkenness or sleep is not admitted as a plea. For, though punishment be annexed to personality, and personality to consciousness, and the drunkard perhaps be not conscious of what

he did, yet human judicatures justly punish him; because the fact is proved against him, but want of consciousness cannot be proved for him. But in the Great Day, wherein the secrets of all hearts shall be laid open, it may be reasonable to think, no one shall be made to answer for what he knows nothing of, but shall receive his doom, his conscience accusing or excusing him.

* * * * *

26. *"Person" a forensic term.* Person, as I take it, is the name for this self. Wherever a man finds what he calls himself, there, I think, another may say is the same person. It is a forensic term, appropriating actions and their merit; and so belongs only to intelligent agents, capable of a law, and happiness, and misery. This personality extends itself beyond present existence to what is past, only by consciousness, — whereby it becomes concerned and accountable; owns and imputes to itself past actions, just upon the same ground and for the same reason as it does the present. All which is founded in a concern for happiness, the unavoidable concomitant of consciousness; that which is conscious of pleasure and pain, desiring that that self that is conscious should be happy. And therefore whatever past actions it cannot reconcile or appropriate to that present self by consciousness, it can be no more concerned in than if they had never been done: and to receive pleasure or pain, i.e. reward or punishment, on the account of any such action, is all one as to be made happy or miserable in its first being, without any demerit at all. For, supposing a man punished now for what he had done in another life, whereof he could be made to have no consciousness at all, what difference is there between that punishment and being created miserable? And therefore, conformable to this, the apostle tells us, that, at the great day, when every one shall "receive according to his doings, the secrets of all hearts shall be laid open." The sentence shall be justified by the consciousness all persons shall have, that they themselves, in what bodies soever they appear, or what substances soever that consciousness adheres to, are the same that committed those actions, and deserve that punishment for them.

27. *Suppositions that look strange are pardonable in our ignorance.* I am apt enough to think I have, in treating of this subject, made some suppositions that will look strange to some readers, and

possibly they are so in themselves. But yet, I think they are such as are pardonable, in this ignorance we are in of the nature of that thinking thing that is in us, and which we look on as ourselves. Did we know what it was, or how it was tied to a certain system of fleeting animal spirits; or whether it could or could not perform its operations of thinking and memory out of a body organized as ours is; and whether it has pleased God that no one such spirit shall ever be united to any but one such body, upon the right constitution of whose organs its memory should depend; we might see the absurdity of some of those suppositions I have made. But taking, as we ordinarily now do (in the dark concerning these matters), the soul of a man for an immaterial substance, independent from matter, and indifferent alike to it all; there can, from the nature of things, be no absurdity at all to suppose that the same soul may at different times be united to different bodies, and with them make up for that time one man: as well as we suppose a part of a sheep's body yesterday should be a part of a man's body to-morrow, and in that union make a vital part of Meliboeus himself, as well as it did of his ram.

b. From Book IV, Chapter III, Section 6 [Concerning the possibility of thinking matter]

[This second selection from the *Essay* is from Book IV, Chapter III, section 6. Here Locke is speculating about what we will perhaps never be able to know. It is in this context that he claims it is just as possible that God has made matter organized in the proper way able to think as that he has added an immaterial soul to a body. It is this claim about the possibility of thinking matter that is the centerpiece of the debate in the Clarke-Collins correspondence.]

But yet after all, I think I may, without injury to human perfection, be confident, that our knowledge would never reach to all we might desire to know concerning those ideas we have; nor be able to surmount all the difficulties, and resolve all the questions that might arise concerning any of them. We have the ideas of a square, a circle, and equality; and yet, perhaps, shall never be able to find a circle equal to a square, and certainly know that it is so. We have the ideas of matter and thinking, but possibly shall never be able to know whether any mere material being thinks or no; it being impossible for us, by the contemplation of our own ideas, without revelation, to discover whether Omnipotency has not given to some systems of matter, fitly disposed, a power to perceive and think, or else joined and fixed to matter, so disposed, a thinking immaterial substance: it being, in respect of our notions, not much more remote from our comprehension to conceive that GOD can, if he pleases, superadd to matter a faculty of thinking, than that he should superadd to it another substance with a faculty of thinking; since we know not wherein thinking consists, nor to what sort of substances the Almighty has been pleased to give that power, which cannot be in any created being, but merely by the good pleasure and bounty of the Creator.

—*Whether Matter may not be made by God to think is more than man can know.* For I see no contradiction in it, that the first Eternal thinking Being, or Omnipotent Spirit, should, if he pleased, give to certain systems of created senseless matter, put together as he thinks fit, some degrees of sense, perception, and thought: though, as I think I have proved, Bk. iv. ch. 10, SS 14, &c., it is no less than a contradiction to suppose matter (which is evidently in its own nature void of sense and thought) should be that Eternal first-thinking Being. What certainty of knowledge can any one have, that some perceptions, such as, v.g., pleasure and pain, should not be in some bodies themselves, after a certain manner modified and moved, as well as that they should be in an immaterial substance, upon the motion of the parts of body: body, as far as we can conceive, being able only to strike and affect body, and motion, according to the utmost reach of our ideas, being able to produce nothing but motion; so that when we allow it to produce pleasure or pain, or the idea of a colour or sound, we are fain to quit our reason, go beyond our ideas, and attribute it wholly to the good pleasure of our Maker. For, since we must allow He has annexed effects to motion which we can no way conceive motion able to produce, what reason have we to conclude that He could not order them as well to be produced in a subject we cannot conceive capable of them, as well as in a subject we cannot conceive the motion of matter can any way operate upon? I say not this, that I would any way lessen the belief of the soul's immateriality: I am not here speaking of probability, but knowledge; and I think not only that it becomes the modesty of philosophy not to pronounce magisterially, where we want that evidence that can produce knowledge; but also, that it is of use to us to discern how far our knowledge does reach; for the state we are at present in, not being that of vision, we must in many things content ourselves with faith and probability: and in the present question, about the Immateriality of the Soul, if our faculties cannot arrive at demonstrative certainty, we need not think it strange. All the great ends of morality and religion are well enough secured, without philosophical proofs of the soul's immateriality; since it is evident, that he who made us at the beginning to subsist here, sensible intelligent beings, and for several years continued us in such a state, can and will restore us to the like state of sensibility in another world, and make us capable there to receive the retribution he has designed to men, according to their doings in this life. And therefore it is not of such mighty necessity to determine one way or the other, as some, over-zealous for or against the immateriality of the soul, have been forward to make the world believe. Who, either on the one side, indulging too much their thoughts immersed altogether in matter, can allow no existence to what is not material: or who, on the other side, finding not cogitation within the natural powers of matter, examined over and over again by the utmost intention of mind, have the confidence to conclude — That Omnipotency itself cannot give perception and thought to a substance which has the modification of solidity. He that considers how hardly sensation is, in our thoughts, reconcilable to extended matter; or existence to anything that has no extension at all, will confess that he is very far from certainly knowing what his soul is. It is a point which seems to me to be put out of the reach of our knowledge: and he who will give himself leave to consider freely, and look into the dark and intricate part of each hypothesis, will scarce find his reason able to determine him fixedly for or against the soul's materiality. Since, on which side soever he views it, either as an unextended substance, or as a thinking extended matter, the difficulty to conceive either will, whilst either alone is in his thoughts, still drive him to the contrary side. An unfair way which some men take with themselves: who, because of the inconceivableness of something they find in one, throw themselves violently into the contrary hypothesis, though altogether as unintelligible to an unbiassed understanding. This serves not only to show the weakness and the scantiness of our knowledge, but the insignificant triumph of such sort of arguments; which, drawn from our own views, may satisfy us that we can find no certainty on one side of the question: but do not at all thereby help us to truth by running into the opposite opinion; which, on examination, will be found clogged with equal difficulties. For what safety, what advantage to any one is it, for the avoiding the seeming absurdities, and to him unsurmountable rubs, he meets with in one opinion, to take refuge in the contrary, which is built on something altogether as inexplicable, and as far remote from his comprehension? It is past controversy, that we have in us something that thinks; our very doubts about what it is, confirm the certainty of its being, though we must content ourselves in the ignorance of what kind of being it is: and it is in vain to go about to be sceptical in this, as it is unreasonable in most other cases to be positive against the being of anything, because we cannot comprehend its nature. For I would fain know what substance exists, that has not something in it which manifestly baffles our understandings. Other spirits, who see and know the nature and inward constitution of things, how much must they exceed us in knowledge? To which, if we add larger comprehension, which enables them at one glance to see the connexion and agreement of very many ideas, and readily supplies to them the intermediate proofs, which we by single and slow steps, and long poring in the dark, hardly at last find out, and are often ready to forget one before we have hunted out another; we may guess at some part of the happiness of superior ranks of spirits, who have a quicker and more penetrating sight, as well as a larger field of knowledge.

c. From Book IV, Chapter X, Sections 14-17 [Locke's proof of the immateriality of God]

[The final selection from the *Essay* is Locke's argument from Book IV, Chapter X for the immateriality of God. This plays a role in the Clarke-Collins correspondence because it is quite similar to Clarke's argument that human intelligence could never come from matter, though the fact that Locke's argument is about God and Clarke's about humans is no small difference, as Collins points out.]

14. *Not material*: first, because each particle of matter is not cogitative. But now let us see how they can satisfy themselves, or others, that this eternal thinking Being is material. I. *I would ask them,*

whether they imagine that all matter, every particle of matter, thinks? This, I suppose, they will scarce say; since then there would be as many eternal thinking beings as there are particles of matter, and so an infinity of gods. And yet, if they will not allow matter as matter, that is, every particle of matter, to be as well cogitative as extended, they will have as hard a task to make out to their own reasons a cogitative being out of incogitative particles, as an extended being out of unextended parts, if I may so speak.

15. II. *Secondly,* because one particle alone of matter cannot be cogitative. If all matter does not think, I next ask, Whether it be only one atom that does so? This has as many absurdities as the other; for then this atom of matter must be alone eternal or not. If this alone be eternal, then this alone, by its powerful thought or will, made all the rest of matter. And so we have the creation of matter by a powerful thought, which is that the materialists stick at; for if they suppose one single thinking atom to have produced all the rest of matter, they cannot ascribe that pre-eminency to it upon any other account than that of its thinking, the only supposed difference. But allow it to be by some other way which is above our conception, it must still be creation; and these men must give up their great maxim, *Ex nihilo nil fit* [From nothing, nothing comes. –ed.]. If it be said, that all the rest of matter is equally eternal as that thinking atom, it will be to say anything at pleasure, though ever so absurd. For to suppose all matter eternal, and yet one small particle in knowledge and power infinitely above all the rest, is without any the least appearance of reason to frame an hypothesis. Every particle of matter, as matter, is capable of all the same figures and motions of any other; and I challenge any one, in his thoughts, to add anything else to one above another.

16. III. *Thirdly, because a system of incogitative matter cannot be cogitative.* If then neither one peculiar atom alone can be this eternal thinking being; nor all matter, as matter, i.e. every particle of matter, can be it; it only remains, that it is some certain system of matter, duly put together, that is this thinking eternal Being. This is that which, I imagine, is that notion which men are aptest to have of God; who would have him a material being, as most readily suggested to them by the ordinary conceit they have of themselves and other men, which they take to be material

thinking beings. But this imagination, however more natural, is no less absurd than the other: for to suppose the eternal thinking Being to be nothing else but a composition of particles of matter, each whereof is incogitative, is to ascribe all the wisdom and knowledge of that eternal Being only to the juxta-position of parts; than which nothing can be more absurd. For unthinking particles of matter, however put together, can have nothing thereby added to them, but a new relation of position, which it is impossible should give thought and knowledge to them.

17. *And that whether this corporeal system is in motion or at rest.* But further: this corporeal system either has all its parts at rest, or it is a certain motion of the parts wherein its thinking consists. If it be perfectly at rest, it is but one lump, and so can have no privileges above one atom. If it be the motion of its parts on which its thinking depends, all the thoughts there must be unavoidably accidental and limited; since all the particles that by motion cause thought, being each of them in itself without any thought, cannot regulate its own motions, much less be regulated by the thought of the whole; since that thought is not the cause of motion, (for then it must be antecedent to it, and so without it,) but the consequence of it; whereby freedom, power, choice, and all rational and wise thinking or acting, will be quite taken away: so that such a thinking being will be no better nor wiser than pure blind matter; since to resolve all into the accidental unguided motions of blind matter, or into thought depending on unguided motions of blind matter, is the same thing: not to mention the narrowness of such thoughts and knowledge that must depend on the motion of such parts. But there needs no enumeration of any more absurdities and impossibilities in this hypothesis (however full of them it be) than that before mentioned; since, let this thinking system be all or a part of the matter of the universe, it is impossible that any one particle should either know its own, or the motion of any other particle, or the whole know the motion of every particle; and so regulate its own thoughts or motions, or indeed have any thought resulting from such motion.

Appendix B: After the Correspondence

1. From David Hume, *A Treatise of Human Nature* (1739)

[David Hume (1711-76) commented on the Clarke-Collins correspondence. As Robin Attfield notes in his article "Clarke, Collins and Compounds," Hume offered strictures on both sides of the dispute. "Fundamentally, the issue between Clarke and Collins was the nature of the substance to which the consciousness belonged, and Hume may have had them in mind when he contended that as there may be no substance which underlies consciousness, disputes about whether it is material or not may be idle." Still, as Robin Attfield asserts, Hume's reasons for holding this position "cannot be true." But Hume does not stop with these even-handed strictures. His new account of causality, as he is well aware, is devastating to what (following Ezio Vailati) I have been calling the Homogeneity Principle as deployed by, among others, Cudworth, Bayle, and Clarke. Hume's new account of causality refutes that principle and in doing so removes all of the alleged contradictions that Clarke claims afflict Collins' attempts to produce properties that belong to wholes without belonging to their parts. This is because Hume rejects heirloom accounts of causality, i.e. accounts that require that the cause should resemble the effect. In this respect, Collins is a precursor of Hume. The passages from David Hume's *A Treatise of Human Nature* are from the three-volume edition by L.A. Selby-Bigge (Oxford: Clarendon Press, 1888).]

From Book I Sect. V: Of The Immateriality Of The Soul

Having found such contradictions and difficulties in every system concerning external objects, and in the idea of matter, which we fancy so clear and determinate, we shall naturally expect still greater difficulties and contradictions in every hypothesis concerning our internal perceptions, and the nature of the mind, which we are apt to imagine so much more obscure, and uncertain. But in this we should deceive ourselves. The intellectual world, though involved in infinite obscurities, is not perplexed with any such contradictions, as those we have discovered in the natural. What is known concerning it, agrees with itself; and what is unknown, we must be contented to leave so.

It is true, would we hearken to certain philosophers, they promise to diminish our ignorance; but I am afraid it is at the hazard of running us into contradictions, from which the subject is of itself exempted. These philosophers are the curious reasoners concerning the material or immaterial substances, in which they suppose our perceptions to inhere. In order to put a stop to these endless cavils on both sides, I know no better method, than to ask these philosophers in a few words, What they mean by substance and inhesion? And after they have answered this question, it will then be reasonable, and not till then, to enter seriously into the dispute.

This question we have found impossible to be answered with regard to matter and body: But besides that in the case of the mind, it labours under all the same difficulties, it is burthened with some additional ones, which are peculiar to that subject. As every idea is derived from a precedent impression, had we any idea of the substance of our minds, we must also have an impression of it; which is very difficult, if not impossible, to be conceived. For how can an impression represent a substance, otherwise than by resembling it? And how can an impression resemble a substance, since, according to this philosophy, it is not a substance, and has none of the peculiar qualities or characteristics of a substance?

But leaving the question of what may or may not be, for that other what actually is, I desire those philosophers, who pretend that we have an idea of the substance of our minds, to point out the impression that produces it, and tell distinctly after what manner that impression operates, and from what object it is derived. Is it an impression of sensation or of reflection? Is it pleasant, or painful, or indifferent? Does it attend us at all times, or does it only return at intervals? If at intervals, at what times principally does it return, and by what causes is it produced?

If instead of answering these questions, any one should evade the difficulty, by saying, that the definition of a substance is something which may exist by itself; and that this definition ought to satisfy us: should this be said, I should observe, that this definition agrees to every thing, that can possibly be conceived;

and never will serve to distinguish substance from accident, or the soul from its perceptions. For thus I reason. Whatever is clearly conceived may exist; and whatever is clearly conceived, after any manner, may exist after the same manner. This is one principle, which has been already acknowledged. Again, every thing, which is different, is distinguishable, and every thing which is distinguishable, is separable by the imagination. This is another principle. My conclusion from both is, that since all our perceptions are different from each other, and from every thing else in the universe, they are also distinct and separable, and may be considered as separately existent, and may exist separately, and have no need of any thing else to support their existence. They are, therefore, substances, as far as this definition explains a substance.

Thus neither by considering the first origin of ideas, nor by means of a definition are we able to arrive at any satisfactory notion of substance; which seems to me a sufficient reason for abandoning utterly that dispute concerning the materiality and immateriality of the soul, and makes me absolutely condemn even the question itself. We have no perfect idea of any thing but of a perception. A substance is entirely different from a perception. We have, therefore, no idea of a substance. Inhesion in something is supposed to be requisite to support the existence of our perceptions. Nothing appears requisite to support the existence of a perception. We have, therefore, no idea of inhesion. What possibility then of answering that question, Whether perceptions inhere in a material or immaterial substance, when we do not so much as understand the meaning of the question?

There is one argument commonly employed for the immateriality of the soul, which seems to me remarkable. Whatever is extended consists of parts; and whatever consists of parts is divisible, if not in reality, at least in the imagination. But it is impossible anything divisible can be conjoined to a thought or perception, which is a being altogether inseparable and indivisible. For supposing such a conjunction, would the indivisible thought exist on the left or on the right hand of this extended divisible body? On the surface or in the middle? On the back or fore side of it? If it be conjoined with the extension, it must exist somewhere within its dimensions. If it exist within its dimensions, it must either exist in one particular part; and then that particular part is indivisible, and the perception is conjoined only with it, not with the extension: Or if the thought exists in every part, it must also be extended, and separable, and divisible, as well as the body; which is utterly absurd and contradictory. For can any one conceive a passion of a yard in length, a foot in breadth, and an inch in thickness? Thought, therefore, and extension are qualities wholly incompatible, and never can incorporate together into one subject.

This argument affects not the question concerning the substance of the soul, but only that concerning its local conjunction with matter; and therefore it may not be improper to consider in general what objects are, or are not susceptible of a local conjunction. This is a curious question, and may lead us to some discoveries of considerable moment.

The first notion of space and extension is derived solely from the senses of sight and feeling; nor is there any thing, but what is coloured or tangible, that has parts disposed after such a manner, as to convey that idea. When we diminish or increase a relish, it is not after the same manner that we diminish or increase any visible object; and when several sounds strike our hearing at once, custom and reflection alone make us form an idea of the degrees of the distance and contiguity of those bodies, from which they are derived. Whatever marks the place of its existence either must be extended, or must be a mathematical point, without parts or composition. What is extended must have a particular figure, as square, round, triangular; none of which will agree to a desire, or indeed to any impression or idea, except to these two senses above-mentioned. Neither ought a desire, though indivisible, to be considered as a mathematical point. For in that case it would be possible, by the addition of others, to make two, three, four desires, and these disposed and situated in such a manner, as to have a determinate length, breadth and thickness; which is evidently absurd.

It will not be surprising after this, if I deliver a maxim, which is condemned by several metaphysicians, and is esteemed contrary to the most certain principles of human reason. This maxim is that an object may exist, and yet be no where: and I assert, that this is not only possible, but that the greatest part of beings do and must exist after this manner. An object may be said to be no where, when its parts are not so situated with respect to each other, as to form any figure or quantity; nor the whole with respect to other bodies so as to answer to our notions of contiguity or distance.

Now this is evidently the case with all our perceptions and objects, except those of the sight and feeling. A moral reflection cannot be placed on the right or on the left hand of a passion, nor can a smell or sound be either of a circular or a square figure. These objects and perceptions, so far from requiring any particular place, are absolutely incompatible with it, and even the imagination cannot attribute it to them. And as to the absurdity of supposing them to be no where, we may consider, that if the passions and sentiments appear to the perception to have any particular place, the idea of extension might be derived from them, as well as from the sight and touch; contrary to what we have already established. If they APPEAR not to have any particular place, they may possibly exist in the same manner; since whatever we conceive is possible.

It will not now be necessary to prove, that those perceptions, which are simple, and exist no where, are incapable of any conjunction in place with matter or body, which is extended and divisible; since it is impossible to found a relation but on some common quality. It may be better worth our while to remark, that this question of the local conjunction of objects does not only occur in metaphysical disputes concerning the nature of the soul, but that even in common life we have every moment occasion to examine it. Thus supposing we consider a fig at one end of the table, and an olive at the other, it is evident, that in forming the complex ideas of these substances, one of the most obvious is that of their different relishes; and it is as evident, that we incorporate and conjoin these qualities with such as are coloured and tangible. The bitter taste of the one, and sweet of the other are supposed to lie in the very visible body, and to be separated from each other by the whole length of the table. This is so notable and so natural an illusion, that it may be proper to consider the principles, from which it is derived.

Though an extended object be incapable of a conjunction in place with another, that exists without any place or extension, yet are they susceptible of many other relations. Thus the taste and smell of any fruit are inseparable from its other qualities of colour and tangibility; and whichever of them be the cause or effect, it is certain they are always co-existent. Nor are they only co-existent in general, but also co-temporary in their appearance in the mind; and it is upon the application of the extended body to our senses we perceive its particular taste and smell. These relations, then, of causation, and contiguity in the time of their appearance, betwixt the extended object and the quality, which exists without any particular place, must have such an effect on the mind, that upon the appearance of one it will immediately turn its thought to the conception of the other. Nor is this all. We not only turn our thought from one to the other upon account of their relation, but likewise endeavour to give them a new relation, viz. that of a CONJUNCTION IN PLACE, that we may render the transition more easy and natural. For it is a quality, which I shall often have occasion to remark in human nature, and shall explain more fully in its proper place, that when objects are united by any relation, we have a strong propensity to add some new relation to them, in order to complete the union. In our arrangement of bodies we never fail to place such as are resembling, in contiguity to each other, or at least in correspondent points of view:

Why? but because we feel a satisfaction in joining the relation of contiguity to that of resemblance, or the resemblance of situation to that of qualities. The effects of this propensity have been [Sect. 2, towards the end.] already observed in that resemblance, which we so readily suppose betwixt particular impressions and their external causes. But we shall not find a more evident effect of it, than in the present instance, where from the relations of causation and contiguity in time betwixt two objects, we feign likewise that of a conjunction in place, in order to strengthen the connection.

But whatever confused notions we may form of an union in place betwixt an extended body, as a fig, and its particular taste, it is certain that upon reflection we must observe this union something altogether unintelligible and contradictory. For should we ask ourselves one obvious question, viz. if the taste, which we conceive to be contained in the circumference of the body, is in every part of it or in one only, we must quickly find ourselves at a loss, and perceive the impossibility of ever giving a satisfactory answer. We cannot rely, that it is only in one part: For experience convinces us, that every part has the same relish. We can as little reply, that it exists in every part: For then we must suppose it figured and extended; which is absurd and incomprehensible. Here then we are influenced by two principles directly contrary to each other, viz. that inclination of our fancy by which we are determined to incorporate the taste with the extended object, and our reason, which shows us the impossibility of such an union.

Being divided betwixt these opposite principles, we renounce neither one nor the other, but involve the subject in such confusion and obscurity, that we no longer perceive the opposition. We suppose, that the taste exists within the circumference of the body, but in such a manner, that it fills the whole without extension, and exists entire in every part without separation. In short, we use in our most familiar way of thinking, that scholastic principle, which, when crudely proposed, appears so shocking, of TOTUM IN TOTO & TOLUM IN QUALIBET PARTE [the whole is in the whole and the whole in every part]: Which is much the same, as if we should say, that a thing is in a certain place, and yet is not there.

All this absurdity proceeds from our endeavoring to bestow a place on what is utterly incapable of it; and that endeavor again arises from our inclination to complete an union, which is founded on causation, and a contiguity of time, by attributing to the objects a conjunction in place. But if ever reason be of sufficient force to overcome prejudice, it is certain, that in the present case it must prevail. For we have only this choice left, either to suppose that some beings exist without any place; or that they are figured and extended; or that when they are incorporated with extended objects, the whole is in the whole, and the whole in every part. The absurdity of the two last suppositions proves sufficiently the veracity of the first. Nor is there any fourth opinion. For as to the supposition of their existence in the manner of mathematical points, it resolves itself into the second opinion, and supposes, that several passions may be placed in a circular figure, and that a certain number of smells, conjoined with a certain number of sounds, may make a body of twelve cubic inches; which appears ridiculous upon the bare mentioning of it.

But though in this view of things we cannot refuse to condemn the materialists, who conjoin all thought with extension; yet a little reflection will show us equal reason for blaming their antagonists, who conjoin all thought with a simple and indivisible substance. The most vulgar philosophy informs us, that no external object can make itself known to the mind immediately, and without the interposition of an image or perception. That table, which just now appears to me, is only a perception, and all its qualities are qualities of a perception. Now the most obvious of all its qualities is extension. The perception consists of parts. These parts are so situated, as to afford us the notion of distance and contiguity; of length, breadth, and thickness. The termination of these three dimensions is what we call figure. This figure is moveable, separable, and divisible. Mobility, and separability are the distinguishing properties of extended objects. And to cut short all disputes, the very idea of extension is copied from nothing but an impression, and consequently must perfectly agree to it. To say the idea of extension agrees to any thing, is to say it is extended.

The free-thinker may now triumph in his turn; and having found there are impressions and ideas really extended, may ask his antagonists, how they can incorporate a simple and indivisible subject with an extended perception? All the arguments of Theologians may here be retorted upon them. Is the indivisible subject, or immaterial substance, if you will, on the left or on the right hand of the perception? Is it in this particular part, or in that other? Is it in every part without being extended? Or is it entire in any one part without deserting the rest? It is impossible to give any answer to these questions, but what will both be absurd in itself, and will account for the union of our indivisible perceptions with an extended substance.

This gives me an occasion to take anew into consideration the question concerning the substance of the soul; and though I have condemned that question as utterly unintelligible, yet I cannot forbear proposing some farther reflections concerning it. I assert, that the doctrine of the immateriality, simplicity, and indivisibility of a thinking substance is a true atheism, and will serve to justify all those sentiments, for which Spinoza is so universally infamous. From this topic, I hope at least to reap one advantage, that my adversaries will not have any pretext to render the present doctrine odious by their declamations, when they see that they can be so easily retorted on them.

The fundamental principle of the atheism of Spinoza is the doctrine of the simplicity of the universe, and the unity of that substance, in which he supposes both thought and matter to inhere. There is only one substance, says he, in the world; and that substance is perfectly simple and indivisible, and exists every where, without any local presence. Whatever we discover externally by sensation; whatever we feel internally by reflection; all these are nothing but modifications of that one, simple, and necessarily existent being, and are not possessed of any separate or distinct existence. Every passion of the soul;

every configuration of matter, however different and various, inhere in the same substance, and preserve in themselves their characters of distinction, without communicating them to that subject, in which they inhere. The same substratum, if I may so speak, supports the most different modifications, without any difference in itself; and varies them, without any variation. Neither time, nor place, nor all the diversity of nature are able to produce any composition or change in its perfect simplicity and identity.

I believe this brief exposition of the principles of that famous atheist will be sufficient for the present purpose, and that without entering farther into these gloomy and obscure regions, I shall be able to show, that this hideous hypothesis is almost the same with that of the immateriality of the soul, which has become so popular. To make this evident, let us [Part II, Sect. 6.] remember, that as every idea is derived from a preceding perception, it is impossible our idea of a perception, and that of an object or external existence, can ever represent what are specifically different from each other. Whatever difference we may suppose betwixt them, it is still incomprehensible to us; and we are obliged either to conceive an external object merely as a relation without a relative, or to make it the very same with a perception or impression.

The consequence I shall draw from this may, at first sight, appear a mere sophism; but upon the least examination will be found solid and satisfactory. I say then, that since we may suppose, but never can conceive a specific deference betwixt an object and impression; any conclusion we form concerning the connection and repugnance of impressions, will not be known certainly to be applicable to objects; but that on the other hand, whatever conclusions of this kind we form concerning objects, will most certainly be applicable to impressions. The reason is not difficult. As an object is supposed to be different from an impression, we cannot be sure, that the circumstance, upon which we found our reasoning, is common to both, supposing we form the reasoning upon the impression. It is still possible, that the object may differ from it in that particular. But when we first form our reasoning concerning the object, it is beyond doubt, that the same reasoning must extend to the impression: And that because the quality of the object, upon which the argument is founded, must at least be conceived by the mind; and could not be conceived, unless it were common to an impression; since we have no idea but what is derived from that origin. Thus we may establish it as a certain maxim, that we can never, by any principle, but by an irregular kind [Such as that of Sect. 2, form the coherence of our perceptions.] of reasoning from experience, discover a connection or repugnance betwixt objects, which extends not to impressions; though the inverse proposition may not be equally true, that all the discoverable relations of impressions are common to objects.

To apply this to the present case; there are two different systems of being presented, to which I suppose myself under a necessity of assigning some substance, or ground of inhesion. I observe first the universe of objects or of body: The sun, moon and stars; the earth, seas, plants, animals, men, ships, houses, and other productions either of art or nature. Here Spinoza appears, and tells me, that these are only modifications; and that the subject, in which they inhere, is simple, incompounded, and indivisible. After this I consider the other system of beings, viz. the universe of thought, or my impressions and ideas. Then I observe another sun, moon and stars; an earth, and seas, covered and inhabited by plants and animals; towns, houses, mountains, rivers; and in short every thing I can discover or conceive in the first system. Upon my enquiring concerning these, Theologians present themselves, and tell me, that these also are modifications, and modifications of one simple, uncompounded, and indivisible substance. Immediately upon which I am deafened with the noise of a hundred voices, that treat the first hypothesis with detestation and scorn, and the second with applause and veneration. I turn my attention to these hypotheses to see what may be the reason of so great a partiality; and find that they have the same fault of being unintelligible, and that as far as we can understand them, they are so much alike, that it is impossible to discover any absurdity in one, which is not common to both of them. We have no idea of any quality in an object, which does not agree to, and may not represent a quality in an impression; and that because all our ideas are derived from our impressions. We can never, therefore, find any repugnance betwixt an extended object as a modification, and a simple uncompounded essence, as its substance, unless that repugnance takes place equally betwixt the perception or impression of that extended object, and the same uncompounded essence. Every idea of a quality in an object passes through an impression; and therefore every perceivable relation, whether of connection or repugnance, must be common both to objects and impressions.

But though this argument, considered in general, seems evident beyond all doubt and contradiction, yet to make it more clear and sensible, let us survey it in detail; and see whether all the absurdities, which have been found in the system of Spinoza, may not likewise be discovered in that of Theologians. [See Bayle's dictionary, article of Spinoza.]

First, It has been said against Spinoza, according to the scholastic way of talking, rather than thinking, that a mode, not being any distinct or separate existence, must be the very same with its substance, and consequently the extension of the universe, must be in a manner identified with that, simple, uncompounded essence, in which the universe is supposed to inhere. But this, it may be pretended, is utterly impossible and inconceivable unless the indivisible substance expand itself, so as to correspond to the extension, or the extension contract itself, so as to answer to the indivisible substance. This argument seems just, as far as we can understand it; and it is plain nothing is required, but a change in the terms, to apply the same argument to our extended perceptions, and the simple essence of the soul; the ideas of objects and perceptions being in every respect the same, only attended with the supposition of a difference, that is unknown and incomprehensible.

Secondly, It has been said, that we have no idea of substance, which is not applicable to matter; nor any idea of a distinct substance, which is not applicable to every distinct portion of matter. Matter, therefore, is not a mode but a substance, and each part of matter is not a distinct mode, but a distinct substance. I have already proved, that we have no perfect idea of substance; but that taking it for *something, that can exist by itself*, it is evident every perception is a substance, and every distinct part of a perception a distinct substance: And consequently the one hypothesis labors under the same difficulties in this respect with the other.

Thirdly, It has been objected to the system of one simple substance in the universe, that this substance being the support or *substratum* of every thing, must at the very same instant be modified into forms, which are contrary and incompatible. The round and square figures are incompatible in the same substance at the same time. How then is it possible, that the same substance can at once be modified into that square table, and into this round one? I ask the same question concerning the impressions of these tables; and find that the answer is no more satisfactory in one case than in the other.

It appears, then, that to whatever side we turn, the same difficulties follow us, and that we cannot advance one step towards the establishing the simplicity and immateriality of the soul, without preparing the way for a dangerous and irrecoverable atheism. It is the same case, if instead of calling thought a modification of the soul, we should give it the more ancient, and yet more modish name of an *action*. By an action we mean much the same thing, as what is commonly called an abstract mode; that is, something, which, properly speaking, is neither distinguishable, nor separable from its substance, and is only conceived by a distinction of reason, or an abstraction. But nothing is gained by this change of the term of modification, for that of action; nor do we free ourselves from one single difficulty by its means; as will appear from the two following reflexions.

First, I observe, that the word, action, according to this explication of it, can never justly be applied to any perception, as derived from a mind or thinking substance. Our perceptions are all really different, and separable, and distinguishable from each other, and from everything else, which we can imagine: and therefore it is impossible to conceive, how they can be the action or abstract mode of any substance. The instance of motion, which is commonly made use of to shew after what manner perception depends, as an action, upon its substance, rather confounds than instructs us. Motion to all appearance induces no real nor essential change on the body, but only varies its relation to other objects. But betwixt a person in the morning walking a garden with company, agreeable to him; and a person in the afternoon inclosed in a dungeon, and full of terror, despair, and resentment, there seems to be a radical difference, and of quite another kind, than what is produced on a body by the change of its situation. As we conclude from the distinction and separability of their ideas, that external objects have a separate existence from each other; so when we make these ideas themselves our objects, we must draw the same conclusion concerning them, according to the precedent reasoning. At least it must be confessed, that having no idea of the substance of the soul, it is impossible for us to tell how it can admit of such differences, and even contrarieties of perception without any fundamental change; and consequently can never tell in what sense perceptions are actions of that substance. The use, therefore, of the word, action, unaccompanied with any meaning, instead of that of modification, makes no addition to our knowledge, nor is of any advantage to the doctrine of the immateriality of the soul.

I add in the second place, that if it brings any advantage to that cause, it must bring an equal to the cause of atheism. For do our Theologians pretend to make a monopoly of the word, action, and may not the atheists likewise take possession of it, and affirm that plants, animals, men, &c. are nothing but particular actions of one simple universal substance, which exerts itself from a blind and absolute necessity? This you'll say is utterly absurd. I own it is unintelligible; but at the same time assert, according to the principles above-explained, that it is impossible to discover any absurdity in the supposition, that all the various objects in nature are actions of one simple substance, which absurdity will not be applicable to a like supposition concerning impressions and ideas.

From these hypotheses concerning the substance and local conjunction of our perceptions, we may pass to another, which is more intelligible than the former, and more important than the latter, viz. concerning the cause of our perceptions. Matter and motion, it is commonly said in the schools, however varied, are still matter and motion, and produce only a difference in the position and situation of objects. Divide a body as often as you please, it is still body. Place it in any figure, nothing ever results but figure, or the relation of parts. Move it in any manner, you still find motion or a change of relation. It is absurd to imagine, that motion in a circle, for instance, should be nothing but merely motion in a circle; while motion in another direction, as in an ellipse, should also be a passion or moral reflection: That the shocking of two globular particles should become a sensation of pain, and that the meeting of two triangular ones should afford a pleasure. Now as these different shocks, and variations, and mixtures are the only changes, of which matter is susceptible, and as these never afford us any idea of thought or perception, it is concluded to be impossible, that thought can ever be caused by matter.

Few have been able to withstand the seeming evidence of this argument; and yet nothing in the world is more easy than to refute it. We need only reflect on what has been proved at large, that we are never sensible of any connection betwixt causes and effects, and that it is only by our experience of their constant conjunction, we can arrive at any knowledge of this relation. Now as all objects, which are not contrary, are susceptible of a constant conjunction, and as no real objects are contrary [Part III. Sect. 15.]; I have inferred from these principles, that to consider the matter *a priori*, any thing may produce any thing, and that we shall never discover a reason, why any object may or may not be the cause of any other, however great, or however little the resemblance may be betwixt them. This evidently destroys the precedent reasoning concerning the cause of thought or perception. For though there appear no manner of connection betwixt motion or thought, the case is the same with all other causes and effects. Place one body of a pound weight on one end of a lever, and another body of the same weight on another end; you will never find in these bodies any principle of motion dependent on their distances from the center, more than of thought and perception. If you pretend, therefore, to prove *a priori*, that such a position of bodies can never cause thought; because turn it which way you will, it is nothing but a position of bodies; you must by the same course of reasoning conclude, that it can never produce motion; since there is no more apparent connection in the one case than in the other. But as this latter conclusion is contrary to evident experience, and as it is possible we may have a like experience in the operations of the mind, and may perceive a constant conjunction of thought and motion; you reason too hastily, when from the mere consideration of the ideas, you conclude that it is impossible motion can ever produce thought, or a different position of parts give rise to a different passion or reflection. Nay it is not only possible we may have such an experience, but it is certain we have it; since every one may perceive, that the different dispositions of his body change his thoughts and sentiments. And should it be said, that this depends on the union of soul and body; I would answer, that we must separate the question concerning the substance of the mind from that concerning the cause of its thought; and that confining ourselves to the latter question we find by the comparing their ideas, that thought and motion are different from each other, and by experience, that they are constantly united; which being all the circumstances, that enter into the idea of cause and effect, when applied to the operations of matter, we may certainly conclude, that motion may be, and actually is, the cause of thought and perception.

There seems only this dilemma left us in the present case; either to assert, that nothing can be the cause of another, but where the mind can perceive the connection in its idea of the objects: Or to maintain, that all objects, which we find constantly conjoined, are upon that account to be regarded as causes and effects. If we choose the first part of the dilemma, these are the consequences. First, We in reality affirm, that there is no such thing in the universe as a cause or productive principle, not even the deity himself; since our idea of that supreme Being is derived from particular impressions, none of which contain any efficacy, nor seem to have any connection with any other existence. As to what may be said, that the connection betwixt the idea of an infinitely powerful being, and that of any effect, which he wills, is necessary and unavoidable; I answer, that we have no idea of a being endowed with any power, much less of one endowed with infinite power. But if we will change expressions, we can only define power by connection; and then in saying, that the idea, of an infinitely powerful being is connected with that of every effect, which he wills, we really do no more than assert, that a being, whose volition is connected with every effect, is connected with every effect: which is an identical proposition, and gives us no insight into the nature of this power or connection. But, secondly, supposing, that the deity were the great and efficacious principle, which supplies the deficiency of all causes, this leads us into the grossest impieties and absurdities. For upon the same account, that we have recourse to him in natural operations, and assert that matter cannot of itself communicate motion, or produce thought, viz. because there is no apparent connection betwixt these objects; I say, upon the very same account, we must acknowledge that the deity is the author of all our volitions and perceptions; since they have no more apparent connection either with one another, or with the supposed but unknown substance of the soul. This agency of the supreme Being we know to have been asserted by [As father Malebranche and other Cartesians.] several philosophers with relation to all the actions of the mind, except volition, or rather an inconsiderable part of volition; though it is easy to perceive, that this exception is a mere pretext, to avoid the dangerous consequences of that doctrine. If nothing be active but what has an apparent power, thought is in no case any more active than matter; and if this inactivity must make us have recourse to a deity, the supreme being is the real cause of all our actions, bad as well as good, vicious as well as virtuous.

Thus we are necessarily reduced to the other side of the dilemma, viz. that all objects, which are found to be constantly conjoined, are upon that account only to be regarded as causes and effects. Now as all objects, which are not contrary, are susceptible of a constant conjunction, and as no real objects are contrary: it follows, that for ought we can determine by the mere ideas, any thing may be the cause or effect of any thing; which evidently gives the advantage to the materialists above their antagonists.

To pronounce, then, the final decision upon the whole; the question concerning the substance of the soul is absolutely unintelligible: All our perceptions are not susceptible of a local union, either with what is extended or unextended: there being some of them of the one kind, and some of the other: And as the constant conjunction of objects constitutes the very essence of cause and effect, matter and motion may often be regarded as the causes of thought, as far as we have any notion of that relation.

It is certainly a kind of indignity to philosophy, whose sovereign authority ought every where to be acknowledged, to oblige her on every occasion to make apologies for her conclusions, and justify herself to every particular art and science, which may be offended at her. This puts one in mind of a king arraigned for high-treason against his subjects. There is only one occasion, when philosophy will think it necessary and even honorable to justify herself, and that is, when religion may seem to be in the least offended; whose rights are as dear to her as her own, and are indeed the same. If any one, therefore, should imagine that the foregoing arguments are any ways dangerous to religion, I hope the following apology will remove his apprehensions.

There is no foundation for any conclusion *a priori*, either concerning the operations or duration of any object, of which it is possible for the human mind to form a conception. Any object may be imagined to become entirely inactive, or to be annihilated in a moment; and it is an evident principle, that whatever we can imagine, is possible. Now this is no more true of matter, than of spirit; of an extended compounded substance, than of a simple and unextended. In both cases the metaphysical arguments for the immortality of the soul are equally inconclusive: and in both cases the moral arguments and those derived from the analogy of nature are equally strong and convincing. If my philosophy, therefore, makes no addition to the arguments for religion, I have at least the satisfaction to think it takes nothing from them, but that every thing remains precisely as before.

2. From John Stuart Mill, *A System of Logic* (1843)

[In *A System of Logic*, John Stuart Mill (1806-73) makes a distinction between compounding and heteropathic causes. This distinction captures and illuminates the distinction between the kind of wholes that are the sum of their parts and wholes that have properties not possessed by their parts. Thus, Mill's distinction looks forward to the distinction between wholes with and without emergent properties and backwards to Collins' attempt to argue that in addition to wholes that are the sum of their parts, there are many wholes whose organization gives them different properties than their parts. It is notable that there is no reference to the role of God in the chapter below, and that Mill does not treat the distinction as if it were a matter of intense controversy, though he does call it "radical." There are also repeated references to causal laws that we do not find in the correspondence between Clarke and Collins. The chapter from J.S. Mill's *A System of Logic* is from the eighth edition published by Harper & Brothers (New York, 1882).]

Book III, Chapter VI

On The Composition Of Causes

1. To complete the general notion of causation on which the rules of experimental inquiry into the laws of nature must be founded, one distinction still remains to be pointed out: a distinction so radical, and of so much importance, as to require a chapter to itself.

The preceding discussions have rendered us familiar with the case in which several agents, or causes, concur as conditions to the production of an effect; a case, in truth, almost universal, there being very few effects to the production of which no more than one agent contributes. Suppose, then, that two different agents, operating jointly, are followed, under a certain set of collateral conditions, by a given effect. If either of these agents, instead of being joined with the other, had operated alone, under the same set of conditions in all other respects, some effect would probably have followed, which would have been different from the joint effect of the two, and more or less dissimilar to it. Now, if we happen to know what would be the effect of each cause when acting separately from the other, we are often able to arrive deductively, or *a priori*, at a correct prediction of what will arise from their conjunct agency. To render this possible, it is only necessary that the same law which expresses the effect of each cause acting by itself, shall also correctly express the part due to that cause of the effect which follows from the two together. This condition is realized in the extensive and important class of phenomena commonly called mechanical, namely the phenomena of the communication of motion (or of pressure, which is tendency to motion) from one body to another. In this important class of cases of causation, one cause never, properly speaking, defeats or frustrates another; both have their full effect. If a body is propelled in two directions by two forces, one tending to drive it to the north and the other to the east, it is caused to move in a given time exactly as far in both directions as the two forces would separately have carried it; and is left precisely where it would have arrived if it had been acted upon first by one of the two forces, and afterward by the other. This law of nature is called, in dynamics, the principle of the Composition of Forces; and in imitation of that well chosen expression, I shall give the name of the Composition of Causes to the principle which is exemplified in all cases in which the joint effect of several causes is identical with the sum of their separate effects.

This principle, however, by no means prevails in all departments of the field of nature. The chemical combination of two substances produces, as is well known, a third substance, with properties different from those of either of the two substances separately, or of both of them taken together. Not a trace of the properties of hydrogen or of oxygen is observable in those of their compound, water. The taste of sugar of lead is not the sum of the tastes of its component elements, acetic acid and lead or its oxide; nor is the color of blue vitriol a mixture of the colors of sulphuric acid and copper. This explains why mechanics is a deductive or demonstrative science, and chemistry not. In the one, we can compute the effects of combinations of causes, whether real or hypothetical, from the laws which we know to govern those causes when acting separately, because they continue to observe the same laws when in combination which they observe when separate: whatever would have happened in consequence of each cause taken by itself, happens when they are together, and we have only to cast up the results. Not so in the phenomena which are the peculiar subject of the science of chemistry. There most of the uniformities to which the causes conform when separate, cease altogether when they are conjoined; and we are not, at least in the present state of our knowledge, able to foresee what result will follow from any new combination until we have tried the specific experiment.

If this be true of chemical combinations, it is still more true of those far more complex combinations of elements which constitute organized bodies; and in which those extraordinary new uniformities arise which are called the laws of life. All organized bodies are composed of parts similar to those composing inorganic nature, and which have even themselves existed in an inorganic state; but the phenomena of life, which result from the juxtaposition of those parts in a certain manner, bear no analogy to any of the effects which would be produced by the action of the component substances considered as mere physical agents. To whatever degree we might imagine our knowledge of the properties of the several ingredients of a living body to be extended and perfected, it is certain that no mere summing up of the separate actions of those elements will ever amount to the action of the living body itself. The tongue, for instance, is, like all other parts of the animal frame, composed of gelatine, fibrine, and other products of the chemistry of digestion; but from no knowledge of the properties of those substances could we ever predict that it could taste, unless gelatine or fibrine could themselves taste; for no elementary fact can be in the conclusion which was not in the premises.

There are thus two different modes of the conjunct action of causes; from which arise two modes of conflict, or mutual interference, between laws of nature. Suppose, at a given point of time and space, two or more causes, which, if they acted separately, would produce effects contrary, or at least conflicting with each other; one of them tending to undo, wholly or partially, what the other tends to do. Thus the expansive force of the gases generated by the ignition of gunpowder tends to project a bullet toward the sky, while its gravity tends to make it fall to the ground. A stream running into a reservoir at one end tends to fill it higher and higher, while a drain at the other extremity tends to empty it. Now, in such cases as these, even if the two causes which are in joint action exactly annul one another, still the laws of both are fulfilled; the effect is the same as if the drain had been open for half an hour first, and the stream had flowed in for as long afterward. Each agent produces the same amount of effect as if it had acted separately, though the contrary effect which was taking place during the same time obliterated it as fast as it was produced. Here, then, are two causes, producing by their joint operations an effect which at first seems quite dissimilar to those which they produce separately, but which on examination proves to be really the sum of those separate effects. It will be noticed that we here enlarge the idea of the sum of two effects, so as to include what is commonly called their difference, but which is in reality the result of the addition of opposites; a conception to which mankind are indebted for that admirable extension of the algebraical calculus, which has so vastly increased its powers as an instrument of discovery, by introducing into its reasonings (with the sign of subtraction prefixed, and under the name of Negative Quantities) every description whatever of positive phenomena, provided they are of such a quality in reference to those previously introduced, that to add the one is equivalent to subtracting an equal quantity of the other.

There is, then, one mode of the mutual interference of laws of nature, in which, even when the concurrent causes annihilate each other's effects, each exerts its full efficacy according to its own law — its law as a separate agent. But in the other description of cases, the agencies which are brought together cease entirely, and a totally different set of phenomena arise: as in the experiment of two liquids which, when mixed in certain proportions, instantly become, not a larger amount of liquid, but a solid mass.

2. This difference between the case in which the joint effect of causes is the sum of their separate effects, and the case in which it is heterogeneous to them — between laws which work together without alteration, and laws which, when called upon to work together, cease and give place to others — is one of the fundamental distinctions in nature. The former case, that of the

Composition of Causes, is the general one; the other is always special and exceptional. There are no objects which do not, as to some of their phenomena, obey the principle of the Composition of Causes; none that have not some laws which are rigidly fulfilled in every combination into which the objects enter. The weight of a body, for instance, is a property which it retains in all the combinations in which it is placed. The weight of a chemical compound, or of an organized body, is equal to the sum of the weights of the elements which compose it. The weight either of the elements or of the compound will vary, if they be carried farther from their centre of attraction, or brought nearer to it; but whatever effects the one effects the other. They always remain precisely equal. So, again, the component parts of a vegetable or animal substance do not lose their mechanical and chemical properties as separate agents, when, by a peculiar mode of juxtaposition, they, as an aggregate whole, acquire physiological or vital properties in addition. Those bodies continue, as before, to obey mechanical and chemical laws, in so far as the operation of those laws is not counteracted by the new laws which govern them as organized beings; when, in short, a concurrence of causes takes place which calls into action new laws bearing no analogy to any that we can trace in the separate operation of the causes, the new laws, while they supersede one portion of the previous laws, may co-exist with another portion, and may even compound the effect of those previous laws with their own.

Again, laws which were themselves generated in the second mode, may generate others in the first. Though there are laws which, like those of chemistry and physiology, owe their existence to a breach of the principle of Composition of Causes, it does not follow that these peculiar, or, as they might be termed, *heteropathic* laws, are not capable of composition with one another. The causes which by one combination have had their laws altered, may carry their new laws with them unaltered into their ulterior combinations. And hence there is no reason to despair of ultimately raising chemistry and physiology to the condition of deductive sciences; for though it is impossible to deduce all chemical and physiological truths from the laws or properties of simple substances or elementary agents, they may possibly be deducible from laws which commence when these elementary agents are brought together into some moderate number of not very complex combinations. The Laws of Life will never be deducible from the mere laws of the ingredients, but the prodigiously complex Facts of Life may all be deducible from comparatively simple laws of life; which laws (depending indeed on combinations, but on comparatively simple combinations, of antecedents) may, in more complex circumstances, be strictly compounded with one another, and with the physical and chemical laws of the ingredients. The details of the vital phenomena, even now, afford innumerable exemplifications of the Composition of Causes; and in proportion as these phenomena are more accurately studied, there appears more reason to believe that the same laws which operate in the simpler combinations of circumstances do, in fact, continue to be observed in the more complex. This will be found equally true in the phenomena of mind; and even in social and political phenomena, the results of the laws of mind. It is in the case of chemical phenomena that the least progress has yet been made in bringing the special laws under general ones from which they may be deduced; but there are even in chemistry many circumstances to encourage the hope that such general laws will hereafter be discovered. The different actions of a chemical compound will never, undoubtedly, be found to be the sums of the actions of its separate elements; but there may exist, between the properties of the compound and those of its elements, some constant relation, which, if discoverable by a sufficient induction, would enable us to foresee the sort of compound which will result from a new combination before we have actually tried it, and to judge of what sort of elements some new substance is compounded before we have analyzed it. The law of definite proportions, first discovered in its full generality by Dalton, is a complete solution of this problem in one, though but a secondary aspect, that of quantity; and in respect to quality, we have already some partial generalizations, sufficient to indicate the possibility of ultimately proceeding farther. We can predicate some common properties of the kind of compounds which result from the combination, in each of the small number of possible proportions, of any acid whatever with any base. We have also the curious law, discovered by Berthollet, that two soluble salts mutually decompose one another whenever the new combinations which result produce an insoluble compound, or one less soluble than the two former. Another uniformity is that called the law of isomorphism; the identity of the crystalline forms of substances which possess in common certain peculiarities of chemical composition. Thus it appears that even heteropathic laws, such laws of combined agency as are not compounded of the laws of the separate agencies, are yet, at least in some cases, derived from them according to a fixed principle. There may, therefore, be laws of the generation of laws from others dissimilar to them; and in chemistry, these undiscovered laws of the dependence of the properties of the compound on the properties of its elements, may, together with the laws of the elements themselves, furnish the premises by which the science is perhaps destined one day to be rendered deductive.

It would seem, therefore, that there is no class of phenomena in which the Composition of Causes does not obtain: that as a general rule, causes in combination produce exactly the same effects as when acting singly: but that this rule, though general, is not universal: that in some instances, at some particular points in the transition from separate to united action, the laws change, and an entirely new set of effects are either added to, or take the place of, those which arise from the separate agency of the same causes: the laws of these new effects being again susceptible of composition, to an indefinite extent, like the laws which they superseded.

3. That effects are proportional to their causes is laid down by some writers as an axiom in the theory of causation; and great use is sometimes made of this principle in reasonings respecting the laws of nature, though it is encumbered with many difficulties and apparent exceptions, which much ingenuity has been expended in showing not to be real ones. This proposition, in so far as it is true, enters as a particular case into the general principle of the Composition of Causes; the causes compounded being, in this instance, homogeneous; in which case, if in any, their joint effect might be expected to be identical with the sum of their separate effects. If a force equal to one hundred weight will raise a certain body along an inclined plane, a force equal to two hundred weight will raise two bodies exactly similar, and thus the effect is proportional to the cause. But does not a force equal to two hundred weight actually contain in itself two forces each equal to one hundred weight, which, if employed apart, would separately raise the two bodies in question? The fact, therefore, that when exerted jointly they raise both bodies at once, results from the Composition of Causes, and is a mere instance of the general fact that mechanical forces are subject to the law of Composition. And so in every other case which can

be supposed. For the doctrine of the proportionality of effects to their causes can not of course be applicable to cases in which the augmentation of the cause alters the kind of effect; that is, in which the surplus quantity superadded to the cause does not become compounded with it, but the two together generate an altogether new phenomenon. Suppose that the application of a certain quantity of heat to a body merely increases its bulk, that a double quantity melts it, and a triple quantity decomposes it: these three effects being heterogeneous, no ratio, whether corresponding or not to that of the quantities of heat applied, can be established between them. Thus the supposed axiom of the proportionality of effects to their causes fails at the precise point where the principle of the Composition of Causes also fails; viz. where the concurrence of causes is such as to determine a change in the properties of the body generally, and render it subject to new laws, more or less dissimilar to those to which it conformed in its previous state. The recognition, therefore, of any such law of proportionality is superseded by the more comprehensive principle, in which as much of it as is true is implicitly asserted.

The general remarks on causation, which seemed necessary as an introduction to the theory of the inductive process, may here terminate. That process is essentially an inquiry into cases of causation. All the uniformities which exist in the succession of phenomena, and most of the uniformities in their co-existence, are either, as we have seen, themselves laws of causation, or consequences resulting from, and corollaries capable of being deduced from, such laws. If we could determine what causes are correctly assigned to what effects, and what effects to what causes, we should be virtually acquainted with the whole course of nature. All those uniformities which are mere results of causation might then be explained and accounted for; and every individual fact or event might be predicted, provided we had the requisite data, that is, the requisite knowledge of the circumstances which, in the particular instance, preceded it.

To ascertain, therefore, what are the laws of causation which exist in nature; to determine the effect of every cause, and the causes of all effects, is the main business of Induction; and to point out how this is done is the chief object of Inductive Logic.

3. From Charles Darwin, *The Descent of Man* (1871)

[In these brief passages from Charles Darwin's (1809-82) *The Descent of Man*, we can hear a clear echo of Collins' account of memory in the Clarke-Collins correspondence and the eighteenth-century arguments against it. These passages thus connect issues about personal identity with issues of the emergence of consciousness. Darwin's account of the evolutionary origins of what he called the higher capacities of human beings (e.g. consciousness) allows for a materialist account of mind without a violation of the Homogeneity Principle — since these capacities do have things in common with the forms from which they are derived. The passages from Charles Darwin's *The Descent of Man* are from a facsimile of the first edition online at *The Complete Work of Charles Darwin Online*, Director, Dr. John van Wyhe.]

Chapter 2

My object in this chapter is solely to show that there is no fundamental difference between man and the higher mammals in their mental faculties. Each division of the subject might have been extended into a separate essay, but must here be treated briefly. As no classification of the mental powers has been universally accepted, I shall arrange my remarks in the order most convenient for my purpose; and will select those facts which have most struck me, with the hope that they may produce some effect on the reader. (p. 35)

It is almost superfluous to state that animals have excellent *Memories* for persons and places. A baboon at the Cape of Good Hope, as I have been informed by Sir Andrew Smith, recognized him with joy after an absence of nine months. I had a dog who was savage and averse to all strangers, and I purposely tried his memory after an absence of five years and two days. I went near the stable where he lived, and shouted to him in my old manner; he showed no joy, but instantly followed me out walking and obeyed me, exactly as if I had parted with him only half-an-hour before. A train of old associations, dormant during five years, had thus been instantaneously awakened in his mind. (p. 45)

That animals retain their mental individuality is unquestionable. When my voice awakened a train of old associations in the mind of the above-mentioned dog, he must have retained his mental individuality, although every atom of his brain had probably undergone change more than once during the interval of five years. This dog might have brought forward the argument lately advanced to crush all evolutionists, and said, "I abide amid all mental moods and all material changes.... The teaching that atoms leave their impressions as legacies to other atoms falling into the places they have vacated is contradictory of the utterance of consciousness, and is therefore false; but it is the teaching necessitated by evolutionism, consequently the hypothesis is a false one."[1] (p. 63)

1 The Rev. Dr. J. M'Cann, "Anti-Darwinism," 1869, p. 13.

Select Bibliography

Books

Ayers, Michael. *Locke*. 2 vols. London and New York: Routledge, 1991.

Bayle, Pierre. *Historical and Critical Dictionary, Selections*. Ed. and trans. Richard H. Popkin. Indianapolis, IN: Hackett Publishing Co., 1991.

Bentley, Richard. *Eight Boyle Lectures on Atheism 1692*. Facsimile edition. New York and London: Garland Press, 1976.

Boyle, Robert. *The Works of Robert Boyle*. Ed. Michael Hunter and Edward Davis. 14 vols. London: Pickering and Chatto, 1999.

Care, Norman and Robert Grimm, eds. *Perception and Personal Identity: Proceedings of the 1967 Oberlin Colloquium in Philosophy*. Cleveland, OH: The Press of the Case Western Reserve University, 1969.

Clarke, Samuel. *A Demonstration of the Being and Attributes of God and Other Writings*. Ed. Ezio Vailati. Cambridge: Cambridge UP, 1998.

——. *The Works of Samuel Clarke*. 4 vols. New York: Garland Press, 1978 [1738].

Cudworth, Ralph. *The True Intellectual System of the Universe*. Facsimile edition. Stuttgart-Bad Cannstatt: Friedrich Frommann Verlag, 1964 [1678].

Darwin, Charles. *The Descent of Man and Selection in Relation to Sex*. Online at <Darwin-online.org.uk/content/frameset?itemID=F937.1&viewtype=side&pageseq=1>.

Descartes, René. *Descartes: Selected Philosophical Writings*. Trans. John Cottingham, Robert Stoothoff, and Dugald Murdoch. Cambridge: Cambridge UP, 1988.

Fergusen, James. *Dr. Samuel Clarke and his Critics*. New York: Vantage Press, 1974.

Fox, Christopher. *Locke and the Scriblerians: Identity and Consciousness in Early Eighteenth-Century England*. Berkeley: U of California P, 1988.

Holden, Thomas. *The Architecture of Matter*. Oxford: Clarendon Press, 2004.

Hume, David. *A Treatise of Human Nature*. Ed. David and Mary Norton. New York: Oxford UP, 2000.

Jacob, Margaret. *The Newtonians and the English Revolution 1689-1720*. Ithaca, NY: Cornell UP, 1976.

Kargon, Robert. *Atomism in England from Hariot to Newton*. Oxford: Clarendon Press, 1966.

Lennon, Thomas M. and Robert J. Stainton, eds. *The Achilles of Rationalist Psychology*. Studies in the History of Philosophy of Mind, Vol. 7, 2008.

Locke, John. *An Essay Concerning Human Understanding*. Ed. Peter Nidditch. Oxford: Clarendon Press, 1975.

——. *The Correspondence of John Locke*. Ed. E.S. De Beer. 8 vols. Oxford: Clarendon Press, 1989.

Martin, Raymond and John Barresi. *The Naturalization of the Soul: Self and Personal Identity in the Eighteenth Century*. London and New York: Routledge, 2004.

Mijuskovic, Benjamin. *The Achilles of Rationalist Arguments*. The Hague: Martinus Nijhoff, 1974.

Mill, John Stuart. *A System of Logic*. 8th ed. New York: Harper & Brothers, 1882.

More, Henry. *A Collection of Several Philosophical Writings*. 2 vols. New York and London: Garland Press, 1978 [1662].

O'Higgins, James. *Anthony Collins: The Man and His Work*. The Hague: Martinus Nijhoff, 1970.

——. *Determinism and Freewill: Anthony Collins'* A philosophical inquiry concerning human liberty*: with a discussion of the opinions of Hobbes, Locke, Pierre Bayle, William King and Leibniz*. The Hague: Martinus Nijhoff, 1976.

Perry, John. *Personal Identity*. 2nd ed. Los Angeles: U of California P, 2008.

Sullivan, John. *John Toland and the Deist Controversy: A Study in Adaptations*. Cambridge, MA: Harvard UP, 1982.

Uzgalis, William. *Locke's Essay Concerning Human Understanding: A Reader's Guide*. London: Continuum, 2007.

Vailati, Ezio. *Leibniz and Clarke: A Study of their Correspondence*. Oxford: Oxford UP, 1997.

Yolton, John. *Locke and the Compass of Human Understanding*. Oxford: Clarendon Press, 1956.

——. *Thinking Matter: Materialism in Eighteenth Century Britain*. Minneapolis, MN: U of Minnesota P, 1983.

Articles

Attfield Robin. "Clarke, Collins and Compounds." *Journal of the History of Philosophy* 15 (1977): 45-54.

Berman, David. "Anthony Collins: Aspects of his thought and writings." *Hermathena* (1975): 49-70.

Chisholm, Roderick. "The Loose and Popular and the Strict and Philosophical Senses of Identity." In Care and Grimm, 82-106.

Ducharme, Howard. "Personal Identity in Samuel Clarke." *Journal of the History of Philosophy* 24.3 (July 1986): 359-83.

Flew, Anthony. "Locke and the Problem of Personal Identity." *Philosophy* 26 (1951): 53-68.

Hutton, Sarah. "The Cambridge Platonists." *Stanford Encyclopedia of Philosophy* (Fall 2008). Ed. Edward N. Zalta. Online at <http://plato.stanford.edu/archives/fall2008/entries/cambridge-platonists/>.

Prior, Arthur. "Opposite Number." *Review of Metaphysics* 11 (December 1957): 196-201.

Rozemond, Marleen. "The Achilles Argument and the Nature of Matter in the Clarke Collins Correspondence." In Lennon and Stainton.

Russell, Paul. "Hume's *Treatise* and the Clarke-Collins Controversy." *Hume Studies* 21.1 (April 1995): 95-115.

Uzgalis, William. "Anthony Collins." *Stanford Encyclopedia of Philosophy* (Winter 2008). Ed. Edward N. Zalta. Online at <http://plato.stanford.edu/archives/win2008/entries/collins/>.

——. "Locke and Collins, Clarke and Butler On Successive Persons." In Perry.

——. "Anthony Collins on the Emergence of Consciousness and Personal Identity." *Philosophy Compass* 4.2. Online at <http://www3.interscience.wiley.com/journal/122241243/abstract?CRETRY=1&SRETRY=0>.

Vailati, Ezio. "Clarke's Extended Soul." *Journal of the History of Philosophy* 21.3 (July 1993): 387-403.

——. "Samuel Clarke." *Stanford Encyclopedia of Philosophy* (Winter 2008). Ed. Edward N. Zalta. Online at <http://plato.stanford.edu/archives/win2008/entries/clarke/>.

Williams, Bernard. "Personal Identity and Individuation." *Proceedings of the Aristotelian Society* 57 (1957): 229-52.

Index

The following abbreviations are used in this index:

I	Introduction
C	Chronology
LD	Collins' Letter to Dodwell
D	Clarke's Defense of an Argument
RD	Collins' Reply to Mr. Clarke's Defense of an Argument
SD	Clarke's Second Defense of an Argument
RSD	Collins' Reflections on Mr. Clarke's Second Defense
TD	Clarke's Third Defense
ATD	Collins' Answer to Mr. Clarke's Third Defense
FD	Fourth Defense
HM	Henry Moore
RC	Ralph Cudworth
PB	Pierre Bayle
JL	John Locke
DH	David Hume
JSM	John Stuart Mill
CD	Charles Darwin

⋆ indicates multiple occurrences of the word on that page

For a list of abbreviations used in this index, please see p. 349.

For a list of abbreviations used in this index, please see p. 349.

For a list of abbreviations used in this index, please see p. 349.

For a list of abbreviations used in this index, please see p. 349.

For a list of abbreviations used in this index, please see p. 349.

For a list of abbreviations used in this index, please see p. 349.

For a list of abbreviations used in this index, please see p. 349.

For a list of abbreviations used in this index, please see p. 349.

For a list of abbreviations used in this index, please see p. 349.

For a list of abbreviations used in this index, please see p. 349.

For a list of abbreviations used in this index, please see p. 349.

For a list of abbreviations used in this index, please see p. 349.

550 lb(s) de Rolland Enviro100 Print
100% post-consumer

Environmental savings
Based on the products you selected compared to products made of 100% VIRGIN FIBERS of the industry are:

5 trees

4,550 gal. US of water
49 days of water consumption

575 lbs of waste
5 waste containers

1,495 lbs CO_2
2,835 miles driven

7 MMBTU
35,460 60W light bulbs for one hour

4 lbs NOx
emissions of one truck during 6 days

For a list of abbreviations used in this index, please see p. 349.